The Learning Process

The BEF's Art of War on the Western Front, 1914-18

Andrew Rawson

Helion & Company Limited

Helion & Company Limited
Unit 8 Amherst Business Centre
Budbrooke Road
Warwick
CV34 5WE
England
Tel. 01926 499 619

Email: info@helion.co.uk
Website: www.helion.co.uk
Twitter: @helionbooks
Visit our blog http://blog.helion.co.uk/

Published by Helion & Company 2019
Designed and typeset by Mary Woolley (www.battlefield-design.co.uk)
Cover designed by Paul Hewitt, Battlefield Design (www.battlefield-design.co.uk)

Text and maps © Andrew Rawson 2019

ISBN 978-1-911628-96-5

British Library Cataloguing-in-Publication Data.
A catalogue record for this book is available from the British Library.

For details of other military history titles published by Helion & Company Limited contact the above address, or visit our website: http://www.helion.co.uk.

We always welcome receiving book proposals from prospective authors.

Contents

List of Maps

Introduction

My interest in the tactics of the British Expeditionary Force (BEF) in the Great War were sparked many years ago after listening to Paddy Griffith at a Western Front Association meeting. His book *Battle Tactics of the Western Front, The British Army's Art of Attack, 1916-1918* (Yale University Press, New Haven, 1996) took my interest and knowledge to new levels. For the first time, I could see how lessons were being learnt and conclusions were being drawn, even if they were sometimes the wrong ones.

Over the period 2013 to 2018, I wrote ten books on the BEF's campaigns on the Western Front for the First World War centenary. This extended period of research gave me the opportunity to learn about soldier's experiences during different types of attack and defence, while writing up the narratives. I was able to assemble the evidence concerning the methods used by the BEF as it planned each attack. It was then possible to compare the anticipated outcome with the actual result and see what lessons were learnt.

The term 'Learning Curve' was first used to counter the 'Lions led by Donkeys' argument, which stemmed back to the 1960s. Allan Clark's book 'The Donkeys' (Hutchinson, 1961) coined the phrase which had allegedly come from a conversation between two German generals. Erich Ludendorff is supposed to have said 'English soldiers fight like lions.' Max Hoffmann allegedly replied 'true. But don't we know that they are lions led by donkeys.' I say supposed and allegedly because no evidence for the conversation has ever been found.

The term has stuck, and the theme has been repeated in films, articles and documentaries over the years. Films such as 'Oh What a Lovely War', television comedies such as 'Black Adder Goes Forth' and the continued interest in the melancholy side of war poetry (because there were sanguine and patriotic sides too, which rarely get the same coverage) have perpetuated the pessimistic view of the BEF's role in the Great War. The incompetence of chateau dwelling generals and the pitiful heroism of the 'poor bloody infantry' are views regularly pushed by the press.

The term 'Learning Process' was first used by Professor Peter Simkins, a military historian for over fifty years, many of them working at the Imperial War Museum, and recently retired president of the Western Front Association. The term appeared in the mid-1980s and it was criticised by some because it implied a constant improvement throughout the war, which is incorrect. Like any manager in business, generals sometimes drew incorrect conclusions from experiences and made the wrong choices, resulting in setbacks. We also have to remember that problems were often caused by the steps taken by German generals who were looking to defeat their enemy; because they too were neither stubborn nor stupid.

Whatever the results of a battle, it does mean that the generals were deliberating over the results of their plans rather than repeating the same mistake. In other words, they were acting contrary to the qualities usually attributed to a donkey; stubbornness and stupidity. If you ask anyone who deals with these animals, they will tell you they are strong, intelligent, independent thinkers with a strong sense of self-preservation. As Professor John Bourne has said, the phrase 'Lions led by Tigers' is more apt for describing the generals of the Great War because they are powerful, cautious, energetic and dangerous.

Simkins' book *Somme to Victory: The British Army's Experience on the Western Front, 1916-1918* (Barnsley, Pen and Sword, 2014) contains a series of essays detailing what is referred to as the 'Learning Process'. The term acknowledges that the BEF improved in how it conducted operations during the Great War. The narrative examines each campaign and its component battles in turn. The method for studying the decisions taken, the innovations introduced and the lessons learned use the following procedure. Firstly, the planning is discussed and the motives behind choosing zero hour, the preliminary bombardment, the creeping barrage and the infantry attack are explained. The impact of new innovations, such as tank involvement, aerial support and special bombardments, on the planning stage are also looked at. Secondly, the successes and failures are described from left to right along the front, unless the fighting dictates otherwise. Finally, the reasons behind the outcomes are given; whether it was due to faulty planning, mistakes made or enemy action.

The two leading members of the Western Front Association have been very influential in my personal learning process. Vice-President Professor John Bourne has been my mentor for the past twenty-five years, regularly providing guidance, suggestions and assistance on countless occasions. President Professor Gary Sheffield was my tutor between 2007 and 2011, providing direction and advice, while I completed my Master of Philosophy in History at the University of Birmingham. Both have furthered my interest and moulded my studies of the Great War for a long time.

Recent research into the First World War is sometimes referred to as revisionist, because it overturns popular conceptions of the conflict. However, these views were formed in the 1960s and 1970s and it is now clear, through serious study that they were in fact the revisionist views. Modern study is pulling back the layers of pessimism and romanticism which have been obscuring history for the past fifty years, to reveal what really happened between 1914 and 1918.

Sources for any conflict fall into several categories which differ with the length of time they are written after the battle. With the First World War it starts with the mass of paperwork created by the men involved around the time of the fighting. This includes orders, war diaries, training pamphlets and summaries, or what the US military refers to as after-action reports. Two types of sources appeared in the years between the two world wars. The first were the national official histories, such as the British series overseen by Brigadier General James Edmonds. But the multi-volume work is controversial because further study makes it clear that many important details were missed out, while others were tucked away in the footnotes and appendices. It is as if Edmonds did not want anyone to read the tactical details of the BEF's learning process. Other national official histories, particularly the Australian one, are more detailed because they had smaller contingents to cover. It can also be said they had a desire to prove their countrymen had done their best, despite their British generals.

The second type is the unit history and they fall into two categories; the divisional history and the regimental history. They were published by members of the unit and most came out before the Official History, so they rely heavily on war time documents, personal diaries and interviews. The quality of information varies and while some are copies of the war time paperwork, others rely on members memories to give the bare details. Despite their limitations, they all provide extra information about the successes and the failures which their members endured. However, they do tend to blame the actions of others, rather than their own, when there was problem.

I have picked out the information from all these sources which were relative to the BEF's learning process. This includes the planning decisions, the mistakes made, the conclusions drawn, and the steps taken to rectify problems and improve performance. Focusing on one aspect of the BEF's battles has made it possible to go into detail on this important aspect of warfare during 1914-18. It scrapes back the tiers of information (and mis-information) which have been added over the years to look at what was involved in planning and executing offensive and defensive operations on the Western Front.

A lot of the information comes from the basic facts given in the official histories. I found the information I wanted was often there, if only I bothered to look for it. Planning information is always given, often in the appendices where few people care to look because the military jargon can be complicated, or the amount of information is over bearing. The time-consuming part was extracting the details relevant to the learning process from the narratives of the action.

With the infantry, we will see how they deployed, what time of day they advanced, the tactics they used and how they consolidated their objectives. The evolution of artillery methods will be explained by looking at the different approaches to the preliminary bombardment and the types of ammunition used before zero hour. The speed of the creep, the layering of the barrage and some unusual methods the gunners used to deal with different types of targets will also be explained.

The introduction of the tank in the autumn of 1916 started to change how the BEF fought battles. The different tactics tried as improved models were introduced to the battlefield over the next twelve months will be explained. They had become as important as the artillery in the planning of an offensive, by the time of the battle of Cambrai in November 1917. However, the German attacks in the spring of 1918 meant the tank crews had to wait until the summer before they could demonstrate their real worth in the offensive.

Warfare became three dimensional during the Great War and the contribution of the pilots is considered. There are discussions about how they improved the work of the infantry and the artillery through observation and later through ground support. The evolution of communications is also covered, illustrating how this most tricky of problems was tackled with the use of vision, sound, light and finally, radio.

One important aspect is the steps that both sides devoted to covert methods. Secrecy was employed to deploy troops and subterfuge was used to trick their enemy and keep zero hour a secret until the last moment. But we also see how the Germans used deception to improve their defensive position. The effects of the weather and the struggle to understand its impact on operations are discussed when they are relevant. Changing temperature, a morning mist, heavy rain, unexpected snow, a setting sun, a rising moon all impacted on the planning, the timing and the execution of an attack.

Finally, I would like to thank Dr Michael LoCicero for his guidance and advice throughout the process of researching, writing and editing. I am also indebted to all the team at Helion & Company who were involved in the production this book.

Professor Bourne once told me that bringing together all these pieces of information had been called 'tactical snippeting' by the late Paddy Griffith. I have likened the process to creating an 'electronic scrapbook' so it was possible to study one aspect of the Western Front from beginning to end. It has been a long process, involving the consultation of many sources to reconstruct the BEF's Learning Process between August 1914 and November 1918. I think the effort has been worth it, I hope you do too.

Andrew Rawson
February 2019

1

The 1914 Campaign
4 August-11 November

A State of War

Gavrilo Princip assassinated Archduke Franz Ferdinand of Austria and his wife Sophie in Sarajevo on 28 June 1914.[1] The political crisis culminated with Austria-Hungary declaring war on 28 July, the same day the British Government ordered the Home Fleet to its war stations. The British Army's General Staff put all Regular troops on standby the following day, as Russia, Germany, Austria, Turkey and France started mobilising.

The British ultimatum to Germany expired at midday on 1 August and German troops then entered France and Luxembourg.[2] King Albert asked Great Britain for help and both the Territorial Force and the Naval Reserves were mobilised on 3 August. Germany declared war on France and Belgium, before crossing the border the following morning.

A state of war between Great Britain and Germany began at 11 pm on 4 August[3] but embarkation was delayed until 9 August, so Territorial Force units could return from their summer training camps. Mobilisation was carried out according to the 'War Book', which detailed the deployment of troops across Great Britain and Ireland with the help of 1,800 special trains.[4] Ships sailed around the clock to Le Havre, Rouen and Boulogne, on the French coast, and all units of the British Expeditionary

---

1   Sir James E. Edmonds, *Military Operations: France and Belgium, 1914, Vol. I: Mons, the Retreat to the Seine, the Marne and the Aisne, August to October 1914* (London, HMSO, 1922), pp. 23-4.

2   Edmonds, *Military Operations: France and Belgium, 1914, Vol. I.* The final days before war are covered on pp. 25-8.

3   Ibid. The Foreign Office announcement is given on p. 29.

4   Ibid. The BEF's mobilisation and movement to France are detailed on pp. 31-2.

Force (BEF) arrived with their transport, ready to march. Nearly 100,000 men and 120,000 horses had been deployed according to plan.

The British and French General Staffs had made peacetime plans for deploying a British Expeditionary Force (BEF) to France.[5] They had agreed that four infantry divisions, one cavalry division and one cavalry brigade would be ready to advance alongside the French armies, as part of their Plan XVII, on day sixteen after mobilisation.

A German invasion of neutral Belgium had not been anticipated, so the Allied plans had been altered by the time the BEF's General Headquarters (GHQ) arrived in France on 16 August.[6] Field-Marshal Sir John French was the Commander-in-Chief and Lieutenant General Sir Douglas Haig headed I Corps. Lieutenant General Sir James Grierson was the first choice to command II Corps but he died the following day and was replaced by Lieutenant General Sir Horace Smith-Dorrien.

The BEF advanced north-east towards Mons on 20 August, unaware that it faced five times its strength. By the time British cavalry engaged German patrols, the Belgian Army had been fighting against overwhelming odds for eighteen days, giving the British and French time to deploy. Aerial observers reported all German movements as the BEF dug in along the Condé Canal and around Mons but the First German Army knew little about the British strength or where they were.

Mons, 23 August

As II Corps dug in along the canals west and north of Mons, I Corps was deployed east of the town. Germans scouts probed the British line, the artillery then shelled it and the first attack hit 3rd Division's salient around Mons. The British troops held shallow entrenchments covering the canal bridges, while the reserves had barricaded the streets in the town, in case it had to be evacuated.

Materials were stacked to block the canal bridges, while the engineers prepared them for demolition in spite of a lack of leads.[7] The German field guns destroyed the barricades, but the infantry were wary of crossing bridges, correctly believing they had been booby trapped. The British infantry waited while the engineers finished their work and the explosions were the signal to withdraw.

The German infantry advanced by rushes, taking cover behind hedges as they moved east of the town.[8] The British infantry used roadside ditches for cover and held their fire until the advancing troops moved past the last hedge line. The German field guns often deployed too far forward, and British scouts employed cover to get close

5   Mutual military assistance was agreed in April 1904 and planning began a year later. Great Britain's strategy in case of war was decided in August 1911, following the Agadir Crisis, a territorial challenge between France and Germany in Morocco.
6   Edmonds, *Military Operations: France and Belgium, 1914, Vol. I*, pp. 49-50, 51-4.
7   Ibid., pp. 77-8.
8   Ibid., pp. 82-6.

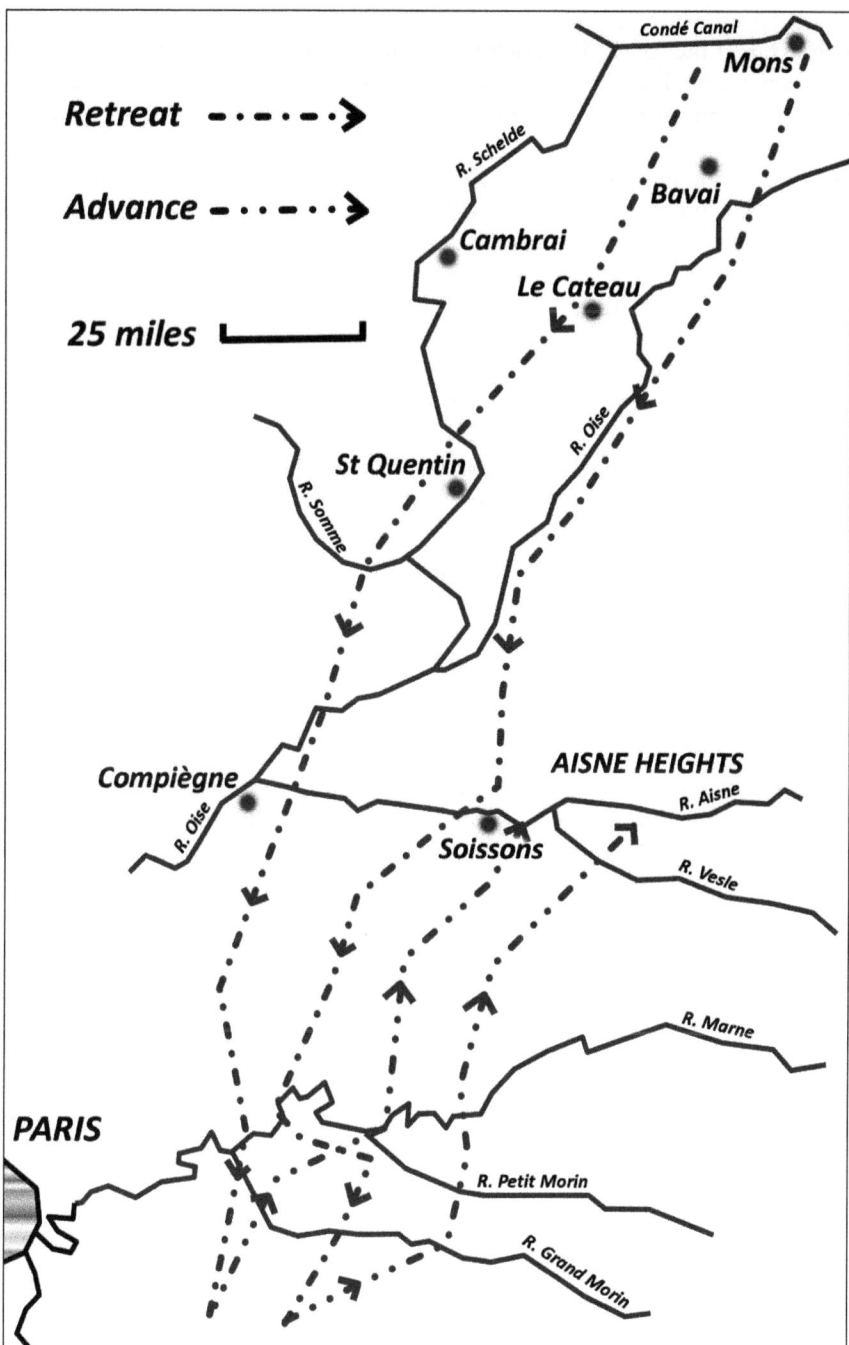

Map 1. Opening Campaign: 23 August -11 November: The BEF's long retreat south beyond the River Marne and its advance north to the River Aisne.

enough to target the crews. The machine-gun teams were far harder to spot and they in turn stopped the British reinforcements. The Germans infantry assembled under cover of the suppressive fire which made it impossible to get the withdrawal message along the British line.

There were running battles through the streets of Mons and the surrounding mining villages. The plan had been to withdraw east of the town after nightfall, but it took time to get the orders out to all the units and the German infantry kept creeping forward. Rear guards kept the enemy at bay while the infantry escorted the artillery along the dark lanes to safety.[9]

Outposts covered the bridges across 5th Division's 7-mile-front along the Condé Canal while cyclists went up ahead to locate the German columns.[10] Some dug false trenches in the open, to draw artillery fire, waiting in hidden ones nearby for the right time to fire. Field gun teams had found it difficult to find suitable battery positions near the canal while machine-gun teams and artillery observers used houses and slag heaps to get a good view of the waterway. Attempts to rush the bridges failed, so the Germans then crept forward to form a firing line along the canal.

The sound of the main bridges being blown up was the signal to withdraw.[11] The outposts made a run for it, escaping on boats and then sank them but it was too late for some. The men of 5th Division dug false trenches make the Germans think they were staying but the Germans were soon crossing the canal on pontoon bridges.

Withdrawal from Mons to Le Cateau, 24-25 August

The Germans had not contacted I Corps on 23 August and it was able to withdraw without any incident. But II Corps had delayed First Army's advance by a day, causing many casualties. There had been no disasters, only two of guns had been lost and the men were in high spirits. But they soon became tired on the long march, many of them suffering from their side effects of their inoculations.[12] The reservists struggled the most, because they were out of shape, and some hitched a lift on passing wagons. A few of II Corps units were caught by the Germans because Smith-Dorrien had deployed according to French's original stand order. In particular, the 1st Lincolns 'hung on with the greatest determination and pluck and stuck it out to the end', delaying an entire German division.[13]

The Cavalry Division's regiments harassed the German columns, forcing them to deploy off the roads. General Edmund Allenby sent three officers to ask General Charles Fergusson if he was withdrawing but none returned. So, he took the decision

9   Ibid., p. 91.
10   Ibid., pp. 78-81, 87-9.
11   Ibid., pp. 89-90.
12   Ibid., p. 52.
13   Ibid., p. 85 and 115. Also, Major General C R Simpson, *The History of the Lincolnshire Regiment, 1914-1918* (London: Medici Society, 1931). p. 13.

to withdraw, exposing 5th Division's left flank. Cavalry squadrons were deployed to help the infantry settle down around Elouges.

The British artillery kept firing until the last minute and then man-handled the guns into cover and limbered up. The 1st Norfolks withdrew after the order was received at 2.30 pm but all three runners sent to the 1st Cheshires were hit. Cavalry troopers gave the impression that the Cheshires were retiring as well but the Norfolks' commander had seniority and two hours passed before the Cheshires' commander went looking for him. He was captured, leaving it down to the company commanders to decide what to do and while some escaped, the engagement ended with a suicidal charge.[14]

The Germans were reluctant to attack some of the rearguards because they had suffered so many casualties along the canal but the 2nd Duke's had to fight off six battalions.[15] There were arguments over who should use which road and German planes circled overhead marking the columns for their artillery. II Corps had escaped to fight another day and while it had lost no guns, the men were tired after twenty-four hours of fighting and marching.

The BEF marched around the Mormal Forest on 25 August, with II Corps west of it.[16] The Germans reached the Escaut bridges around Valenciennes first while a French Cavalry Corps and refugees blocked the road. So, it was evening 5th Division and 3rd Division bivouacked west of Le Cateau and dark when 4th Division arrived. Meanwhile, I Corps had marched through the night to get clear of the forest but civilians reported that the enemy were approaching Landrecies and Maroilles.

The 1st Berkshires struggled through the mass of refugees to defend the bridge over the Sambre at Maroilles[17] but the Germans found 1st Division behind barricades in Landrecies.[18] They first tried rushing the garrison loaded in lorries before trying to crawl across the fields to reach the Guardsmen.[19] A third attempt involved a soldier with a horse and wagon pretending to be a French farmer, while the fourth try involved men dressed as French soldiers singing French songs at the head of a column of troops. The final attempt involved a field gun blasting at a barricade after nightfall while infantry set fire to haystacks to illuminate the area for their artillery. The Guardsmen fought them all off before escaping Landrecies.

14 Edmonds, *Military Operations: France and Belgium, 1914, Vol. I.* The engagement at Elouges is chronicled pp. 105-10.
15 Ibid., p. 110. The Duke's never received their order, again illustrating how difficult it was to pass on messages.
16 Ibid., the difficulties in getting past the Mormal Forest are discussed on pp. 119-21.
17 Ibid., p. 133.
18 Ibid., pp. 134-5.
19 Lieutenant Colonel Rt Hon Sir Frederick Ponsonby, *The Grenadier Guards in the Great War* (London; MacMillan and Co., 1920), pp. 26-8.

The Battle of Le Cateau, 26 August

The cavalry found the Germans were far closer than expected early on 26 August while II Corps' infantry and artillery were not ready to march, having had only a few hours' sleep. Smith-Dorrien told GHQ he intended to stand and fight and French replied: 'Although you are given a free hand as to method, this telegram is not intended to convey the impression that I am not as anxious for you to carry out the retirement and you must make every endeavour to do so.'[20] Dawn would find battalions and batteries camped where they had stopped rather than ready to fight and it was too dangerous to redeploy in the morning mist. They would have to fight were they were.

On the left, 4th Division was already 'at it hammer and tongs' when Smith Dorrien's order to fight arrived.[21] The infantry found themselves in an exposed position while the 60-pounders and the support troops were already on the road. Rapid fire drove off the Germans, but it was soon time to withdraw by platoons and the Germans surged forward when the volume of fire reduced. A few Germans shouted 'retire' to interfere with the withdrawal and a few groups were cut off. The infantry redeployed alongside the guns and they then withdrew, battery by battery. Units became mixed up as the day wore on and some did not get the retire order, so they escaped when it was dark, joining the night march south.

In II Corps' centre, 3rd Division had improved trenches dug by the locals with their hand tools and wire taken from nearby gardens.[22] German infantry probed the trenches around Caudry and then withdrew so the artillery could shell it. The salient had to be abandoned but the rest of the line held on until the afternoon, when mounted officers rode along the line to pass on the order. It was too dangerous for some to retire and nine field guns and several hundred men were captured.

German scouts again located 5th Division's line on the heights around Le Cateau for their artillery.[23] It soon became clear that the guns were aiming at the mounds of earth dug by the infantry,[24] so they redeployed in the open. Most of the British guns were hidden behind sheaves of corn and their crews came under sniper and artillery fire, while they fired at the German infantry.

It was impossible to see into the Selle valley from the heights south-west of Le Cateau, so the Germans could advance past, before climbing the slope and using

---

20 Edmonds, *Military Operations: France and Belgium, 1914, Vol. I.* General Smith-Dorrien's predicament and his decision to stand and fight are explained on pp. 140-3.
21 Ibid. The 4th Division's fight is covered on pp. 146-9 and 164-9.
22 Ibid. The 3rd Division's engagement is described on pp. 155-7 and 163-4.
23 Ibid. The early fighting on 5th Division front is described on pp. 153-5.
24 These shallow ditches were just deep enough to lie in; the spoil formed a small heap to cover a man's head and shoulders. They would have looked like a mass of large mole hills from a distance.

ditches to get behind 5th Division's flank.[25] The order to retire was issued too late to act on in the afternoon and several infantry units were overrun, while around twenty-five guns were lost.[26] Lieutenant Colonel Bond's orders to the 2nd King's Own Yorkshire Light Infantry was typical of the desperate situation; 'There will be no retirement for the fighting troops. Fill up your trenches, as far as possible, with water, food and ammunition.'[27]

There was a running battle across the Selle stream, as cavalry squadrons helped the rest of 5th Division escape. German planes dropped smoke signals, so their artillery knew where to fire while the late issue of the withdrawal order ended in 'confusion but no disorganisation; disorder, but no panic.'[28]

Plans to make a stand were abandoned and it 'looked like the breakup of an army' as the cavalry covered II Corps' retreat. Sorting out the mess took most of the night, with staff officers dividing troops into divisions or transport, then into brigade groups and finally into battalions and batteries. Only then could the surviving officers lead their tired men into the night.

Le Cateau had been a close-run battle but French supported Smith-Dorrien's decision to fight at Le Cateau: 'I say without hesitation that the saving of the left wing of the army under my command could never have been accomplished unless a commander of rare and unusual coolness, intrepidity, and determination had been present to personally conduct the operation.'[29]

As the men of II Corps fought for their lives on 26 August, I Corps endured a tedious march. The only action occurred when French cavalry and infantry fled through the 2nd Connaughts at Le Grand Fayt. An attack disorganised the Germans, but 300 men were lost.[30]

The Retreat Begins in Earnest

The BEF crossed the Somme and the Oise, but it was unable to deploy and counter-attack, like General Joseph Joffre wanted, because the Germans were too close behind. Interpreters went ahead to look out for spies and check routes but false information occasionally added miles to a journey. Staff officers cleared civilian traffic through

25 Edmonds, *Military Operations: France and Belgium, 1914, Vol. I,* the narrative of 5th Division's fight is continued pp. 157-62.
26 Ibid. The 5th Division's chaotic withdrawal is covered on pp. 172-80.
27 Ibid., Lieutenant Colonel Bond's actions are covered on p. 175.
28 Ibid., p. 180.
29 Field Marshal French's first despatch of the 1914 campaign was printed in the third supplement to the London Gazette issued on 8 September 1914. He may have publicly supported II Corps stand at Le Cateau but a long running feud between the two generals came to a head in May 1915 when Smith-Dorrien was sacked for suggesting a withdrawal from the Ypres Salient.
30 Edmonds, *Military Operations: France and Belgium, 1914, Vol. I,* pp. 202-3.

towns but the columns still concertinaed and the troops and wagons had to move 'double banked' through the streets.[31] Officers manned junctions and side roads out in the country, to prevent wrong turnings, while the hourly halts had to be cancelled because it took too long to get the tired men moving again. Wagons dumped all the spare equipment and ammunition, to make space for those too exhausted to march, because fighting a battle and marching nearly 70 miles in forty-eight hours was just too much for some.

The Royal Flying Corps searched for the German columns, the cavalry watched the roads and the rear guards covered the British columns. There were few incidents, but one serious affair occurred at Etreux on 27 August, after the messengers did not reach the 2nd Royal Munster Fusiliers in time.[32] Most were killed or captured as they fought along the ditches and hedges for six hours. Their sacrifice, however, allowed 1st Division to escape.

The BEF rested on 29 August, while a new base opened at St Nazaire, to keep pace with the retreat south.[33] The march towards the River Aisne resumed the following day and aerial observers confirmed the Germans were wheeling south-east, to follow the BEF. A captured order said their plan was to drive the French and British away from Paris, brought about by the need to send troops to capture the fortresses of Antwerp and Maubeuge.[34] On hearing the news, Joffre decided to draw the Germans into a trap.

The BEF thought it only needed a short march on 1 September, but a cavalry brigade and artillery battery were caught in the mist at Néry, confirming that the German cavalry were close.[35] More cavalry caught 5th Division's rearguards at Crépy-en-Valois and Raporie while I Corps came under fire as it marched towards Villers Cottéréts Forest.[36] A confused fight in the undergrowth and trees delayed the Germans and while most of the rearguard rallied south-west of the town, some of the Guardsmen were overrun or surrounded. These small actions meant that the rest of the British soldiers had to march late into the night to shake off the Germans.

The BEF may have been reunited for the first time in a week, but a gap was opening with the French armies to the east. So, Lord Kitchener was sent to France to confirm full cooperation with President Raymond Poincaré and General Joffre, but it was impossible to defend the River Marne; the Germans were too close.[37] So, the march had to continue to the River Seine, 40 miles further south.

The Marne was crossed on 3 September and all but one of the bridges had been demolished before the engineers ran out of explosives. The cavalry then found

31   Ibid., pp. 219-220. Double banked means two lines of traffic travelling side-by-side in the same direction.
32   Ibid., pp. 221-6.
33   Ibid., pp. 286.
34   Ibid., pp. 287.
35   Ibid., pp. 256-8.
36   Ibid., pp. 259-62.
37   Ibid., Kitchener's visit is detailed on p. 260.

crossings over the Grand Morin and Petit Morin, ahead of the infantry and artillery, on 4 September. General Joseph Galliéni, Military Governor of Paris, and General Michel Maunoury, commander of the new Sixth French Army, visited GHQ and spoke to his Chief of the Staff, General Archibald Murray, in French's absence. They agreed to continue marching south, to draw the First German Army past the east side of Paris.[38]

Aerial observers watched the First German Army cross the Ourcq and the Marne on 6 September and it became apparent that it was ignoring the BEF, believing it was a spent force. General Alexander von Kluck was also unaware that the French had formed a Sixth Army in Paris, behind its flank.

Everyone was exhausted after eleven days on the road and while discipline never broke, the reservists suffered the most because civilian life had made them unfit. The march continued and those with the furthest to go sometimes marched through the night, to take advantage of the cooler weather. The relocation of the BEF's base to St Nazaire was completed on 5 September and 20,000 men, 7,000 horses and 60,000 tons of supplies had been moved in just six days.[39] It was completed just in time to help the BEF respond to Joffre's order to turn around.[40]

The BEF had to march fast back to the Grand Morin and a bridgehead was formed by nightfall. Abandoned equipment was seen alongside the roads to the Petit Morin, indicating that German discipline was breaking down. There were skirmishes at the bridges but units waded across and outflanked the German rear guards until a thunderstorm stopped all offensive action.

The Chief of the German General Staff, General Helmuth von Moltke, assumed everything was going well, so he sent Lieutenant Colonel Richard Hentsch to assess the situation, with full powers to give orders to check if 'rearward movements have already been initiated'.[41] Hentsch found General Karl von Bülow in a pessimistic mood, because the BEF had crossed the Marne behind Second Army. He then encountered columns of troops in disarray on the roads, en route to First Army's headquarters. General von Kluck left it to his Chief of Staff, General Hermann von Kuhl, to speak to Hentsch. He regretted the decision because First Army was placed under Second Army's command and they were both ordered to withdraw behind the Aisne and Vesle rivers. Hentsch also cancelled OHL's order for Third Army to stay south of the Marne; an order which was approved on his return.

Joffre correctly believed a gap was opening between First German Army and Second German Army and he wanted the BEF to advance into it. The British engineers did not have enough equipment to bridge the Marne, so the artillery shelled the river bank until the Germans withdrew on 9 September. On III Corps' front some men

38   Ibid., p. 278.
39   Ibid., p. 287.
40   Ibid., p. 295-7.
41   Ibid. Hentsch's momentous journey is dealt with in detailed on pp. 348-56.

crossed on small ferries, while others ran across lock gates, a weir and a railway bridge which were impossible to blow up.[42] A floating bridge was soon ready to carry the artillery across. Meanwhile, II Corps used two bridges to cross and it had advanced 3-miles north of the river by nightfall.[43] The cavalry crossed first in I Corps' area, holding the high ground while the infantry caught up.[44] The 500 strong German rear guard at Charly-sur-Marne were captured, as they slept off their hangovers in the nearby chateau.[45] By nightfall, the entire corps was across without a shot being fired. Aerial observers could see German cavalry only 3-miles ahead and they were covering the 25-mile gap which had opened up between the First German Army and Second German Army.

The BEF was snapping at the German heels but it was difficult to get enough artillery and supply wagons across the Marne. There was disappointment when column of fifty-four heavy guns escaped from Oulchy-le-Chateau, but morale soared when the troops saw how many prisoners had been taken.[46]

The BEF advanced north-east on 11 September and the march continued beyond the River Ourcq, despite bad weather preventing aerial reconnaissance. The Aisne was next, but the bridges had been either been blown up or were covered by machine guns. A few crossed the damaged Venizel bridge during the night to encounter German cavalry dug in along the Chemin des Dames height.[47]

For three difficult weeks, Field Marshal French had always respected the Government's instruction that the 'greatest care must be exercised towards a minimum of losses and wastage'.[48] We, the reader, must remember that Great Britain only had one expeditionary force and it had suffered 20,000 men casualties and lost over forty guns in just two battles, at Mons and Le Cateau. French now had to conserve what remained in a new style of fighting; trench warfare.[49]

The Aisne Heights

The cavalry checked the Aisne crossings before the infantry climbed the slopes on the north bank. The men of 4th Division crossed a bridge, aware that their guns were

42   Ibid., pp. 337-9.
43   Ibid., pp. 334-7.
44   Ibid., pp. 332-4.
45   Everard Wyrall, *History of the Second Division 1914-1918, Vol. 1* (London: Thomas Nelson, 1921), p. 67.
46   Edmonds, *Military Operations: France and Belgium, 1914, Vol. I*, p. 362.
47   Ibid., p. 370.
48   Ibid. Instruction from Lord Kitchener to Field Marshal French issued at the beginning of the campaign and quoted in Appendix 8, pp. 499-500.
49   The British Army only had enough troops for defending the British Isles and the Empire until troops could be recalled from overseas stations.

soon too far away to give support.[50] A slender bridgehead was established but the few heavy guns could not silence the German artillery at such a long distance. Around Missy, 5th Division sailed over on rafts but it was unable to advance from the river bank, while 3rd Division crossed a damaged bridge at Vailly and then waited.[51] A boat ferried 2nd Division over around Chavonne, while others crossed the damaged bridge at Pont-Arcy.[52] On the right, 1st Division crossed a bridge and aqueduct at Bourg while the cavalry explored the Chemin des Dames ridge beyond.

Captured documents and aerial observers made Joffre believe that the Germans were retiring but the BEF needed more bridges across the Aisne before it could attack the Chemin des Dames ridge in force. The advancing infantry found the Germans holding trenches at the summit and while wire and heavy fire stopped 5th Division around Chivres and Missy, 3rd Division fell back to the river bank. Heavy fire around Braye took 2nd Division by surprise, while 3rd Division's retreat left it in a precarious situation. At one point, 200 Germans waved white flags but those who went forward to accept their surrender were shot at.[53] White flags were also waved at men of 1st Division when they reached the summit, but nobody moved, and many prisoners were taken. However, the summit position around Cerny-en-Laonnois had been lost by the time the gunners found suitable battery positions.

The Aisne bridgehead was precarious, and it was proving difficult to carry ammunition forward and the wounded back across the river. Crossing the river was dangerous because the bridges were easy to spot, and they often had to be repaired. The troops used a mixture of pontoon and trestle bridges while barges covered in decking shuttled supplies and casualties across the river.[54]

The BEF had no reserves while French had no idea how strong the Germans were. The men dug shallow trenches but there were no dug outs and there was little wire.[55] A daily routine soon developed in which the artillery and snipers dominated the ground during the day while the infantry attacked at night, with the help or hindrance of flares.

The field guns struggled to find safe battery positions, while the 60-pounders were the only guns with the range to hit most targets.[56] An artillery officer was attached to each infantry brigade to report targets, but they found it difficult to spot the German trenches. Each division only had a single aeroplane to spot targets and the pilot flew over the enemy lines every morning while an artillery observer noted targets on a

50 Edmonds, *Military Operations: France and Belgium, 1914, Vol. I*, III Corps' crossing is detailed on pp. 378-9.
51 Ibid. II Corps' crossing is covered on pp. 381-2.
52 Ibid. I Corps' crossing is explained on pp. 382-3.
53 Ibid. White flag incidents are chronicled on pp. 397 and 405.
54 Ibid. Bridging the Aisne is covered on pp. 438-9.
55 Ibid. The development of trenches is detailed on pp. 434-5.
56 Ibid. The challenges faced by the British gunners are detailed on 434-7.

crude map. Some even photographed the trenches and the images were studied to help improve the crude maps being plotted.

The Germans had observation balloons which could see for miles from the summit of the ridge, while their pilots dropped metal shavings on targets, to mark them.[57] The British gunners had to withdraw their limbers and carry shells forward to the camouflaged battery positions at night. Dummy guns drew fire, but the real guns had to be shifted if spotted. Guns were aimed at their targets before dusk and then lamps were used during the hours of darkness.

Artillery fire soon started reducing, as both sides ran out of ammunition. Before long, it was clear that many of the German shells were failing to explode.[58] The British guns were probably firing a similar number of duds.

By 15 September there was stalemate along the Aisne, with neither side strong enough to defeat the other. Then rain turned the trenches into muddy ditches and trench foot was seen for the first time.[59] Entrenching tools started arriving on 17 September and crude hand grenades made from slabs of gun cotton tied to wooden handles were used for the first time on 27 September.[60] Trench warfare was starting to develop its own rules.

The Race to the Sea

Minister of War General Erich von Falkenhayn took over the post of Chief of the General Staff on 14 September. He planned three operations 'to bring the northern coast of France and the control of the English Channel into German possession.'[61] Antwerp would be put under siege, his cavalry would cross Flanders heading for the coast, while the rest of his troops headed for Arras. The Allied response was to protect the coalfields between Béthune and Lens, resulting a rapid extension of the front line across the Somme and Artois regions. The plan also included transferring the BEF to Flanders, to shorten its lines of communication and protect the Channel ports. The first British troops left the Aisne valley late on 1 October and the last ones handed over their trenches eleven days later.

---

57   Ibid. The work of the German observers and gunners is covered on p. 434 and 437.
58   It has been suggested they were using shells which were out of date.
59   A painful swelling of the feet caused by standing in mud or water for too long.
60   Stephen Bull, *Trench: A History of Trench Warfare on the Western Front* (Oxford: Osprey, 2014). The early development of grenades is covered p.99. These entrenching tools were replacements for the ones dumped during the long march from Mons.
61   Edmonds, *Military Operations: France and Belgium, 1914, Vol. I,* p. 429. Falkenhayn's plans are discussed in detail on p. 454-5.

Antwerp and Ghent, 28 September-10 October

The Belgian Field Army was deployed along the River Dendre and while the 65,000 strong Field Army was permitted to withdraw towards Ostend, if necessary, the 80,000 strong Antwerp garrison had to fight to the end. The Belgian troops had cleared vegetation and flooded low lying areas but it sometimes made it easier to see the forts. Ominously, the first fort had to be evacuated on 28 September; it had only been shelled for a few hours.

The Belgians asked for a British presence, so officers were sent to assess the naval plan, the tactical situation and the fortifications. First Lord of the Admiralty Winston Churchill also visited King Albert to confirm that reinforcements were on their way under the command of Lieutenant General Sir Henry Rawlinson.[62] Unfortunately, the Marines and Naval troops had little training, poor equipment, few service troops and no transport. They also faced the German super heavy guns, which had crossed the River Nethe to shell Antwerp's inner forts. General Rawlinson arrived on 6 October and his first task was to withdraw all his troops behind the River Schelde. The Naval troops and the Marines were instructed to hold on around Antwerp, but they were not to get trapped.

The 7th Division had reached Zeebrugge on 7 October, only to learn the Germans were crossing the River Schelde, looking to surround Antwerp.[63] The following day, it made its escape only to find that the Germans had cut the two railway lines. There were a few wagons on a nearby single track but the rest of the men had to walk. Meanwhile, 3rd Cavalry Division had landed at Ostend and Zeebrugge only to hear that strong German forces were advancing north from Lille. Rawlinson was told to cover the evacuation of Antwerp and cover the Belgian Army's retirement while his command was renamed IV Corps, to bring it in line with the rest of the BEF.[64]

The ad hoc Royal Naval Division was also told to leave Antwerp on 8 October.[65] Two brigades reached the rendezvous point but a runner delivered the message to a battalion headquarters rather than the third brigade headquarters. It meant three battalions did not leave until nightfall and they missed their trains. Half would escape across the border into neutral Holland but the other half were captured after their train was derailed by shell fire.

62   Sir James E. Edmonds, *Military Operations: France and Belgium, 1914, Vol. II: Antwerp, La Bassée, Armentières, Messines and Ypres, October and November 1914* (London, HMSO, 1925), p. 47-8.
63   Edmonds, *Military Operations: France and Belgium, 1914, Vol. II*, pp. 49-50. The 7th Division was made up of units gathered from across Britain and the Empire.
64   Ibid., pp. 55, 60-65.
65   Ibid. The evacuation of Antwerp is covered on pp. 52-3, 55-60.

The Germans discovered that the forts had been abandoned on 9 October and they accepted the surrender of Antwerp.[66] It had taken just eleven days to capture the city, but it had tied up a large number of German infantry and artillery.

First Encounters, 8 -19 October

On 6 October, Joffre and French agreed the BEF would fill the gap between the French and the Belgians.[67] Three days later French cavalry stopped their German counterparts interfering with the BEF's deployment at Abbeville, St Omer and Hazebrouck and the new Cavalry Corps headed for Messines Ridge. It would link with IV Corps around Ypres. Meanwhile, II Corps advanced east of Béthune while III Corps headed for Armentières on 11 October.[68]

The Belgian Army came under attack as it concentrated along the River Yser and Yprelee Canal, but the Antwerp garrison joined it on 11 October.[69] It meant that 7th Division could head for Ypres and it deployed around the town on 15 October. Meanwhile, the Cavalry Corps had reached Messines Ridge, to the south only to discover that their 13-pounder guns were virtually useless for stopping the Germans. Everyone found that the mist interfered with observation, the rain slowed progress across the fields and the dykes restricted mounted troops and artillery to the roads. Planks had to be used to cross ditches while the gunners had to man-handle their artillery pieces along the roads, so they could give the infantry close support.

The rest of the Cavalry Corps reached the River Lys on 17 October and linked the two wings of the BEF along the Messines Ridge, together two days later. It left the BEF holding 25 miles of front, which was far too long for the number of troops it had. I Corps arrived at Hazebrouck on 19 October and headed for Ypres.

It is now time to look at each corps in turn, starting with IV Corps and I Corps around Ypres. The Cavalry Corps on the Messines Ridge will be followed by III Corps at Ploegsteert and II Corps around Neuve Chapelle.

IV Corps' Advance East of Ypres, 17-19 October

Field Marshal French had wanted to capture Menin but he used the word 'move' rather than 'attack' in IV Corps' order, so Rawlinson told Major General Thompson to proceed cautiously. Aerial observers had spotted German troops concentrating around Menin by the time a GHQ staff officer reported Rawlinson's misinterpretation. The

---

66   Ibid. The capitulation of Antwerp is covered on pp. 60-2.
67   Ibid., p. 69.
68   Ibid., pp. 70-2.
69   Ibid., pp. 66-7.

misunderstanding had stopped 7th Division running into the Germans, but Rawlinson was still told to continue the advance at dawn.[70]

IV Corps covered an area 5 miles wide, with waves of men at intervals up to three miles deep, as it moved forward. All was going well until the Royal Flying Corps observers took to the air when the mist cleared and spotted an evident increase in the number of German troops. Rawlinson ordered General Capper to abandon the attack, but it took time to get the message to the front and his troops were under fire by the time they started to withdraw in succession from the left.[71]

III Corps, 13-19 October[72]

Rain delayed the advance past Bailleul on 13 October, giving the Germans time to withdraw across the River Lys and demolish all the bridges. By 16 October 4th Division was moving astride the Lys while 6th Division was on the far bank. Prisoners said two infantry corps were moving into the area on 18 October, but Lieutenant General William Pulteney concluded there was only a thin screen of Germans on Aubers Ridge overlooking his right flank. His plan was to halt 4th Division, so 6th Division could change direction and turn the enemy's flank.

I Corps and IV Corps, 21-23 October

The French were driven out of Houthulst Forest on 20 October, forcing 3rd Cavalry Division to withdraw towards St Julien, but the arrival of 2nd Division secured a semi-circle around Ypres. I Corps was delayed by traffic at the Yser Canal bridges on 21 October, thwarting Haig's plan to advance north-east through Poelcappelle and Passchendaele. It eventually advanced at 9.20 am, only to see the French cavalry withdrawing on their left flank, as large numbers of German troops emerged from the Houthulst Forest. Meanwhile, 2nd Division had advanced through St Julien as far as s'Gravenstafel.

At the same time, 7th Division faced a strong attack from Terhand and Gheluwe. The men endured the bombardments before shooting down the German reservists, as they advanced en mass time after time. Eventually they had to abandon a blazing Zonnebeke, as ammunition ran low and weapons jammed. The German infantry then tried a night attack, but the British lookouts spotted the white arm bands they were wearing for identification purposes.

The French were supposed to advance through 1st Division's front between Steenstraat and Langemarck on 22 October but a surprise counter-attack stopped them getting beyond the British trenches. The Germans then set fire to haystacks, to

---

70   Ibid., pp. 115-6.
71   Ibid., pp. 131-5.
72   Ibid. III Corps advance across the Lys and onto Aubers Ridge is covered on pp. 94-110.

create a smoke screen to cover their deployment, but the waves of infantry were shot down when they advanced at dusk.

Only Kortekeer Cabaret had been lost, so 1st Division organised an attack to retake it the following day. One battalion advanced in the open, to draw fire, while two battalions crept forward, cutting gaps through the hedges, in case the Germans were watching the gates.[73] A bugle call sounded 1st Division's successful charge.[74]

The Germans again lit fires, so smoke hid the troops massing to attack, and they then sang as they marched forward; rapid fire routed them. Dense formations were also stopped in front of 2nd Division's positions around Poelcappelle.[75]

There was a breakthrough in 7th Division's line around Reutel when one battalion's machine guns were knocked out, but the Germans fell back when their own artillery started firing short. By this time the battalions were just 'holding a chain of posts', making communications difficult, especially during daylight hours.[76] Spies were thought to be operating behind 7th Division's lines, posing as stragglers, so officers were instructed to put orders in writing, while verbal instructions were to be viewed with suspicion.

Cavalry Corps, 20-23 October

The Cavalry Corps chose to withdrew to a safer line late on 20 October but the troopers were short of tools to make new trenches and they either had to dig by hand or borrow tools from the locals.[77] However, they were found to be in an equally exposed position at dawn on 21 October and the German artillery could range in on the overhead cover some men had installed over their trenches.[78]

General Hubert Gough issued instructions suggesting lines of retreat, if they were required, except General John Vaughan thought they were retirement orders.[79] He withdrew his men from Hollebeke, exposing 7th Division's flank but most of the area was retaken. Meanwhile, 2nd Cavalry Division fell back from Hollebeke, opening a gap between Zandvoorde and Hollebeke.

The Germans inched up the Messines Ridge to locate the cavalry line, while aerial spotters reported the columns of troops crossing the River Lys before they massed around Warneton and Houthem. On 26 October 3rd Cavalry Division reinforced

---

73 Wyrall, *History of the Second Division 1914-1918, Vol. 1*, p. 113. The Germans occasionally wove wire into the hedges, so the soldiers had to rely on field gates if they had no wire cutters. For their part, the defenders had their machine-guns trained on the evident gaps.
74 Edmonds, *Military Operations: France and Belgium, 1914, Vol. II*, pp. 185-6.
75 Ibid., pp. 186-8.
76 Ibid., pp. 189-90.
77 Ibid., pp. 143-4.
78 Ibid., pp. 152-3.
79 Ibid., pp. 153.

Zandvoorde while the 2nd Cavalry Division advanced west of the Comines Canal.[80] The cavalry then returned to the defensive as the Germans dug trenches and fortified farms close to their front line.

III Corps, 20-23 October[81]

The Germans captured Prémesques and Ennetières from 6th Division on 20 October but the attack against Ploegsteert Wood failed because No Man's Land was too wide. So, they ran towards 4th Division's line at dusk and then dropped to the ground before digging a new trench.[82] The attacks then slackened off because the Germans were concentrating on the situation around the Ypres Salient. III Corps was exhausted, so Pulteney made his engineers prepare a rear position called the 'Lines of Torres Vedras'.[83] He also made his artillery reorganise, so individual batteries were ready to support the infantry brigades at short notice.

II Corps, 13-23 October

III Corps made slow progress along the north bank of the La Bassée Canal, unaware that the Germans outnumbered them three to one.[84] Observers used mine workings, slag heaps, factory towers and church steeples to keep a watch on each other, but thick mist made observation impossible on 13 October. Smith-Dorrien allocated a field artillery brigade and a field howitzer battery to each brigade, while field gun sections were added to each battalion, to give close support. The advance came to a standstill the following day after the 1st Dorsets were massacred accepting a surrender.[85]

The advance onto the Aubers Ridge ended when 3rd Division encountered large numbers of Germans on 18 October.[86] Most fell back to a line the engineers had marked out with straw but the 2nd Royal Irish Regiment was surrounded in Pilly the following day. The Germans probed II Corps' new line and overran part of it in the mist, early on 22 October. It forced Smith-Dorrien to order another withdrawal of up to 2 miles to trenches dug by civilians under engineer supervision. Nevertheless, men

---

80   Ibid., pp. 250-1.
81   Ibid., pp. 138-142.
82   Ibid., p. 143.
83   Ibid., p. 355. Torres Vedras (Green Towers) was the Duke of Wellington's last stand line in Portugal during the Peninsular War (1808-14) over one hundred years before.
84   Ibid. II Corps' advance is detailed on pp. 80-5.
85   Brigadier General A. H. Hussey, *The Fifth Division in the Great War* (London: Nisbet, 1921), p. 37. Some Germans with their hands up dropped to the floor as the Dorsets went forward to take them prisoner. Others then opened fire from a hidden position.
86   Edmonds, *Military Operations: France and Belgium, 1914, Vol. II.* The II Corps withdrawal is covered on pp 80-91.

could not dig any deeper because of the high-water table and they had no barbed wire either.[87]

Trench Warfare

The trenches around Ypres were nothing more than ditches was there were no dug outs and little wire. They were disconnected and officers were easy targets for snipers as they ran along the line, passing on orders. Men sat in the mud during the bombardments, rising to their knees when the attack began, waiting until the enemy was close before opening rapid fire. The wounded had to lie in the dirt until they could be evacuated at nightfall and men went hungry and made each shot count, as they waited for the rations and ammunition to be sent forward.

The French artillery chose to cease fire as soon as the infantry left their trenches and the Germans soon learned to man their parapets when they stopped firing.[88] The British artillery fired 'bursts during which the infantry made their rushes', providing the observers could see the ground. After the assault had been delivered, they would establish 'a belt of fire through which its should be impossible for any counter-attack to penetrate.'[89]

Pre-war ammunition estimates had been determined by what had been fired during the war in South Africa (1899-1901). It was soon clear that the amount of shells required during trench warfare was far higher than anticipated, so firing often had to be restricted to critical periods.[90] Stocks eventually fell so low that I Corps had to pull a quarter of its guns out of the line.[91] The primitive wireless equipment was unreliable, there were no observation balloons and the Royal Flying Corps had a lot to learn before counter-battery fire was inefficient. It was decided that the best way to support the infantry was to disperse enemy attacks. but the artillery still had to learn how to prepare SOS barrages.[92]

The line was too fluid and there were too few resources to establish a telephone system yet, while the misty autumn weather made visual signalling unreliable. The most effective way to call down a barrage was for forward observers to note targets on a map and hand the information to a mounted officer who could take it to a battery.

---

87   Ibid., pp. 206. Sandbags and wire did not start arriving until 28 October.
88   Ibid., p. 91
89   Ibid., p. 91. Taken from 5th Divisional Artillery memorandum, dated 16 January 1915.
90   Ibid., pp. 13-15 details pre-war estimates, available shell stocks on the outbreak of war and steps taken to increase production.
91   Ibid., p. 13. For example, each of the 324 18-pounder field guns had a reserve of 1,000 rounds prior to the war. Factories could only to manufacture 10,000 shells a month – less than one shell per day per gun.
92   A pre-calculated barrage designed to be fired at No Man's Land when the infantry signalled an attack was under way.

Defending Ypres, 24-27 October

The BEF looked on as the French advanced ½ mile towards Passchendaele on 24 October but they had not gone far enough for I Corps to become involved. The Germans retaliated by using snipers and machine-gun teams to dominate the ground, firing from the upper storeys of houses when possible. The rest of the infantry crawled closer to the British and dug new trenches. Attacks were always preceded by artillery fire which flattened the trenches, buried men and jammed weapons with mud. But French and Rawlinson believed 7th Division lost more men than necessary because General Capper insisted on placing trenches on forward slopes with overhead cover, rather than digging them on the reverse slope.

The German infantry crawled even closer, ready to charge, while their guns fired a bombardment, but they were often stopped by rapid fire, sometimes followed by a counter-charge. But each time the battalions lost more men, while it was a dangerous business relieving them in the dark. Even more so, after German soldiers were found behind the lines dressed in Belgian and British uniforms taken from dead soldiers.

The artillery had been shelling 7th Division's salient around Kruiseecke throughout 25 October when a few men came forward when it was dark and asked if they could surrender. The 2nd Scots Guards were suspicious and then saw that several hundred were crawling forward behind them.[93] Others shouted, 'don't shoot, we are the Scots Guards and South Staffords', unaware their Pickelhaube helmets were silhouetted against burning buildings.

On 26 October, GHQ intercepted two conflicting messages; one threatened a major attack against 2nd Division while the other said the Germans were struggling. GHQ was also hearing about a lot of train movements behind the enemy line from its aerial observers.

At the front, mass attacks were replaced with subterfuge as men crept along the hedges towards Kruiseecke, shouting, 'retire' when they were close enough. Around 300 of the 2nd Staffords believed the order and many were shot down as they ran back.[94] The salient then collapsed and while some men were cut off, officers stopped the rest on a rally line.

Counter-attacks were usually pointless affairs which resulted in many casualties, as proved by the 2nd Division when they advanced on 27 October. The men gained a small amount of ground and then had to dig in after being pinned down, leaving them vulnerable to counter-attack.[95]

---

93   Edmonds, *Military Operations: France and Belgium, 1914, Vol. II*, pp. 239-40.
94   Ibid., pp. 245-6.
95   Wyrall, *History of the Second Division 1914-1918, Vol. 1*, p. 129-30.

II Corps, 24-30 October

German infantry crept along ditches towards 3rd Division's line around Neuve Chapelle early on 25 October. There was no wire and lookouts had no flares to light up the area when they realised the enemy were in their trenches. But the Germans just took what prisoners and documents they could and then withdrew, in possibly the first trench raid on the Western Front.[96] Tit-for-tat fighting for Neuve Chapelle followed, culminating in the loss of the village on 27 October.[97] The bombardment was delayed until 11 am by mist the following morning and it then lifted 500 yards in one jump fifteen-minutes later. It proved to be too far to support the infantry because it gave the Germans time to man their parapets.[98] The advance was uncoordinated and each group was shot down in turn, as they left their trenches. The problem was it had been made by seven units, composed of men speaking three languages.[99] Three staff officers had been sent to help the attack, but they were too few to make a difference. The Indian engineers suffered heavy casualties, because they had been deployed as storm troops. Field Marshal French had to issue a reminder to ban such practices because they needed engineers for their technical skills.[100]

The Germans abandoned Neuve Chapelle to regroup late on 29 October. They then tried three different ways to recapture it the following day. The first attack involved advancing through the morning mist; the second attempt was an impromptu affair, made as a French bombardment fell short on 3rd Division's trenches; their final effort involved sneaking into the village in the dark.[101] They were stopped each time and then the men of the Meerut Division[102] found it a struggle to take over the area. There were no communication trenches and the men had to crawl along ditches, so as not to alert the enemy.[103]

Summary, 24-28 October

The German reservists were being deployed en mass in divisions only to be mown down in their hundreds. Meanwhile, the British soldiers were proving they were more than a match for the Germans and while the reservists lacked training and stamina,

---

96   Ibid., p. 209 describes this action as an attack and successful counter-attack.
97   Ibid., the loss of the village is covered on pp. 211-5.
98   Edmonds, *Military Operations: France and Belgium, 1914, Vol. II*. The counter-attack against the village is described on pp. 216-20.
99   English, French and Indian.
100 Edmonds, *Military Operations: France and Belgium, 1914, Vol. II*, p. 218.
101 Ibid., p. 221-2.
102 One of the two Indian divisions dispatched to the Western Front in the autumn of 1914.
103 Ibid., p. 220.

they were being distributed amongst the seasoned regulars.[104] The question was, did the BEF have enough men to keep fending off large attacks?

Flying Corps' observers reported that many troops were heading for Flanders while GHQ could only expect six Territorial Force battalions until regular battalions returned from overseas stations. Ammunition trains were also arriving at Menin and Courtrai, while the BEF was being told there was no extra ammunition in Britain, so corps and divisions needed to conserve what they had.[105] Despite the bad news, Field Marshal French believed the Germans were 'quite incapable of making any strong and sustained attack', having suffering heavy casualties over the past few days.[106] Despite his optimism, officers had been sent to Boulogne and Calais, to sketch out defensive positions in case the BEF had to abandon Flanders.

Flooding the Yser, 28-30 October

The Belgian Army was struggling to hold the coastal sector, so locks and sluices along the Yser had been opened to flood the canal with sea water.[107] Arches and culverts had been blocked in such a fashion to make the water flood the German held area. The floodwaters spread 10 miles south to Dixmude and up to 5 miles wide. The Belgians might have been made safer, but the Germans responded by moving several divisions to fight the BEF around Ypres.

Ypres, 28-30 October

German troops had assembled north of the Menin Road during the hours of darkness. The men of 1st Division could see little through the morning mist on 29 October, while the artillery was busy with counter-battery fire.[108] Jamming weapons and defective bullets then left men searching bodies for rounds.[109] The Germans were already heading for Gheluvelt by the time reinforcements intervened. News of the breakthrough was dismissed by 7th Division as a false alarm, because it could not be seen from the lower ground south, of the Menin Road. A disaster was only averted because the mist cleared and the Germans were pinned down. A counter-attack reinforced by cooks, orderlies and servants regained the line. A fake message issued

---

104 Ibid., p. 210. The BEF's policy meant that veterans could help the reservists adapt to trench warfare; time and ammunition permitting. The German policy meant there was no cadre of experienced men, limiting what they could be ordered to do.
105 Ibid. Two examples are given on p. 208 and 379.
106 Ibid., p. 252.
107 Ibid., pp. 299-301.
108 Ibid., pp. 265-72.
109 Ibid., pp. 265. As many as 50 per cent of issue bullets were defective while a shortage of rifle oil and too much mud made it impossible to keep the rifles serviceable.

by the Germans sent the men retiring through Gheluvelt and the troops preparing to counter-attack mistook them for the enemy in the heavy rain.[110]

Probing attacks on 30 October located 7th Division's line around Broodseinde and the German infantry then crept along hedgerows while field guns were man-handled forward, ready to support the attack. Again, jamming weapons and a shortage of ammunition resulted in a withdrawal through the woods east of Zandvoorde.[111] Platoons worked in pairs as they escaped, taking in turns for one to run back on a pre-arranged signal, while the other opened rapid fire to keep the enemy pinned down.

The Cavalry Corps, 28-30 October

The Cavalry Corps was stretched thin across 9 miles, south of Ypres.[112] There were only around 1,000 rifles per mile to defend the line and men were sheltering in shallow and unconnected trenches, with little artillery to support them. A heavy bombardment forced 3rd Cavalry Division to abandon its position astride the Comines Canal but 2nd Cavalry Division held onto Messines Ridge, even after the troopers had been shelled out of their trenches.[113]

Assaults All Along the Line, 31 October

The hard-pressed British Tommies around Ypres were tired, dirty, unshaven and clothed in rags. Nevertheless, they held onto trenches as long as they had weapons and ammunition to fight with. There were, however, complaints about a new German mortar (*Minenwerfer*) were employed for the first time.[114] It could fire a 10-lb shell up to 300 yards and could flatten the defenders shallow trenches.

Gheluvelt was the target for the next big attack, because 1st Division's trenches were exposed on forward slopes. A counter-attack by the 1st South Wales Borderers stopped the first probe towards Gheluvelt Chateau, but the main attack drove the line back next to the Menin Road.[115] It was difficult to pass messages along the line but most of the men rallied on a reserve line.

Some Germans headed west into Gheluvelt while others turned north, towards the chateau. A burning farm helped the Germans enfilade the trenches and they were soon clearing the village.[116] Meanwhile, their artillery extended their range to catch the British reinforcements moving forward during the attack. The sight of the guns

---

110 Ibid., pp. 272-3.
111 Ibid., pp. 286-90.
112 Ibid., pp. 274-5.
113 Ibid., pp. 290-2.
114 Ibid., p. 341.
115 Ibid. The initial assault is described on pp. 312-20.
116 Ibid., pp. 317-20

being pulled out undermined morale[117] but rumours of prisoners being murdered and robbed made the infantry determined to fight on. One group held the west side of Gheluvelt until they were overrun, giving staff officers time to form a rally line at Veldhoek.[118]

A German spotter plane directed artillery fire onto Hooge Chateau, knocking out the staffs of both 1st and 2nd Divisions at a critical point in the battle.[119] But replacement officers were immediately appointed, new headquarters were opened, and staff officers were sent forward, to see what was happening. Haig returned from a visit to the front line to learn about the disaster and he sent every man forward to either reinforce the firing line or form a rally line.[120]

Senior officers had cantered around looking for reinforcements following the loss of Gheluvelt but they could only find the 2nd Worcesters.[121] Just 300 men advanced in columns of fours, only to find the Germans resting in Gheluvelt. They were driven out. Then the Germans who had advanced towards Veldhoek fell back Gheluvelt, only to find the Worcesters waiting for them.

The attack widened to include 7th Division's line through Herenthage Wood and Shrewsbury Forest in the afternoon.[122] Telephone lines were cut and all the runners were hit as they moved back making it difficult to pass messages along the line; one battalion was overrun because it never received its withdrawal order. The supports held on while the battalions to the flanks turned to hit the Germans with cross-fire. The generals and their staffs then gathered the few reserves they could find and their counter-attack restored the line.[123]

Bulfin's Group fell back to stay in line with 7th Division, only to see the counter-attack regain the line. General Edward Bulfin was moving his headquarters, and was unable to contact his troops, so he sent a staff officer forward to tell them to stand and fight. Another officer collected three cavalry regiments from I Corps headquarters and they reinforced the counter-attack through the wood. Officers encouraged their men to shout and cheer, convincing the Germans that there more men than there were.[124]

A two-hour bombardment was followed by an attack which drove 2nd Cavalry Division out of Hollebeke woods, near Wytschaete. The cavalry's field guns could do little,[125] but the 1/14th London Regiment (London Scottish) reinforced the ridge.[126]

117 Ibid. The disastrous episodes behind Gheluvelt are covered on p. 318.
118 Ibid. The defence of Veldhoek is detailed on pp. 330-331.
119 Ibid. The catastrophe is detailed on pp. 323-7.
120 Ibid., p. 327.
121 Ibid. The Worcester counter-attack is covered on pp. 328-30.
122 Ibid. The attack against 7th Division is explained on pp. 332-5.
123 Ibid., pp. 334-5.
124 Ibid. The counter-attack is detailed on p. 337.
125 Cavalry divisions were armed with 13-pounder guns and they were short of ammunition.
126 The London Scottish was the first Territorial Force infantry battalion to go into action.

They had never fired a shot in anger, their rifles could only fire single shots and they often jammed.[127] The cavalry south of Wytschaete also had defective machine-gun ammunition but the line still held.

German soldiers wore fake turbans during a night relief around Messines, confusing the incoming 2nd Inniskillings, and then overran the waiting Indian troops.[128] They eventually got into the village and the gunners man-handled their field guns down the roads to find targets, while engineers blew holes in walls so the infantry could move under cover. Reinforcements were needed if the Messines ridge was to be held.

I Corps, 1-10 November

On 1 November, scouts located 1st Division's position around Gheluvelt for the artillery to shell, while the attack went in against 7th Division, in the woods to the south.[129] Bulfin was wounded when the Germans broke through his line, but the flanks again turned to defeat them. A platoon of Irish Guards never received the message to withdraw and they stood their ground, disrupting the attack. The 2nd Grenadier Guards then fixed bayonets and charged through the wood to restore the line.

On 2 November, I Corps' artillery stopped firing, but a promised French infantry attack north of the Menin Road never materialised. The German infantry surged forward when the British guns went silent and they overran one battalion before spreading out behind 1st Division's line.[130] It needed French help to retake the lost trenches.

On 3 and 4 November, I Corps had to withdraw one in three guns from the line due to a lack of shells.[131] There were no infantry reserves left either, so GHQ's Chief Engineer, Brigadier General Spring Rice, decided it was time to build strongpoints behind the line.[132] Farms would be fortified and garrisoned, while nearby trenches would serve as rally points for stragglers and reinforcements. They would act as rendezvous points for reinforcements to head towards.[133]

Heavy rain and fog interfered with operations over the days that followed and 7th Division was relieved after being in action for twenty-four days. Gleichen's Group was

---

127 A shortage of Mark III Lee-Enfield rifles had resulted in Mark I*** rifles being converted to fire Mark VII ammunition. However, they became difficult to fire when they overheated.
128 Edmonds, *Military Operations: France and Belgium, 1914, Vol. II*, the attack against Messines is covered on pp. 304-7. Also J. Mereweather and Sir Frederick Smith, *The Indian Corps in France* (New York: E. P. Dutton, 1918) p. 38. Indian troops sometimes confused German and French soldiers.
129 Edmonds, *Military Operations: France and Belgium, 1914, Vol. II*, p. 358.
130 Ibid., pp. 366-370. The battalion was 1st King's Royal Rifle Corps.
131 Ibid., p. 379.
132 Ibid., pp. 377-8.
133 It meant reinforcements could be directed to pre-determined points.

compromised on 7 November, after an unauthorised order caused the 1st Bedfords to withdraw south of the Menin Road.[134] General Cavan assembled 1,000 men to clear the area, but it was too misty to arrange artillery support. Only some of the officers heard the single artillery gun shot, which signalled the attack at dawn, but the line was still restored.[135] The shelling of I Corps' line intensified around the Menin Road, starting on 8 November and it took every available man to hold the line in front of Veldhoek Chateau and Herenthage Woods.[136]

Cavalry Corps, 1-7 November

French troops took over 2nd Cavalry Division's trenches astride the Comines Canal but they were driven out of Wytschaete early the following morning.[137] A counter-attack was ambushed because the Germans shouted they were Indian troops and the troops fell back after hearing shouts to retire.[138] However, no one told the German artillery and they shelled the village all night. The German infantry withdrew before the dawn bombardment began, only to be shot at by their comrades who mistook them for British troops in the morning mist. The French and British cavalry were then able to occupy an abandoned Wytschaete.

The London Scottish were alerted by the sounds of German regimental bands, before they were driven off the Messines ridge by superior numbers. Both Wytschaete and Messines had to be abandoned during the night, because they were targets for the German artillery. The Cavalry Corps had too few heavy guns to retaliate with, so the troopers had to withdraw to a safe distance from the Messines Ridge.[139] Only then did they receive bayonets and entrenching tools.

The Germans dug saps ahead of their trenches, around the Comines Canal, and then emerged from them on 6 November to capture trenches from the French around Zillebeke.[140] The Germans were only 2 miles from Ypres until British cavalry recaptured the lost ground.

III Corps

There was little activity around Ploegsteert Wood, except when some Germans unsuccessfully tried to pass themselves off as Scottish soldiers with home-made kilts on 2 November. The final German attempt to take the wood from 4th Division failed on 9 November.

---

134 Ibid., p. 401.
135 Ibid., pp. 399-400.
136 Ibid., pp. 407-8.
137 Ibid., p. 364.
138 Simpson, *The History of the Lincolnshire Regiment, 1914-1918*, p. 63-4.
139 The low ground west of the ridge was observed and unsafe to hold.
140 Edmonds, *Military Operations: France and Belgium, 1914, Vol. II*, pp. 394-7.

11 November

A final attempt to break the line between Polygon Wood and Messines started with the heaviest bombardment of the battle at dawn on 11 November. The guns increased their range at 9 am and twenty-five battalions advanced as a plane flew low overhead to mark zero hour.[141] In places the bombardment had overshot 2nd Division's front line but the lookouts could not see the advancing infantry through the mist. A few men were in strongpoints. but the rest fought on south of Polygon Wood, throwing bandoliers along the line of rifle pits when ammunition ran short.[142]

The attack overran 1st Division's line between Polygon Wood and the Menin Road and then the mist cleared.[143] The machine-gun teams could then fire accurately from their strongpoints, splitting up the waves of Germans, driving many to seek cover in Nonne Bosschen. The survivors emerged from the far side, right in front of the artillery lines, and then turned tail not knowing how close they had been to breaking through.[144] Every spare man of 1st Division then counter-attacked through Nonne Bosschen, restoring the line as the heavens opened.[145]

Many men had been withdrawn from the trenches astride the Menin Road, to escape the worst of the preliminary bombardment, but a surprise attack captured them before they could be reoccupied.[146] Again, the clearing mist was the Germans' downfall and attacks against 3rd Division's position in Herenthage Wood and Shrewsbury Forest were carried out 'without enthusiasm and in a sort of dazed way as if [the Germans] were drugged'.[147]

Heavy rain started on 12 November and it turned to snow three days later, culminating in a blizzard on 19 November. Rain, wind, snow and ice hampered every aspect of military operations for the next four months. It interfered with observation, covered roads in mud and filled trenches with water. Soldiers had to learn how to survive in such conditions as they dug in and adapted to trench life.

The battle had shattered the BEF and while 2nd and 7th Divisions were around 30 percent of their full strength, 1st Division was down to 15 per cent. A new division, the 8th Division had deployed to France, using units from overseas postings, but there were no more regular soldiers or reservists to send. All that was left were new recruits and 'old, worn, drunken wasters' from the depots.[148]

---

141 Ibid., pp. 433-4.
142 Ibid., pp. pp. 440-1.
143 Ibid., pp. 432-6.
144 Ibid., pp. 438-9.
145 Ibid., pp. 440-3.
146 Ibid., pp. 427-32.
147 TNA WO 95/1571/1: 1st Cheshire War Diary.
148 Edmonds, *Military Operations: France and Belgium, 1914, Vol. II*, p. 449.

The 1914 Campaign Summary

The British Army had discussed strategy with the French Army and had made detailed deployment plans to move a 100,000 strong expeditionary force to France in the event of war. Both worked without a hitch but the rapid German advance across Belgium meant the BEF had no idea that it was greatly outnumbered around Mons on 23 August.

Many years employed as a colonial police force across the British Empire had resulted in a professional approach to training and it paid off in the early days of the campaign. Time and again small groups of men held off many times their number before withdrawing from contact. Inevitably, rudimentary communications meant that some units were overrun during the long retreat south.

Lord Kitchener reminded Field Marshal French that Britain only had one expeditionary force and he did well to keep it out of harm's way most of the time. Lieutenant General Smith-Dorrien had little option but to stand and fight at Le Cateau but the battle illustrated how easy it would have been to lose the BEF if it was caught.

The cavalry soon got into its stride, tracking and harassing the German columns, and their information was supplemented by the Royal Flying Corps' aerial observers. Cavalry units were also successful at protecting the rear of the BEF during its long withdrawal to the Marne and then covering its front during the advance to the Aisne.

The soldiers quickly adapted to static warfare, coming up with new ways to improve their fortunes in the trenches. However, the BEF was not powerful enough to break through the enemy line on the Aisne and it was barely strong enough able to defend its own around Ypres, in the face of superior number. It meant there was little time to learn from their lessons because everyone was too busy defending the line.

2

The Early Offensives
December 1914-June 1916

Winter 1914-15

The British Expeditionary Force spent the winter resting and reorganising, digging trenches and mapping trenches while rotation schedules were drawn up. Roads were improved, tracks were added, and billets, baths and laundries were built.[1] Plenty of work had to be done on creating two lines of communication to the coast.[2] There was a shortage of everything because the BEF had not planned for trench warfare, so the Royal Engineers set up parks to stockpile stores and workshops to repair weapons and equipment.[3] The Army Service Corps also opened depots and workshops to organise, service and repair transport. But the biggest shortage was in shells, because the Royal Artillery's estimates had been based on the Boer War experience.[4] It would be a couple of years before Britain's factories could supply enough ammunition and weapons for its army in the field.[5]

Field Marshal Sir John French also had a manpower problem, because some of the Reservists recalled to the army were unfit while others were unwilling to fulfil their obligation. In the meantime, Regular units were being recalled from across the Empire, while the Canadian Division and the Territorial Force Divisions were due to arrive in the spring.[6] Over 600,000 civilians had volunteered across Britain in just

---

1   Sir James E. Edmonds, *Military Operations: France and Belgium, Vol. I: Battle of Neuve Chapelle and Battles of Ypres* (London, HMSO, 1927), p. 5.
2   Edmonds, *Military Operations: France and Belgium, 1915, Vol. I*, p. 34-6 explains routes and base ports, the regulating stations (where men and material waited to be called forward) and the railheads (where it was collected from).
3   Ibid., p. 6.
4   Ibid., p. 38 to 50 discusses the steps (and problems they caused) the War Office Armaments Output Committee took to increase shell production.
5   Ibid., pp. 50-8 details weapon and munition deliveries to France in 1915.
6   Ibid., p. 27.

a few weeks and they all had to be trained and equipped. It was a monumental task and the Derby Scheme had been introduced on 16 October 1914, to regulate the flow of volunteers.[7] The expanding BEF was divided into two armies on Christmas Day 1914, with General Sir Douglas Haig in charge of First Army and General Sir Horace Smith-Dorrien at Second Army.[8]

Trench fighting required new weapons, and many were invented in the trenches or in factories across Britain. The troops acquired personal weapons for trench fighting, including dangerous home-made grenades while a dozen designs were sent to France and Flanders.[9] The first mortars were also inaccurate and unsafe, particularly the catapults used to lob hand-grenades across No Man's Land.[10]

The new style of warfare also needed new training establishments. A Machine-Gun School was opened in November 1914 and an Officer Cadet School the following month. The Officer Training Corps and universities also stepped up recruitment to train men to lead the tens of thousands of men who were flocking to the colours.[11]

The BEF's first attack in Flanders took place on the night of 14 December, between Messines and Warneton.[12] The plan was to support a French attack between Hollebeke and Wytschaete and while 3rd Division was told to attack with the *utmost determination*, 5th Division would only *convey the impression that an attack is going to be delivered*. Meanwhile, III Corps was to *make demonstrations against the enemy with the object of holding him to his trenches*. There had been no reconnaissance nor artillery preparation and the assault troops encountered hedges laced with wire and flooded trenches.

Ten small mines exploded around Givenchy on 20 December 1914, the first sign that warfare had gone below ground.[13] There were raids along the La Bassée Canal early in the New Year; a deserter warned of another mine under Givenchy on 25 January.[14] Another loss on 1 February was countered, following a short barrage by the heavy howitzers, the first coordination of infantry and artillery activities in an attack.

Field Marshal French was concerned about the increase in German activity, so a few days later he issued instructions to carry out raids, to keep the initiative and take prisoners to identify German units.[15]

Then 2nd Division overran the Brickstacks at 2.30 pm on 6 February, following another short barrage and many German tunnels were found. The response was to

7   Ibid., pp. 51-2 discusses the organisation of over 2.4 million men into those who immediately enlisted and those who attested (to enlist when called up).
8   Ibid., p. 23.
9   Ibid., p. 7.
10   Ibid., p. 8.
11   Ibid., p. 11.
12   Ibid., p. 18.
13   Ibid., p. 20.
14   Ibid., pp. 29-30.
15   Ibid., pp. 31-2.

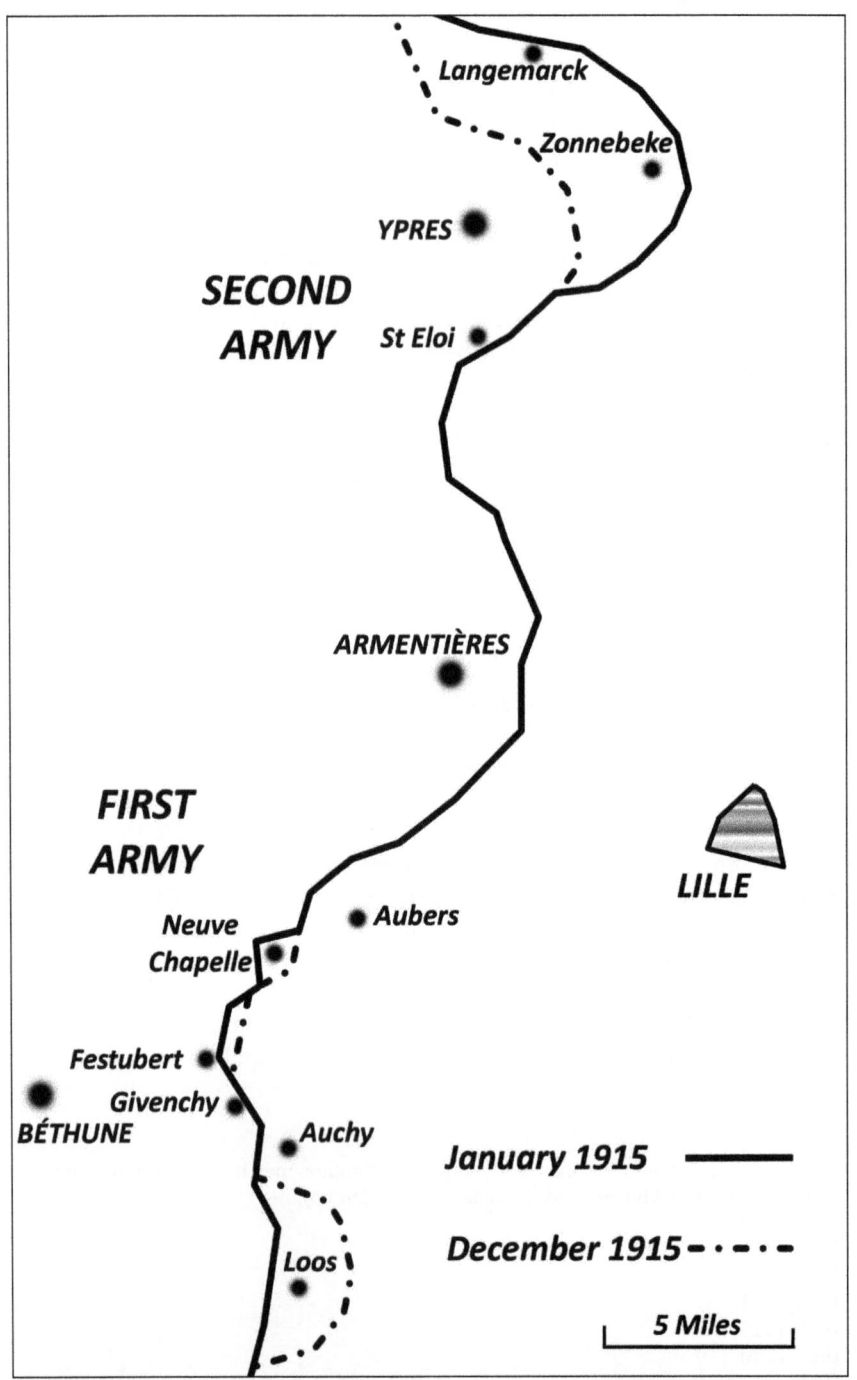

Map 2. 1915 Battles, 10 March–13 October 1915: The front barely moved in 1915 and early 1916, as the BEF struggled to come to terms with offensive warfare.

recruit professional miners and the first group arrived from Britain at the end of the month. They were organised into Tunnelling Companies and put to work digging tunnels.[16] Mining activity was stepped up and there was prolonged fighting for St Eloi between 14 and 17 March, because it overlooked the south side of the Ypres Salient.[17]

The politicians were considered sending resources to the Dardanelles, a new theatre, in the Eastern Mediterranean.[18] Both General Joffre and Field Marshal French wanted all the resources on the Western Front, ready to launch a combined offensive as soon as the weather permitted.

Planning for Neuve Chapelle

On 12 February 1915, Field Marshal French approved General Haig's plan to attack Neuve Chapelle on 9 March,[19] even though First Army only had enough ammunition for a few days offensive action.[20] Staff presented feasibility studies, while GHQ's intelligence estimated that 20,000 German troops could reinforce the area in just thirty-six hours. So, they agreed that Second Army would feint an attack, to pin reserves east of Ypres.

First Army designed the first attack timetable, which set a precedence for the rest of the war. It included a deployment plan, a preliminary bombardment, a barrage which jumped forward in bounds according to a timetable and plans for holding and consolidating the enemy trenches.

Tests had proved that high-explosive shells tended to throw wire entanglements into the air, creating equally difficult obstacles. But they had also proved that blasts of shrapnel balls could cut a gap in a belt of wire in just thirty minutes. Further tests proved that the artillery needed thirty-five minutes to blast gaps in the German parapets.[21] Batteries moved into camouflaged positions during the hours of darkness and registered their targets a few at a time, while ground observers adjusted the fall of shot.

Map fire was very inaccurate at this stage of the war because maps were poor, the guns were not calibrated and the weather was not monitored.[22] Therefore, the Royal Flying Corps helped adjust the registration of the guns onto distant targets, including

---

16   Ibid., pp. 32-3.
17   Ibid., pp. 33-4.
18   Ibid. Plans for the Gallipoli campaign are discussed on pp. 62-5.
19   Ibid. First Army's plan for Neuve Chapelle is outlined on pp. 76-7.
20   Ibid. Available shell quantities are on p. 95.
21   Ibid. These tests are covered on p. 78.
22   The efficiency of an artillery piece decreased due to wear and tear while air pressure and wind affected the range. These adjustments would eventually be factored in towards the end of 1916.

enemy gun batteries. There were also plans to photograph the enemy trenches, so accurate maps could be drawn, but misty weather interfered with the flying schedules.[23]

The plan was to have all the batteries in place ten days before the attack, but many arrived late and their deployment was rushed.[24] The engineers then had difficulties building gun platforms, while the observers found it hard to find look out posts in houses and trees. GHQ's Heavy Artillery Reserve only had six heavy batteries and only one of two 15-inch howitzers turned up in time with faulty ammunition.[25]

The infantry had dug assembly trenches, where the troops could deploy but a high-water table meant that they needed breastworks. The real ones were hidden behind canvas screens while dummy ones were prepared to draw enemy artillery fire. The assault troops rehearsed the advance behind the lines, while every officer visited the front, to see their objective, returning to explain the task to their men.[26]

The engineers had improved roads and tracks and laid tramways behind the lines. It made it easier to fill the depots with tools and stores and dumps with ammunition and rations. Each infantry brigade formed a grenade company of 120 men while each battalion had twenty bombers; they each carried ten bombs.[27]

Communications would be limited to the messages that runners carried back to their headquarters, while observers had to watch for coloured flags which indicated trenches or buildings had been captured.[28]

Each field battery was given a specific target and the bombardment started at 7.35 am on the day of the attack, giving the gunners only thirty minutes to fire at their designated targets.[29] The 18-pounders targeted the wire, the howitzer batteries hit the trenches and the heavy howitzers shelled batteries and other targets around the village. Extra field batteries shelled the trenches either side of the attack, to confuse the enemy.[30] They all extended their ranges at 8.05 am, as the infantry advanced across No Man's Land. The gunners continued to extend their range at set times, according to a strict time-table, while the infantry advanced between coloured objective lines marked on their maps. It was the first time an artillery barrage set the pace of the advance and it was soon discovered that the jumps were too large to give much protection.

---

23 Edmonds, *Military Operations: France and Belgium, 1915, Vol. I.* The beginnings of aerial photography is discussed on pp. 85-6.
24 Ibid., p. 84.
25 Ibid., heavy artillery organisation is detailed on pp. 86-7.
26 Ibid., p. 82.
27 Ibid., p. 120.
28 The problem was, the flags could also be seen by German observers.
29 Edmonds, *Military Operations: France and Belgium, 1915, Vol. I.* Further explanation of the bombardment is given on p. 77.
30 Ibid. Details on the preliminary bombardment are provided on pp 91-3 and appendix on p. 391.

Attack on Neuve Chapelle

Gaps were made in the British entanglement during the night and then camouflaged by moveable sections called 'knife-edges'. The 15-inch howitzer fired the warning shot at 7.30 am and the bombardment started five minutes later. Unfortunately, the aerial observers had failed to spot that the support trench had been abandoned due to flooding, so many shells were wasted. Meanwhile, eight spotter planes reported the enemy guns which retaliated to the heavy batteries by wireless. The field artillery lifted east of the village at 7.40 am, creating the first example of a box barrage.

Two siege batteries had not had time to register targets on 8th Division's left, so they missed their target and the infantry attack failed.[31] Two more bombardments eventually convinced the Germans to surrender around 10 am. The advance was then stopped by the British barrage and there was no way to tell the gunners. The right brigade had advanced fast until it was stopped by the British guns; they eventually extended their range at 8.35 am. It was around midday before 7th Division could be ordered forward but its advance was soon stopped by machine-gun fire and again there was no way to ask the artillery for assistance.

Smoke obscured the tree which marked 7th (Meerut) Division's direction of advance and the right flank veered into uncut wire.[32] The rest of the division discovered that Smith-Dorrien Trench was full of water, so a new one had to be dug, while high officer casualties meant that no attempt was made to locate the German trench. The order to attack again at 3.30 pm arrived at zero hour, and the barrage was moving as infantry filed across planks placed over the Layes stream. The Indians then chose to dig in after a prisoner reported that the large wood in front of them was occupied in strength; the line needed to be secured before it was dark.[33]

The orders for 7th Division to resume the advance were eventually issued at 2.55 pm, but there had been no time to re-register the guns.[34] At 3.30 pm the single brigade headed east, rather than north-east, only to be pinned down by the British bombardment. It was impossible to contact the artillery before nightfall, so the men dug in.

A few small attacks and bombardments were made at other points along the BEF's line, including Chinese attacks which involved shooting and cheering but no advance; just dummies to fire at.[35] The main effort was made by 2nd Division at Givenchy, where

---

31   Ibid., 8th Division's attack is given on pp. 95-9 and 100-1.
32   J. Mereweather and Sir Frederick Smith, *The Indian Corps in France* (New York: E. P. Dutton, 1918), pp. 227-9. The Indian trench was at an angle to the German, increasing the problem.
33   Ibid., p. 244-5. The wood was known as Bois de Biez.
34   Edmonds, *Military Operations: France and Belgium, 1915, Vol. I*, details the delay in orders is on 101-2; 7th Division's attack is provided on pp. 106-8.
35   False trenches were also dug in other locations in order to draw attention away from the attack front.

the artillery opened fire when the assault started at Neuve Chapelle. The infantry were stopped by wire which had lain hidden behind a mound in No Man's Land.

Neuve Chapelle Continues

Battalion commanders had wanted a longer bombardment on 11 March, but First Army only had enough shells for fifteen minutes. The gunners did not know where the British or German trenches were and they had to fire blind into the mist before the 7 am attack.

Men of both 7th and 8th Divisions were pinned down crossing ditches and a message reported that Layes stream had been reached on the left flank.[36] An observer then saw British troops moving around the Moated Grange, not realising they were prisoners being sent to the rear. The guns were told to extend their range and they overshot a new German trench, which had been dug in front of 7th Division during the night. The late decision to renew the attack at 2 pm and the loss of many runners meant that both 7th and 8th Divisions' battalions received their orders just before zero hour; no more progress was made.[37]

The bombardment overshot a new trench dug in front of the Meerut Division and they never saw 8th Division moving past their left flank in the mist; their signal to advance.[38] The Indians also received the afternoon order just before zero hour and again they did not move due to a misunderstanding with 8th Division.[39]

The plan was to attack again at 10.30 am on 12 March, once the morning mist had cleared, but the German guns opened fire at 4.30 am and their infantry advanced thirty minutes later.[40] Bombing attacks against 7th Division were stopped, while the only success in 8th Division's sector occurred when Germans were mistaken for men returning from a listening post in the mist. The Indians mistook Germans wearing greatcoats for Scottish troops in kilts until they noticed they had spikes on their helmets.[41] Flares were used to light up No Man's Land, so the troops could see to stop the final attack against Port Arthur strongpoint.

A heavy morning mist postponed First Army's attack for two hours[42] but the runners carrying the delay order were killed, so 7th Division advanced at the original time. The troops went prone when they realised there was no barrage and then crept

36   Edmonds, *Military Operations: France and Belgium, 1915, Vol. I,* the morning attack is detailed on pp. 122-6.
37   Ibid. The afternoon attack is covered on pp. 126-30.
38   Mereweather and Smith, *The Indian Corps in France,* p. 250.
39   Ibid., p. 250. The 8th Division battalion on the Indian flank reported that 'nothing was known of any intended attack at 2.15 pm.'
40   Ibid. The German attack is covered on pp. 130-6.
41   TNA: WO 95/3946/1: 2/3rd Gurkha Rifles War Diary.
42   Edmonds, *Military Operations: France and Belgium, 1915, Vol. I.* First Army's afternoon attack is described on pp. 137-42.

towards the Quadrilateral when the guns eventually opened fire. Unfortunately, the barrage fell short in 8th Division's sector and no one could contact the guns, so the infantry withdrew to safety. Battalion commanders initially refused to send their men forward, but their divisional commander overruled them. A second attempt at 5.15 pm got nowhere. The delay order did not get to all the Meerut Division's battalions in time and the men who went over the top were pinned down. They then had to endure two hours laid in No Man's Land until the guns opened fire at the revised zero hour.[43]

Reports talked of a breakthrough, so Haig told the 2nd Cavalry Division to exploit the imaginary success.[44] The afternoon bombardment landed too far ahead of the front line and so 7th Division's battalion commanders ignored the order to advance. It was dark by the time 8th Division's battalion commanders were told to attack, and the messengers got lost while the gunners fired blind into the night. An attack at 6.05 pm failed in the darkness, while further attempts were cancelled.

One final attack on 7th Division's front at 9.30 am the following morning was a disaster. The British trenches were full of men, so many spent spend the night laid in the open, behind them. Observers mistook the prone figures for Germans when the morning mist cleared, and the gunners opened fire on their own.[45] They had to wait until dusk before they could withdraw.

Gas Attack at Ypres, 22 April

Second Army took over more of the Ypres Salient from the French on 15 April, only to hear that they thought the Germans were planning to use gas, as soon as the wind was blowing in the right direction.[46] Prisoners said they seen large numbers of cylinders in their trenches and they contained 'a gas which is intended to render the enemy unconscious or to asphyxiate him'.[47] Second Army had insufficient men to carry out raids, so the artillery was told to fire random barrages to try and provoke a reaction and even puncture some cylinders.

There was a diversion when Second Army attacked Hill 60, south-east of Ypres at 7.05 pm on 17 April. Three mines exploded, the artillery opened fire and then 5th Division's infantry took the observation post.[48] Tit-for-tat fighting stopped on 22 April because of the gas attack but the Germans succeeded in retaking the hill on 1 May, using gas.

43   Mereweather and Smith, *The Indian Corps in France,* p. 253
44   Edmonds, *Military Operations: France and Belgium, 1915, Vol. I.* The evening attack is detailed on pp. 142-7.
45   TNA: WO 95/1656/2: 2nd Gordon Highlanders War Diary.
46   Colonel G. Nicholson, *Canadian Expeditionary Force, 1914-1919* (Ottawa: Roger Duhamel, 1962), p. 60.
47   Edmonds, *Military Operations: France and Belgium, 1915, Vol. I,* p. 164.
48   Ibid., pp. 166-70.

German batteries registered their targets early on 22 April and then opened a heavy bombardment of the rear areas at 5 pm. Chlorine gas was released from 5,730 cylinders at the same time and around 160 tons drifted across No Man's Land, north-east of Ypres, in less than ten minutes.[49] They produced *'a cloud of green vapour several hundred yards in length'[50]* which drifted slowly over the 2-mile length of trenches between Steenstraat and Langemarck.

Canadian and French soldiers became aware of an acrid smell and then their eyes watered, throats were irritated, and noses tingled.[51] Most of the French infantry and artillery fell back, followed by German infantry, heading for Boesinghe, Pilckem and Langemarck. There were chaotic scenes as the Germans moved past the Canadian Division's flank.[52] Battalions from 27th and 28th Divisions deployed along the canal north of Ypres, and around at St Jean and Potijze without waiting for any orders. Many Canadian field batteries were caught in the process of being relieved and they were unable to give covering fire. The heavy batteries also had to withdraw to safe distance and re-establish communications before they could help.

By nightfall, there was a huge gap in the line north-east of Ypres and there were few troops to stop the Germans reaching Ypres.[53] The Germans had halted 2-miles from the town for two reasons. They were no reserves to go advance further while the troops stayed a respectful distance from the gas because they had no masks. In summary, German high command had underestimated how effective the gas would be.

Plugging the Breach, 23 and 24 April

A counter-attack during the night had taken Kitchener's Wood but the troops had to withdraw at dawn, because the position was surrounded by Germans.[54] At dawn, British aerial spotters confirmed that there was 2-mile gap between the Yser Canal and Kitchener's Wood. Second Army formed two ad-hoc brigades and they had orders to capture Mauser Ridge, taking any troops they found forward with them. Brigadier General Mercer's group advanced at 5.25 am but there was little artillery support and there was no sign of the French. The French eventually attacked at 7 am but they could not retake Mauser Ridge either. It took Brigadier General Geddes all morning to find the seven battalions sent to him because he had been given no extra staff officers; so all he could do was deploy on Hill Top Ridge.[55]

49   Nicholson, *Canadian Expeditionary Force,* p. 62.
50   TNA: WO95/3717: 1st Canadian Division War Diary, April 1915 Appendices.
51   Edmonds, *Military Operations: France and Belgium, 1915, Vol. I,* pp. 177-8.
52   Nicholson, *Canadian Expeditionary Force,* pp. 62-4.
53   Edmonds, *Military Operations: France and Belgium, 1915, Vol. I,* pp. 180-3.
54   Nicholson, *Canadian Expeditionary Force,* p. 66.
55   Edmonds, *Military Operations: France and Belgium, 1915, Vol. I,* pp. 196-7.

A second attempt at 2.45 pm was postponed, to give the infantry time prepare, but no one told the artillery.[56] It left the guns short of ammunition by the time Mercer's group advanced at 4.25 pm while French troops interfered with its advance. Geddes group advanced thirty minutes late on Mauser Ridge, only to withdraw from the exposed position, as soon as it was dark.[57] No one supervised the digging and some of the trenches were found to be in the wrong position when they were checked at dawn. It left Geddes' men overlooked by Mauser Ridge, holding ground they could have occupied without a fight and in an organised manner under cover of darkness.

The Germans had captured St Julien by midday and the British battalion commanders agreed they had to withdraw a short distance, because their trenches were under observed artillery fire. Major General Richard Turner misunderstood his orders and issued instructions for everyone to head back to the GHQ Line.[58] Some officers followed their orders, but others decided to stand and fight astride the Steen stream because it was too dangerous to retire. Reinforcements then arrived, only to find there were no trenches for them to shelter in; so they had to dig their own. They then made a hasty counter-attack, which stopped the Germans leaving the village.

Meanwhile, the Canadian Division had been under attack on both days, falling each back time the Germans threatened to overrun their line or outflank it. More gas drifted across the line on 24 April and the Canadians tied handkerchiefs soaked in water or urine around their faces. They struggled with their Ross rifles, because they often jammed in the muddy conditions.[59]

Ypres, 25 April to 2 May

General Hull was told the rest of the Northumbrian Division was marching forward and he had to attack Kitchener's Wood and St Julien at 3.30 am. It left him having to find and organise fifteen battalions in the dark and rain with no staff officers or signal company. They had to file through two narrow gaps in the GHQ Line wire, meaning hardly anyone made it to briefing. So, Geddes was forced to postpone the attack until 5.30 am, knowing that it would be light. His men would be advancing 'without adequate artillery preparation and support, on ground unknown and reconnoitred...'[60]

Some battalions advanced at the original time, some moved at the new time, some were late, and the rest never received their orders. They all heard the guns fire at 3.30 am because no one had told the artillery of the change in time. It left the gunners

---

56 Nicholson, *Canadian Expeditionary Force*, p. 69-70.
57 Edmonds, *Military Operations: France and Belgium, 1915, Vol. I*, pp. 202-6.
58 Ibid., pp. 225-6.
59 Nicholson, *Canadian Expeditionary Force*, p. 156 explains the problems with the Ross Rifle. The British had refused to supply Lee-Enfield rifles to Canadian units in the Boer War, so Canada had made her own. They often clogged up in muddy trenches while the British supplied ammunition often jammed. They would be replaced in the summer of 1916.
60 Edmonds, *Military Operations: France and Belgium, 1915, Vol. I*, p. 240.

short of shells to support the attack, while mist at zero hour meant the observers could not see that some batteries were overshooting their targets. Two battalions advanced towards Fortuin at 3.30 am and then withdrew in the wrong direction when Germans approached. Five battalions advanced at 5.30 am, only to be pinned down in front of Kitchener's Wood and St Julien. The British guns were firing short and there was no way of contacting them in the dark, while snipers hiding in the crops started targeting the officers as soon as it was light. Everyone fell back to a safe distance as soon as the mist cleared but the reserves had to cover the gap left by the two missing battalions. It had been a costly attack, but Hull's men had stopped a counter-attack from St Julien.[61]

The Canadians around s'Gravenstafel endured a nine-hour bombardment and then there was a two-hour break, while the German spotter planes checked the targets. The German infantry crept towards the Stroom stream when the guns restarted at 3.30 pm and the Canadians were 'simply blown out of their trenches'.[62] It was impossible to get ammunition and reinforcements forward or casualties back, so the battalion commanders sent as many men back as they dare at dusk; those who remained behind were overrun during the night. Overnight, 4th Division arrived but its guides struggled to find the battalions they supposed to relieve.

Smith-Dorrien protested when the French asked for zero on 26 April to be brought forward three hours to 2 pm, but GHQ insisted. There was the usual shortage of heavy guns while the field batteries west of the canal were too far away to be effective. The Lahore Division's six battalions became mixed up as they crossed hedgerows and ditches and they were all pinned down close to the enemy trench.[63] A gas release caused panic amongst the Indian battalions, while the British battalions withdrew when it was dark.[64] Four battalions were sent forward to restore the line but they found few men holding it.

The Northumbrian Brigade never received its order to attack St Julien, but it followed the Lahore Division into action; it was the first time a territorial brigade had made an attack. But the men were given no any extra ammunition and they came under shell fire as they filed through the few gaps in the GHQ Line wire. The delay meant the barrage had finished by the time they advanced and the Indian troops then veered into their path.[65] The brigade was pinned down in front of St Julien and it withdrew at dusk, having lost over two-thirds of its strength.[66] Germans dressed in British uniforms probed the line around s'Gravenstafel during the night, shouting

---

61   Ibid. There is a detailed account of the attack on pp. 240-3.
62   Nicholson, *Canadian Expeditionary Force*, pp. 81-2. Brigadier General (later Lieutenant General) Arthur Currie's words.
63   Edmonds, *Military Operations: France and Belgium, 1915, Vol. I*, p. 256-8.
64   Mereweather and Smith, *The Indian Corps in France*, p. 304-5.
65   Ibid., p. 316. Heavy fire aimed at hedges and ditches (where men were likely to seek cover) drove the Indians off course.
66   Ibid., pp. 261-3.

messages in English to try and locate the line.[67] Two more attacks on 27 April failed to make any headway because Second Army's line had stabilised.

French sacked Smith-Dorrien for daring to suggest pulling back to a tighter defensive position around Ypres. General Herbert Plumer took over the salient and was told to do what had been proposed, so the surplus troops and guns could be moved move west of the town.[68] Mist helped covered the withdrawal, which started on 1 May, but the Germans attacked the following day. The eight-hour bombardment culminated in gas shells being fired at the British gun batteries, to interfere with the counter-barrage.[69]

Gas was released thirty minutes later but the cloud was only waist high, so the men climbed into the open to fire and stopped the attack.[70] The Germans incorrectly assumed that the gas had been too weak, so they planned another attack with more cylinders. However, the retirement resumed when it was dark, and the guns were followed by the infantry who withdrew in three stages before midnight. A few men remained behind to fire weapons and flares while medics stayed with the seriously wounded.

End of Second Ypres

Only one sentry saw the gas creeping over Hill 60 at 8.45 am on 5 May and he was unable to raise the alarm to stop the Germans seizing the summit.[71] A second gas release at 11 am sparked a withdrawal from the nearby Zwarteleen salient. The counter-attack started from the support trench by accident and the troops were unable to catch up with the creeping barrage.

The rest of Second Army was left holding a semi-circle of new trenches, only 3-miles from Ypres. Plumer planned a support line of strong points and a reserve line along the canal and the town ramparts but the Germans attacked before they were completed. A small break was made in 28th Division's line, north of Frezenberg, at dawn on 8 May and it soon spread to almost 2-miles wide. A rocket signal signalled a second attack in the afternoon and several battalions were overrun in the charge that followed. The Germans then bombed to the flanks, widening the gap across 27th Division's line.[72] A withdrawal order was misinterpreted by some as a general retirement, but the rest fought on, because it was too dangerous to leave their trenches. Plumer sent his remaining reserve forward but 500 men could not cover the ½ mile wide gap. A gas release panicked more men, expanding the gap from Mousetrap Farm to the Zonnebeke railway; a distance of 2-miles. It was only the refusal of the

---

67   TNA: WO 95/2277/3: 1st Suffolks War Diary.
68   Edmonds, *Military Operations: France and Belgium, 1915, Vol. I*, pp. 275-6.
69   This would evolve into a standard artillery tactic for the rest of the war.
70   Edmonds, *Military Operations: France and Belgium, 1915, Vol. I*, pp. 290-1.
71   Ibid., pp. 304-6.
72   Ibid., pp. 314-20.

Germans to advance over the Frezenberg Ridge that gave Second Army time to rally enough men to form a new line.[73]

The Aubers Ridge offensive and the Artois plateau on 9 May meant there was a lull in the fighting in the Ypres Salient. Second Army was so short of troops, that it had to deploy dismounted cavalry regiments, even though they had no experience of trench fighting. A few Germans dressed in British uniforms and shouted warnings not to fire but no one around Mousetrap Farm was fooled. The next attack began with the heaviest bombardment of the battle during the early hours of 13 May. The attack began around 8 am and it drove the Cavalry Force off the Verlorenhoek Ridge.[74]

Lieutenant-Colonel Ferguson, 28th Division's medical officer, suggested using lint masks soaked in a bicarbonate of soda solution and officers were sent to Paris to buy the materials.[75] GHQ opened an experimental laboratory and while Professors Watson, Haldane and Baker designed a full-face respirator, Major Cluny McPherson of the Newfoundland Medical Corps designed a gas helmet with Professor Watson. Units also put in place a range of warning measures, including weather vanes, look outs and alarms.

A gas helmet which consisted of a flannel sack, soaked in a chemical solution which neutralised the chlorine gas, was designed. Sixteen were issued to each battalion in the middle of May, to protect the machine-gun teams. They were uncomfortable, unreliable and the soldier could barely see through the celluloid eye-piece. However, they were better than nothing and every man would have one by the beginning of July. Chemists had also invented the Vermorel sprayer, which was used to neutralise pockets of gas, particularly in trenches and dug outs.

A series of red flares at 2.45 am on 24 May told the German gunners to start firing. A gas cloud spread across a 5-mile-wide front, the largest release so far. It took a long time to pass over 4th Division's trenches, where they bent around Mouse Trap Farm, and the position was lost. It also prompted another breakthrough around Bellewaarde Lake, but the clearing skies meant the assault troops were spotted in the moonlight and could be stopped. The two breaks meant an exposed section of the GHQ Line around Wieltje had to be abandoned, leaving the Germans only 1-mile from Ypres' ramparts.

Aubers Ridge, 9 May

GHQ was confident it had the formula for breaking the German line after Neuve Chapelle. *By means of careful preparation as regards details and thorough previous registration of the enemy's trenches by our artillery, it appears that a sector of the enemy's*

---

73   Ibid., pp. 320-2.
74   Ibid., pp. 332-4.
75   Ibid., the design and making of the first gas masks is covered on p. 217.

front-line defence can be captured with comparatively little loss.[76] What it did not know was that the Germans had changed the rules. They increased the number of troops holding the front line, thickened parapets and built machine-guns posts and dug-outs under them. Extra wire entanglements had been added while communication trenches were turned into fire trenches. More importantly, a second line reinforced by strongpoints had been built where the front-line troops could rally, or the reserves could deploy.[77]

Air patrols flew over the battlefield for four days but the flat ground meant the batteries had to deploy a long way back, making registration difficult.[78] The bombardment began at 5 am but First Army only had enough ammunition for a forty-minute bombardment and it merely 'raised a curtain of dust and smoke' which alerted the Germans.[79] The observers could not see the barrage in the early morning light but they would have seen two problems if they had. Many shells were falling short, because the guns were worn out, and many shells were failing to explode, because of poor quality control in the factories.[80]

The field guns again cut the wire and two had been deployed in the front line so the gunners could fire directly at their target. Unfortunately, one smashed its emplacement floor after opening only one gap and the artillery had no time to remedy the situation.[81] Field howitzers targeted the trenches and 'Infantry Artillery Groups' hit strongpoints, while two Heavy Artillery Groups targeted enemy batteries and other long-range targets. The infantry deployed in No Man's Land during the final ten minutes of intense shelling, but signs of activity in the German trench meant that it was having little effect.[82]

Only a few trenches were captured on IV Corps' left before 8th Division's assault was pinned down, leaving the support waves laid in No Man's Land. On the right, the assault wave crowded through the single gap in the wire only to find their way forward blocked by a ditch filled with wire. It left IV Corps with three lodgements in the enemy trenches and the artillery had no idea where they were.[83]

Heavy fire made it impossible to cross No Man's Land, so ammunition ran out and men started falling back. Prisoners running for cover were even mistaken for

76   Sir James E. Edmonds, *Military Operations: France and Belgium, 1915, Vol. II: Battles of Aubers Ridge, Festubert, and Loos* (London: HMSO, 1928), p.13.
77   Edmonds, *Military Operations: France and Belgium, 1915, Vol. II*. Details of the German counter measures are on pp. 14-5.
78   Ibid., p. 20. Sound ranging had been rejected as because experts 'did not consider it worth pursuing'. Flash spotting was in its infancy. Both systems used observers to denote angles to an enemy battery, so it could be located by mathematical triangulation.
79   Ibid. The bombardment and barrage are explained in full on pp.17-9, 41.
80   New factories had opened but they were turning out sub-standard shells as they tried to meet orders because quality control was not fully understood. Fuses did not fit or failed to work, casings were the wrong size and propellant charges did not work.
81   Edmonds, *Military Operations: France and Belgium, 1915, Vol. II*, p. 34.
82   Ibid., p. 33.
83   Ibid. A description of 8th Division's attack is provided on pp. 33-6.

a counter-attack. Haig wanted Rawlinson to *press the attack vigorously and without delay*[84] but the trenches were full of injured men and it would take until nightfall to reorganise the line for defence, never mind another assault.

The Germans had seen the Meerut Division open gaps in the wire and put bridges across the dykes around Rue du Bois. The waves of Indians were shot down in turn as they clambered over the parapet until battalion commanders stopped any more going forward.[85] Another thirty-minute barrage and a second attempt at 7 am also ended in disaster.[86]

On I Corps' front, 1st Division's assault wave kept advancing, expecting others to clear the trenches around the Cinder Track behind them. However, machine-gun fire stopped the support wave in No Man's Land. The British artillery then started firing short and it took time to tell them to extend their range.[87]

A second forty-five-minute bombardment ended at 7 am but no one advanced because the trenches were filled with wounded men. Organising a final attempt at Rue de Bois was virtually impossible and it had to be postponed until 4 pm. The Germans were so confident of success, that they stood on the parapet to shoot at the men when they clambered into No Man's Land.[88] After 9,500 casualties, no ground had been taken.

Festubert, 15-27 May

Neuve Chapelle and Aubers Ridge had proved that narrow break-ins were easy to contain, because cross fire from the flanks stopped reinforcements from going forward. Haig wanted to immediately try again, and he planned a two-pronged attack which would converge, isolating part of the German line and the potential for a large gap. There would be a night attack on the left, because 2nd Division knew the ground, so the first objective could be captured in the dark. The attack on the right would made at dawn, because 7th Division was new to the area. The two attacks would link up, cutting off part of the German Line, before a second bombardment supported the next advance beyond La Quinque Rue.[89]

Over 430 guns and howitzers started shelling the German defences on the morning of 13 May, firing over three two-hour periods each day. Some of the field guns hit the wire while the 6-inch howitzers hit the front trench, smashing the parapet. The rest of the field guns and the 4-5-inch howitzers hit the support trenches. Artillery officers now worked with each infantry division, to improve cooperation, while observers had

---

84   Ibid., p. 36.
85   Mereweather and Smith, *The Indian Corps in France*, pp. 344-5.
86   Ibid. An account of the Meerut Division's assault is given on pp. 20-3.
87   Ibid. An explanation of 1st Division's attack is provided on pp. 19-20.
88   Ibid. The details of this disastrous attempt are on pp26-9.
89   Ibid., pp. 50-1.

started helping individual battery commanders register their guns. Haig made the heavy artillery play a bigger part, but many shells still failed to detonate.

Continuous rain postponed the assault until 15 May, using up First Army's ammunition reserve. Three Chinese attacks were made on 14 May, each involving a three-minute bombardment, two minutes of cheering and finishing with a two-minute barrage to catch the Germans manning their parapet.

The weather eventually cleared on 15 May and two short bombardments kept the Germans under cover while the troops deployed. The men who would advance in the dark wore a white patch on their chest and back for identification and they were told to follow old plough marks in the soil, because they pointed towards the enemy trench.[90] At 8.30 pm the Lahore Division to the north began firing, with the idea of keeping the Germans under cover as 2nd Division deployed in No Man's Land. However, all it did was put them on their guard and flares lit up the sky while a search light started scanning No Man's Land.[91] The German machine-gun teams targeted the bridges over the ditch in front of the 2nd Division's trench the moment the British guns extended their range. They also fired SOS rockets to tell their artillery to fire pre-arranged barrages at No Man's Land. The left was pinned down, but the right captured some trenches and vehicle head-lamps and torches guided the support wave towards the foothold. A thirty-minute bombardment was followed by a second attempt at 3.15 am but 2nd Division's companies struggled to get through the congested trenches and the Germans were ready for them when they advanced.

Six field guns had smashed holes in the German parapet opposite 7th Division by firing high explosive shells from the front trench.[92] The thirty minutes of intense shelling before zero again alerted the German artillery and the men preferred to run through their own barrage than be hit by the enemy counter-barrage. The few guns shelling the line to the flanks had to stop at zero due to the shortage of shells.

Flares were fired when indicated the first trench had been taken but most men found it impossible to cross a ditch. Those who did find a way to reach the North Breastwork, were stopped by the British guns firing short.[93] Another fifteen-minute bombardment was organised but it made no difference and 7th Division was starting to lose ground. A further attempt on 2nd Division's front had been repeatedly postponed due to the congested trenches and it failed when it was finally made at 4 pm.

A plan to close the gap between 2nd and 7th Division at 10 am on 16 May ended with the men pinned down by machine-gun fire in half-dug trenches and ditches. A second attempt at 2.30 pm was easily stopped by artillery fire.[94] Both divisions were

---

90   Ibid., p. 56.
91   Ibid. This 'abnormal procedure' consisted of four controlled bursts of fire p.57.
92   Ibid. The guns were mounted on vehicle tyres, 'to deaden the sound of movement'. pp 59.
93   Ibid. The 7th Division's attack is explained in detail on pp.59-62.
94   Ibid. The fighting either side of this gap on 16 May is described on pp. 62-3.

finding it difficult to get fresh troops or ammunition forward, while the Germans were reinforcing the area.

A new bombardment started at 2.45 am on 17 May and it convinced the Germans to withdraw from the salient between the two divisions. Aerial observers reported they had pulled out at dawn, but it took time to react to the withdrawal. Zero was postponed to 10.30 am, to give time to rearrange plans, but then several hundred Germans ran across No Man's Land waving white flags at 9.30 am. Lieutenant General Henry Horne gave the order to attack at once, only it resulted in the infantry advancing at different times around 3 pm and some came under fire from their own guns. German machine-gun teams fired through gaps opened in the parapets while the infantry waved white flags, when they had no intention of surrendering.[95]

First Army and I Corps thought the attack had been a success, but they soon discovered it was untrue. Rain then interfered with the artillery registration for the 9 am attack and the two-hour bombardment eventually started at 4.30 pm. The infantry orders were issued late, the trenches were overcrowded, and companies advanced at different times, often crawling along ditches to get forward. The Canadian Division's attack at 5.25 pm *collapsed after a few minutes*[96] while a second attempt by 7th Division at 7 pm was doomed because the guns still had no idea where the front line was.

Lieutenant General Edwin Alderson[97] was given control of the attack front but he had insufficient staff to control all four divisions under his command. Reliefs took too long in the damaged trenches, while No Man's Land was so narrow that the heavy artillery could not shell the German parapet. It meant that Alderson's Force struggled to make any progress.

First Army had run out of heavy calibre ammunition by now and it was down to the field gunerss, who only had shrapnel shells to fire when the barrage started at 5 pm on 21 May. The German guns had plenty of high-explosive shells and the trenches were in such a mess that the infantry had to exit via two holes made in the parapet at 8.30 pm. Machine-gun fire annihilated one group, while the other had to withdraw across No Man's Land before dawn. Haig was so disappointed that he dissolved Alderson's Force.[98]

The Canadians tried again at 2.30 am on 24 May, only to fall back from the South Breastwork because their Ross rifles kept jamming in the mud. The attack by 47th Division started thirty minutes late and it too failed. Another attempt by the two divisions the following day failed because the troops were inexperienced, the trench maps were inaccurate, and the Germans were listening into the Londoners trench telephones.[99] The two divisions finally linked up on 27 May.

---

95   Ibid. The problems associated with the German withdrawal are detailed on p. 67-9.
96   Nicholson, *Canadian Expeditionary Force*, p. 99.
97   Commander-in-Chief of the Indian Corps.
98   Edmonds, *Military Operations: France and Belgium, 1915, Vol. II*, pp. 73-5. Anderson's Force illustrates the pitfalls of organising an ad-hoc command.
99   Ibid., pp. 75-6.

Second Action of Givenchy, 15-16 June

An attack at Givenchy had to wait until enough ammunition had been delivered and extra attention was given to air observation, to conserve shells. The heavy artillery eventually joined in on the evening of 13 June. A twelve-hour bombardment of the wire and the trenches began two days later but it was difficult to see the enemy trenches because long grass covered a low rise in No Man's Land.

The plan was for the assault troops to signal with Very Lights and rockets to indicate when trenches had been taken, but the Germans were again listening into the British telephones. It meant they knew when zero hour was, and they spotted the men moving into position. The mine exploding under the Duck's Bill two minutes before zero confirmed the attack was about to start.[100] Everyone struggled to negotiate uncut wire, both above ground and in ditches, and they were pinned down as soon as barrage lifted off the German trenches.

A morning mist meant the attempt the following day was postponed until 4.45pm. The artillery only had enough ammunition for a two-hour barrage, while a German shell blew up the British bomb stores. The attack was a disaster.[101]

Bellewaarde, 16 June

The Germans had a good view of the Ypres Salient from Bellewaarde ridge and 3rd Division was ordered to make a pre-dawn attack on 16 June. Limited manpower meant that assembly trenches were only dug along the attack front, so it was obvious to the German observers what was about to happen and where.[102] Extra efforts were put into reporting progress and the troops were given flags to signal with and carrier pigeons to send messages back. Three sets of communication cables were laid from the battalion to brigade headquarters, to increase the chance of the message getting through.[103]

It had been noted that it was difficult to use an enemy trench because it faced the wrong way, so every man was given two empty sandbags to build new parapets, while some platoons were equipped with shovels to dig a new fire step. The problem of carrying ammunition forward was overcome by giving each man two bandoliers of

---

100 Ibid., pp. 93-5.
101 Ibid., pp. 95-6.
102 Ibid., p. 99. The counter-barrage was so accurate that zero had to be set for dawn, so the observers did not see the assault troops entering the assembly trenches.
103 Ibid., the steps to improve communications between the assault troops and their headquarters, so that the reserves and artillery could be used effectively, are explained on pp. 98-9.

ammunition to carry over their shoulders.[104] A new type of gas helmet was available and it tucked under the collar to form a seal.[105]

The barrage began at 2.30 am and there were three pauses in the firing to encourage the Germans to come out of their dug-outs. Zero hour was at 4.15 am and the Germans machine gunners struggled to see through the darkness as the first objective was taken.[106] The plan had been for the infantry to tell the artillery when to start the creeping barrage to the second and third objectives but the observers could not see the flags through the smoke. It meant the artillery had to fire at set times and they hit the support battalions, who had advanced early in their eagerness to get forward.[107] Lack of control resulted in nine mixed up battalions racing to get to the final objective first. A counter-barrage delayed the reserves, while the extra ammunition proved to be insufficient and the objective had to be abandoned. An attempt to retake it at 3.30 pm ended in disaster, leaving Bellewaarde ridge in German hands.

Hooge, 19-30 July and 9 August[108]

A mine exploded under Hooge Chateau on 3.15 am on 30 July and then flamethrower teams advanced; it was the first time a *Flammenwerfer* had been used.[109] The British response was to dig false assembly trenches and make fake attacks. There were plenty of shells, so the artillery fired a variety of barrages at different times every morning to confuse the Germans. No Man's Land varied in width, but the infantry deployed in a straight line along No Man's Land, so they all entered the enemy trench at the same time. Both division and brigade headquarters had been issued with portable wireless sets for the first time, to speed up communications but the main problem was still how to talk to the assault troops. The attack was a success, even though the wireless sets did not work. The first batch of Brodie steel helmets had also been issued but some mistook the wearers for German, resulting in friendly fire incidents.[110]

The Royal Engineers had continued surveying the British trenches while the Royal Flying Corps photographed the enemy ones, and they were all plotted on different scales of maps. The troops had started to name their trenches back in March, but every trench, farm, wood and road had a name by the summer of 1915. The Geographical

---

104 Ibid., p. 100.
105 The British smoke hood had just been issued. There was no breathing valve and the man had to inhale and blow air through a bag soaked in glycerine and sodium thiosulphate of soda. Around 2.5 million were manufactured before it was superseded in September 1915.
106 Ibid., p.100.
107 Ibid., 100-1.
108 Ibid. The fighting around Hooge is explained on pp. 100-8.
109 Ibid., p. 104 explains the workings of the *Flammenwerfer*.
110 The Type 'A' Brodie Helmet was immediately superseded by the Type B, which was made of steel toughened with manganese known as 'Hadfield steel'.

Section of the General Staff started to include the names on trench maps because they were far easier to refer to than map coordinates.[111]

Loos Offensive: The Plan

The Allies may have condemned the use of chlorine gas in Ypres Salient in April 1915, but GHQ decided to use it as a substitute for guns and shells. Scientists devised a system for releasing gas from pressurised cylinders, providing the wind was blowing in the right direction (it rarely was). Tests in England in June 1915 discovered how fast it moved in different wind conditions.[112]

Britain's chemical industry could not supply enough gas cylinders for the size of attack that GHQ wanted. More tests had proved that the mining masks issued to German machine-gunners lasted for around thirty minutes. So, a plan had to be devised to produce the illusion of a forty-minute long gas cloud with the aid of 7,500 smoke candles.

First Army's meteorological officer started monitoring hourly weather reports, sent from stations as far away as London and Paris. Chemistry students from universities and across the army were recruited and they were taught how to report wind speed and direction.[113]

Around 3,000 cylinders, code named 'Accessory Number One', were delivered to the front and placed in a shallow trench, ahead of the front line. Members of the new Special Brigade opened half of them at 5.50 am, followed by the lighting of smoke candles twelve minutes later.[114] The other half of the cylinders were opened eight minutes later with more candles being lit after another twelve minutes. The remaining candles were lit two minutes before zero. Haig became nervous about the weather but he dithered until it was too late to cancel the attack. At 6.30 am six divisions advanced through a dense cloud of gas and smoke across a 6-mile front.

The heavy artillery had been organised into two groups, composed of thirty-seven guns and howitzers of 4-inch to 15-inch calibre. There were thirty-six guns dedicated to counter-battery fire and another 460 for wire and trenches; they were placed under corps artillery officers. Divisional batteries were divided into sub-groups which were allocated to an infantry brigade. Over one thousand miles of cabling were buried, sometimes in triplicate, to provide safe communications between the batteries, their

---

111 Edmonds, *Military Operations: France and Belgium, 1915, Vol. II*, p. 5. Brigadier-General Hunter-Weston had first christened trenches on the Aisne in September 1914.

112 Major General Charles Foulkes, *Gas! The Story of Special Brigade* (London: Blackwood & Sons, 1934). A description of the experiments with gas is given on pp. 42-3. Also, covered on Edmonds, *Military Operations: France and Belgium, 1915, Vol. II*, p.151.

113 Foulkes, *Gas!* The formation and training of the Special Brigade – the Gas Brigade's codename – is covered in Chapter IV, pp. 49-65.

114 Edmonds, *Military Operations: France and Belgium, 1915, Vol. II*. The gas discharge programme is discussed on pp. 159-60.

brigade headquarters and the infantry headquarters.[115] The number of guns First Army had was larger than it had for Festubert but the amount ammunition stocks it could call on was over eight times higher than in May.[116]

I Corps, 25 September

The attack by 2nd Division was affected by three problems. The attack north of the La Bassée Canal was timed to start thirty minutes early and it alerted the Germans south of the canal. Several mines were detonated before zero hour and the Germans withdrew, fearing more, taking them beyond the range of the gas. They returned as the wind pushed it north, along the British trenches.

At least two gas officers wanted to stop the release, but they were overruled. The assault troops were cut down as they bunched up to get around the craters across the Brickstacks. The support troops could not get along the congested trenches and a plan to attack again at 9 am was called off because the battalion commanders protested.[117]

A lack of night patrols meant 9th Division did not know about a wire filled ditch covered with netting and turf in No Man's Land. The German artillery opened fire as soon as the cloud appeared and they shelled the assembly trenches, puncturing several cylinders which filled the trenches with gas. The cloud drifted back as crossfire from Railway Redoubt, Mad Point and Strongpoint stopped the left brigade. The first messages were optimistic, but the support battalions were delayed moving along the crowded communications and some company commanders held their men back, after realising there had been no advance.[118]

Hohenzollern Redoubt and the slag heap called the Dump overlooked 9th Division's right, so it had been impossible to dig assembly trenches. Shallow tunnels dug under No Man's Land were opened up and connected by a shallow assembly trench the night before. Phosphorous grenades and Stokes mortars firing smoke shells made the cloud too dense and some men became disorientated or were overcome. But the rest crossed the Redoubt and the Dump, before clearing the Fosse 8 pithead. Several battalions went as far as Haisnes, only to become pinned down in Pekin Trench.

Orders for a second attempt by the left brigade took too long to get to the assault troops, despite a fifteen-minute delay, and the attack was another disaster. The reserve brigade struggled to get along the crowded trenches and the four battalions became scattered across 9th Division's front.[119]

Assembly trenches had been dug in front of the original trenches, but 7th Division still had 400 metres to go to reach the enemy trenches.[120] Some engineers struggled

---

115 Ibid. The organisation of the artillery for Loos is detailed on pp. 174-6.
116 Ibid. Approximately 250,000 shells for Loos as opposed to only 30,000 for Festubert. p. 177.
117 Ibid. The 2nd Division's unsuccessful attack is detailed on pp. 253-7.
118 Ibid. 9th Division's partial success is chronicled on pp. 236-245.
119 Ibid., pp. 245-9.
120 Ibid. 7th Division's attack is covered on pp. 227-32.

to open the cylinders and the gas was still pouring into No Man's Land at zero hour, while machine-gun teams posted in saps No Man's Land caused many casualties. A few companies advanced too fast, emerged from the gas cloud and were silhouetted right in front of wire. Many were then hit cutting gaps through low aprons of wire which had not been seen in the long grass. The front trenches were taken but casualties were so high that the survivors had to stop before Cité St Elie and along the Lens-La Bassée road, to wait for support.

The reinforcements were delayed moving along the congested trenches and then by fire from strongpoints which refused to surrender.[121] They would arrive six hours after zero hour, by which time it was too late. The few men who had entered the trenches north of Hulluch had to withdraw when German reinforcements arrived. An attempt to enter Cité St Elie at 4 pm was then cancelled because the artillery shelled the empty village rather than the occupied trench in front of it.

IV Corps, 25 September

The German artillery opened fire when the gas cloud appeared, again bursting several cylinders in 1st Division's trenches. Machine-gun teams hidden in two saps in No Man's Land hit many men but most casualties occurred because the wind blew the gas back. A lack of wind meant the gas suffocated the assault companies on the right, leaving it to the support companies to attack. Two machine-gun outposts caused many casualties before the advance was stopped in front of a belt of wire hidden in the long grass.

Again, there were many casualties cutting through the wire and only a few men reached the Lens Road.[122] However, the message to divisional headquarters made it sound like Hulluch had been captured when only thirty men had entered it. A message stated that the right brigade had also entered the German trenches, but the four battalions sent forward discovered it to be false.

Around 600 Germans held the Lone Tree position for six hours, only surrendering after a battalion accidentally moved behind them.[123] It was late afternoon before the survivors reached the Lens-La Bassée road and it was late in the night before the 1,200-yard gap in First Army's line was closed. The only counter-attack during the night involved Germans shouting *'Don't shoot, we are the Welsh'* in foreign accents; they were annihilated.[124]

Gas also settled in 15th Division's trench but the Scots still overran Jew's Nose Trench and entered the valley north of Loos.[125] The left brigade moved rapidly to

121 Ibid. 7th Division's afternoon attacks are covered on pp. 232-4.
122 Ibid. 1st Division's successful attack on its left flank is on pp. 212-3
123 Ibid. 1st Division's unsuccessful attack on its right flank is on pp. 210-2 and 213-21.
124 TNA: WO 95/1281/2: 2nd Welsh Regiment War Diary.
125 Edmonds, *Military Operations: France and Belgium, 1915, Vol. II.* The advance through Loos is described on pp. 191-205.

Puits 14 on the far slope, only to find no one on their flanks. The right brigade took the Loos garrison by the surprise and some engaged them, while the rest climbed Hill 70 beyond. A lack of officers meant the disorganised Scots chased the Germans south, towards Cité St Laurent, rather than east, towards Cité Auguste. They had advanced 2 miles but they were also pinned down in front of the second German trench with no chance of arranging artillery support.

A counter-attack drove them back and they rallied on the support battalions on the summit of Hill 70. The day ended in stalemate and while the Germans had plenty of artillery support, the Scots would have to wait for their guns to move forward.[126] Major General Frederick McCracken made the senior surviving officers recall their experiences to make some sense of battle; an early form of after-action report.[127]

The gas crept down the slope on 47th Division's left flank, only to disperse before Loos village.[128] A few machine-gun teams caused casualties, but the rest ran, only to be caught by an overhead machine-gun barrage. The Londoners cleared the village, its colliery and the adjacent huge slag heap but few officers had survived to organise the advance through Welwyn Garden City estate towards Chalk Pit Copse. The gas allowed the centre brigade to secure a defensive flank by converting a communications trench into a fire trench. The flank was secured after one battalion clambered up Double Crassier slag heap while the right brigade carried out a Chinese attack.

The gas had caused as many problems as it had solved. The cloud was the sign for the German artillery to fire on trenches filled with cylinders. The weather conditions mean that zero hour was unpredictable right up to the last moment and even then, the wind might not push the gas across No Man's Land. The damp air around the La Bassée Canal could have interfered with the cloud while the slope of the ground does not seem to have been considered. The cloud moved far faster when the slope was downhill, as on 47th Division's sector.[129] The density of cloud was hard to control, and the men became disorientated and chocked when it was too thick. However, the biggest problem was that the attack had used up Britain's stock of chlorine.

126 Ibid. The advance beyond Hill 70 is explained on pp. 205-7.
127 TNA: WO 95/1911: 15th Division, Headquarters, Branches and Services, General Staff, War Diary. Surviving officers of each brigade and battalion (and there were not many) gave an account of the attack.
128 Edmonds, *Military Operations: France and Belgium, 1915, Vol. II*, 47th Division's attack is chronicled on pp. 183-191.
129 John W. Jenkins, *The World War and Historic Deeds of Valour from Official Records and Illustrations of the United States and Allied Governments, Vol. 5* (Minnesota: National Historic Publishing Association, 1919), p. 186. Chlorine is 2 ½ times heavier than air and had a tendency to drift downhill.

IX Corps, 26 September

By nightfall on 25 September, both I and IV Corps were through the first German line but fresh troops were needed to attack the second German line. Both 21st and 24th Divisions of IX Corps had been marching for several days to reach First Army's rear area and the tired men had no battle experience. The first brigade was released at midday on 25 September and was told to reinforce the line east of Loos. All the battalion commanders were told was, *we do not know what has happened on Hill 70. You must go and find out: if the Germans hold it, attack them; if our people are there, support them; if no one is there, dig in.*[130]

The battalions advanced along the Lens road without maps or guides and their transport was smashed by artillery fire as soon as they crossed the Grenay ridge. Two battalions ignored warnings not to approach Chalk Pit Copse and the rear ranks opened fire after the front ranks panicked under fire and fell back. The other two battalions moved through Loos but the Scots through the scouts were the start of the relief. It would take until dawn to sort out the line around Hill 70.[131]

The second of 21st Division's brigades became split up as it crossed the battlefield in the dark. The brigadier never received the order to wait until morning and it was fortunate that there were no friendly fire incidents as his men marched through 1st Division's area. By dawn, it was holding Bois Hugo while the third brigade halted north of Loos. However, *there was a complete absence of information as to the general situation and the exact position of the various battalions.*[132] Poor planning, insufficient staff work, and a change of plan had left 21st Division scattered around Loos.

Attacking the Second Line, 26 September

The Fosse 8 situation was precarious, so 24th Division's leading brigade had been sent to I Corps' sector to relieve 9th Division. Some companies became lost in the dark while others were spotted moving over the top, but the brigade managed to take over the colliery.[133] The brigadier could not cope with the situation and his replacement soon discovered that *no communication of any kind had been established with my battalions either by wire or orderly and I attribute this to the fact that all battalions and the brigade staff were quite ignorant of the rudiments of what to do in the trenches ...*[134]

Meanwhile, a gap had been left in the line during 7th Division's night relief, allowing the Germans to infiltrate the Quarries. A new line had to be established in the old

---

130 Edmonds, *Military Operations: France and Belgium, 1915, Vol. II*, p. 296.
131 Ibid., pp. 297-8.
132 Ibid., pp. 297-8.
133 Ibid. The difficulties of carrying out a night relief in a network of battered trenches is explained on p. 303.
134 Ibid., p. 350.

German front line and an attempt to recapture the area by a single inexperienced battalion ended in disaster the following morning.[135]

The Germans cleared Chalet Wood and then Bois Hugo, and the retreating men took two 21st Division battalions with them. Another four battalions advanced southeast up Hill 70 rather than east towards Bois Hugo, having mistaken the Scots in their gas helmets for Germans. They were decimated by enfilade fire from Bois Hugo and Chalet Wood and ran back down the slope.[136]

The men of 15th Division should have cleared Hill 70 at 9 am but their heavy artillery had not had time to move forward while their field batteries had not had time to register.[137] Mist obscured the flags marking the front line and the Scots were hit by friendly fire. The summit was cleared but the Scots again went too far and were soon driven back. Two battalions from 21st Division were caught up in the retreat and Hill 70 was lost.

Two of 24th Division's brigades were given vague orders at the last minute, telling them they were to advance across the Lens-La Bassée road at 11 am.[138] Snipers targeted the officers before they fell back, closing the gaps in the wire covering the second trench. The left flank was enfiladed from Hulluch village and the right from Bois Hugo, while Strongpoints III and IV[139] pinned down the centre. They were shelled by both the German and British artillery, because it was impossible to contact the gunners. Then there was a general retreat and while some say it was controlled withdrawal, others said they *bolted in a wild panic*.[140] Those left behind escaped when it was dark, while the wounded were rescued from what the Germans called the *Field of Corpses*.

It had been a disastrous day for First Army and a huge lesson in how not to use New Army divisions.[141] Colonel Stewart, 21st Division's chief staff officer, gave the following explanation about the disaster:

> It was that these two divisions would be in reserve in a big operation at Loos on the idea that not having been previously engaged in this way. They would go into

---

135 Ibid., p. 303.
136 Ibid. The angle of the slope also encouraged 21st Division's men to advance towards the summit of Hill 70, rather than towards the two woods.
137 Ibid. The difficulties of coordinating a bombardment of a new line at short notice, are explained on pp. 311-4.
138 Edmonds, *Military Operations: France and Belgium, 1915, Vol. II.* The attack is covered on pp. 329-32.
139 The German *Stutzpunkts III* and *IV*.
140 TNA: WO 95/1281/2: 2nd Welsh Regiment War Diary. The retreat is also described in Edmonds, *Military Operations: France and Belgium, 1915, Vol. II*, pp. 332-5.
141 Major General J Capper, 24th Division's new commander stated that the 'best trained troops in the British, or any other army, would have found it difficult to succeed.' Edmonds, *Military Operations: France and Belgium, 1915, Vol. II*, pp. 332.

action for the first time full of esprit and élan and being ignorant of the effects of fire and the intensity of it, they would go forward and do great things.[142]

The fact that inexperienced divisions advanced ignorant of the effect of firing would not be forgotten when planning the Somme offensive, the following summer.[143]

Guards Division Attack, 27 September

After sending in the inexperienced New Army battalions, it was the turn of the Guards Division to try and break the deadlock.[144] The initial plan was scaled down but the revised orders arrived as the ninety-minute bombardment came to an end, so the men had to advance at the double at 4 pm. A smoke screen to the north dispersed and the left flank was soon back where it started. The rest of the Guardsmen had to march across the Loos valley under artillery fire before struggling to get through the ruins of Loos village. Some got lost while others joined the attack towards Puits 14. It meant one battalion was left to capture Hill 70, rather than two brigades. Star-shells lit up the summit when the attack went in and the survivors had to rally below the crest.[145] A final attempt to take Puits 14 on 28 September was wiped out.

Hohenzollern Redoubt, 27 September to 13 October

Three enemy parties infiltrated the perimeter when two red rockets were fired at dawn on 27 September and machine-gun teams then climbed to the top of the Dump. Fosse 8 colliery was lost, and a new line was eventually established along the East Face of Hohenzollern Redoubt.[146]

A surprise counter-attack late on 27 September against the Dump was spotted and flares stopped it going further than Dump Trench. A plan to attack at dawn the following day was postponed because the 'congested state of the trenches due

---

142 TNA: WO 95/2128: 21st Division Headquarters Branches and Services, General Staff War Diary.

143 Experienced divisions tended to go to ground as soon they came under heavy fire (for example 2nd, 7th and 1st Divisions) and Field Marshal French called them 'sticky and disinclined to push forward, on account of the trench habit.' New Army divisions (for example, 9th, 15th, 21st and 24th Divisions) were 'better for the pursuit, following upon a successful assault...' Or, as in the case of 1 July 1916, taking on an enemy defeated by a prolonged bombardment. Edmonds, *Military Operations: France and Belgium, 1915, Vol. II*, p. 274.

144 Edmonds, *Military Operations: France and Belgium, 1915, Vol. II*. The changes in orders came about by the loss of Fosse 8, on I Corps' front. pp. 355-6.

145 Edmonds, *Military Operations: France and Belgium, 1915, Vol. II*. The attack is described on pp 355-9.

146 Ibid., pp. 350-1.

to dead, wounded and units waiting to be relieved, admitted very slow progress.'[147] The shortage of communication trenches would hinder 28th Division's operations about Hohenzollern Redoubt and the Dump throughout the battle; delaying reliefs, resupply and the evacuation of the wounded.

The Germans stopped the advance along South Face while a second attack against the Dump, timed for 9.30 am, started late. A combination of German and British artillery fire drove the troops back before the German counter-attack entered Dump Trench, splitting the British position in two. Bombs refused to light[148] in the rain while the shortage of communication trenches made it difficult to bring ammunition forward or carry wounded back. Guides failed to turn up and both Dump Trench and South Face were lost during the delayed relief. Big Willie Trench was then evacuated by mistake and the Germans sprayed chlorine gas into the trenches to stop anyone entering them. Eventually, West Face was abandoned at dusk.[149]

A fresh brigade was unsure if either West Face and Big Willie Trench were still held when it arrived on 30 September. Only two guides turned up to lead the hundreds of men into the trenches, so many lost their way. The Germans again attacked when they realised there was a relief under way and it took until nightfall to secure the position.[150] Troops deploying to make a surprise midnight attack against Little Willie Trench were spotted, so they ran forward only to find that their objective trench had been levelled by artillery fire; they withdrew after their bombs ran out.

An appeal to cancel an attack over the top against Little Willie, because the trenches were congested, was refused. Some men advanced early while the rest advanced the wrong way and then a counter-attack drove 28th Division from Hohenzollern Redoubt. A final attack to retake the redoubt by the division's third brigade involved four waves of men deploying in No Man's Land before zero. They were spotted and pinned down while the bombers followed the wrong trench. It had been a painful lesson in trench fighting, one in which the Germans had maintained the upper hand.[151]

---

147 TNA: WO 95/2279/2: 2nd Buffs War Diary. At least double the number would be dug in future; an 'Up Trench' for fresh troops and supplies and a 'Down Trench' for tired troops and the wounded.

148 Anthony Saunders, *Reinventing Warfare 1914-18: Novel Munitions and Tactics of Trench Warfare* (London: Continuum, 2012), p. 106. Early bomb striking mechanisms worked on friction and failed in wet conditions. The Mills bomb (Service pattern No. 5 grenade) solved the issue with a spring-loaded strike lever, which was released by the removal of a safety pin. The lever was held down until thrown and it then activated the four second fuse. The first batch reached France in March 1915 but many of the old pattern grenades were still in use at Loos and they often failed in the damp conditions.

149 Edmonds, *Military Operations: France and Belgium, 1915, Vol. II*, pp. 352-4.

150 Ibid., pp. 369-70.

151 The British had to deploy across the broken ground into trenches they were unfamiliar with, while the Germans fighting over ground they knew well. The German bombers were also better organised, as described on Edmonds, *Military Operations: France and Belgium, 1915, Vol. II*, pp. 373-4.

Lieutenant General Richard Haking's IX Corps took over the line but a counter-attack was driven off on 8 October, leaving insufficient time to dig a separate trench for the gas cylinders.[152] Zero was postponed to 13 October, meaning 46th Division had to attack Hohenzollern Redoubt, in its first offensive action. The commander's request to attack by bombing was denied because the Germans had better bombs.

Officers were given a tour of the trenches while everyone visited a large-scale model of the battlefield behind the lines.[153] There were insufficient gas cylinders, but it was hoped that the mere smell of gas would make the Germans run. Each officer would release just five gas cylinders over fifty minutes and then mortars, candles and grenades would create a smoke screen.[154] The bombardment began at midday on 13 October, but the counter-barrage caused panic when several cylinders were damaged.

The first waves on the left advanced at 2 pm, only to find their objective trench had been obliterated by artillery fire. A third wave struggled to deploy out of the congested trenches and was shot to pieces because the smoke had cleared. The right brigade had to advance from a split front and three waves were pinned down in an abandoned trench. The fourth wave did not see the disaster through the smoke and they too were shot to pieces. The division suffered nearly 3,000 casualties and gained nothing.[155]

There were insufficient smoke candles to cover 12th Division's three-pronged assault against the Quarries and the screen was clearing by zero. The left attack was shot down from a new trench which had been missed. The right one was stopped because the trench mortars failed to fire. The centre one reached its objective but had to withdraw when the bombs ran out.[156]

Tactical Operations, December 1915 to June 1916

The Loos offensive brought an end to major British offensive operations for nine months, giving the BEF time to build up its reserve of men and material. Meanwhile, attentions were drawn to the Verdun region in February 1916, when the Germans tried to capture the important town from the French. But both sides continued to carry out small operations against tactical points along the British front, to gain a local advantage.

Phosgene Attack, Ypres Salient, 19 December 1915

Prisoners reported that gas cylinders were being placed in the trenches north-east of Ypres, ready to use when the wind was right. So, sentries were posted next to alarms,

---

152 Edmonds, *Military Operations: France and Belgium, 1915, Vol. II*, p. 372.
153 TNA: WO 95/2662: 46th Division's 1915 War Diary.
154 Edmonds, *Military Operations: France and Belgium, 1915, Vol. II*. The gas plan is explained on p. 384-7.
155 Ibid. The attack on Hohenzollern Redoubt is described on pp. 380-3.
156 Ibid. The attempt to take the Quarries is covered on pp. 382-3.

signal offices and dug-outs. Officers monitored the wind direction and inspected the new P gas helmets twice a day. They had glass eye-pieces and an improved breathing valve but the men carried their old H helmet as a spare. A parachute flare and red rockets signalled the attack at 5.15 am on 19 December.[157] It was the first use of phosgene gas, a chemical which stops the lungs absorbing oxygen. The attack was soon called off because the British calmly dealt with the few men who dared leave their trenches. A PH helmet was introduced the following month, to give protection against phosgene.[158]

The Bluff, 14 February-1 April 1916

Army doctrine was that a unit always held both sides of a terrain feature, so the defence could be coordinated. However, one of 17th Division's battalions was left in a difficult position astride the Ypres-Comines Canal after three mines exploded under an embankment called the Bluff on 14 February.[159] An inexperienced battalion commander waited for permission to counter-attack rather than just doing it, giving the Germans time to consolidate their position. Parties of eight bombers were sent forward but they needed too many men to carry the bombs, making them difficult to control. So, a brigade practised an attack across a full-scale model of the trenches, created from aerial photographs, while enough steel helmets were collected for everyone to wear.

The bombardment was composed of four parts. A fake bombardment was fired late on the afternoon of 1 March, to check the German reaction.[160] A short but heavy bombardment then smashed the wire at dusk while a slow bombardment through the night stopped the Germans repairing the damage. An intense two-minute barrage at 4.30 am drove the Germans under cover and then the troops attacked. The approach to the Bluff was exposed, so a 60-pounder battery had fired double salvoes throughout the night, to condition the sentries. The attack went in after the first salvo was fired at zero and the Germans were found waiting under cover for the second.

---

157 Ibid., the gas attack is covered on pp. 158-61.
158 Sir James E. Edmonds, *Military Operations: France and Belgium, 1916, Vol. I: Sir Douglas Haig's Command to the 1st July: Battle of the Somme* (London: HMSO, 1932), a description of the helmets is given on pp. 79-80. The Phenol Hexamine (PH) helmet improved over the P Helmet (P) by having two bags (one treated and one untreated), an exhaust tube on the breathing tube and double eyepieces. The addition of hexamethylene tetramine to the anti-gas solution dealt with the phosgene.
159 Edmonds, *Military Operations: France and Belgium, 1916, Vol. I*, pp. 163-7.
160 Ibid: *Vol. I*, the bombardment and attack are described on pp.170-1.

Hohenzollern Redoubt, 2-18 March 1916

German tunnellers were discovered digging under Hohenzollern Redoubt, so small mines, known as camouflets, were detonated to collapse them. The British tunnellers then hand dug several shallow tunnels, detonating a camouflet every time they heard the Germans, before continuing. At the same time, machines were used to drill three tunnels deep underneath the redoubt.[161] After three months and fifty camouflets,[162] the tunnellers detonated 25 tonnes of ammonal under the Hohenzollern Redoubt at 5.45 pm on 2 March. Men of the 12th Division captured the three craters but the objective, a trench called the Chord, had been flattened. Tit-for-tat mining attacks would rage until 18 March, ending with the men separated by a line of craters which neither side could hold.

St Eloi Craters, 27 March-16 April

Thirty mine craters surrounded St Eloi, but the plan was to capture the nearby high ground, to stop the Germans looking over the south part of the Ypres Salient.[163] The artillery opened fire at 4.15 am on 27 March and seven mines exploded. Those who charged straight away captured their objective but those who waited thirty seconds for the debris to fall were pinned down.[164] Crater fighting followed and the Germans held them all by the time the Canadians took over the area on 3 April.

The infantry held a series of isolated posts while the artillery had no idea where the front line was. There was only one communication trench and the Germans captured more ground during a relief.[165] Daytime bombing parties were annihilated while night time raiding parties got lost crossing the crater field. Trench foot, jammed weapons and a shortage of bombs made it impossible to defend the area while a lack of aerial photography and accurate trench maps made it difficult to plan.[166] The Canadians abandoned the craters after a difficult week.[167]

---

161 Ibid., pp. 175.
162 Camouflets were small charges designed to collapse tunnels and killed miners without disturbing the surface.
163 Nicholson, *Canadian Expeditionary Force.* The extensive mining is covered on p. 138.
164 Edmonds, *Military Operations: France and Belgium, 1916, Vol. I,* pp. 181-4. It was clear that enemy sectors could be captured. However, small ones were easily retaken, because the artillery could concentrate on a small area. Meanwhile, attacks against large sectors were prone to failure.
165 Nicholson, *Canadian Expeditionary Force.* The need for more communications trenches is detailed on pp. 140-1.
166 Ibid., p. 145. General Turner listed fourteen ways the Canadians could improve operations and 'no less than seven dealt with methods of securing and transmitting reliable information, the absence of which had been one of the greatest obstacles to the success of the enterprise.'
167 Edmonds, *Military Operations: France and Belgium, 1916, Vol. I.* The difficult conditions faced by the Canadians are described on pp. 185-90.

The St Eloi fighting demonstrated two things; the BEF were now able to seize important tactical points but the German artillery would make them impossible to hold. The question was, what frontage was 'small enough to ensure success but large enough to prevent the enemy's artillery making it impossible to hold the captured ground.'[168]

Gas Attacks at Hulluch, 27 and 29 April

A deserter said a gas attack was planned near Hulluch and rats were then seen leaving the German trenches because of leaking cylinders. Early on 27 April, a cloud crept across No Man's Land but the infantry following were soon stopped.[169] The only unfortunate incident occurred when an inexperienced officer told his men to dispose of their helmets, believing they only worked once. The wind then changed direction and blew the gas back over his position.[170] A second attempt at 3.45 am on 29 April included smoke, to make up for the lack of gas cylinders, but a change in wind direction forced the Germans to run back.[171] A second attempt at dawn caused many casualties because the anti-gas chemicals had not been applied to the PH helmets properly.[172]

Gas Attacks at Wulverghem, 30 April and 17 June

Deserters confirmed cylinders were in the trenches west of Messines and so the alert was sounded when the wind changed on 25 April. Rifle fire at 12.35 am hid the sound of the release and the infantry followed short releases of gas, while longer releases along the rest of the line disguised the location of the attacks.[173]

Snipers and Lewis gunners had been issued with new box respirators which gave far better protection than the hood helmets. It meant snipers could stay in No Man's Land, ready to shoot the men cutting the wire, while the Lewis gunners stopped the attack. A second attack planned for 12.20am on 17 June was called off because the wind changed direction and blew the gas back over the German lines.

The Kink, 11 May

The German artillery hit several targets around Hohenzollern Redoubt on the afternoon of 11 May, to disguise their plan to capture the Kink. Observers could not see the SOS calls though the smoke and dust while the battalion headquarters had

---

168 Nicholson, *Canadian Expeditionary Force*, p. 145.
169 Edmonds, *Military Operations: France and Belgium, 1916, Vol. I*, pp. 193-5.
170 TNA: WO 95/1937/2: 9th Black Watch War Diary.
171 Edmonds, *Military Operations: France and Belgium, 1916, Vol. I*, pp. 196.
172 TNA: WO/1979: 46 Brigade War Diary.
173 Edmonds, *Military Operations: France and Belgium, 1916, Vol. I*, pp. 199-203.

been knocked out by the time the attack was made at 6 pm.[174] The Germans seized the British tunnel entrances and went no further.[175] The counter-attack was made over the top at 1.30 am the following morning because the trenches were so battered.

Vimy Ridge, 21 May 1916

British troops took over Vimy Ridge at the beginning of March 1916, to find that the trenches were *merely shell holes joined up; hastily organized positions in mine craters; a line of detached posts, accommodated in grouse butts; straight trenches without traverses.*[176] The live and let live attitude the Germans promoted was a just a ruse because they were tunnelling under 47th Division's position. The artillery opened fire at 3.40 pm on 21 May and a mine explosion at 7.45 pm, signalling the start of the attack. The infantry stopped after capturing the British tunnel entrances and their artillery fired a box barrage around the objective.[177]

A deserter provided the details of the night counter-attack, so the German artillery shelled the assembly area. Meanwhile, the British guns were short of ammunition[178] and poor weather grounded the aerial observers. The hour-long bombardment began 7.25 pm but the counter barrage was far heavier. One company did not get the order cancelling the attack and it was wiped out. Instead ground had to be gained by digging forward.[179]

Tor Top and Mount Sorrel, 2-13 June

The Germans wanted the summit of the low ridge east of Ypres, so they could see across the Salient. The infantry connected saps together to narrow No Man's Land, while the trench mortars and artillery registering targets. The guns stopped firing at dusk on 1 June, to let the infantry cut gaps in the wire, and resumed when they finished. The bombardment began in earnest at 8.30 am, silencing many guns and cutting communications to the rest.[180]

Three mines exploded under Mount Sorrel at 1.07 pm while white rockets signalled zero hour.[181] The first wave bombed their way into the trenches held by 3rd and 1st Canadian Divisions. The support waves then silenced strongpoints along Observatory Ridge. Troops held an outpost line until the captured trenches had been repaired and

---

174 TNA: WO 95/1946/2: 13th Royal Scots War Diary.
175 Edmonds, *Military Operations: France and Belgium, 1916, Vol. I*, pp. 205-8.
176 Ibid., pp. 211-2.
177 Ibid., pp. 217-8.
178 All the shells were being sent to the Somme, ready for the upcoming offensive.
179 Edmonds, *Military Operations: France and Belgium, 1916, Vol. I*, pp. 220-1.
180 Ibid. The German bombardment is described on pp. 231-2.
181 Nicholson, *Canadian Expeditionary Force*. The Canadian account of the German attack is detailed on pp. 148-50.

communication trenches had been dug across No Man's Land. They then withdrew to the objective when it was dark.[182]

Orders to retake the ridge gave 1st Division insufficient time to get ready, so zero was postponed from 2 am until 7.10 am. The thirty-minute barrage was supposed to be followed by six green flares to mark zero, but they would not light in the damp conditions.[183] Some troops wondered if they had seen the correct signal while others did not see any flares. The German machine gunners dealt with each company as soon as they left the trenches.

Lieutenant General Julian Byng wanted to employ more artillery and less infantry, but bad weather made it impossible to register the heavy guns and the Germans struck first. They detonated four mines on 6 June and then captured trenches south of Hooge.[184] Two clear days allowed the aerial spotters to photograph the enemy trenches and then the rain returned. Random thirty-minute barrages were fired around the clock, to make the Germans take cover and the troops deployed while one was being fired at 8 pm on 12 June.

A barrage and smoke screen made it look as though the attack would extend north of the Menin Road.[185] The final bombardment lasted forty-five minutes to confuse the Germans and the 1.30 am attack recaptured most of the ridge. Both sides then established bombing posts in shell holes along the crest.[186] The Canadian Corps had suffered 8,500 casualties in less than two weeks.

Early Offensives Summary

The basic rules for attacks from trenches were decided during 1915. Neuve Chapelle introduced a preliminary bombardment which broke down the enemy defences and a creeping barrage to protect the infantry. A timetable with objectives and timings used the artillery to set the speed of the advance. Deception was used to hide the infantry and artillery deployment while steps were taken to train the troops, so they knew what to achieve. All these concepts would be improved on during the course of the war.

The attack at Aubers Ridge on 9 May was an example of over-confidence on GHQ's part. It thought it had the solution to breaking the enemy line, without realising that the Germans had changed their plans. A lack of ammunition meant the artillery failed to deal with the extra measures put in place, resulting in a disaster. Festubert was an attempt to make two breaches, which could be linked up to create a large hole

---

182   Edmonds, *Military Operations: France and Belgium, 1916, Vol. I.* The German attack against the Canadians is chronicled on pp. 232-4.
183   Ibid. The failed attack is chronicled on pp. 236-7.
184   Nicholson, *Canadian Expeditionary Force,* pp. 152-3.
185   Ibid. The Canadian version of events is on pp. 153-4.
186   Edmonds, *Military Operations: France and Belgium, 1916, Vol. I.* The British version of events is explained on pp. 205-8.

in the enemy line. Chinese attacks may have confused the Germans but they also alerted them.

A lack of artillery ammunition made GHQ consider using chlorine gas for its attack at Loos on 25 September. The innovative plan to make up for the lack of cylinders with smoke may have deceived the Germans but the lack of wind and poor visibility caused as many problems as it solved. Too many casualties meant it was impossible to reach the second line of defences on the first day, while poor handling of the reserves meant it could not be reached on the second day. Inexperience in trench fighting and a shortage of trenches then led to the loss of the Hohenzollern Redoubt, while the mishandling of a second gas attack meant it could not be retaken on 13 October.

Several actions in the spring of 1916 gave the BEF time to hone its trench fighting skills. Deception by the artillery and the miners helped take short sections of line but they were easily retaken because the Germans could concentrate their artillery and infantry against them. The BEF needed far more divisions, batteries and ammunition before a large enough breach could be made in the enemy line.

3

The Somme Campaign
1 July-18 November 1916

Planning for 1 July

On 16 May, British GHQ announced there would be a major attack on the Somme and General Rawlinson told his six corps commanders the following day.[1] Orders were issued on 14 June and the final corps commanders' conference was held on 22 June. They worked to the booklet called 'Preparatory Measures to be taken in Armies and Corps before undertaking Offensive Operations on a Large Scale',[2] which covered all aspects of trench warfare for the arms and services.

The infantry plan was to deploy in four lines, so the German machine gunners could not concentrate on detachments. Each wave would add impetus to the attack by passing through or 'leap-frogging', while some groups were engaged in the 'clearing up and consolidation of a position'. Fourth Army's memorandum, 'Tactical Notes',[3] stated that the first wave would advance 100 metres apart behind the barrage, because the 'only safe method of artillery support during an advance is a fixed time-table of lifts.' Divisional commanders also had to consider the memorandum called 'Training of Divisions for Offensive Action',[4] which said the New Army soldiers needed more training. But there was too little time and too few instructors.

The bombardment plan allocated the wire to the mortars and field guns while the large calibre guns hit machine-gun positions and observation posts; they both shelled the trenches and strongpoints. The heavy guns switched to billets, roads and tracks during the night. Each corps had a Heavy Artillery Group which worked from the 'Active Hostile Battery List'. Ground observers noted the times and angles to gun

---

1 Haig notified Rawlinson verbally on 6 May. See Edmonds, *Military Operations: France and Belgium, 1916, Vol. I*, pp. 258.
2 Edmonds, *Military Operations: France and Belgium, 1916, Vol. I*, Appendix 11.
3 Ibid., Appendix 18.
4 Ibid., Appendix 17.

flashes, so enemy batteries could be located through trigonometry. Sound ranging equipment used low frequency microphones to estimate the range to batteries.[5]

Each corps had one spotter plane adjusting the heavy howitzers fall of shot, while two others searched for batteries. They also had two contact planes searching for different targets and while one reported by wireless, the other dropped messages at the headquarters. Sixteen planes would fly reconnaissance and bombing missions while another nine took photographs. Aerial photography was relatively new and the gunners preferred to have their shots adjusted by spotter aircraft.[6]

The five-day bombardment started on 24 June and the gunners fired in two-hour cycles; shooting for eighty minutes and then resting for forty minutes.[7] The plan was to have two registration days and three destructive days with the attack on the sixth day. However, rain resulted in a two-day postponement and the final barrages used up part of the shell reserve. Altogether, 1,010 field guns, 427 heavy guns, 40 French guns, 316 medium and heavy mortars had fired over 1.7 million rounds by the end of the bombardment.[8]

A large number of casualties were anticipated, and the battalion stretcher bearers would carry the wounded to the regimental aid posts, where the Royal Army Medical Corps took over. They were given first aid at advanced dressing stations, (ADS) while main dressing stations (MDS), walking wounded centres and rest areas administered the necessary medical care. Casualty clearing stations (CCS) operated in pairs and while ambulances carried the seriously wounded to one, lorries carried the lightly injured to the other. Those requiring emergency operations were taken to advanced operating centres.[9]

Ambulance trains carried patients to the base hospitals around Le Harve and Boulogne, where they rested until their wounds had healed and they could be put through an exercise programme at a convalescent centre. Hospital ships took men who needed prolonged treatment or who were going to be discharged across the English Channel. Trains then took them to a station near their home and they ended their journey at a hospital specialising in their type of injury.

Raids made in the days leading up to the attack discovered that the Germans were alert and expecting the offensive to start soon. They also reported that damage to the wire was patchy, particularly on the steep sided slopes either side of the River Ancre. On the night before the battle, each man was issued with 220 rounds, two grenades, two sandbags, an entrenching tool, increasing his load to 66 pounds (30 kilograms).[10] Officers and NCO's carried four flares, ready to signal progress to the contact planes.

5   Ibid., artillery methods are explained on pp. 294-6.
6   Ibid., the Royal Flying Corps part is explained on pp. 297.
7   Ibid., Fourth Army's preliminary bombardment programme is given on pp. 302-6 and in Appendix 19.
8   Ibid., Gun, howitzer and ammunition statistics are given on pp. 300-2.
9   Ibid., the work of the Royal Army Medical Corps is explained on p. 281.
10   Ibid. The infantryman's equipment is described on p. 314.

Rawlinson had wanted a 7 am zero hour but Foch wanted the attack to start at 9 am, so the last part of the barrage could be observed; they compromised on 7.30 am. All the battalions were in place by 5.15 am on 1 July and the final bombardment began at 6.25 am. The first wave deployed into No Man's Land when the guns increased their rate of fire at 7.25 am; five minutes later the guns extended their range. Rawlinson had assured his corps commanders that 'nothing could exist at the conclusion of the bombardment'; the question was, would Fourth Army's first wave reach the enemy trench before the parapet was manned?[11]

The heavy artillery jumped from trench to trench according to a strict timetable, while the field artillery fired a curtain of shrapnel ahead of the infantry. Artillery commanders could not change targets or adjust their range unless ordered to do so by corps headquarters. Correcting the fall of shot was difficult because the battery observers were too far back. The forward observing officers were with the assault troops and often out of contact with their battery.

The troops were to advance 2 miles in just 107 minutes. The creep of the barrage was crude, but it was attempted, and it would set the standard for future battles. VIII Corps' artillery orders stated that the 'success or otherwise of the assault largely depends on the infantry thoroughly understanding the creeping method of the artillery.'[12] III Corps wanted the field guns to 'rake back gradually to the next line'[13] whilst XIII Corps' artillery orders were more specific: 'The field artillery barrage will creep back by short lifts …'[14]

Fourth Army's artillery understood the need to move barrage slowly forward, in time with the advance. However, it did not have the means to fire an accurate creeping barrage close enough to give the infantry the support they required. Matters such as mapping the batteries, calibrating the guns and appreciating the weather effects still had to be addressed.

The Germans were aware that a large attack was coming after such a long bombardment. A listening post near La Boisselle had also heard zero hour being discussed during the early hours, although how far the information was spread is not known. The answer was provided for all in earshot when 18 tons of ammonal exploded under the Hawthorn Ridge, west of the River Ancre, at 7.20 am. Anyone who looked into No Man's Land would have seen the waves of men deploying minutes later. Another 27 tons exploded near La Boisselle just eight minutes later.

11   Ibid., p.292.
12   Ibid., p. 428.
13   Ibid., p. 373-4.
14   Dale Clarke, *World War I Battlefield Artillery Tactics* (Oxford: Osprey, 2014), p. 43.

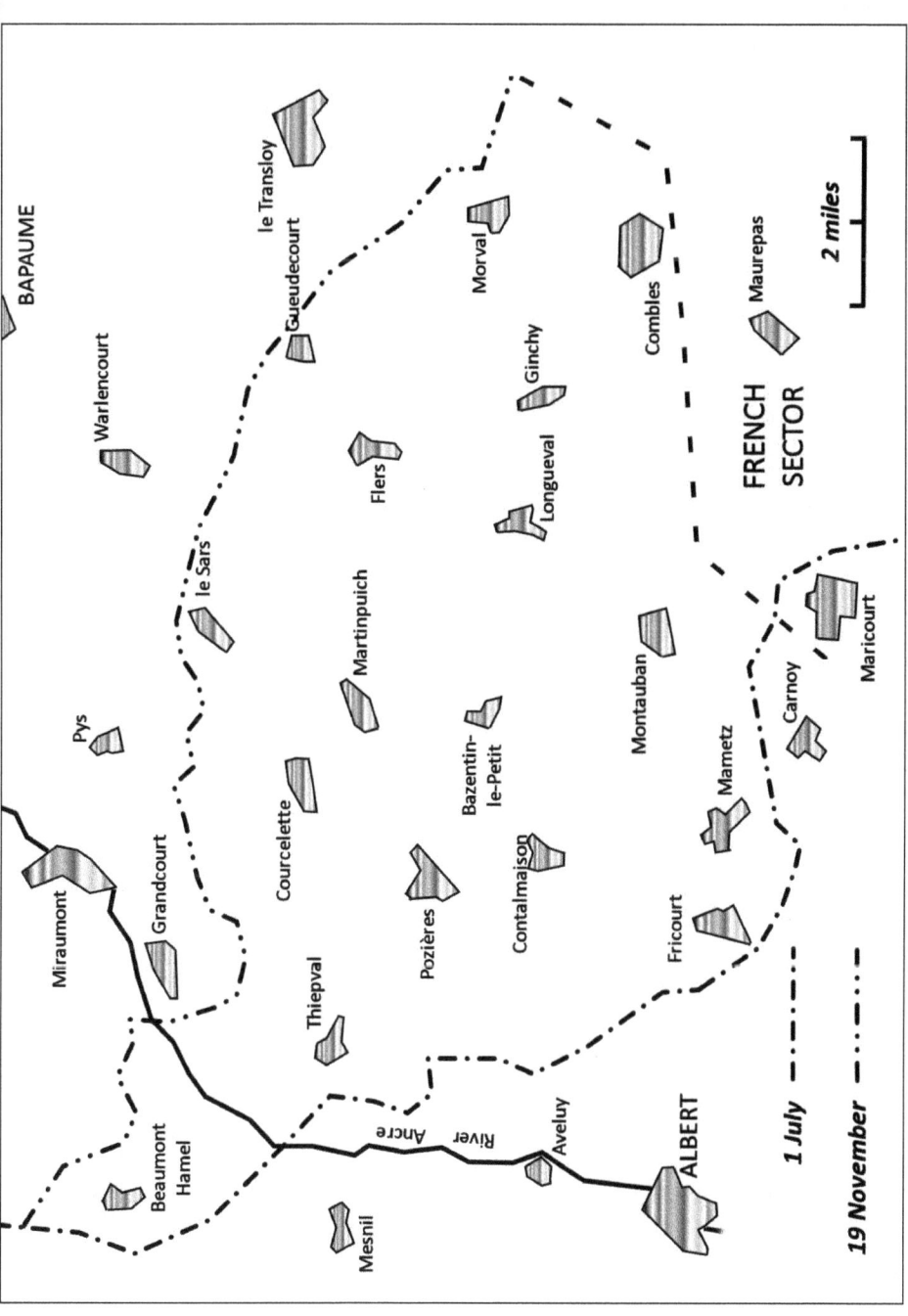

Map 3. Somme Campaign, 1 July –19 November 1916: The BEF learned many costly lessons during the painfully slow advance across the Somme.

VII Corps, Gommecourt Salient

A pincer attack would take Gommecourt, 2 miles north of the main attack. Half the heavy guns had to switch to the inside flanks of the advance at two minutes before zero, leaving insufficient firepower on the frontline trenches. The divisional commander north of the village, had told the heavy artillery not to shell the first trench because he wanted 46th Division to use it. It was his second bad decision, because his men were tired after ten days digging assembly trenches. The wind did not carry the smoke far enough and the troops were silhouetted as they squeezed through the gaps in the enemy wire. The support waves mistook their own trenches for German ones in the smoke, while a counter-barrage forced others to take cover in them.[15]

Smoke had been released south of Gommecourt for several days, but the Germans realised it was much thicker on 1 July. The men of 56th Division then found that the wire had been repaired during the night and it took time to cut through it. Those who made it into the enemy trenches, soon found themselves under counter-attack, because the assault north of the village had failed.[16] A second attack was made by 46th Division after midnight, because it was believed men were still in the German trenches. They were not and flares lit up No Man's Land as the men cut through the wire.

VIII Corps

Lieutenant General Sir Aylmer Hunter-Weston had wanted to detonate the mine under Hawthorn Redoubt four hours before zero. The Inspector of Mines wanted to fire it at zero, because the Germans usually won crater battles. Rawlinson compromised at ten minutes before zero and the artillery would lift from area, so the crater could be occupied.[17] However, VIII Corps' artillery order instructed all the heavy guns to extend their range at 7.20 am. Five minutes later the howitzers shelling the support trench would lift to the reserve trench. It meant that only the field guns were firing at the enemy trenches while the infantry formed up in No Man's Land.

A smoke screen failed to cover 31st Division's open flank, while machine-gun fire stopped all but a few men reaching Serre; they were never seen again.[18] A German mine accidentally detonated under the Quadrilateral, killing the garrison, so 4th Division's first wave advanced beyond it.[19] However, cross fire from Serre and Ridge Redoubt stopped the support waves in No Man's Land. Then there was confusion over the signals because single white flares reported that the infantry were held up on the

---

15   Edmonds, *Military Operations: France and Belgium, 1916, Vol. I.* The 46th Division's attack is on pp. 465-70.
16   Ibid., 56th Division's attack is on pp. 462-4.
17   Ibid., p. 429.
18   Ibid. 31st Division's attack is on 441-4.
19   Ibid. 4th Division's initial attack is covered on pp. 437-8.

wire, while three white flares meant they were on the first objective. The plan to hold back the rest of the battalions was thwarted because they had set off early and four and a half battalions were shot to pieces when they advanced into No Man's Land at 9.30 am.[20]

The Hawthorn Ridge mine had warned the Germans that the attack was due, and their artillery shelled the assembling troops. The Germans won the battle for the crater and then half the field artillery lifted at 7.27 am, 'to avoid a pause at zero'. It meant the German machine-gun teams were ready to decimate 29th Division's assault troops at the wire.[21] The support battalions requested a new bombardment but white flares had been seen, indicating the objective had been taken; it had not, because they were German flares.[22] A second attack at 8.05 am was also shot down but progress reports were being exaggerated. A third attempt was delayed until after 9 am because the trenches were congested; it too failed.

Reports across VIII Corps' front were few and far between but they were also optimistic and inaccurate. Both 31st and 29th Divisions called off further attacks, while the Germans closed in on 4th Division. The Quadrilateral would be abandoned the following morning.

X Corps

The advance by 36th Division's left, along the west bank of the Ancre, was stopped by wire hidden in a gully. Permission to bring the barrage back for a second attempt was refused.[23] The advance across the Schwaben Redoubt, on the east bank, was going well until the Ulstermen had to wait for the barrage to lift. They came under fire from three sides as they entered the Grandcourt Line and Stuff Redoubt; then they were told to halt indefinitely, because there was no one on their flanks.[24]

Battalion commanders had been forbidden from going forward with their men, but signalling was impossible through the dust and the runners were taking too long to get back. Heavy fire made it was impossible to cross No Man's Land while corps reserves were being sent towards Thiepval, because it had been incorrectly reported that the village had been taken. By mid-afternoon the Ulstermen were low on ammunition and back in Schwaben Redoubt; they would have to abandon it the following morning.

The two heavy howitzers detailed to destroy Thiepval's machine guns had been destroyed by a dud shell,[25] so 32nd Division suffered heavy casualties crossing No Man's Land. Only a few men entered Leipzig Salient while a second attempt was

---

20   Ibid. 4th Division's later attack is on p. 439.
21   Ibid. 29th Division's initial attack is described on pp. 431-5.
22   Ibid. This mistake is explained on p. 434.
23   Ibid., pp. 405-6.
24   Ibid., pp. 404-8.
25   Ibid., p.399.

cut to pieces.[26] A contact plane confirmed a written message that troops were in Thiepval, so the guns extended their range. They were both wrong and the battalions sent forward behind a smoke screen were shot to pieces. A third attempt to reach the imaginary troops in Thiepval failed at midday.[27] Around the same time 49th Division made an uncoordinated attack against the north side of Thiepval. It was late afternoon before X Corps understood there were no British troops in the village, and it called off further attacks.

III Corps

The divisional commander facing the Ovillers area had wanted the high ground either side of his objective captured before zero hour, but Rawlinson refused. Only a few men of 8th Division crossed No Man's Land and they then discovered that the German trenches had been levelled by the British barrage. The support waves were delayed moving through the British congested trenches before they were pinned down in No Man's Land; a second attempt was called off.[28]

Two mines detonated[29] at 7.28 am and 34th Division's two flanking columns advanced two minutes later. The two centre columns had been told to wait another five minutes, for the debris to land. Hardly any men reached the far side of Mash Valley or Sausage Valley because the German machine-guns were able to concentrate on each column in turn.[30] By 10 am most of 34th Division was either dead or injured in No Man's Land while the rest were scattered around Schwaben Höhe crater (Lochnagar crater) or on the wrong side of the Fricourt spur. III Corps made no more attacks.

XV Corps

The front line curved around Fricourt and Mametz. The plan was for the outer wings of the two divisions to advance at 7.30 am and meet at the north-east corner of Fricourt Wood. The inner flanks would then move through the village and wood, starting at 2.30 pm.

During the night, a Russian sap (shallow tunnel) had been turned it into an assembly trench for 21st Division. Three mines exploded in the Tambour area at 7.28 am but there were many casualties crossing the first set of trenches.[31] Counter-attacks delayed the advance north of Fricourt, so the barrage was lost and requests for artillery support were acted on too late.

---

26   Ibid. 32nd Division's attack on Thiepval is covered on pp. 400-3.
27   Ibid. The mistaken messages are discussed on p. 400.
28   Ibid. 8th Division's attack is explained on pp. 385-90.
29   Creating Y Sap and Lochnagar craters.
30   Ibid., pp. 34th Division's advance is covered on pp. 375-386.
31   Ibid. 21st Division's attack is explained on 356-60 and 366-8pp.

The front trenches had been flattened across 7th Division's sector, so the first wave had to deploy from the support trenches. Five small mines exploded at zero but enfilade fire from the left (where there was no attack) hit the men as they cut through wire hidden in a dip in No Man's Land.[32] The support battalions went forward at 9.30 am but they could not go any further. Two more attempts meant Danzig Alley and Mametz were reached.

Both 21st and 7th Divisions were ordered the second attack to begin at 2.30 pm, after the contact planes reported the Germans were withdrawing. One of 21st Division's brigades heard about the attack after the bombardment had lifted while the other was shot to pieces.[33] Meanwhile, 7th Division bombed forward until the Germans began withdrawing from Fricourt and Mametz at nightfall.[34]

XIII Corps

The Germans had filled its battered front trench with barbed wire and withdrawn to their support line. Three small mines exploded and a Livens Projector spewed flames across No Man's Land just before 18th Division advanced. Bombers and Lewis gunners outflanked Pommiers Redoubt on the left flank, before advancing over 1 mile.[35] But the right flank struggled to clear the Carnoy crater field, giving the Germans time to man their trenches. Success elsewhere meant it moved forward later.

Enfilade fire from 18th Division's area struck 30th Division's left flank as it waited for the barrage to lift; it then exploited a weak spot to reach Glatz Redoubt.[36] The right found that Dublin Trench had been levelled and so they dug a new one. Stokes mortars fired smoke and candles were lit to screen the advance towards Montauban. By nightfall the village had been taken and the division had advanced over 1 mile.

Fourth Army, 2-13 July

Rawlinson was aware of the disastrous outcome by nightfall on 1 July but he still gave orders to attack 'under corps arrangements, as early as possible compatible with adequate previous artillery preparations.'[37] He wanted to extend the break in the first German line around Montauban by pushing towards Contalmaison, getting closer to the second German line between Bazentin-le-Petit and Longueval. General Hubert Gough's Reserve Army took over of the line north of the Bapaume road on 4 July, so Fourth Army could focus on its task, but a general shortage of ammunition meant it could do little.

---

32   Ibid. 7th Division's initial assault is explained on pp. 351-6.
33   Ibid. 21st Division's disastrous later attack is described on 361-364.
34   Ibid. 7th Division's later attack is covered on pp. 364-6.
35   Ibid. 18th Division's advance is explained on pp. 329-34 and 338-41.
36   Ibid. 30th Division's attack is detailed on pp. 326-9 and 334-8.
37   Ibid., p.482

Fourth Army's three corps carried out unconnected attacks over the next eleven days, so we shall look at each in turn in two phases; first between 2 and 6 July and then between 7 and 13 July.

X Corps, 2-6 July

The men of 36th Division were still in Schwaben Redoubt by dawn on 2 July, so the artillery fired a box barrage while reinforcements carried supplies to them. It was too little, too late, and the area had to be abandoned.

X Corps was unable to support a 3.15 am attack against Ovillers on 3 July and smoke failed to cover 12th Division's open flank, leaving it exposed to enfilade fire. But there was plenty of smoke on the objective, so the moppers up missed many dugouts in the dark. It was clearing by the time the reinforcements were ready to advance and they could not cross No Man's Land.[38]

A plan to attack with three divisions against Thiepval was reduced to just one due to a shortage of ammunition. An extra three hours were given to deploy but it still left 32nd Division insufficient time to check the ground before zero at 6.15 am.[39] The gunners did not hear of the postponement until they had fired off most of their shells, leaving them insufficient ammunition to make a creeping barrage. The battalions were told to cover double the expected frontage, only to be 'mowed down, line after line', when they went over the top.[40]

General Sir Hubert Gough took over both VIII Corps and X Corps at midday on 3 July. His Reserve Army would play a defensive role for three weeks, while Rawlinson and Fourth Army focused on clearing the Bazentin Ridge.[41]

III Corps, 2-6 July

It took six hours longer than expected to get 19th Division into line in front of La Boisselle. Even then only one battalion was ready to attack at 4.30 am and it found a deep trench blocking its way.[42] A barrage against Ovillers, was followed by a smoke screen at 4 pm on 2 July. It drew the Germans' attention from the real objective, La Boisselle and half the village was captured. The rest was taken during the early hours of the following morning, but the Germans fired flares, to signify it had been lost,

---

38   Captain Wilfrid Miles, *Military Operations: France and Belgium, 1916, Vol. II: 2 July 1916 to the end of the Battles of the Somme* (London, HMSO, 1938); pp, 13-14.

39   Miles, *Military Operations: France and Belgium, 1916, Vol. II,* 32nd Division's fateful attack is covered on pp. 13-4.

40   TNA: WO 95/2250/1: 11th Cheshire's War Diary.

41   The shortage of ammunition meant the attack front had to be reduced to just 2 miles.

42   Senior officers were repeatedly underestimating how long it took to carry out a relief. Battalions struggled to prepare and rarely had time to check the ground they were to cross.

so a counter-attack could be launched.[43] The bombing continued until the evening of 6 July. It was the turn of 23rd Division next and it cleared Horseshoe Trench, even though its orders for the 7 July morning attack were issued late.[44]

XV Corps, 2-6 July

The Germans had abandoned Fricourt and the area north of Mametz late on 1 July, so both 17th Division and 7th Division followed them up. A contact plane spotted a counter-attack aimed at 21st Division the following day, so reinforcements were able to stop it and then take both Shelter Wood and Birch Tree Wood.[45] Meanwhile, the artillery never heard about 17th Division's attack on Crucifix Trench and the Germans were taken by surprise.[46]

Patrols reported that Mametz Wood was unoccupied on 3 July, but Horne waited until the following evening before ordering troops to enter it. However, 7th Division's instructions were vague and while one battalion asked for more information, a second found Germans holding the wood and withdrew.[47]

Heavy rain postponed operations against Quadrangle Trench and Wood Trench until 5 July and they were again delayed for forty-five minutes for the same reason. The artillery eventually opened fire at 12.15 am on 5 July while the assault troops crept forward. Thirty minutes later the guns lifted and while 17th Division captured Quadrangle Trench, 7th Division was pinned down by fire from Mametz Wood as it cut the wire in front of Wood Trench.[48]

X Corps, 7-13 July

German observers spotted the new trench dug to reduce the width of No Man's Land and their artillery hammered it. The wind did not carry the smoke far enough at the end of the sixty-minute barrage, but 12th Division still took 1,400 prisoners in front of Ovillers when it attacked at 8 am. More ground was taken by bombing before dawn while a surprise attack at 8 pm secured more ground around the village. Lamps

---

43   Miles, *Military Operations: France and Belgium, 1916, Vol. II*, p. 7.
44   Ibid., pp. 33-4. Senior officers were also underestimating how long it took to get orders out to the infantry and artillery, in time for them to prepare for a coordinated attack.
45   Ibid., pp. 15-16. This example of good air-to-ground cooperation resulted in the taking of 800 prisoners.
46   A.H. Atteridge, *The History of the 17th (Northern) Division* (Glasgow: Robert Maclehose & Co, 1929), pp. 117-9.
47   Miles, *Military Operations: France and Belgium, 1916, Vol. II*, p. 21. It would have been unwise to push only a few troops into the wood, ahead of the troops on the flanks, during the dark, rainy night.
48   Ibid., p. 21.

were used to report the objective had been taken, but some men went well beyond the objective; only a few returned.[49]

III Corps, 7-13 July

The attack was planned for 8 am on 7 July, however 19th Division hesitated for fifteen minutes, northeast of La Boisselle, because 23rd Division had found that its jumping off position had been lost. The infantry then walked into the creeping barrage because it moved forward late, due to a mix up over times. The attack was eventually made at 9.15 am and it took the Germans completely by surprise.[50]

The attack against Contalmaison was compromised because 23rd Division had to advance at different times to cooperate with the attacks to the flanks. The men who entered Contalmaison had to withdraw after running out of ammunition while the bombers were unable to make any progress in the muddy trenches.[51]

For four days between 9 to 13 July 32nd Division and 25th Division edged closer to Ovillers. Meanwhile 23rd Division found the trenches around Contalmaison were plotted incorrectly or damaged beyond repair, while there was no ammunition for a smoke barrage. The attack at 4.30 pm at 10 July had to cut through hedges woven with netting but they still captured the village, along with nearly 400 prisoners.[52]

XV Corps, 7-13 July

The divisional commander had argued against advancing up the slope between Contalmaison and Mametz Wood because his men would be subjected to crossfire. He was overruled and so 17th Division was instructed to crawl across No Man's Land during a thirty-five-minute bombardment. They charged headlong into a German attack at 2 am before encountering uncut wire.[53] The failure to capture Quadrangle Support Trench meant that zero hour for the main attack was delayed by thirty minutes, to give the artillery time to cut the entanglement. The late change to 8 am meant that part of 17th Division advanced a few minutes late, while the rest did not get far.[54] A second attempt at 8 pm also failed because there was too much fire in the open, while the trenches were filled with mud.

---

49   Ibid., p. 35, p. 41-2. 12th Division – with an attached brigade of 25th Division – attempted three types of attack at three different times of day in just twenty-four hours; with artillery support, pre-dawn bombing and a post dusk surprise attempt without artillery.
50   Ibid., p. 32. Fourth Army was accidently learning that surprise attacks could take objectives with little loss.
51   Ibid., p. 33-4.
52   Ibid., pp. 55-6.
53   Ibid., p. 29.
54   Ibid., pp. 29-30. There were no reliable telephone communications from brigade headquarters to the battalions.

A series of late afternoon and evening attacks captured Quadrangle Trench and then Wood Trench on 7 and 8 July. The first attempt against Quadrangle Support had to be abandoned because it was deep in mud while a second surprise attack late on 9 July failed because part of 17th Division advanced just four minutes late. The trench was cleared by bombers the following afternoon but there could be no further progress towards Contalmaison until Mametz Wood had been cleared.

Three attacks were made by 38th Division against the Hammerhead, on the east side of Mametz Wood, on 7 July but the wind dispersed smoke screen.[55] Then a mistake over orders meant that only patrols entered Mametz Wood during the night and became spooked in the abandoned wood, so they withdrew.[56]

Mametz Wood was next approached from the south at 4.15 am on 10 July after a forty-five-minute bombardment and a smoke screen. But 38th Division's orders were issued late and while some battalions hesitated, they all became disorganised in the wood as many low trajectory shells exploded in the tree tops.[57] It was impossible to keep going because the artillery could not be contacted, so the Germans moved back into the north part of wood. It was eventually cleared over twelve hours after zero hour but the troops had to pull back inside the wood, to avoid the counter-barrage.[58] The artillery barrage lifted late at 3.30 pm the following day, due to a communications delay, and the Welshmen could not hold a line any further forward because of the machine guns in Bazentin-le-Petit Wood.

XIII Corps, 8-13 July

Howitzers set Bernafay Wood on fire with thermite shells and the Germans pulled back to Trônes Wood. The first attempt by 30th Division failed to reach Trônes Wood at 8 am on 8 July but a second attempt at 1 pm cleared the south end. Fighting then moved back and forth through the wood over the next five days, at times troops abandoning parts so the heavy artillery could shell them. Few men advanced on time when 18th Division tried to take it at 7 pm on 13 July, following a two-hour bombardment. It was finally cleared during the early hours of 14 July. The men were led in single file through the south end of the wood on a compass. They then fixed bayonets and walked north through the trees while firing from the hip.[59]

---

55   Ibid., p. 30-1.
56   Ibid., p. 40.
57   Ibid., pp. 49-52. The barrage moved too fast through the wood, at 100 yards every two minutes, with halts on the two objective lines.
58   It was dangerous to hold the edge of a wood because it was easy to range in on. Troops usually dug in around 200 yards inside the tree line.
59   Miles, *Military Operations: France and Belgium, 1916, Vol. II*, pp. 74-8 covers the last-minute clearance of Trônes Wood.

Fourth Army, 14-20 July

Rawlinson postponed an attack against Bazentin Ridge on 10 July, to give the artillery time to register targets and the infantry time to clear Mametz Wood and Trônes Wood on his flanks. The Germans could see all of the ½ mile wide No Man's Land from Bazentin ridge, so the corps commanders suggested a night attack. Haig was against the idea, but Rawlinson persisted.[60]

The bombardment started on 11 July and 6-inch howitzers blasted craters ahead of the jumping off line, so Lewis gun teams could use them to cover the deployment. Officers placed white tapes in No Man's Land while it was dark[61] and sentries then directed the companies into position, as they deployed in silence. Over 20,000 men were ready two hours before zero hour and no one had been seen.[62]

One telephone operator thought their line was being tapped, so a fake message calling off the operation was sent.[63] The Reserve Army then discharged smoke twenty minutes around Pozières before zero, to draw the Germans' attention away from Fourth Army's sector.

The bombardment ended with an intense five-minute barrage, to drive the German infantry underground and to warn the British infantry that zero was approaching. The barrage lifted at 3.25 am and the assault troops followed the large explosions caused by high explosive shells armed with delay fuses in the darkness. The Bazentin-le-Petit area was cleared by 21st Division, while 7th Division took the Bazentin-le-Grand area. Uncut wire on the reverse slope stopped 3rd Division's right, so snipers and bombers moved through the gap made by the left brigade. Wire had also delayed 9th Division and it could not get through Longueval.[64] A large gap had been opened in the German line but the divisions had been told not to go beyond their objectives, while the fight for Longueval was making Rawlinson nervous.[65]

The 2nd Indian Cavalry Division was alerted at 7.40 am and while High Wood had been abandoned, there was still heavy fighting around Bazentin-le-Petit and Longueval. Offers of help from 7th and 3rd Divisions were turned down because everyone expected to follow up a cavalry breakthrough. Only the cavalry was taking too long to get forward, so Rawlinson wanted 7th Division to advance as soon as Longueval was secure. That took until 3 pm, so the orders to advance towards High

---

60   Ibid. Preliminary discussions over the 14 July attack are explained in detail on pp. 61-6.
61   They used one pull to move the tapes to the left, two pulls to move it to the right and a long pull to stop.
62   Miles, *Military Operations: France and Belgium, 1916, Vol. II*, pp. 67-75 chroncles the remarkable deployment in silence in detail.
63   TNA: WO 95/2151/1: 62 Brigade War Diary.
64   Miles, *Military Operations: France and Belgium, 1916, Vol. II*, pp. 78-82 covers the capture of 1,400 prisoners on the Bazentin ridge.
65   Ibid., pp. 83-84. High Wood was for there the taking on 14 July, but it would be another two months before it was cleared.

Wood were issued as late as 6.15 pm; twelve hours after it had been abandoned.[66] Orders reached the front late and one infantry brigade entered High Wood as it was getting dark, while a cavalry brigade was pinned down to the east of it. The order never reached 33rd Division but the nearest brigadier used his initiation and deployed west of the wood.[67]

Fourth Army faced a variety of problems when it advanced from a ragged line which snaked past High Wood and Delville Wood at 9 am on 15 July. The rain meant 34th Division's damp flares failed to light, so companies advanced at different times and the German machine-gun teams dealt with each one in turn. Observers could not see that the British artillery halted 1st Division's advance around Bazentin-le-Petit Wood. Meanwhile, a lack of reconnaissance meant that 33rd Division was stopped by wire hidden in long grass while 7th Division struggled to locate Switch Trench. The infantry eventually had to pull back, so the heavy artillery could shell High Wood.[68]

On the right flank, 9th Division had to attack in two directions from a salient. Hedges laced with wire and machine-gun teams covering the main street meant Longueval could not be cleared, while the South Africans over extended themselves in Delville Wood. The British artillery then found it difficult to give them support because it could not see the enemy trenches beyond the trees; the German gunners could not fail to miss the wood.[69]

An advance through Longueval before dawn on 16 July was broken up because the Germans emerged from their dug outs and lit up the ruins with flares. Two days later, 3rd Division deployed into No Man's Land to take the wired hedges west of the village in the flank, while it was dark.[70] However, 9th Division made the mistake of letting the infantry set zero and no one told the gunners that their deployment had been delayed. It meant the infantry was left without a covering barrage.[71]

The plan for 20 July was to crawl forward during a thirty-minute intense barrage, ready to rush the German trench when it lifted at 3.05 am. However, the gunners had to fire blind in the dark, misty night. A counter-attack overran 33rd Division's gains in High Wood, while 7th Division was shot down by the machine-gun teams which had hidden in the long grass, in front of Wood Lane. The problem was, the trench had been dug behind a low ridge, making it impossible to see from the ground.[72]

The fight for Longueval and Delville Wood ended in disaster for 3rd Division. One battalion was late because its guide got lost; a second battalion never received the order, while flares lit up the sky as the third battalion charged. The French had cancelled their advance because of the mist but 35th Division was made to attack

66   Ibid. The delay to the attack on High Wood is explained on pp. 85-6.
67   Ibid. The ineffectual advance around High Wood is covered on pp. 86-7.
68   Ibid. The attacks on 15 July are covered on pp. 95-7.
69   Ibid. 9th Division's problems fighting out of a corner into a wood are described on pp. 91-3.
70   Ibid. The confused fighting around High Wood and Longueval can be found on pp. 93-4.
71   TNA: WO 95/2040/1: 8th Norfolk's War Diary.
72   Ibid., XV Corps attack is explained on pp. 107-8.

Guillemont. An enemy gas barrage incapacitated many men and it was light by the time they advanced into machine-gun fire. A second attempt would have succeeded, except that the British bombardment had levelled the trenches on the objective.[73]

Fromelles, 19-20 July

Lieutenant General Charles Monro was informed that his First Army had to attack at Fromelles, to create a diversion to the Somme battle.[74] Lieutenant General Richard Haking's XI Corps believed a methodical bombardment would *'reduce the defenders to a state of collapse before the assault'*, despite the experience on 1 July.[75] The field artillery started cutting the wire on 14 July and the heavy artillery began registering targets two days later.[76] Gas was released to the south on 15 July only the cloud drifted back and all the cylinders had to be removed from the trenches, to avoid any accidents. Instead the artillery hit targets in the same area the following day, hoping the Germans would redeploy their guns.

Starting on 17 July, four dummy barrages were made, each followed by a Chinese attack at 'zero hour'. The guns reduced their range a few minutes later, catching the Germans as they manned the parapet. But the aerial observers failed to see that the support trenches were flooded, or that the Germans had built strongpoints inside buildings, so the later stages of the barrage would be hitting empty trenches.

Haig's Deputy Chief of Staff, Major General Richard Butler, had reported the success on the Somme on 14 July and Monro was told to attack if he had enough resources. XI Corps only had only two inexperienced divisions but Haking was confident of success, so Monro went ahead with the final planning. He then decided to cancel the operation when it rained heavily, rain but GHQ urged him to press on.[77] Zero hour was set for 6 pm on 19 July, to give the observers time to assess the gunners' work, but the Germans suspected an attack and a counter-barrage hit the assembling troops and batteries. Even more Chinese attacks in the afternoon failed to mislead the Germans.[78]

The men of 5th Australian Division discovered that the German support trench was full of water when they came under enfilade fire and they had to take cover where they could find it.[79] Machine-gun fire hit so many men as they filed out of sally-

---

73 Miles, *Military Operations: France and Belgium, 1916, Vol. II*, XIII Corps attack is covered on pp. 109-11.
74 Ibid., pp. 121. 'Thus the operation was to be purely a local attack intended to hold the enemy to his ground and teach him that he could not, with impunity, reinforce the main battle by thinning the line on this front.'
75 Ibid., p. 124.
76 Ibid., the bombardment is covered on pp. 122-4.
77 Ibid. The discussions over whether to attack is covered on pp. 124-5.
78 Ibid. The problems caused by the late zero hour are described on p. 126.
79 Ibid. The assault by the 5th Australian Division is explained on pp. 130-2.

ports (holes in the parapet), that 61st Division's support waves had to climb over the parapet instead. Stokes mortars had been unable to knock out the machine guns in the Sugarloaf salient, so enfilade fire hit many as they cut through the wire. Few men made it across No Man's Land and it soon became a battle to save the wounded.[80] Pipes filled with ammonal were used to create ditches which were then expanded into trenches to assist the rescue attempt.

Haking cancelled a second attack planned for 9 pm and the bombardment covered the withdrawal instead. Counter-attacks and artillery fire intensified as soon as the Germans worked out where the Australians where and the withdrawal was disorganised, because so many officers had been hit. Many groups never got the order while others were unable to escape.[81]

The Australian official historian, Charles Bean, summed up the indecisiveness which had led to 7,000 casualties: *Suggested first by Haking as a feint-attack; then by Plumer as part of a victorious advance; rejected by Monro in favour of attack elsewhere; put forward again by GHQ as a "purely artillery" demonstration; ordered as a demonstration but with an infantry operation added, according to Haking's plan and through his emphatic advocacy; almost cancelled [due to the] weather and the doubts of GHQ and finally reinstated by Haig, apparently as an urgent demonstration...*[82]

Reserve Army, 23-30 July

Back on the Somme, the four-day bombardment increased at dusk on 22 July before intensifying west of Pozières five minutes before zero hour, to draw attention away from the objective. A counter-barrage forced 1st Australian Division to move forward, 'crawling low, [they] were mostly hidden by the fall of the ground and by thistle tufts.'[83] They advanced through Pozières at 12.30 am on 23 July only to discover they were holding a salient which was easy to target because the ruins were on the summit of a ridge.[84]

Gough ordered the divisional commander to set zero hour, as soon as his men were ready, and he chose to attack in two stages early on 25 July.[85] An intense barrage hit the OG trenches on the east flank for two minutes as the troops wheeled ninety degrees into No Man's Land, to face their objective. They advanced at 2 am, only to find that the OG2 Trench had been obliterated while a counter-attack forced them out

---

80   Ibid. 61st Division's attack is described on pp. 127-9.
81   Charles E.W. Bean, *The Official History of Australia in the War, Vol. III: The Australian Imperial Force in France, 1916* (Angus and Robertson, Sydney, 1941), pp. 427-435
82   Bean, *The Official History of Australia in the War, Vol. III*, p. 350.
83   Ibid., p. 496.
84   Miles, *Military Operations: France and Belgium, 1916, Vol. II*. The capture of Pozières is covered on pp. 141-4.
85   Ibid. The advance beyond Pozières is explained on pp. 149-51.

of the OG1 Trench. The 3.45 am attack north of Pozières was a success, even though the bombers advanced late because the wrong date had been written on their orders.[86]

Early on 29 July, the men of 2nd Australian Division were spotting moved towards the OG trenches as the guns fired at a normal rate.[87] They only increased in tempo at 12.14 am and the men charged one minute later. The left flank went well beyond their objective and many were never seen again, while the right was pinned down in front of the OG2 Trench. Trench mortars had failed to silence the machine-gun teams south of the Bapaume road, where No Man's Land was narrow, so no progress was made at 12.19 am. Smoke and dust meant the artillery could not see the infantry's signal lamps, leaving them unable to protect the captured territory, so the Australians fell back.[88]

Fourth Army, 23-30 July

Several early zero hours were chosen for an attack spread over the night of 22 and 23 July, so Fourth Army could coordinate with the Reserve Army's attack on the left and compensate for the French cancelling their attack on the right. Times were also different across XV Corps' sector, where No Man's Land varied in width, so the assault troops would reach their objective at the same time. It was a recipe for disaster because the first attack alerted the Germans all along Fourth Army's front.[89]

The advance at 10 pm on 22 July east of High Wood initially went well, however, flares lit up 5th Division's attack before it could reach Wood Lane.[90] A counter-barrage disrupted 19th Division's assembly, west of High Wood, making one battalion late for the 12.30 am advance. Flares then lit up the advance and 1st Division was cut down by the machine-gun teams hiding in the long grass in No Man's Land.[91] It also alerted the Germans holding High Wood and flares illuminated the sky as 51st Division cut through the Switch Line wire at 1.30 am.[92] A second attack by 5th Division cleared the area west of Longueval at 3.20 am but it had to fall back because no one else had advanced.

The final attack on Longueval was due to start at 3.40 am but 3rd Division's assault troops found other units occupying their trenches. There was no last-minute intense barrage on Delville Wood, as promised, and the minutes ticked by while zero hour was confirmed. It gave the Germans in Piccadilly trench time to deploy and the attack

---

86   Bean, *The Official History of Australia in the War, Vol. III*, p. 571.
87   Ibid. No jumping off line had been pegged out and the Germans spotted the troops moving forward, p. 628.
88   Ibid. Attack particulars are provided on p. 631-9.
89   Miles, *Military Operations: France and Belgium, 1916, Vol. II*, p. 147.
90   Ibid., pp. 136-7.
91   Ibid., p. 138. They had deployed far forward to avoid the British barrage.
92   Ibid., p. 137.

stood no chance.[93] Meanwhile, smoke shells had exploded in 30th Division's trenches before zero hour and then failed to cover the open flank, instead drifting across Guillemont and disorientating the men.[94]

Haig told Rawlinson to straighten Fourth Army's line, but bad weather disrupted the necessary counter-battery work. The dog-leg shape of Fourth Army's line required new target boundaries, resulting in each corps having to rely on another corps' Heavy Artillery Groups, complicating communications. A one-hour bombardment started at 6.10 am on 27 July and 5th and 2nd Divisions cleared most of Longueval and Delville Wood.[95] A trench was dug just inside the tree line (make it harder to register) and a second attack at 3.30 pm on 29 July secured more of the wood.

XV Corps next attack either side of High Wood was set for 30 July. Mist delayed 19th Division's deployment but Intermediate Trench was secured at 4.45 am, while smoke screened the west side of the wood.[96] Zero had been set for 6.10 am east of the wood, to allow for observed fire during the final stages of the bombardment, but it allowed the Germans time to fire an accurate counter-barrage, which forced the Stokes mortar teams to withdraw. It meant the machine-gun teams at the east corner of High Wood could enfilade 51st Division, as the Scots cut through the Wood Lane wire.[97] The final parts of Longueval and Delville Wood were cleared by 5th Division, after two weeks of fighting.

On XIII Corps front, the artillery had failed to silence the German machine-gun teams, so 2nd Division was unable to advance north-west of Guillemont. That allowed the Germans to enfilade 30th Division's attack on the village. Some men were delayed by wire while others were disorganised by a counter-barrage and the mist made it difficult to get any messages back. The Germans had used an elastic defence, in which the outposts disrupted the advance before the reserves counter-attacked, when the British were at their most vulnerable. The lack of information meant the artillery put down a protective barrage beyond Guillemont, far ahead of 30th Division, and the village had to be abandoned during the night.[98]

By the end of July, two problems were apparent. Firstly, many lessons were being learnt but they were not being distributed between armies, corps and divisions fast enough. Secondly, there were enough replacements but those who had recovered from their injuries were being sent to weak battalions rather than their original units. The decision was reducing both efficiency and morale.[99]

93   TNA: WO 95/1430/3: 1st Northumberland Fusiliers War Diary.
94   Miles, *Military Operations: France and Belgium, 1916, Vol. II*, p. 140. The wind direction had been misjudged and the smoke caused more problems than it solved.
95   Ibid., p. 157-8. Rawlinson had been worried about a counter-attack from Longueval and Delville Wood.
96   Ibid., pp. 168-9.
97   Ibid., p. 262.
98   Ibid. The problems experienced by 30th Division are explained in detail on pp. 163-5.
99   Ibid., p.147.

Reserve Army, August

General Gough wanted to clear Skyline Ridge before tackling the Thiepval ridge, but it took 12th Division eleven days to capture Ration Trench and Skyline Trench.[100] The German artillery targeted the ridge every time it was taken, so strongpoints had to be built to protect the minimum number of men needed to hold the exposed position. Posts were eventually established in front of Skyline Trench on 15 August.[101]

I Anzac Corps' heavy artillery fired distraction barrages around Pozières every day, while the field artillery and mortars targeted the enemy wire. Unfortunately, 2nd Australian Division advanced beyond the OG2 Trench on 4 August, because it had been obliterated by the bombardment, and they ran into their own barrage.[102] It was 4th Australian Division's turn to advance towards Mouquet Farm at 10.30 pm on 12 August, but the order did not reach some of the companies in time. A second attempt at 10 pm on 13 August failed because the men were too exhausted to advance.[103]

The trenches around Nab Valley had to be cleared one at a time, to avoid enfilade fire across the depression. Smoke and artillery fire isolated the Leipzig Salient, while 48th Division captured the position on 18 August.[104] Hindenburg Trench was taken three days later, but a third attack at 3 pm on 23 August failed because the barrage stopped a few minutes early, giving the Germans time to man their parapet.[105] Smoke smothered Thiepval while a bombardment surprised the Germans in the Hindenburg Trench on 25 August but the gunners fired short on 27 August, interrupting 48th Division's attack on Pole Trench.[106]

At the same time, I Anzac Corps was pushing north towards Mouquet Farm. The first attack was timed for 9 pm on 18 August, but one battalion had not been told the barrage timetable and it landed on top of them. The 1st Australian Division was unable to advance beyond the crest because the gunners had no idea where the German trenches were.[107] Three practice barrages were fired to confuse the Germans and register the guns before a second attempt on 21 August. However, a German spotter aircraft called down a barrage on the assembling assault troops, making some companies late for the 6 pm zero hour. Fabeck Graben was captured but the garrison of Mouquet Farm emerged from the cellars to retake part of the trench.[108]

---

100 Ibid., pp. 209, 213, 217 and 219.
101 The British artillery found it difficult to fire accurate barrages beyond the ridge, especially as communications were cut so often.
102 Miles, *Military Operations: France and Belgium, 1916, Vol. II*, p. 211.
103 Ibid. Both attacks are covered on p. 217-9.
104 Ibid., p. 221.
105 TNA: WO 95/2764/1: 1/4th Oxford and Buckinghamshire Regiment War Diary.
106 TNA: WO 95/2756/1: 1/7th Warwicks War Diary.
107 Bean, *The Official History of Australia in the War, Vol. III*, p. 787-90.
108 Ibid. It was the first time the Australians had made a daylight attack and they suffered for it.

It was 2nd Australian Division's turn to attack at 4.45 am on 26 August but some captured the wrong trench while others became disorientated around Mouquet Farm.[109] Orders to withdraw to a safe distance never reached 4th Australian Division on 29 August and the assault troops were hit by a bombardment from both sides before zero hour. Heavy rain and mud meant they could not keep up with the barrage, when they advanced at 11 pm.[110]

Fourth Army, August

The heavy artillery again had to be reorganised, because XIII Corps had two objectives. It left XV Corps' guns having to hit Ginchy and Guillemont, while III Corps' guns shelled High Wood. Counter-battery work also had to be shared out, further complicating communications. The field artillery struggled to support 17th Division's attempts to advance north of Longueval and Delville Wood at 12.40 am on 4 August and 4.30 pm on 7 August. The problem was the ground observers could not see the new trenches dug around Delville Wood, because they were behind a low ridge.[111]

An intense bombardment, west of High Wood, during the evening of 12 August was followed by fifteen minutes of normal artillery fire. It made the Germans in the Switch Line think an attack had been cancelled, and 15th Division took them by surprise at 10.30 pm. It had always been a problem moving reinforcements and ammunition to a captured trench, so pipe pushers had been burrowed under No Man's Land.[112] They were detonated once the objective had been taken, so communication trenches could be dug quicker.[113]

After 34th Division failed to take Intermediate Trench west of High Wood, 1st Division found that that its maps were inaccurate. It took part of the trench at 4.15 am on 17 August, only to discover it was much longer than expected and the bombardment had missed the undetected part.[114]

XIII Corps' artillery fired six barrages at Guillemont on 7 August. Each time, it intensified, crept forward and then dropped back to the front trench, to encourage the Germans to stay under cover.[115] Mist caused many problems during the 4.20 am

109 Ibid., p. 811-20.
110 Ibid., p. 828.
111 Miles, *Military Operations: France and Belgium, 1916, Vol. II*, p. 186. 'The German trench system now appeared to be more elaborate and better organised...'
112 Ibid. Both the artillery hoax and the pipe-pushers are mentioned on p. 189.
113 F. W. Bewsher, *The History of the 51st (Highland) Division 1914–1918* (London, Blackwood, 1921), p. 83. The Barlett Forcing Jack drove iron pipes loaded with tin canisters of ammonal at a depth of from four to five feet under the ground. It turned out the labour required to carry the equipment forward was too much.
114 TNA: WO 95/1271/2: 1st Northamptonshire Regiment War Diary.
115 Miles, *Military Operations: France and Belgium, 1916, Vol. II*, p. 178.

attack the following morning. Many dug-outs were missed and the Germans emerged to reoccupy their trench behind 2nd Division, north-west of the village. No one knew how well 55th Division was doing south-west of the village until the mist cleared. An aerial observer spotted movement in the ruins, but messages from the infantry were confusing; then they stopped altogether.[116] The British artillery was unable to give useful support while the German counter-barrage stopped any reinforcements reaching the village.

A counter-barrage delayed the deployment for a second attempt at 4.20 am on 9 August. The Germans had reinforced the area and neither 2nd nor 55th Division captured any ground.[117] No Man's Land was narrow south of Guillemont, so 55th Division withdrew to a safe distance, while the heavy artillery targeted Lonely Trench. It proved impossible to hit, because it was behind a low ridge, and the 5.15 pm advance on 12 August failed. Another bombardment on 15 August but there was a mix up over 3rd Division's zero hour. The infantry advanced at 10 pm and the Germans had pinned them down before the artillery opened fire.[118]

Stokes mortars were used to target Lonely Trench ahead of the attack on 16 August. XIII Corps' barrage intensified at 5.37 pm and the infantry advanced three minutes later.[119] A shower of grenades stopped 24th Division taking Arrow Head Copse while 3rd Division discovered that the mortars had failed to knock out the machine guns covering Lonely Trench.

XV Corps' creeping barrage fell short at 4.15 am on 18 August, disrupting 1st Division's attempt to take Intermediate Trench in thick mist.[120] A heavy calibre shell blocked the assembly trench just before a second attempt at 2.45 pm. Some men advanced early, and ran into the creeping barrage, but enough reached Intermediate Trench to hold it.[121]

Everything went wrong during 33rd Division's attempt to clear High Wood at 2.45 pm on 18 August.[122] The preliminary bombardment fell short, knocking out the flamethrower teams, while the thirty drums of burning oil failed to kill the Germans in their dug outs. The pipe-pushers under No Man's Land had failed to penetrate the tree roots, so the charges exploded short of the Switch Line. The smoke bombs were fired late, so they failed to create a screen, and then the creeping barrage fell short, hitting the assault troops.

116 Ibid. The infantry carried flares, lamps, panels pigeons, mirrors, and even tin discs on their backs. Regular signal posts and runner relays were set up, while a wireless station had been set up. They were still insufficient.
117 Ibid., p. 179-80.
118 TNA: WO 95/1432/2: 12th West Yorkshires' War Diary.
119 Miles, *Military Operations: France and Belgium, 1916, Vol. II*, p. 184-5.
120 Ibid., p. 195-6.
121 TNA: WO 95/1270/3: 1st Loyal North Lancashire War Diary.
122 Miles, *Military Operations: France and Belgium, 1916, Vol. II*, p. 194-5.

The disaster to 33rd Division meant that 14th Division's attack came under enfilade fire from the east of the wood. A combination of German artillery and British trench mortar fire stopped the attack against Edge Trench, east of Delville Wood, but both Beer Trench and ZZ Trench, to the south-east, were captured.[123]

XIV Corps' gunners continued firing at a steady rate right up to the 2.45 pm zero hour, so as not to alert the Germans. But the lack of a final intense burst of shelling meant 24th Division did not notice that the barrage was creeping forward through the mist for several minutes.[124] A counter-barrage on No Man's Land was so heavy that the support waves could not cross but the limited objective around Guillemont, meant the artillery could continue to give covering fire. To the south, 3rd Division had mixed success against Lonely Trench, but the Germans evacuated the position during the night.

Rawlinson had received a letter from GHQ on 17 August, regarding a new weapon called the 'tank'. He received a second on the 19th, telling him to secure a good start line for them before mid-September. They would help Fourth Army secure the 'enemy's last line of prepared defences between Morval and Le Sars'.[125]

The Germans abandoned the Switch Line and Wood Lane, either side of High Wood, between 19 and 21 August, because Fourth Army's artillery had finally ranged in on them. However, they continued to hold High Wood, because it dominated the surrounding area. Fighting also continued around Intermediate Trench, until 15th Division surrounded it on 30 August. Small gains were also made around Longueval and Guillemont, sometimes because accurate artillery fire convinced the Germans to abandon their trenches. However, it was proving impossible to push beyond Delville Wood, because the artillery could not see well enough to help.

An attack by 35th Division against Arrow Head Copse at 10 pm on 21 August failed, because the British heavy artillery hit the assembly trenches both before and after zero hour.[126] Some also complained that the replacements for the original Bantam soldiers (men shorter than the Army's minimum height) were 'either half grown lads or degenerates.' A heavy counter-barrage on 24 August meant that a large-scale attack by 35th Division was cancelled. Instead a single battalion advanced towards Falfemont Farm in support of a French attack. The battalion commander's protests had been overruled and, as he predicted, his men were cut down by enfilade fire.[127]

The German bombardment of Delville Wood intensified on 31 August while their infantry assembled, some of them wearing British uniforms.[128] Planes then flew low over the British lines, reporting targets to the gunners before they fired their final

123 Ibid., p. 193-4.
124 Ibid., p. 192.
125 Ibid., p. 196-7.
126 Ibid., p. 199.
127 Ibid., p. 200-1.
128 TNA: WO 95/1670/2: 1st South Staffordshire Regiment War Diary.

barrage.[129] Tea Trench and Orchard Trench were taken from 24th Division, while part of the wood was taken from 7th Division. Bad weather then delayed further attacks until 3 September.

Reserve Army, September

Zero hour was set between 5.10 am and 5.13 am on 3 September, so that everyone reached the far side of No Man's Land at the same time. Unfortunately, the artillery had underestimated its width along the west bank of the River Ancre, so the creeping barrage jumped forward before 39th Division reached the German trenches. Across the river, 49th Division suffered many casualties taking their objective but they could not clear the Pope's Nose salient. No one could see the signals calling for help through the mist while all the runners were hit. So, no reinforcements were sent forward and the position had to be abandoned.

The Wonder Work, south of Thiepval, held out against 25th Division while 4th Australian Division could not capture Mouquet Farm nor Fabeck Graben. The Germans spotted the 1st Canadian Division moving into line early on 8 September and they recaptured Fabeck Graben before the relief was complete. The Canadians retook it the following afternoon.[130] Another attempt to take the Wonder Work by the 11th Division failed at dusk on 14 September because the artillery overshot Turk Trench.

Fourth Army, Early September

Rawlinson's plan was to straighten out Fourth Army's line and that involved making a series of small attacks over the following week. The bombardment started at 8 am on 2 September and while III and XV Corps' heavy artillery continued at the same rate of fire on High Wood and Delville Wood until zero the following day, the bombardment intensified before XIV Corps' attack on Guillemont. The field guns had also started searching the ground between the trenches, to silence the German machine-gunners hiding in shell holes.[131]

A mine destroyed the strongpoint at the east corner of High Wood but the rest of 51st Division's attack was a disaster. The Stokes mortars fired short, hitting the oil drums, while the pipe-pushers again blew up short of their target. The crater was soon lost, and German machine gun teams returned to make the ground around Wood Lane untenable.[132]

129 Miles, *Military Operations: France and Belgium, 1916Vol. II*, p. 205-7.
130 Nicholson, *Canadian Expeditionary Force*, p. 166.
131 Miles, *Military Operations: France and Belgium, 1916, Vol. II*, p. 251.
132 TNA: WO 95/3948/2: 1st Black Watch War Diary.

A midday attack beyond Longueval and Delville Wood was cancelled because the runners carrying the messages about zero hour to 24th Division were killed. It was rearranged to 4 pm but the creeping barrage moved forward at the wrong time, leaving the infantry unprotected.[133] The attack south-east edge of Delville Wood started on time and 7th Division used fumite grenades to clear out the dugouts.[134] The idea worked but the grenades gave off smoke, which the Germans used to range in on. A contact plane reported flares in Ginchy but 7th Division had no reinforcements left to secure the village.

A false creeping barrage was fired along 20th Division's front at 8.50 am, the same time the French planned to attack on its right flank. The real one crept forward at noon but the infantry went too fast through Guillemont and the mopping up teams overlooked a German stronghold based in a quarry. Men had to be sent back to deal with it when they came under fire from behind. The supports were sent beyond Guillemont after the contact plane reported the first objective had been taken.[135]

The French attack failed to materialise at 8.50 am, so the single battalion of 5th Division sent to capture Falfemont Farm stood no chance. The main effort at midday cleared Wedge Wood ravine but the creeping barrage landed behind the troops facing the farm, leaving them unprotected.[136]

Ginchy could not be shelled because 7th Division reported it had troops in it, so the 8 am attack on 4 September was a disaster. A surprise attack planned at 3.30 am the following morning never took place, because one battalion lost all its officers before zero while the other was late deploying. The troops advanced in the wrong direction when a third attempt was made at 5 am on 6 September. A fourth attempt at 2 pm the same day only held Ginchy for a time, because the counter-barrage stopped the reinforcements getting forward.[137]

Bad weather interfered with the bombardment which supported 20th Division's 3.10 pm attack on 4 September, making it impossible to take the Quadrilateral. Bouleaux Wood was cleared by 56th Division but the French again failed to support the attack on Falfemont Farm on 4 September; the ruins were finally taken during the night. Two attempts to reach Leuze Wood by 16th Division at 6.30 pm the same evening and 8.30 am the following morning were stopped by the British guns firing short.

The creeping barrage hit 15th Division and 1st Division at 6 pm on 8 September but they still cleared Intermediate Trench, west of High Wood. Machine-gun fire then stopped the reinforcements getting forward, so it had to be abandoned.[138]

133 Miles, *Military Operations: France and Belgium, 1916, Vol. II*, p. 267.
134 Ibid., pp. 262-4. Fumite was normally employed to fumigate confined spaces.
135 Ibid., pp. 254-5.
136 Ibid., pp. 252-3.
137 TNA: WO 95/1666/2: 91 Brigade War Diary.
138 Miles, *Military Operations: France and Belgium, 1916, Vol. II*, p. 270.

The barrage restarted at 7 am on 9 September and the aim was to straighten out the line by attacking at three points; High Wood, Ginchy and Leuze Wood. The barrage intensity did not increase before zero hour at 4.45 pm, so the Germans in High Wood were surprised when a mine exploded under the strongpoint at the east corner. It meant 1st Division could finally clear the Switch Line and Wood Lane and hold them.[139]

Assembly trenches had been dug in front of 16th Division's front trench, to reduce the width of No Man's Land, but no one had told the artillery and the barrage landed on the assault troops.[140] A camouflaged trench delayed 55th Division's advance east of Delville Wood, so it lost the barrage, leaving 16th Division holding a salient around Ginchy. The creeping barrage for 56th Division's attack was 'practically non-existent', while observers could not see that the heavy artillery was firing short in the mist. One battalion cleared Leuze Wood, even though it set off late, but the second went the wrong way and failed to clear the Quadrilateral.[141]

An advance from Leuze Wood the following morning failed because cut telephone lines meant no one could tell the batteries to fire a creeping barrage. Stokes mortars failed to knock out the Quadrilateral's machine guns in the afternoon, while the infantry again advanced in the wrong direction when they tried again at 12.15 am the following morning. Even 6th Division could not take it at 6 am or 6 pm on 13 September and Lieutenant General Cavan eventually admitted that the *'situation must be accepted'*.[142]

Planning for the Tanks

Winston Churchill had submitted a memorandum on caterpillars to the War Committee on 3 December 1915. Two months later, Lieutenant Colonel Sir Ernest Swinton, Assistant-Secretary of the War Committee, summarised what the tank (the machine's codename) could do. Haig later said that he wanted to deploy many of them 'in one great combined operation.'[143]

The Male version of the Mark I tank was armed with two six-pounder guns and four Hotchkiss machine-guns while the Female version had five Vickers and one Hotchkiss. They would work in pairs to silence strongpoints and pin down infantry. Instructions said that 'its safety lies in surprise, in rapid movement, and in getting to close quarters',[144] however, the 28-ton monster could only crawl across the battlefield at ½ mile an hour; or 100 yards every eight minutes.

Rawlinson wanted to achieve a break through over three successive nights but Haig wanted to use all the tanks on the first day, opening a gap for the cavalry. Haig heard

139 Ibid., p. 276.
140 Ibid., p. 274.
141 Ibid. 56th Division's difficulties around the Quadrilateral are explained on pp. 272-3.
142 Ibid., p. 278. The position had held out against all forms of attacks for two weeks.
143 Ibid., p. 238.
144 Ibid., p. 240.

the first batch of sixty tanks were due to start arriving on 1 September and he wanted to use them straight away, even though it gave would be no time to train with the infantry. He had told Robertson that he wanted to 'use what I have got, as I cannot wait any longer for them and it would be folly not to use every means at my disposal in what is likely to be our crowning effort for this year.'[145]

Flers-Courcelette, 15 September

The attack was delayed until 15 September because the bad weather had delayed preliminary operations against Ginchy and Guillemont; it meant the barrage had to be extended to three days and nights. 'The preliminary bombardment differed little in character from artillery preparations, but the fire was more intense.[146] It was recognised that the tanks would be vulnerable to artillery fire, so the gunners regularly ceased fire to let the aerial observers report on damage.

Details for deploying tanks had been outlined in Lieutenant Colonel Ernest Swinton's February 1916 memo for the War Committee.[147] Zero was set so it would be light enough for the crews to see to navigate, but dark enough to stop the German artillery spotters seeing the tanks. The tanks would drive ahead of the infantry and 100-yard gaps would be left in the barrage as far as the first objective, so the infantry could stay close to it. The artillery could close the gaps if some tanks did not turn up, but they would be unable to respond quick enough if any were put out of action.

The artillery was expected to smash the first belt of wire, so the tanks could crawl to the enemy trench, turning parallel to it as the assault troops approached. They would then drive parallel to a communication trenches to the objective.[148] The tanks could crush gaps in the wire beyond field artillery range, allowing the infantry to advance 3 miles by midday.[149]

That left eight hours of daylight for the artillery, then the cavalry and finally the ammunition wagons to move forward. The usual communication systems were put in place and the messages started coming in as soon as the smoke and dust from the bombardment cleared. Both ground observers and pigeons were able to confirm the reports made by the contact planes.[150]

A single tank helped 15th Division clear its objective near Martinpuich and the Germans later abandoned Prue Trench.[151] Two more tanks led 50th Division to the

---

145 Ibid., p. 235.
146 Ibid., p. 298. Over 600,000 rounds were fired.
147 Ibid., p. 238-40 and Appendix 18.
148 Ibid. Detailed instructions for the tank crews are given on p. 297.
149 Ibid. The full timetable is detailed on p. 295. Cutting wire at long range had always been a problem. The artillery was not accurate enough and it took too long to move the batteries forward, while the infantry struggled to cut through by hand.
150 Ibid., p. 325.
151 Ibid., pp. 334-5.

Starfish Line but the men had to withdraw because it was under accurate artillery fire.[152] The problem was that the trench had been dug on the reverse slope for the Germans, which meant that it was exposed to their artillery.[153] An attack by the reserve brigade was postponed three times because the guides got lost and it was then unable to reach the Starfish Line.

Four tanks could not get through High Wood, as Major General Charles Barter had warned, leaving 47th Division advancing alone and without a protective barrage.[154] They eventually took Crest Trench but casualties had been so high that the reserve brigade had to be sent forward. Some followed the barrage at 5.30 pm only to be pinned down while those who were late were shot down by the Germans holding the Starfish Line.

The tanks followed the infantry across XV Corps' front (rather than led), so there were no gaps in the barrage. The New Zealanders captured the Switch Line, before digging in beyond it because the trench 'would certainly prove a ranging mark for German guns. The assumption proved correct...'[155] The four tanks struggled to catch up with the advance towards Flers, and the barrage had moved on by the time they had crushed the wire. Three tanks were soon out of action and the New Zealanders stopped when they saw the Germans preparing to counter-attack. Three of 41st Division's tanks broke down early on, while the rest struggled to catch up with the infantry.[156] They advanced together through Flers but there were too few men to go any further, while there were no tanks left to support them.

Only two out of six tanks were able to join 14th Division's advance towards Gueudecourt.[157] Some men had to crowd into the Switch Line to escape the counter-barrage, while others advanced thirty minutes late without tanks or creeping barrage. Despite the problems, 14th Division ended up ahead of the divisions to its flanks with no tanks, beyond the range of its artillery and its reinforcements 4 miles behind the front.

The Guards Division had to deploy in slit trenches which had been dug in a small area, because Ginchy was a shell trap.[158] Nine tanks either broke down or 'lost all sense of direction and wandered around aimlessly', and there was no time to close up the gaps in the barrage.[159] Only one tank joined the advance, but the left brigade drifted

---

152 Ibid., pp. 333-4.
153 The German gunners also knew exactly where their own trenches were.
154 Ibid., p. 331-3.
155 Colonel H Stewart, *The New Zealand Division 1916-1919: The New Zealanders in France, Vol. II* (Uckfield: Naval and Military Press; 2009 reprint of 1921 edition), p. 85.
156 Miles, *Military Operations: France and Belgium, 1916, Vol. II*. 41st Division's attack is detailed on pp. 321-3 and 327-8.
157 Ibid., 14th Division's advance is chronicled on pp. 318-21, 326-7.
158 Ibid. The Guards Division is covered on p. 310-4.
159 Cuthbert Headlam, *History of the Guards Division in the Great War, 1915-1918. Vol. II* (Edinburgh: John Murray, 1924), p. 161.

north-east of its line of advance, because of the dust and smoke. The commanders incorrectly reported they had reached their third objective, and the support battalions approached Serpentine Trench in artillery formation. They lost heavily redeploying but still took the German position.[160]

Major General Ross heard that two of the tanks had broken down, but his instruction to close the gap in the barrage never reached 6th Division's artillery.[161] A third tank fired on 6th Division's trench before it headed north, leaving the infantry pinned down in front of the Quadrilateral. Three tanks were supposed to lead 56th Division; one broke down, another advanced too early and the third was knocked out.[162] The Londoners still made progress through Leuze Wood.

Contact planes reported XIV Corps' true situation when the mist cleared. A plan for the Guards Division to outflank the Quadrilateral was cancelled, because it was too far north. An attack by 6th and 56th Divisions was postponed but Major General Hull's staff did not have time to tell the battalions and 56th Division's advance was a disaster. Ross rearranged 6th Division's attack for 7.30 pm, only to see his artillery miss the Quadrilateral, while his infantry advanced in the wrong direction. A surprise attack by 56th Division at 11.00 pm also failed to capture the position.[163]

As soon as the contact plane reports reached Fourth Army headquarters, it was clear there had been no breakthrough. Rawlinson stopped further advances and sent the three cavalry divisions back. The spotter planes had also located much more German artillery than expected. It was estimated that Fourth Army's batteries could only engage one third of them at a time and they first had to redeploy and register.

Reserve Army, 15-17 September

Seven tanks covered 2nd Canadian Division's advance towards Courcelette at 6.20 am, before turning on machine-gun posts around a sugar factory.[164] Gough ordered the Canadian Corps to extend the advance north of the Bapaume road, as soon as he heard III Corps was approaching Martinpuich.[165] The preliminary bombardment overshot Fabeck Graben at 5.30 pm, but the creeping barrage was on target when the 2nd Canadian Division advanced thirty minutes later. Some men captured the wrong part of the trench, because they had been given no time to check the ground, while others were hit by the counter-barrage, while crossing No Man's Land.

---

160 Ibid., p. 156.
161 Miles, *Military Operations: France and Belgium, 1916, Vol. II*, pp. 309-10.
162 Ibid., pp. 307-9.
163 Ibid. XIV Corps' later attempts to take the Quadrilateral are covered on pp. 315-6.
164 Ibid., the Canadian Corps' two-part attack is chronicled on pp. 169-71.
165 Ibid., p. 170.

The tanks led the advance through Courcelette but Lieutenant-General Byng still thought they were 'a useful accessory to the infantry, but nothing more'.[166] They had given the infantry 'a feeling of superiority and security'[167] but they had headed back early, due to insufficient communication with the infantry. One had even laid 400 metres of telephone cable from a drum, proving that tanks were useful for carrying heavy items.

The barrage overshot Zollern Graben on 16 September, so 3rd Canadian Division only captured the west half, when it attacked at 5 pm. The next attempt at 5 am on 20 September started with a bombing attack on the flank, to distract the Germans, followed by a charge over the top. The Germans used a smoke screen and a shower of rifle grenades to retake the trench at their fifth attempt.[168]

Fourth Army, 16 to 20 September

Both 41st Division and 14th Division tried to straighten out the line around Flers on 16 September but the artillery had not been given time to move across the broken ground and register their guns.[169] The heavy guns missed their targets and the creeping barrage landed too far ahead, while cut telephone wires, damp flares and a counter-barrage meant the gunners never realised their mistake. The brigade sent to help 41st Division had a nightmare journey through the dark, wet night and it deployed to attack too far back. It passed through the front line some time later and was pinned down in front of Gird Trench. A shell then destroyed the brigade signal headquarters, preventing further attempts. Wire and hidden machine-gun teams pinned 14th Division's men down in the wrong trench south of Gueudecourt and it was some time before they realised it was not Gird Trench.

The Guards Division was due to attack at 1.30 pm on 16 September but the orders were issued late to one brigade and it was spotted assembling at dawn; the Guardsmen then had to endure the German barrage for six hours. The other brigade advanced late, never caught up with the creeping barrage and was pinned down facing the wrong way, having mistaken Gueudecourt for Lesboeufs.[170] Orders for a complicated deployment for an attack at 6.30 pm the following afternoon were issued late by 20th Division. The artillery had insufficient time to prepare a barrage plan or bring ammunition forward and so the attack was a disaster.[171]

---

166 Nicholson, *Canadian Expeditionary Force*, p. 170 and Miles, *Military Operations: France and Belgium, 1916, Vol. II*, p. 368 covers the Canadian feedback on the tanks.
167 Miles, *Military Operations: France and Belgium, 1916, Vol. II*, p. 339.
168 Nicholson, *Canadian Expeditionary Force*. The actions on 16 and 20 September are covered on p. 172.
169 Miles, *Military Operations: France and Belgium, 1916, Vol. II*, p. 351.
170 Ibid., pp. 349-50.
171 Ibid., pp. 355.

The failures on 16 September meant that the New Zealand Division was given extra time to prepare its attack, so it was able to bomb along the Flers Support on 18 September.[172] Advances over the top by 6th Division and 56th Division the same morning were thwarted by thick mud but the bombers were able to clear Straight Trench and Bouleaux Wood. Even the Quadrilateral finally fell, after two costly weeks.[173] The New Zealanders then made a surprise attack without artillery support, at dusk on 20 September, and took the rest of the Flers Trenches and Goose Alley. The Germans finally abandoned Starfish and Prue Trenches, late on 21 September, allowing III Corps to straighten out the line around Martinpuich and High Wood.

An Appraisal of the Tank

Thirty-six tanks had been deployed on 15 September, but two-thirds had broken down, ditched or had been knocked out. The tank commanders had just driven to their objective and returned because there had been no time for training with the infantry. There had been localised panics. The Germans, however, had not been routed, as hoped for. The British infantry had been left exposed by the gaps left in the barrage when the tanks broke down and the artillery had no way of closing them at short notice. However, the consensus was that 15 September had been 'a very valuable try out'[174] and GHQ asked for evaluations. Lieutenant-General Kiggell observed that the tanks were a 'valuable accessory',[175] Gough wanted 'tactical training' but Rawlinson did not want to change the 'normal tactical methods'.[176]

Reserve Army, 26-30 September

Major General Ivor Maxse wanted 18th Division to have enough time to capture and consolidate Thiepval in daylight, leaving the Germans having to counter-attack in darkness.[177] So, zero hour was set for 12.35 pm on 26 September, giving Fifth Army's men three hours before sunset to secure their objectives. The machine guns opened fire at 12.34 pm, giving the infantry one minute's notice to advance and they were moving when the bombardment hit the German trenches.

The assault battalions crossed No Man's Land as the counter-barrage hit the empty assembly trenches, while support battalions ran across in small groups when it had slackened off.[178] Bombers had trapped the garrison of Mouquet Farm in their shelters

172 Stewart, *The New Zealand Division 1916-1919, Vol. II*, p. 91.
173 Miles, *Military Operations: France and Belgium, 1916, Vol. II*, pp. 356-7.
174 Ibid., p. 365.
175 Ibid., p. 368.
176 Ibid., p. 367.
177 *G.H.F. Nicholls, The 18th Division in the Great War (Edinburgh: William Blackwood & Sons, 1922), p. 81.*
178 Ibid., p. 82.

before zero hour, finally securing the area after two months. However, 11th Division had been given insufficient time to take the first objective, so the barrage was creeping towards Zollern Redoubt before the troops were ready to move.[179]

Observers had been unable to determine if the wire protecting Regina Trench had been cut, so 1st Canadian Division sent patrols forward behind the barrage to check before the assault troops advanced.[180] They too were uncertain, but the advance was stopped because Zollern Redoubt had not been taken on the left, while a heavy counter-barrage had stopped 2nd Canadian Division leaving its trench to the left.[181]

The relief in 18th Division's sector finished early on 27 September, so the battalion commander decided to attack at once.[182] The absence of a bombardment took the Germans by surprise and the rest of Thiepval was cleared.[183] Maxse relied on his belief that it took six hours to plan and prepare an attack, but the rest of 18th Division still could not clear Schwaben Redoubt.

The attack against Stuff Redoubt was delayed because 11th Division's relief was taking too long. One battalion did not hear of the change and artillery began their barrage when their observers saw the infantry advance at 3 pm. That left no ammunition to support the second battalion an hour later and while the absence of a barrage took the Germans in Stuff Redoubt by surprise, they still held on.

No one knew how close the Canadians had got to Regina Trench, making it difficult to plan the barrage on 27 September. There was fierce fighting for Kenora Trench and the Germans chose to withdraw, so their artillery could drive 1st Canadian Division out of it. The order was then given to take the position, 'even if it required the last man in the brigade to do it' but an attempt to take it at 2 am on 28 September was spotted and flares lit up the area.[184] The Germans eventually abandoned the Courcelette area on the afternoon of 27 September.

The plan for 28 September was to advance towards Le Sars but heavy rain had filled the trenches with mud while the brigade slated to attack was 'too exhausted and too few in numbers.'[185] The artillery was also 'shooting short', so General Currie had to grant a postponement until the guns had been re-registered.[186]

179 Miles, *Military Operations: France and Belgium, 1916, Vol. II*, p. 399-403.
180 Nicholson, *Canadian Expeditionary Force*, p.174-7.
181 Miles, *Military Operations: France and Belgium, 1916, Vol. II*. The Canadian Corps' attack is covered on pp. 395-9.
182 TNA: WO 95/2043/1: 7th Bedfordshire Regiment War Diary.
183 Nicholson, *Canadian Expeditionary Force*, p. 176. The new German doctrine was to leave their trenches when an offensive was due, to avoid the barrage. They hid in nearby shell holes, ready to take the attacking troops by surprise. Barrages were moved back and forth once this was realised, catching the Germans in the open.
184 Ibid., p. 178. The assault battalion started with only 75 men. It suffered over 400 casualties trrying to take Kenora Trench.
185 Ibid., p. 180.
186 Ibid., p. 180.

Fourth Army, 25-30 September

A five-day bombardment was planned but the autumn mists meant the gunners often had to use map fire, not knowing if they were hitting the enemy batteries. Rain then turned the battlefield into a quagmire and the field artillery had to rely on pack animals to carry shells to their battery positions. The bombardment eventually began in earnest at 7 am on 24 September but morning mist and afternoon haze continued to interfere with the counter-battery work.[187]

Zero was eventually set for 12.35 pm on 25 September because the French artillery wanted to fire the final part of their bombardment after the morning mist had cleared. It meant the assault troops had to deploy before dawn and then sit in the trenches for six-hours. The anticipation of what lay ahead, during the prolonged wait, made them tired and anxious.[188]

Tanks were not used because the ground was open, making them vulnerable to artillery fire.[189] The barrage landed 200 yards ahead of Fourth Army's line and led the troops across the German trenches around Lesboeufs and Morval. The advance went well in most areas, but the Guards Division was delayed clearing a new trench which had been dug in No Man's Land in the night.[190] It gave the Germans the opportunity to pour enfilade fire into 21st Division, and pin it down in front of Gird Trench.

An ingenious combined arms attack was prepared to eradicate the salient the following day. A contact plane fired a flare to start the barrage and the infantry deployed while the Germans took cover. A second flare stopped the bombardment and then the pilot flew low, strafing the trench to keep the Germans under cover. A tank supported the bombers as they cleared the trenches and many prisoners were taken for few casualties.[191]

Reserve Army, October

The wet and misty autumn weather defeated both 18th Division's and 39th Division's attempts to clear Schwaben Redoubt for several days early in October. Stuff Redoubt was finally taken by 25th Division on 9 October and the high point called the Mounds were taken five days later. It meant II Corps' observers could see across the Ancre valley for the first time.

The bombardment either overshot Regina Trench or hit the Canadian Corps' assembly area before zero hour at 3.15 pm on 1 October. The Germans had used concertina wire to repair the damage (because it was quicker to erect) and it left the

---

187 Miles, *Military Operations: France and Belgium, 1916, Vol. II*, p. 372.
188 Ibid. The French preferred later attacks, so observers could direct the final part of the bombardment.
189 Ibid., p. 371.
190 Ibid., p. 373-6.
191 Ibid., p. 384-5.

Canadians pinned down under an accurate counter-barrage. The rain then came down harder and operations had to be cancelled.[192] There were similar problems at 4.50 am on 8 October as 1st Canadian Division reached the arc of wire at different times, giving some of the Germans time to man parts of Regina Trench, which was curved. The few that did get through soon ran out of bombs and had to withdraw.[193]

Byng was against any more pre-dawn attacks and wanted to focus on patrolling instead. He also wanted a rethink on the Canadian Corps' barrages because he faced a dilemma. Large calibre high explosive shells always smashed the wire, but they also churned up No Man's Land. Meanwhile, the field batteries were often unable to cut the entanglements with shrapnel. He also wanted the aerial observers to recheck the position of Regina Trench, to help the heavy artillery register.

The artillery had plenty of ammunition to cut the wire on 21 October, while the barrage crept forward 'like a wall' at 12.06 pm.[194] The Canadians were able to capture most of Stuff Trench and all of Regina Trench. The counter-barrage hit the area in front of the Grandcourt Line, until the Germans realised Fifth Army planned to go no further. The Canadian observers could now see better across the Ancre valley but they were unable to see the Grandcourt Line because of the convex nature of the slope. An oversight meant the artillery plan for 25 October paid 'little attention' to the flanks and even failed to include the Quadrilateral, so the 7 am attack was stopped by enfilade fire.[195] Heavy rain started on 30 October, bringing operations to an end for the time being.

Fourth Army, October and November

Fourth Army's bombardment started at 7 am on 1 October and it intensified at the 3.15 am zero, to avoid alerting the Germans.[196] Both 23rd Division and 50th Division reached Flers Trench around Le Sars but the smoke screen made it difficult to find the Flers Support. Two tanks drove around Eaucourt l'Abbaye, firing into the trenches in support of 47th Division. Meanwhile, projectors had fired burning oil one minute before the New Zealand Division charged at the Gird Trenches.[197]

Heavy rain and low cloud delayed the next attack until 1.45 pm on 7 October. A tank helped 23rd Division clear the Flers Trenches and the Tangle around Le Sars but 47th Division could not get any closer to the Butte du Warlencourt in daylight.[198] So, the Londoners crept forward as soon as it was dark and charged when the guns lifted off Snag Trench at 9 pm.

192 Nicholson, *Canadian Expeditionary Force*, pp. 182-3.
193 Ibid., pp. 184-6.
194 Ibid., pp. 189-91.
195 Ibid., pp. 191-2.
196 Miles, *Military Operations: France and Belgium, 1916, Vol. II*, pp. 430-1.
197 Stewart, *The New Zealand Division 1916-1919, Vol. II*, p. 110-6.
198 Miles, *Military Operations: France and Belgium, 1916, Vol. II*, pp. 436-7.

Burning oil was once again employed against the Gird Trenches on 7 October but thick mud meant that 41st Division could not keep up with the creeping barrage.[199] A counter-barrage had disrupted 12th Division before zero hour, so it too was unable to reach Bayonet and Hilt Trenches.

The Germans had deployed in shell holes and gun pits rather than the trenches around Le Transloy, to avoid the British barrage. The ground observers struggled to spot them, the aerial observers were grounded, and the barrage missed many. Even so, the Germans east of Gueudecourt still surrendered to 20th Division, beaten into submission by the bombardment.[200]

Rainbow, Cloudy and Misty Trenches had been levelled, so new ones had to be dug. A crooked front-line east of Lesboeufs meant that 56th Division faced several problems.[201] No Man's Land was so narrow in places that trench mortars had to be used instead of heavy artillery. Battalions then had to advance at different times towards Hazy, Rainy, Dewdrop and Spectrum Trenches, only to find the machine-gun teams had not been silenced. The men withdrew to a safe distance the following day, so the heavy guns could shell the four trenches, but the men were so exhausted by the time 3.30 pm came, they took too long to haul themselves out of the muddy trenches and missed the barrage.

The rain finally stopped on 9 October, but it had turned the battlefield into a quagmire. At least one divisional commander asked for a postponement, but the request was denied because it would give Germans more time to improve their defences.[202] Dark clouds on 11 October made it difficult to take aerial photographs, but a Chinese attack during the afternoon revealed many new targets for the gunners. Rawlinson set zero hour for 2.05 pm the following day even though the forecast correctly predicted bad weather, resulting in an inaccurate barrage.[203]

Smoke released to cover the Gird Trenches and the Butte, warned the Germans an attack was coming, and the counter-barrage pinned down some of the assault troops. The screen then dispersed, exposing 9th Division to fire from Snag Trench. The late start time meant that the men of 29th and 12th Division were silhouetted by the low sun and they were pinned down while trying to cut through the wire covering Gird, Bayonet and Hilt Trenches. Grease Trench was taken at 3.40 am the following morning, but it gave little shelter and a new trench had to be dug.

The creeping barrage hit part of 6th Division while part of 4th Division advanced into its own barrage. A couple of machine guns hidden in No Man's Land caused many casualties, but the biggest problem was a strongpoint in Zenith Trench, because

---

199 Ibid., pp. 435-6.
200 Ibid., pp. 435.
201 Ibid., pp. 434-5.
202 Major General Furse wanted another forty-eight hours to prepare for 9th Division's attack.
203 Miles, *Military Operations: France and Belgium, 1916, Vol. II,* the attack on 12 October is covered on pp. 440-3. It appears the Germans were 'accustomed to afternoon attacks' by this time.

neither division had been detailed to attack it. Only Rainbow Trench was taken and held.

Rawlinson set zero for 3.40 am on 18 October, two hours before dawn, but he decided against sending any tanks across the muddy battlefield in the dark.[204] The infantry dug extra assembly and communication trenches across the crater field, but the autumn weather continued to hinder the artillery.[205]

Smoke and tear gas smothered the Butte du Warlencourt as 9th Division fought across a 'sea of pewter-grey ooze'. They reached it on 20 October, using flares to tell the artillery when to lengthen their range by 50-yard intervals. The men of 30th Division were exhausted by the time they reached the Gird Trenches, while wire stopped 12th Division securing Bayonet Trench.

No one reached Mild and Cloudy Trenches because they had taken too long to climb out of the wet, slippery trenches and they never caught up with the creeping barrage as they waded through the mud. Some of 6th Division's men went beyond their objective in the darkness, never to be seen again, but 4th Division's bombers managed to clear Rainy, Dewdrop and Frosty Trenches. The rain stopped on 19 October but the soldiers were wet and tired, their rifles were caked in mud and the guns were worn out. An autumn storm blew up three days later, ending all operations.

Morning mist on 23 October made the French decide to postpone zero hour to 2.30 pm, so the artillery could see, but the time change reached some battalions late. The barrage speed had been slowed to 100 yards every two minutes because of the muddy conditions, but 8th Division and 4th Division still took Mild Trench, Zenith Trench and Spectrum Trench. The weather worsened the following day and the attack against Le Transloy was postponed. Instead, 33rd Division captured Dewdrop, Rainy and Boritska Trench early during 28-29 October.

Major General Philip Robertson of 17th Division summarised the awful conditions with the following words: "The weather conditions have been simply appalling and the trenches awful; men buried in mud, several deaths from exposure alone, men drowned in mud... I wonder if those behind the lines have the slightest conception of what it is like?"

The shell holes were full of water, but strong winds dried out the muddy ground until the bad weather returned. Major General James Legge insisted that 2nd Australian Division attacked the Maze at 12.30 am on 5 November, despite protests from his brigadiers.[206] Some battalions advanced on time in the heavy rain, only to see the creeping barrage land behind them. The rest moved off three minutes late, due to a

---

204 Ibid., p. 444. The new moon was hidden by rain clouds, making navigation too difficult in the dark.
205 Miles, *Military Operations: France and Belgium, 1916, Vol. II*. The 18 October attack is covered on pp. 444-7.
206 Ibid., pp. 472-3.

misunderstanding over times, and could not catch the barrage up. The same happened to 1st Australian Division in front of Hilt Trench.

The barrage crept slowly at 100 metres every four minutes towards the Butte du Warlencourt ahead of 50th Division at 11.10 am, on 5 November.[207] Again, the men struggled to haul each other out of the muddy trenches and then could not keep up in the thick mud. The barrage was that slow that it gave the Germans nearly five minutes to man their parapet; more than enough time to stop the attack.

Fifth Army, November

The skies cleared and the temperature dropped on 8 November, so Gough set zero hour for 5.45 am on 13 November.[208] Guns shelled distant targets, to make the attack front seem wider, while regular morning barrages of the German artillery settled the infantry into a routine. An intense barrage signalled zero hour was close and then a mine detonated under Hawthorn Crater. Three out of four guns continued to shell the enemy trenches, the rest reduced their range by 50 yards. Six minutes later the double barrage crept forward at 100 yards every five minutes. This double shrapnel screen got over the problem of the slow barrage because it kept the Germans under cover while the assault troops crossed No Man's Land.[209]

Visibility was so limited in the fog, that the sound of the bombardment was used to coordinate the advance. The gunners ceased firing on each objective, giving the infantry a five-minute-warning. They then fired at double the normal rate; the sudden increase in shelling alerting the troops to move off.[210]

There was an advance towards Serre but there was no advance on 31st Division's north flank, while 3rd Division found it difficult to find the gaps through the wire in the mist.[211] Cut telephone wires meant the few footholds in the enemy line had been abandoned before a second attack could be organised. The Quadrilateral disrupted 2nd Division's advance, so too few men reached the final objective and it had to be abandoned. Two tanks failed to join 51st Division and it took the infantry time to get through the wire. Even so, Beaumont Hamel was taken after a translator convinced the Germans in Y Ravine to surrender.[212]

---

207 Ibid., p. 473.
208 Ibid., p. 476. Commanders had asked for a decision to attack or cancel because repeated postponements were stressful on the men.
209 Ibid., p. 479. One divisional general had suggested slowing the barrage to 100 yards every ten minutes after seeing the state of the ground. It was considered impractical because it would give the German machine-gun teams too long to deploy.
210 Ibid., p. 479. Employing sound to communicate worked effectively but the Germans immediately realised that the cessation of the bombardment warned the next attack was imminent.
211 Ibid., pp. 497-501.
212 Ibid., pp. 491-7.

There were heavy casualties west of the Ancre but a battalion commander rounded up the survivors and led them forward. Unfortunately, there were insufficient men to mop up and the reserve brigade faced a tough fight to clear 63rd Division's rear. Another bombardment was fired as soon as the mist lifted but it took too long to organise the infantry and it was evening before the extent of the advance was known.[213]

Many of the Germans were caught underground east of the Ancre and the dugouts were guarded until the moppers up arrived. Infantry guided the tanks through the Hansa Line and 39th Division trapped the Germans along the river.[214] The flank was successfully covered by 19th Division. Fog had resulted in some units losing their way but it 'concealed the scope and direction of the assault and helped to effect a tactical surprise.'[215]

An attempt to continue the advance the following day was hampered by inaccurate barrages and late orders. The only success was 63rd Division's capture of Beaucourt, but only after the Germans abandoned the mud filled trenches. A final attack early on 18 November ended in disaster because everyone became disorientated in the appalling wintry conditions.[216]

The Somme Campaign Summary

By the summer of 1916, the BEF had enough infantry, artillery and ammunition to make the big breakthrough GHQ had been looking for. It also had the French on its right flank, extending the attack front to 25-miles wide. GHQ did, however, have very little experience of conducting offensives while most of the troops had no experience at all.

An over dependence on the preliminary bombardment and poor judgement about the timing of the detonation of the mines led to catastrophic results across large parts of the front on 1 July. However, there was success on Fourth Army's right flank, illustrating that a deep advance was possible, under the right circumstances.

The surprise attack on 14 July was a complete contrast to what had happened two weeks earlier, demonstrating the BEF's willingness to try different methods to 'bite and hold' small sections of ground. A range of tactics were then tested across the Somme over the next two months. Various zero hours were used, different bombardments were employed and diverse types of attack were tried. Places such as Pozières, High Wood and Delville Wood became bloody testing grounds where lessons were learned and mistakes were made on both sides.

---

213 Ibid., pp. 486-90.
214 Ibid., pp. 480-5.
215 Ibid., p. 485.
216 Ibid., pp. 514-9. The first snow of the year blinded the infantry, gunners and the observers alike.

The deployment of the tank on 15 September changed the face of the battle, as a breakthrough was tried once again. But endeavours to keep the new weapon secret meant there was no opportunity to practice any tactics with the infantry. Changes to the barrage, to accommodate the new weapon, caused many problems due to the tanks' poor reliability.

Bad weather interfered with operations in October but more lessons were learnt as different tactical problems were tackled. One final innovation was to use the sound of the guns to coordinate the artillery barrage and infantry advance in poor visibility on 13 November. This final attempt at bite and hold around Beaumont Hamel demonstrated how far the BEF's art of attack had progressed over the course of the Somme campaign.

4

The Withdrawal to the Hindenburg Line and the Arras Campaign
February-May 1917

Early 1917

Many lessons from the Somme campaign were considered during the winter. The infantry companies had learnt to advance in two waves, around 75 yards apart, while platoons moved in two lines, around 20 years apart. Troops had to stay close to the creeping barrage, while 'moppers up' searched the captured area and others brought equipment and ammunition forward to hold it. But the main lesson learnt was that plans had to be flexible, to deal with a tactical problem and the enemy's response. But a basic attack had Lewis-gunners and rifle-bombers giving covering fire, while the riflemen and bombers moved in on the enemy position behind a smoke screen.

The artillery was proficient at firing creeping barrages at different speeds by now, but they had also learnt to use fake barrages, practice barrages and different intensities to confuse the enemy. They used combinations of shrapnel and high explosive shells while the new graze fuse, which exploded on contact, was proving to be effective. A quarter of field artillery batteries had been taken from the divisions and formed into army brigades, so deployment was more flexible.

The infantry and artillery were learning how to work with the newcomer on the battlefield; the tank. Lessons from the September battle had been noted and improved models were promised. The same went for working with the Royal Flying Corps, as crews learnt how to spot and report targets. It had also increased its number of squadrons in France to thirty-six. The number of spotter planes equipped with wirelesses had been doubled, while the art of taking and reading aerial photographs was improving.

The weather had been monitored for some time, but meteorological stations started issuing daily reports in January 1917. Experiments had determined that temperature, wind speed and air pressure all affected the range of shells, so the information was being used to make the barrages more accurate.

Operations on the Ancre

The changing winter weather made it a struggle to survive in the trenches, which changed from flooded to frozen according to the temperature. Explosives sometimes had to be used to break up the frozen ground, so it could be dug, but it was impossible to screw picquets through the frost. Shells exploded prematurely due to the cold, while men had to tie sandbags around their boots, so they could walk on the ice. But rain filled the trenches with water and duckboards were needed to cross soft mud when it thawed.[1]

Changes in the temperature could also cause more serious problems, as happened at 5.45 am on 17 February near Miraumont. A thaw created a mist, so the artillery observers could not see that the barrage was landing short while the troops became disorientated around Boom Ravine. Many never returned and the blame was placed on two deserters who had given away zero hour.[2]

Fourth Army still wanted to capture tactical points and 29th Division used a variation on the double shrapnel barrage on 27 January. Half the field batteries hit the enemy front line for four minutes and then the rest shelled the area in front of the trenches, so the Germans did not hear or see what was happening. Both lines of shells crept forward a minute later and the Germans left their dug-outs after the first line had passed, only to be caught by the second.[3]

The ground was so hard around Gueudecourt that I Anzac Corps had to rely on the heavy artillery to cut the wire, because the mortar shells were bouncing off the ice. The artillery did not see the SOS signals through the mist when a surprise attack late on 1 February got into trouble and many men were captured.[4] A week later, 17th Division tried the double barrage again, when it attacked near Sailly-Saillisel at 7.30 am, but the worn guns were firing short.

The Germans Prepare to Withdraw

The Germans had built the Siegfried Position, or *Siegfried Stellung*, many miles behind the front over the winter. The British would call it the Hindenburg Line when they realised the full extent of it, at the end of February 1917. It had escaped GHQ's attention because it was dangerous to fly deep into German air space in the winter

1   Charles Bean, *The Official History of Australia in the War, Vol. IV: The Australian Imperial Force in France, 1917* (Sydney: Angus & Robertson, 1941), pp. 20-1 explains the issues associated with trench warfare in winter.
2   Captain Cyril Falls, *Military Operations: France and Belgium, 1917, Vol. I: The German Retreat to the Hindenburg Line and the Battles of Arras* (London: HMSO, 1940), p. 79-82.
3   Falls, *Military Operations: France and Belgium, 1917, Vol. I*, p. 83.
4   Bean, *Australian Official History, Vol. IV*, pp. 27-31. Also covered in Falls, *Military Operations: France and Belgium, 1917, Vol. I*, p. 84.

weather, and it was the beginning of April before a photographic survey was finally completed.[5]

The Hindenburg Line had two trench systems about 2,500 yards apart and each one had three trenches, creating a 3-mile deep defensive zone.[6] Wire aprons were built in irregular patterns with gaps to funnel the Allied troops towards strongpoints. There were surface bunkers for the machine-gun teams, shallow shelters for the infantry and deep dugouts for the headquarters, signal offices and medical facilities. It made strategic sense to withdraw to a purpose-built defensive system, but Ludendorff was aware of the negative effect it would have on his troops. *The decision to retire was not reached without a painful struggle. It implied a confession of weakness bound to raise the moral of the enemy and lower our own. But as it was necessary for military reasons, we had no choice it had to be carried out.*[7]

The plan was to withdraw between three Reserve Lines or *Reserveleitung Stellung*, which had been dug across the 1916 battlefield. On 22 February the German machine guns and mortars were quieter (because they were withdrawing), the artillery was livelier (because they were getting rid of surplus ammunition) and there were fires and explosions in the distance (getting rid of surplus stores).[8] Empty trenches were entered on 22 February and one prisoner said the 'Germans were withdrawing to a line of trenches at Cambrai, 22 miles farther back.'[9] The admission suggested they abandoning 100 miles of trenches, shortening their line by 30 miles. It would upset the Allied plans for a spring offensive and the Anzac Corps' chief of staff, Brigadier General Cyril White, said 'I am afraid it is a very clever thing the Germans have done.'[10]

The Allied troops pushed forward cautiously but 'to strike the mean between rashness and over caution was inevitably difficult.'[11] The German infantry used flares to report their withdrawal, but it was difficult to coordinate their movement with the artillery across the 1916 battlefield because they 'had no experience of rear guard actions. Attempts were made to control troops from too far behind and too much reliance was placed upon field telephones when they should have been abandoned for mounted orderlies and visual signalling.'[12]

5   Falls, *Military Operations: France and Belgium, 1917, Vol. I*, pp. 87-90 explains how the Hindenburg Line was discovered.
6   Ibid., pp. 90-3 details how the Hindenburg Line was built.
7   Erich Ludendorff, *My War Memories, 1914-18, Vol. II* (London: Hutchinson, 1919) p. 407.
8   Falls, *Military Operations: France and Belgium, 1917, Vol. I*, p. 94.
9   Bean, *Australian Official History, Vol. IV*, p. 70.
10   Ibid., p. 70.
11   Falls, *Military Operations: France and Belgium, 1917, Vol. I*, p. 98.
12   G. Nicholls, *The 18th Division in the Great War (Edinburgh: William Blackwood & Sons, 1922), p. 154.*

They found the Germans holding the R1 Line between Bucquoy and Achiet-le-Petit.[13] Howitzers shelled the south end of Irles at 5.15 am on 10 March, while men of 18th and 2nd Divisions crawled across the mud to reach the north end. Lewis gunners fired into Lady's Leg ravine before establishing an outpost line in craters made by the 6-inch howitzers.[14]

The withdrawal to the R2 Position started late on 11 March, but it was twenty-four hours before anyone realised. Captured plans then revealed a faster withdrawal to the Hindenburg Line would begin on 13 March and it would be completed in just three 'Marching Days'.[15] Protests about making a hasty attack against Bucquoy late on 13 March were ignored. The infantry faced a long march in the rain while the gunners had no time to register their targets before it was dark. Pipe-pushers could not be found, so the wire was intact, and then clouds hid the moon, so the artillery could not adjust their barrage. The attack had failed by the time the Germans carried out their planned withdrawal.[16]

The advance guards were increased to brigade sized groups, to fend off small attacks, while the main groups had to build fortifications behind the lines, to meet any large counter-attacks.[17] But it was slow going, because the Germans destroyedeverything they could; buildings, bridges and roads. They also booby-trapped many things, ranging from delay-action bombs to wiring explosives to souvenirs. Dugouts were particularly dangerous.[18] Anything from doors, floorboards and loose planks could be rigged to a tripwire while detonators were set in lumps of coal and chimneys were lined with explosives.[19]

Bridging watercourses was time consuming and many had to be built across the River Somme.[20] Army engineers assessed what was needed at each crossing, while each corps collected the materials. Engineers supervised the clearing of tree trunks, ice and debris from the river and they sometimes built dams or opened new channels to improve the water flow. The infantry established bridgeheads and then pontoons carried supplies and rafts carried field guns across. Only then could the engineers work around the clock, illuminating their work site with bonfires at night. Typically, it took four days to complete a light bridge across the Somme and eight days to open one for heavy wheeled traffic.[21]

13   Falls, *Military Operations: France and Belgium, 1917, Vol. I*, p. 97. The advance to the R.1 Line is covered in detail on pp. 98-104.
14   Ibid., p. 105.
15   Ibid., p. 109.
16   Ibid., pp. 108-9.
17   Ibid. General Rawlinson views on this are explained on p. 123.
18   Ibid., p. 148.
19   Bean, *Australian Official History, Vol. IV*, p. 74.
20   See Falls, *Military Operations: France and Belgium, 1917, Vol. I*, pp. 130-1 for responsibilities details.
21   Ibid. Examples of bridging the Somme are given on pp. 131-3 and 137.

As the Hindenburg Line came into sight, it was clear that the Germans intended to hold the villages in front of it, to give everyone time to settle down.[22] The tanks were all being saved for the Arras offensive, leaving the British infantry to fend for themselves in the fields in front of the defensive position. One-by-one the outpost villages were taken, as the rearguards were forced to fall back. Outposts and platoon sized strong points could then be built and then connected together. Meanwhile, the roads had to be repaired and bridges built, so the front line could be kept supplied. All the time the senior commanders were considering how the German withdrawal would impact on the planned offensive around Arras.

Planning for Arras

Lieutenant General Julian Byng's 'Scheme of Operations' for the Canadian Corps' suggesting starting the bombardment on 20 March, with the attack being made on 8 April.[23] The final objective was at an angle to the front line, leaving the left division with only ½ mile to go, while the right division needed nearly eight hours to advance 2½ miles in stages.

General Edmund Allenby's ambitious plan was for Third Army to advance 4½ miles, east of Arras. Both XVII and VI Corps would clear the Black Line astride the River Scarpe and VII Corps would join the advance to the Blue Line. The field artillery then had to redeploy to cut the Brown Line wire before their final advance, which would clear the trenches some eight hours after zero. Three reserve divisions would then to pass through to the Green Line, making a gap for three cavalry divisions to exploit.

A large model of the ridge was built at First Army headquarters and all officers and NCOs were invited to study it. The men also trained on marked out courses, walking it slowly to learn the objectives before moving at the speed of the barrage. Lieutenant General Montagu Harper's message to 51st Division was typical of the post Somme attitude amongst the divisional generals. The men were to fight 'with their wits and not by a mere display of seeing red and brute courage'. His tactical points were representative of what was being taught across the BEF:

1) Use envelopment to hold the enemy front and attack their flank.
2) Make the maximum use of mechanical weapons and the minimum use of infantry.
3) Troops had to advance in depth.
4) A leader without personality will achieve nothing.

22   Ibid. The capture of the outpost villages is chronicled on pp. 154-60, 162-9.
23   Nicholson, *Canadian Expeditionary Force*, pp. 247-8.

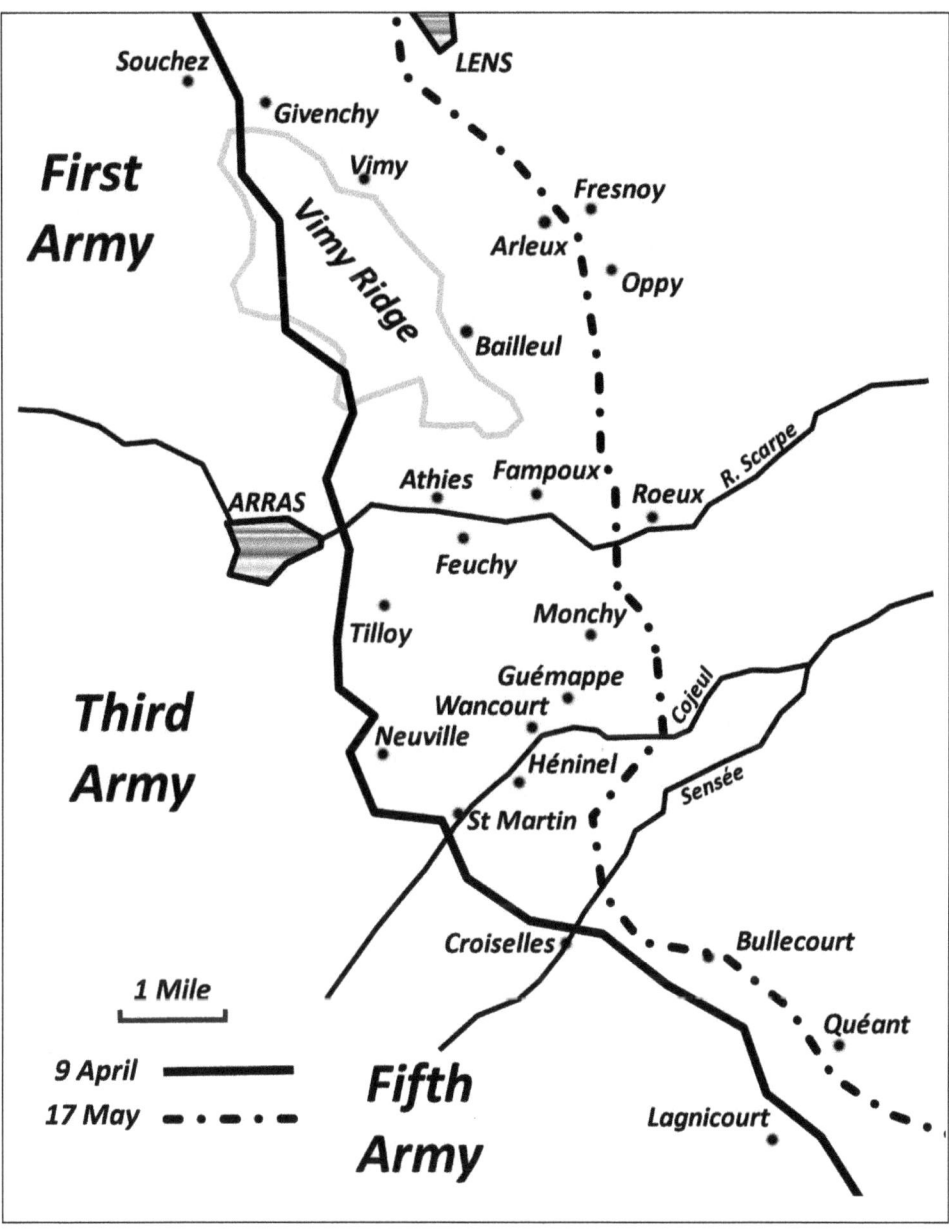

Map 4. Arras and Bullecourt, 9 April -17 May: The rapid advance onto Vimy Ridge and east of Arras soon deteriorated into another blood battle of attrition.

Tanks

The large number of craters on Vimy Ridge meant that only eight tanks had been allocated to the Canadian Corps, and it was thought they would get all bogged down. Third Army had thirty-two tanks and they would join the infantry once they had reached the Black Line because the front line was too rough to fight over. They would advance together to the Blue Line, where the tanks would cut wire and help the infantry tackle the strongpoints. Eighteen tanks would attack Chapel Hill before driving parallel to the Brown Line, to support the infantry. The survivors would then head for Monchy-le-Preux and the Green Line.[24] Maintenance teams would carry ammunition and petrol to pre-arranged rallying points, so the tanks could operate at long range.

Royal Flying Corps

The Royal Flying Corps' pilots struggled to gain the upper hand because the German planes were better, but two squadrons tried to keep them at bay while looking for observation balloons to shoot down. Four squadrons looked for targets and took aerial photographs; two over Vimy Ridge and two beyond it; a squadron of balloon observers also watched the ridge.[25]

Each of Third Army's corps had a squadron which photographed as far as the Brown Line and it would switch to reporting the infantry's progress during the advance. Other squadrons operated beyond the Brown Line while fighter planes protected them. Some attacked observation balloons while others made night bombing raids. Each corps had two balloons, which offered a far better observation platform because they were more stable.[26]

First Army's Preliminary Bombardment

First Army had 377 heavy and 720 field artillery pieces to help the Canadian Corps' stick to its mantra; the 'artillery conquered, and the infantry occupied'. Aerial photography located most of the 212 Germans batteries and they were silenced one-by-one with high explosive and gas shells. Isolated batteries were hit first before the guns combined their firepower to knock out groups of batteries.[27]

---

24   Falls, *Military Operations: France and Belgium, 1917, Vol. I.* The tanks are examined on pp. 186-7.

25   Nicholson, *Canadian Expeditionary Force,* p. 251. The aerial observers located approximately 175 out of 212 German guns. Falls, *Military Operations: France and Belgium, 1917, Vol. I,* p. 311 also covers First Army's air cover.

26   Falls, *Military Operations: France and Belgium, 1917, Vol. I.* Third Army's aerial cover is explained on pp. 187-8.

27   Ibid. First Army's preliminary bombardment is covered on pp. 302-7.

Half of First Army's guns opened fire on 20 March while the rest joined in on 2 April; nine field batteries remained silent close to the front line, ready to cover the later stages of the advance.[28] Aerial observers looked for tracks in the snow, so the artillery and machine-gun teams knew which villages and tracks to target during the hours of darkness. Large calibre mortars hit the trenches while smaller calibres targeted the wire. Medium howitzers hit the wire beyond the range of the field artillery with shells armed with 106 impact fuses.

First Army's final bombardment began at 6.30 am on 4 April and the creeping barrage was practised for the first time two days later.[29] Poor visibility meant the attack had to be put back a day but that gave the artillery an extra day to knock out targets in what the Germans called a 'week of suffering'. Trench mortars and field guns hit the first objective and the wire covering the second objective, while some of the 12-inch batteries hit the strongpoints. They all then fired short, intense barrages to stop any repair work. The 60-pounders and the 6-inch guns shelled nearby and distant billets and roads respectively while 15-inch howitzers hit distant villages and bridges. The 8-inch, 9.2-inch and the rest of the 12-inch howitzers targeted enemy batteries and distant trenches. The medium and heavy howitzers switched to roads and villages, to hit transport and relieving troops, during the hours of darkness.

Every heavy battery turned their attentions to counter-battery fire the day before the attack. Then at dusk, the 4.5-inch howitzers and 60 pounders smothered all the batteries, command posts and communication centres with mustard gas. They switched to tear gas just before zero hour, so that the Canadian troops could capture and occupy them.

Third Army's Preliminary Bombardment

Allenby originally wanted a forty-eight-hour hurricane bombardment but Haig and his Chief of Artillery, Major General Noel Birch, objected for four reasons.[30] Tests had proved that trench mortars could cut the wire in such a short time on the testing grounds but it would be harder under battlefield conditions. They also doubted the heavy artillery could silence the German batteries in such a short time, because many of the gun crews were inexperienced, while such an intensive bombardment would wear out both men and the guns alike. Haig and Birch thought a short bombardment would not lower German morale enough, but Allenby believed it would at its lowest after 48 hours heavy shelling because men became desensitised during lengthy periods of shelling.

---

28 Nicholson, *Canadian Official History*, p. 248-9. 50,000 tons of munitions were fired at the German position on Vimy Ridge.

29 Falls, *Military Operations: France and Belgium, 1917, Vol. I.* Further explanation of the preliminary bombardment and ammunition expenditure is provided on pp. 312-5.

30 Ibid. The dispute is covered on pp. 177-9.

Third Army's new artillery commander, Major General Robert Lecky, agreed with Haig and Birch, so Allenby relented. The 1,134 field guns and 586 heavy howitzers and guns opened fire at 6.30 am on 4 April, following a bombardment of gas shells, Lieven projectors and Stokes mortars.[31]

Additional Preparations

The Canadian engineers built 5 miles of road during the night while labourers repaired the damage during the day.[32] Over 50 miles of light railway were laid while another 50 miles of track was stockpiled, ready to connect to the German system across No Man's Land. Tracks were laid to new battery positions, while timber bases were built to stop the guns sinking into the soft ground. Around 1,500 miles of underground and 1,100 miles of overhead cables had been installed between corps, divisions, brigade, battalions and batteries. Five stations collected messages from the front via a range of visual signals, power buzzers, amplifiers and wireless sets.[33] The German held area had been divided into small areas, each containing a target allocated to single battery. Observers could signal their batteries by day and night, making it easy to monitor progress.

Final Hours

The Canadian troops followed stakes covered in luminous paint and then deployed along tapes in No Man's Land, the night before the attack, while the support troops gathered in fourteen tunnels.[34] Third Army housed 13,000 men in the cellars beneath Arras while another 11,500 men waited in the caves under the suburbs. The Saint Sauveur tunnel connected the caves under the Cambrai road while the Ronville tunnel did the same under the Bapaume road.[35] The deployment of ten divisions started at dusk on 8 April and they were crammed into a 2-mile-deep zone by zero.

The two artillery of the two armies used different types of deception just before zero, to put the Germans off their guard as the men crept forward through a snowstorm. First Army's batteries reduced their rate of fire to make the Germans relax.[36] Nearly 1,000 guns fired rapidly for three minutes at the German front trench at 5.30 am as smoke blinded the German batteries. The barrage crept forward at 100 yards every

---

31   Ibid., p. 185.
32   Nicholson, *Canadian Expeditionary Force*, p. 249-50 covers the Canadian engineers' exploits. Falls, *Military Operations: France and Belgium, 1917, Vol. I.* pp. 189-91 covers similar herculean tasks carried out behind Third Army's front.
33   Falls, *Military Operations: France and Belgium, 1917, Vol. I.* Communications are explained on pp. 193-4.
34   Ibid. First Army's tunnels are described on p. 309.
35   Ibid. Third Army's caves are described p. 192-3.
36   Nicholson, *Canadian Expeditionary Force*, the final preparations are covered on p. 252.

three minutes while over 350 machine-gun teams fired overhead, to catch anyone falling back.

Third Army's guns had targeted the area east of the Black Line at ninety minutes before zero, before dropping back to the front line an hour later. The 18-pounder batteries fired shrapnel for three minutes to warn the infantry to deploy, switching to a fifty-fifty mixture of shrapnel and high-explosive at zero hour. The barrage then crept forward at 100 yards every four minutes. All the time, the 4.5-inch howitzers and 6-inch howitzers continued to target the support trench until the creeping barrage reached it.[37] Heavier guns hit the enemy batteries and ammunition dumps with high-explosive and gas, disabling guns, men and horses. It meant there was little response to the many German SOS flares.

Canadian Corps Attack, 9 April

The biggest factor in the Canadians' favour was that the wind blew the snow into the faces of the German lookouts, blinding them.[38] Two mines exploded opposite 4th Canadian Division but the left flank lost its barrage and then came under machine-gun fire when the smoke covering the Pimple dispersed.[39] One battalion commander had refused to let the artillery demolish one strongpoint, because he wanted to turn it into a defensive position, and his men paid dearly for the mistake. But the entrances to tunnels were missed in the snow and the delay caused when the Germans emerged meant it was impossible to capture Hill 145.

Some of 3rd and 2nd Canadian Divisions ran into their own barrage in the smoke and snow, while others struggled to identify the objectives around Thélus village and Hill 135. However, they both still reached the eastern edge of the ridge and Lewis gun teams moved down the slope through Bois de la Folie while the rest dug in.[40] Meantime, 1st Canadian Division had to advance over 2 miles and men used wire-cutters as soon as they went beyond the range of the field artillery.[41] They then captured several batteries, bringing the total number of guns taken to over thirty. As expected, all eight tanks had bogged down but an important terrain feature had been taken and a brief break in the weather gave a glimpse of the expansive views to the north-east.

The Canadian gunners had no idea where the front line was around Hill 145 on 10 April, so a ten-minute bombardment was cancelled. No one told the bombers and they surprised the Germans as they charged up the trenches. The capture of this important observation point reduced the volume of German artillery fire across the north end of Vimy Ridge.

---

37   Falls, *Military Operations: France and Belgium, 1917, Vol. I,* the creeping barrage is detailed on pp. 184-5 and 319-20.
38   Nicholson, *Canadian Expeditionary Force,* pp. 253-7.
39   Ibid., p. 258-61.
40   Ibid., p. 254-7.
41   Ibid., p. 253-7.

Third Army, 9 April

XVII Corps

Both of 51st Division's tanks were late while the snow and smoke caused several problems.[42] Many officer casualties meant the assault troops on the left flank stopped in the wrong trench; the German had returned by the time the Scots realised their error. One battalion veered across another battalion's front and then stopped in a communication trench, both short of their objective and facing the wrong way. Most of the Germans had retired but enough machine-gun teams stayed behind to delay the Scots; some even detonated a huge store of shells under them.

A contact plane reported that 34th Division's centre and right had reached the Blue Line but the left was in difficult due to 51st Division's problems.[43] Patrols silenced the machine guns in the gap, so the two divisions could clear the Blue Line, but there were many more casualties clearing the Brown Line in front of Bailleul. The right brigade was delayed cutting though the Blue Line wire but the Germans holding the railway beyond surrendered once it was through.

Low-trajectory shrapnel shells would have unsettled the Scots as they crossed the spurs astride the River Scarpe, so the gunners fired high-trajectory high-explosive shells. Unfortunately, smoke shells landed amongst the assault troops, interfering with 9th Division's advance.[44] Only two tanks joined the battle south of the river but neither helped the infantry cut the wire covering Athies. Many dugouts had been missed in the smoke, but both the Blue Line and the Brown Line were taken, despite fire from the rear. The Line and Fampoux were there for the taking but 9th Division's requests to push through their own barrage were denied.

The Scots waited for 4th Division to take over the advance but it was 4 pm by the time the Fampoux-Gavrelle road was reached. The barrage detonated a large ammunition dump in Fampoux but machine-gun teams along the railway embankment, prevented any more progress.[45] At 3 ½ miles, it was the longest advance since the start of trench warfare, but there had not been a breakthrough.

VI Corps, South of the Scarpe

Ten tanks had left Arras Citadel but seven had bogged down driving to the front line. Two mines detonated under the German trenches around Blangy but 15th Division

---

42   Falls, *Military Operations: France and Belgium, 1917, Vol. I*, 51st Division's assault is covered on pp. 234-6.
43   Ibid. 34th Division's attack is chronicled on pp. 231-4
44   Ibid. 9th Division's advance is covered on pp. 227-9.
45   Ibid. 4th Division's attempts to get forward are covered on pp. 229-30.

was stalled en route to Observation Ridge. The field artillery had to reduce their range at 11.30 am, so a tank could help the Scots clear a railway triangle.[46]

The advance towards the Blue Line was postponed to 2 pm but some companies did not get the message and they advanced at 12.50 pm. They then had to take cover in shell holes as their barrage crept over them. Once Observation Ridge had been taken, small parties captured thirty-six guns in Battery Valley beyond. A tank followed the infantry to Feuchy and then crushed the wire so they could enter the Brown Line.

The two tanks assigned to 12th Division were late but smoke hid the trenches on Observation Ridge while the Black Line was cleared.[47] Some men were pinned down in front of Hart Redoubt until a prisoner revealed the layout during questioning.[48] Observation Ridge was crossed and over thirty guns were captured in Battery Valley beyond. The support troops left the St Sauveur caves and followed in artillery formation, but all four tanks detailed to tackle the Blue Line were disabled. The men advanced in short rushes, covered by bursts of Lewis-gun fire, but the trenches around Heron Redoubt held on for longer than expected. There were no tanks left and the Germans returned to the Brown Line while the infantry cut the wire.

Four tanks struggled to help 3rd Division make a pincer move against Tilloy-lez-Mofflaines and only one tank was still running by the time the Harp had fallen.[49] The support waves were then pinned down because there were no tanks to cut the Brown Line wire, including that protecting Feuchy Chapel. Orders to renew the attack at 6.45 pm were late, while the artillery had been unable to cut the wire.

The plan had been for 37th Division to advance towards Monchy, as soon as 12th Division had captured the Brown Line. However, the lead brigade had to wait four hours longer than planned before it was told to head for Monchy-le-Preux.[50] It finally passed through 15th Division, east of Feuchy, at 6.30 pm only to be stopped by fire from the Brown Line and Feuchy Chapel redoubt.

The barrage stopped creeping forward at 7.34 am, to give 14th Division time to bomb their way across Telegraph Hill and the Hindenburg Line.[51] Thirteen tanks were lost crossing the crater field, leaving the infantry to advance alone beyond the Hindenburg Line at 12.30 pm. Some of 56th Division's men exploited a weak spot in the German position but the rest were pinned down because the guns had been unable to cut the wire blocking the streets in Neuville Vitasse.[52] It would take eight hours to

46   Ibid. 15th Division's assault is detailed on pp. 222-4.
47   Ibid. 12th Division's assault is covered on pp. 217-21.
48   Major General Sir Arthur B. Scott, *History of the 12th Division in the Great War, 1914-1918* (London: Nisbet, 1923), p 100
49   Falls, *Military Operations: France and Belgium, 1917, Vol. I*, 3rd Division's attack is detailed on pp. 215-7.
50   Ibid. Delays to 37th Division's advance are provided on pp. 221-2.
51   Ibid. 14th Division's difficult advance is detailed on pp. 227-9.
52   Ibid. 56th Division's slow progress is covered on pp. 207-10.

reach the Blue Line, beyond village, but the Germans still held onto the Hindenburg Support Trench.

Several preliminary operations by 30th Division had cleared the Hindenburg outposts between Hénin and Croisilles. However, the tanks were late, the trench mortars failed to cut the wire and the artillery was too far away to help the 11.38 am advance. Some of the infantry were pinned down in a sunken road which the German artillery were able to range in on.

The right of 30th Division joined the advance at 4.15 pm, but it too could not get through the wire covering the Hindenburg Line south of Héninel. However, smoke shells covered 21st Division as it threaded its way through gaps in the wire. The first Hindenburg trench was taken but the artillery had failed to cut the wire protecting the second.

Third Army's Results

General Byng had been receiving positive reports about a break-in astride the Scarpe throughout the day, so rushed arrangements were made for a combined attack by the 3rd and 14th Divisions against the Brown Line.[53] Brigade headquarters received their written orders only eighty minutes before zero, while the companies heard their verbal orders only five minutes before the barrage crept forward. They were all pinned down.

Byng had also ordered two of the cavalry divisions forward but only a single brigade had been sent forward to Fampoux and it had not been given any orders. All that could be done was to send the troopers back, to spare their horses from a cold night in the open.[54]

Third Army, 10-11 April

XVII Corps

The lack of a barrage at 5 am on 10 April meant that 51st Division surprised part of the Pont du Jour Line garrison. However, the previous day's problems led to some battalions shooting at each other.[55] The Germans ran from the Pont du Jour Line but exhaustion and a counter-attack prevented 34th Division reaching Gavrelle. There was a prolonged bombardment across 4th Division's front but the creeping barrage moved too fast across the marshy ground in front of Roeux and two attacks failed. Blizzard conditions and heavy fire convinced 1st Cavalry Division's brigade to cancel their advance beyond Fampoux.[56]

---

53   Ibid., pp. 212-3.
54   Ibid., pp. 236-7.
55   Ibid. XVII Corps' disappointing results on 10 April are covered on pp. 254-7.
56   Ibid. The cavalry's difficulties are detailed on p. 257.

The attack on 11 April was delayed until 6.30 pm, to give the artillery time to register their guns. By the time 51st and 34th Divisions advanced, the Germans had abandoned both the Pont du Jour Line and the Oppy-Méricourt Line.

VI Corps

Lieutenant General Aylmer Haldane had to postpone the attack against the Wancourt – Feuchy Line until noon on 10 April, to coordinate it with VII Corps' attack to the south.[57] The late change of zero did not reach 15th Division in time, so the Scots advanced north-east side Monchy without artillery support and were hit by machine-gun fire from across the Scarpe. Meanwhile, 12th Division moved through the Scots and wheeled right, clearing Orange Hill and Feuchy Chapel redoubt with the help of a single tank.

The batteries had not had enough time to prepare a barrage for 37th Division's advance, so it was stopped by machine-gun fire from Monchy and Guémappe. A second attempt after dusk was cancelled because the attack orders were received, just as the creeping barrage moved forward. It meant that the Cavalry Corps spent a second day waiting for the breakthrough that never came.[58]

There was more lack of coordination the following morning due to another late postponement of zero hour which never reached the infantry. Four tanks led the advance through Monchy in miserable weather and then the German artillery zeroed in on the ruins. The support battalions failed to capture Infantry Hill, so they reinforced the line around Monchy instead until 12th Division took over the line. The Germans had abandoned Chapel Hill, on the Cambrai road, but 3rd Division found them waiting in Guémappe.

The cavalry regiments had been waiting behind VI Corps front all night and the horses were suffering in the wintry conditions. Just before midday, both 2nd and 3rd Cavalry Divisions were sent forward but they did nothing more than overcrowd the busy roads, so they were withdrawn. Many of the regiments were sent to the rear during the night, so the horses had shelter horses.

The following morning, the cavalry brigades were told to move quickly to Monchy because the German infantry had been seen retiring. They were withdrawing to reorganise while their artillery prepared the ground for another attack. The squadrons came under fire as they cantered along the Cambrai road into Monchy. They found the defence in chaos and the village under a heavy bombardment, so the horses had to be led to the rear. There was no attack, but it was obvious that the Germans were preparing something.

57   Ibid. VI Corps' attack on 10 April is explained on pp. 248-251.
58   Ibid. The difficulties experienced by the cavalry are covered on pp. 251-3.

Meanwhile, there had been no time to register the guns on 3rd Division's front, while the late change in zero hour resulted in a rushed deployment. The disorganised advance which followed ended in front of Guémappe.

VII Corps

There was a mix up over times, so 14th Division's attack against Wancourt was delayed to 12.20 pm to give 56th Division time to clear the Hindenburg Line.[59] A problem then arose because the Germans started withdrawing to drier trenches on Wancourt Ridge and 56th Division decided to wait, without warning 14th Division. It left the advance on Wancourt under enfilade fire from the ridge. A second advance by 14th Division at 2.15 pm failed in blizzard conditions.

Only a little ground was taken by 30th Division, as teams of infantry infiltrated the gaps in the Hindenburg Line next to the Cojeul stream. The British barrage fell short, scattering a counter-attack against 21st Division and it was able to advance when the guns extended their range.

Lieutenant General Snow's plan for 11 April was for the 56th Division to capture Wancourt Ridge, on the right, before 14th Division attacked Wancourt, on the left.[60] However, the artillery did not have time to prepare the ground and the attack failed. Some ground was taken on the west end ridge as four tanks worked closely with the bombers from 56th Division. Two more tanks helped 30th Division's bombers make progress along the Wancourt Valley, once the barrage had been corrected. The artillery had been unable to cut through the Hindenburg Line wire, so 21st Division was unable to advance on the far side of the valley.

First Army, 12-13 April

Blinding snow hid the rate of 24th Division and 4th Canadian Division as they advanced astride the Souchez stream at 5 am on 12 April.[61] The Germans withdrew when the skies cleared because their trenches were overlooked, while the British and Canadian troops could see across the Douai plain. The following day, smoke and explosions were seen opposite First Army's front and patrols then discovered that the Germans had withdrawn. They were found in the Avion Switch and the Oppy-Méricourt Line, 2 miles from Vimy Ridge.[62] It was some time before the roads were fit for wheeled traffic, so the Canadians had to use German guns until their own arrived.

59   Ibid. VII Corps efforts on 10 April are explained on pp. 245-7.
60   Ibid. VII Corps attempt to advance on 11 April is covered on pp. 259-61.
61   Nicholson, *Canadian Expeditionary Force*, p. 262-3.
62   Ibid., p. 264.

Third Army, 12-13 April

Allenby wanted to 'substitute shells for infantry' as his flanks made a slow, deliberate advance, while his centre could advance faster. The heavy artillery did not to increase its fire at zero, so as not to alert the Germans, but several batteries had been instructed to shell Roeux village, rather the chemical works and the station. Aerial observers then noticed a new trench but it was too late to warn the artillery, while the smoke screen failed to cover the flank of the attack. Poor planning left 9th Division having to advance for thirty minutes to reach its first objective and the Scots were shot down in what 'was a sacrifice rather than an attack'. The advance across the River Scarpe by 17th Division then had to be stopped because of the failure to take Roeux.

Neither 14th nor 56th Divisions, could cross the Cojeul in daylight but the Germans withdrew onto a ridge after dusk. It triggered a withdrawal from the Hindenburg Line to the south, allowing 30th Division to cross the stream near Héninel. It was joined by 21st Division as they climbed the slope on the east bank.

VI Corps' attack against Monchy, to the north, had been cancelled, while the artillery had been given the wrong target, to the south. The problem was that 50th Division thought it held Wancourt Tower and it did not, so the hill was not shelled. It meant that 3rd Division was hit by fire from three directions when it advanced at 6.40 pm. The setting sun also silhouetted the men as they advanced, and they were pinned down in front of Guémappe.

Both 50th and 56th Division reached the top of the ridge the following morning, but they had to withdraw because the artillery observers could not see the second ridge the Germans were holding, and so the guns were firing blind. Both of 21st Division's tanks broke down and it was unable to cross the Sensée stream.

First and Third Armies, 14 April

The Germans had abandoned all the ground overlooked by Vimy Ridge by dawn on 14 April, so XVII Corps was able to move close to Arleux, Oppy and Gavrelle. An attack by 29th Division at 5.30 am ended in disaster because the assault troops advanced beyond an abandoned Infantry Hill and were never seen again. The few reserves available had to be thrown into the gap and they stopped attack after attack against Monchy.

The bombardment of Guémappe had been planned to suit the attack on Infantry Hill, which meant the Germans could enfilade 50th Division's advance beyond the Cojeul. A last-minute change of time compromised the attack and it would take until 18 April to secure Wancourt tower spur.

Second Battle of the Scarpe, 23-24 April

General Allenby wanted to continue Third Army's offensive towards the Sensée stream however, VI Corps wanted to secure Monchy-le-Preux first. The main attack was planned for 20 April, but bad weather prevented artillery registration and it was postponed until 23 April. The bombardment began on 20 April, but Horne did not think the Oppy Line wire would be cut in time, so Haig agreed that First Army only had to capture Gavrelle.[63]

The preliminary barrage only lasted two days and the artillery focused on hitting sunken roads, dugouts and enemy batteries with mustard and tear gas. Standard bombardments by medium calibre guns hit the front line while the heavy howitzers hit villages with intense bombardments.

Rain made it difficult to deploy while the Germans expected an attack and the weak barrage meant they had been able to reinforce their front line. Smoke thickened the morning mist as the barrage crept forward at 100 yards every four minutes, starting at 4.45 am on 23 April. Only nineteen tanks were ready for action; Although 51st Division had been given five tanks to clear Roeux, the rest of the divisions only had a pair each, to help them tackle strongpoints.[64]

First Army, 23-24 April

Lieutenant General Arthur Holland thought the Germans were preparing to abandon Lens, so he would only let two of I Corps' companies attack La Coulotte on 23 April. They immediately discovered that he was wrong. Meanwhile, 5th Division found that all the reports of cut wire were incorrect.[65]

Third Army, 23-24 April

An aerial observer patrol had incorrectly reported gaps in the wire in front of 63rd Division and it took time to cut through. Gavrelle was taken but the long wait until the second stage of the advance exhausted the men, so the battalion commanders decided against advancing when the barrage moved forward. It meant they were able to stop the counter-attacks the following afternoon.

The battalions of 37th Division had to wait in half dug assembly trenches for zero hour. It then took time to cut through the wire and the survivors could not reach the summit of Greenland Hill. A rumour that the Germans were withdrawing turned out to be untrue, and so there was a stalemate. The barrage was weak because the gunners supporting 51st Division had been gassed.[66] No one could see the Scots through the dust and smoke, but the late arrival of a tank rallied them. They abandoned Roeux when it returned for fuel and ammunition, while it bogged down on its second foray. SOS flares alerted the gunners while a new power buzzer meant simple message

---

63   Falls, *Military Operations: France and Belgium, 1917, Vol. I*, p. 379.
64   Ibid Preparations for the attack are covered on pp. 382-3.
65   Ibid., pp. 504-5.
66   Ibid., pp. 51st Division's difficult advance is explained on 394-6.

codes identified the target area. Except the messages were one-way and the Scots were driven out of the chemical works after one was misread. A later attempt to send reinforcements across the Scarpe on a single plank bridge failed.

Crossfire from Roeux, across the Scarpe, stopped 17th Division advancing along the south bank. Meanwhile, the artillery found it difficult to form a barrage around the Monchy-le-Preux salient and it hit parts of 29th Division's line. The infantry companies then had to advance different distances, and some ran into their creeping barrage because the gunners continued to fire short. Enfilade fire stopped 15th Division's advance, so one battalion crept forward before charging into Guémappe. It then took so long to clear the ruins that the Scots could go no further.[67]

Counter-attacks drove back parts of 29th Division and 50th Division, delaying 15th Division's attack. The change in orders did not reach all the companies in time and they advanced though the British barrage; the survivors were soon driven back. A late attack by 29th Division cleared Infantry Hill, east of Monchy.

The enemy artillery was quick to react along VII Corps' front while the British barrage was too slow to support 50th Division's advance towards Wancourt. A single tank helped take the first objective, but German infantry infiltrated their line during the four-hour wait for the second part of the attack. There were many casualties before the survivors fell back.[68]

The two tanks supporting 30th Division's attack on Chérisy were knocked out and most of the attackers fell back after suffering heavy casualties.[69] Some ground had to be abandoned after being hit by British artillery and strafed by planes. On the right, a tank helped 33rd Division's bombers take over 700 prisoners in the two Hindenburg trenches.[70] A counter-attack threatened to overwhelm the bombers, so they retired before more Germans emerged from a tunnel to reoccupy their trench. However, there was success on 33rd Division's right flank where twelve machine-gun teams had deployed in No Man's Land before zero hour, ready to cover the crossing of the Sensée. The two tanks were late and the men who cleared the Hindenburg Support Trench were overrun, while their comrades held onto the Hindenburg Front Trench.

At 2.25 pm, General Allenby told his divisional commanders they had to capture the Blue Line in a second attack, but that left them only four hours to prepare; insufficient time to prepare written orders.[71] This time the artillery gave 50th Division good protection and it advanced towards Wancourt. However, the rushed planning meant 30th Division's assault troops did not get the attack order, while no guides turned up to lead the support companies forward. The attack on Chérisy failed.

---

67   Ibid. The attacks by VI Corps' three divisions are covered on pp. 390-2.
68   Ibid. The counter-attacks against VI Corps are described on pp. 392-3.
69   Ibid., pp. 386-7.
70   Ibid., pp. 384-6.
71   Ibid. The afternoon attack is chronicled on pp. 387-9.

There was a similar situation across 33rd Division's front and the creeping barrage then landed on the deployment area. The men that did advance found a line of British dead on the crest; they had all been hit by the machine-gun teams waiting on the far side. Counter-attacks during the night stopped the British interfering with a withdrawal to the Croisilles-Chérisy road.

Battle of Arleux, 28 April

Haig wanted to continue the offensive and he had to keep the pressure on around Arras to help the French who were struggling on the Aisne. But the BEF chose to keep its reserve of divisions 60 miles to the north in Flanders, ready to attack in case the French called off their attacks. It meant that divisions were being used repeatedly around Arras and battalions were often down to 400 men, half of them inexperienced drafts.[72] The guns were also wearing out while the tanks were always breaking down. The next attack was timed for 4.25 am on 28 April and the preliminary barrage focused on the first line of trenches because the support trenches were out of sight, on a reverse slope.

First Army, 28 April

The 2nd Canadian Division stopped in a sunken road, short of its objective, leaving 1st Canadian Division exposed to enfilade fire. The rest of the division was left struggling to get through the wire when the Germans abandoned Arleux.[73] A variation of the double creeping barrage was used by XIII Corps around Oppy and Gavrelle, in which high explosive drove the Germans underground while shrapnel hit them as they emerged to man their parapet.[74] The Germans had chosen to abandon Oppy Wood but 2nd Division found them in the village beyond. The British artillery had no idea where the front line and few men returned. Meanwhile, 63rd Division tried to take Gavrelle with a pincer attack, but the northern arm was driven back by artillery fire while the eastern attack took too long to capture the German strongpoints.

A weak 2nd Division attacked at 4 am the following morning but the few men who reached the Oppy Line fell back after using every grenade they could find. The 63rd Division had organised its brigade into composite battalions but they were unable to gain any ground either.[75]

---

72   Ibid. Manpower shortages are discussed on p. 414. In 34th Division's case, the drafts had not arrived, and battalions were only 200 strong with a couple of officers per company.
73   Nicholson, *Canadian Expeditionary Force*, pp. 270-2. The British historian described it as the 'only tangible success of the whole operation'. Falls, *Military Operations: France and Belgium, 1917, Vol. I*, p. 423-4.
74   Falls, *Military Operations: France and Belgium, 1917, Vol. I*, pp. 422.
75   Ibid. The 29 April attack is covered on pp. 420-2.

Third Army, 28 April

The barrage moved at 100 yards every four minutes in the open and half that speed as it moved through Roeux. There was a breakthrough on the north slopes of Greenland Hill but no one knew what had happened to the weak battalions of 37th Division (no replacements had been received) until the survivors were driven back.[76] Meanwhile, enfilade fire from Roeux chemical works stopped the advance across the south slopes of the hill, while the wrong trench was reported as being taken, so the artillery could not help.

Inexperienced replacements, who had just joined 34th Division, followed an inaccurate creeping barrage 'owing to the lack of reconnaissance and the nearness of the lines in places.[77] It overshot the German front trench and then jumped over Roeux Chateau and then over the chemical works. The Germans hid in their dugouts as the first wave passed through Mount Pleasant Wood, emerging to halt the support waves. The survivors had to withdraw at night and some even had to swim the River Scarpe to escape.[78] Orders for two battalions to carry out a surprise attack without a covering barrage later that night were issued late; only one advanced and that was an hour after zero and so little ground was gained.

The start of the bombardment warned 12th Division to advance only two minutes later, so the deployment was rushed.[79] Some men were pinned down by fire from across the River Scarpe, while others were stopped because the artillery had overshot part of a trench. The reinforcements were also hit by fire from across the river as they crossed Pelves mill ridge.

Third Battle of the Scarpe, 3 May

Haig wanted to end the offensive with First and Third Armies holding a solid defensive position around Arras, and he believed that one big attack would have more success than several little ones. On 30 April, Horne, Allenby and Gough were ordered to attack on 3 May and the barrage started that night.[80] Counter Battery Groups hit the enemy artillery while the Super Heavy Groups fired intense barrages against villages. The Trench Groups hit the infantry defences while 60-pounder batteries shelled No Man's Land at night, to stop parties repairing the wire.

Gough wanted to attack in the dark with artillery support, but Allenby wanted a surprise attack at dawn with no artillery. The compromise was to set zero hour at 3.45 am but the late change meant issues associated with night attacks had not been

---

76   Ibid., pp. 416-7.
77   J. Shakespear, *The Thirty-Fourth Division, 1915–1919* (London: Witherby, 1921), p. 114.
78   Falls, *Military Operations: France and Belgium, 1917, Vol. I*, pp. 415-6.
79   Ibid., pp. 413. Three minutes was the usual warning.
80   Ibid., p. 428.

considered.[81] No one had anticipated that the full moon would silhouette the troop deployment before zero hour. Nor did anyone predict that the creeping barrage would throw up clouds of dust which would blind British troops as they advanced. No one expected that the Germans would shelter in No Man's Land, to avoid the barrage on their trenches, and they would cause mayhem amongst the advancing troops in the darkness. The creeping barrage had been set at 100 yards every two minutes, the typical speed for a daylight advance but too fast in the dark. The late change meant that there was no time to change the infantry objectives from the long bounds, which were typical in daylight, into the short bounds needed to keep control in the dark.

A fake barrage across XIII Corps' front merely alerted the German artillery and the counter-barrage on the deployment areas delayed the advance in some areas. A gas bombardment also forced some gunners to work with their masks on, interfering with the creeping barrage.

First Army, 3-9 May

Wire barred 2nd Canadian Division's advance at 3.45 am on 3 May, so they jumped into a trench only to find it went the wrong way. However, 1st Canadian Division, captured Fresnoy in one of the few successes of the day.[82]

A counter-barrage delayed 2nd Division's deployment and the men then bunched up in the clouds of dust.[83] Their inexperience meant that some captured trenches were overcrowded, while others were left empty; everyone withdrew as soon as they ran out of bombs. The Germans spotted 31st Division assembling in front of Oppy Wood and shelled their assembly area. Then the moon set while the creeping barrage threw up dust, making it difficult to follow. Only a few men made it through the wood and they were soon forced back to their own trenches.

The Fresnoy area was heavily shelled because it was overlooked by the German line and while the first attack on 8 May was stopped, no one saw the SOS flares for the second one and the position was lost. A counter-attack early the following morning failed because only one company received the message to advance.[84]

81   Ibid., the unfortunate consequences of the late change in zero hour are explained on pp. 430-3.
82   Nicholson, *Canadian Expeditionary Force*, p. 273. The capture was the 'relieving feature of a day which many who witnessed it considered the blackest of the War'. Falls, *Military Operations: France and Belgium, 1917, Vol. I*, pp. 448-50.
83   Falls, *Military Operations: France and Belgium, 1917, Vol. I*. The two divisions of XIII Corps are covered on pp. 445-8.
84   Ibid., p.520.

Third Army, 3 May

Dust and inexperienced replacements caused problems across 9th Division's dog-legged front.[85] One battalion failed to see a lamp set to guide them forward, so the first wave of companies went the wrong way, leaving the support companies to stumble on the German trench. A second battalion advanced five minutes later in the right direction only to find the Germans had infiltrated their line; a forlorn rescue attempt only freed a few men. A third battalion attacked its own front line by mistake while the fourth lost direction and fired at friendly troops in the adjacent division's area.[86]

Two battalions captured Roeux chemical works on 4th Division's front but German reinforcements followed a railway cutting, so they could surround them in the dark.[87] Two more battalions were cut down by a single machine-gun team which had been missed. Another battalion had been given an inaccurate map of Roeux and the barrage had moved off by the time it had corrected its line of advance.

The infantry across VI Corps' front found it difficult to follow the creeping barrage through the smoke and dust as it moved at different speeds across the fields and through the villages. They had to fight the Germans who had sheltered in shell-holes to avoid the barrage and then silence the machine-gun teams who fought to the last in the trenches.

The Germans smothered VI Corps' front with high explosive and gas shells just before zero hour. The creeping barrage landed amongst 12th Division, south of the Scarpe, and some men then drifted into 3rd Division's area as they advanced towards Pelves. A counter-attack cut many off in Devil's Trench and it was impossible to reset the barrage because the observers could not see there was a problem. The barrage overshot some of trenches east of Monchy, so 3rd Division was pinned down. Visual signalling was impossible, and it took a long time to get a message back; even longer to lead the support battalions forward.[88]

The support wave worried they would lose contact with the first wave during 56th Division's advance and they bunched up, creating a dense target for the counter-barrage. The British guns had missed the German trenches beyond the crest and the few men who reached St Robart factory had to retire because there was no one to their flanks.[89] The Germans withdrew to avoid 14th Division's barrage, so the first wave advanced too quickly beyond Guémappe, missing many dugouts in the darkness. The Germans emerged to counter-attack the support wave, and then a second attack hit the first wave.[90]

---

85   Ibid., p. 444. One group of drafts from an Army Service Corps unit were dressed in kilts and given rifles; they could not load nor attach bayonets to them.
86   Ibid. 9th Division's disastrous attack is covered on pp. 444-5.
87   Ibid., pp. 442-3.
88   Ibid. The unfortunate experiences of 12th and 3rd Divisions are covered on pp. 439-40.
89   Ibid. 56th Division's attack is covered on p. 438.
90   Ibid., 14th Division's misfortune is explained on p. 437.

A brigadier's objections about 21st Division's exposed deployment area had been overruled and then the three promised tanks failed to turn up. However, 18th Division's advance towards Chérisy was going well until a tank returning for fuel prompted inexperienced men to shout 'retire!'[91] But some men of 18th Division had followed the gradient of the slope in the pitch darkness and they cut across 21st Division's front, delaying its advance even more. Disaster followed because many dugouts had been overlooked in the darkness and the Germans emerged to overrun them. An evening counter-attack captured many more men from the two divisions around Chérisy and Fontaine because they were too inexperienced to drive it off.[92]

Third Army, 11-30 May

Two attacks were planned for the evening of 11 May, so the objectives could be consolidated during the night. It left the men sitting in shallow trenches all day, while anti-aircraft kept German observer planes at bay. A practice creeping barrage triggered a counter-barrage and many battery positions were noted, ready to be shelled at zero hour.

A double layer creeping barrage, of high-explosive followed by shrapnel, led a very weak 4th Division into Roeux at 7.30 pm as the Germans withdrew to allow their heavy artillery to shell the area.[93] A barrage at 8.30 pm helped the infantry of 56th Division take Tool Trench by surprise.[94] An attempt to take Greenland Hill the following day failed because a German plane used flares to mark 17th Division's deployment area for its artillery. The counter-barrage then hit No Man's Land the moment the troops advanced.[95] Later that night, the Germans drove 51st Division from the Roeux chemical works. Another attack at 3.45 am on 16 May retook the Greenland Hill.

A deserter may have compromised the 9 pm zero hour because the Germans were waiting for 56th Division on Infantry Hill on 19 May.[96] A slow bombardment by 600 guns preceded an attack by 33rd Division against the Hindenburg Line at 5.15 am on 20 May.[97] A combined bombing and over the top attack reached the Sensée in the mist. A week later the same division crossed the Sensée stream, after surprising the Germans while they relaxed after their lunch.

There were worries another deserter had betrayed 29th Division's surprise attack against Hill 100, early on 30 May. Zero could not be postponed because the moon

91   Nicholls, *The 18th Division in the Great War. An account of the problems associated with the attack is given on pp. 169-71.*
92   Falls, *Military Operations: France and Belgium, 1917, Vol. I,* p. 437.
93   Ibid., pp. 511-3.
94   Ibid., p. 516.
95   Ibid., pp. 514-5.
96   Ibid., pp. 518-9.
97   Ibid., p 518.

would be up, so a hurried artillery barrage was planned instead.[98] The men were spotted deploying in No Man's Land before 12.40 am and Allenby blamed the inexperienced troops for not waiting until zero hour. It was Third Army's final attack of the campaign and future night operations were banned until the conscripts had be trained.[99]

Fifth Army

Bullecourt, 10-11 April

Fifth Army planned to attack between Bullecourt and Quéant on 9 April, at the same time as the main attack, but the field artillery was short of horses, leaving the heavy artillery struggling to cut the wire at long range.[100] Gough only had twelve tanks and he decided to deploy them en mass, to create a large gap in the wire east of Bullecourt, while the wire west of the village would have to be cut by hand.[101]

Gough's late decision to make a surprise night attack, left 4th Australian Division no time to practice with the tanks (they had never worked with them before). The Australians deployed in the snow during the early hours of 10 April, but the tanks were delayed until dawn due to the bad weather. The attack was called off and the infantry withdrew during a snow storm.

Zero was reset for 4.30 am the following morning and the Australians deployed ready to follow the tanks a second time. The guns continued firing at the same rate, while machine-gun teams fired a barrage to hide the sound of the tanks. Only the tanks were delayed again, this time negotiating a railway embankment; three even got stuck. The first tank commander to reach the infantry suggested they advanced immediately because the tanks would take a long time to cross the soft ground.

One brigade commander agreed and they advanced past the tanks at 4.45 am, only to be lit up by flares as they cut through the wire.[102] The second brigade commander ignored the suggestion and his men advanced twenty-five minutes later.[103] But the creeping barrage had moved on, nine of the tanks had been knocked out and it was light.[104] A few men reached the enemy trenches but requests for artillery were turned down because of false reports that troops were advancing through Riencourt. The Australians soon had to give up their two footholds.

---

98   Ibid., p. 517.
99   Ibid., p. 517. Both General Allenby and Lieutenant General Haldane blamed the failure on the untrained troops.
100   Ibid., pp. 358-9.
101   Bean, *Australian Official History, Vol. IV.* Australian planning is detailed on pp.285-8.
102   Ibid., pp. 289-303.
103   Ibid., pp. 303-11.
104   Ibid. The demise of the tanks is chronicled on pp. 312-6.

Lagnicourt, 15 April

The 1st Australian Division was stretched thin around Lagnicourt, with each battalion holding around 2 miles of trenches. One night it was told to establish outposts, to convince the Germans an attack was imminent, only to find they were overlooked at dawn.[105] At 3.30 am on 15 April the German artillery opened fire with their new instantaneous fuses while exploded as soon as they hit the surface. Flares lit up No Man's Land when the infantry advanced thirty minutes later, but the outposts had no signal flares to warn their own artillery.[106] The Germans were soon amongst the Australian artillery and seven batteries had to be abandoned west of Lagnicourt. Fortunately, the Australians could see where the Germans were at dawn and they either surrendered or ran as the gunners retrieved their guns.[107] A disaster had been averted but divisional sectors had to be made stronger while batteries needed better protection in future.

Bullecourt, 3 May

Another attack was required against Bullecourt, to keep German divisions opposite Fifth Army occupied. Tanks were allocated to 62nd Division but the Australians refused to use them, so they were given extra heavy batteries instead.[108] The village was not going to be attacked frontally and would, instead, be cleared by bombing from both flanks. However, the area was not 'kept under artillery fire'[109]and no one knew that a battalion armed with ninety automatic rifles had just reinforced the area.

The German artillery hit No Man's Land as ten tanks led 62nd Division across No Man's Land, west of Bullecourt, at 3.45 am on 3 May.[110] Some men became disorientated in the dust while others fell back, taking the rest with them. The Australians sought cover in the shell holes, as the barrage stopped on the first trench east of Bullecourt for two minutes.[111] They split into small groups and the Germans were waiting when the barrage lifted. Before long, 400 men came running back and the reinforcements who were sent forward at 5.45 am without an artillery barrage were shot down.[112]

A renewed barrage on the second German trench at 9.30 am let some men of 62nd Division follow three tanks past the west side of Bullecourt but there was little cooperation with the tanks. They had to withdraw for fuel and the infantry followed

105 Ibid pp. 370-1.
106 Ibid., pp. 371-3. The flares lit up the assault troops.
107 Ibid., pp. 374-6.
108 Falls, *Military Operations: France and Belgium, 1917, Vol. I*, pp. 455, 457, 459.
109 Ibid., p. 459.
110 Ibid., pp. 463-5.
111 Ibid., p. 460.
112 Ibid., p. 461.

when they ran out of ammunition.[113] An afternoon attack was postponed to 10.30 pm, to give the artillery time to cut the wire, but it still only gave the 'company commanders time to get their horses and ride forward as near as possible to a point from which they could get an idea of the ground...' A counter-barrage disrupted the deployment, making one battalion late, and the other had to advance slowly to let it catch up.[114] There were too few gaps in the wire and too many dugouts were missed in the darkness, so the Germans were able to disperse the attack.

The Australians in the German trenches east of Bullecourt held on into the afternoon but they were outnumbered, short of bombs and then hit by their own artillery.[115] A bombardment of No Man's Land at dusk prompted most of the Australians to withdraw but fighting along the Hindenburg Line continued well into the night.

A counter-barrage stopped an attempt by 7th Division to enter Bullecourt at 3 am on 4 May before it started. A special barrage, which crept parallel with the trenches supported the Australians during the afternoon.[116] The bombers kept as close as possible to the Germans, so their bombs went over their heads, but they still had to deal with several flamethrowers.

Men of 7th Division advanced past the east side of Bullecourt at 3.45 am on 7 May, but no one could enter the south-west corner of the ruins until two days later.[117] No one returned from 62nd Division's advance east of the village, early on 12 May, but 7th Division cleared the east side of the village.

The decision was taken to withdraw everyone from Bullecourt on 16 May, so it could be hit by the heavy artillery. The plan worked, the Germans were in the process of abandoning the ruins when 58th Division charged through, following a two-minute bombardment at 2 am the following morning.[118] Fifth Army had suffered 14,000 casualties around the village in just two weeks.

The Arras Campaign Summary

The retreat to the Hindenburg Line took the Allies completely by surprise. It gave the Germans a shorter defensive line and a larger reserve but the BEF was also able to increase the number of divisions it had to support an offensive. One important aspect of following up the retreat was learning how to move quickly across devasted ground. The infantry and the artillery came to terms with operating in the open while the engineers bridged rivers, built roads and disarmed booby traps.

113 Ibid., p. 463-5. It was 62nd Division's first attack following several months of trench holding duties..
114 Ibid., pp. 465-6.
115 Ibid., pp. 462-3.
116 Ibid., pp. 467-8.
117 Ibid., pp. 471-4.
118 Ibid., pp. 478.

A rethink on offensive tactics meant the artillery were responsible for demolishing the enemy defences, ready for the infantry to secure, on 9 April. However, it is important to note that First Army and Third Army used very different preliminary barrages. Third Army's plan was for the tanks to then exploit the infantry's break-in, by ripping through the wire beyond field gun range.

The advance on 9 April was the most extensive of the war so far, however, it proved impossible to send forward infantry reserves to exploit the gap; attempts to send cavalry units failed miserably. A long delay meant it was 23 April before a second full scale attack had to be launched; only this time the divisions were weaker, there were fewer guns and tanks, and the ammunition was short supply. The Germans also knew where the attack would be.

Later attacks were hampered by the need to support the French and the desire to keep reserves in Flanders. A late change in zero-hour, poor visibility and the deployment of a large number of inexperienced replacements resulted in disaster on 3 May. The numerous attacks around Bullecourt during this campaign proved that small scale affairs stood little chance against the well-designed defences of the Hindenburg Line.

5

The Messines and Third Ypres Campaigns
6 June-2 December 1917

Flanders Offensive Plan

Haig had been planning to attack east from Ypres ever since he took command of the BEF at the end of 1915. However, the fighting had been focused around Verdun and Somme throughout 1916. But the spring attacks around Arras and on the Aisne were to be followed by a combined British, French and Belgian advance across Flanders. Five divisions would then land on the coast and secure the harbours of Ostend and Zeebrugge.[1]

Messines ridge, to the south of Ypres, had to be seized first and Second Army had been burrowing under the ridge for over eighteen months.[2] Miners had dug shafts deep into the clay before tunnelling under German strongpoints. Mechanical diggers were noisy and slow, so teams of men hand dug passages and the clay was buried under parapets or hidden in woods. The work underground involved new surveying instruments, better shoring techniques, improved rescue equipment and listening devices. The Germans heard nothing and thought the British had given up tunnelling. A couple of tunnels were damaged when camouflets were detonated but new ones were dug. Some of the twenty-two mines were complete months before the attack but the last one was set only hours before zero (only nineteen would be blown because three were outside the attack area).[3] Each mine had an average of 21 tons of ammonal while gun cotton and gelatine would detonate them.[4]

---

1   Sir James E. Edmonds, *Military Operations: France and Belgium, 1917, Vol. II: Messines and Third Ypres (Passchendaele)* (London: HMSO, 1948), pp. 2-3.
2   Tunnelling work had initially been planned to be complete by June 1916, so Second Army could capture the Messines Ridge immediately after a breakthrough on the Somme. The breakthrough never came and the plan to blow up the ridge had to be put off.
3   Edmonds, *Military Operations: France and Belgium, 1917, Vol. II*. The mine locations, tunnel lengths, charge sizes, completion dates and crater sizes are listed on pp. 52-3.
4   Ibid., pp. 35-39 covers the mining operations.

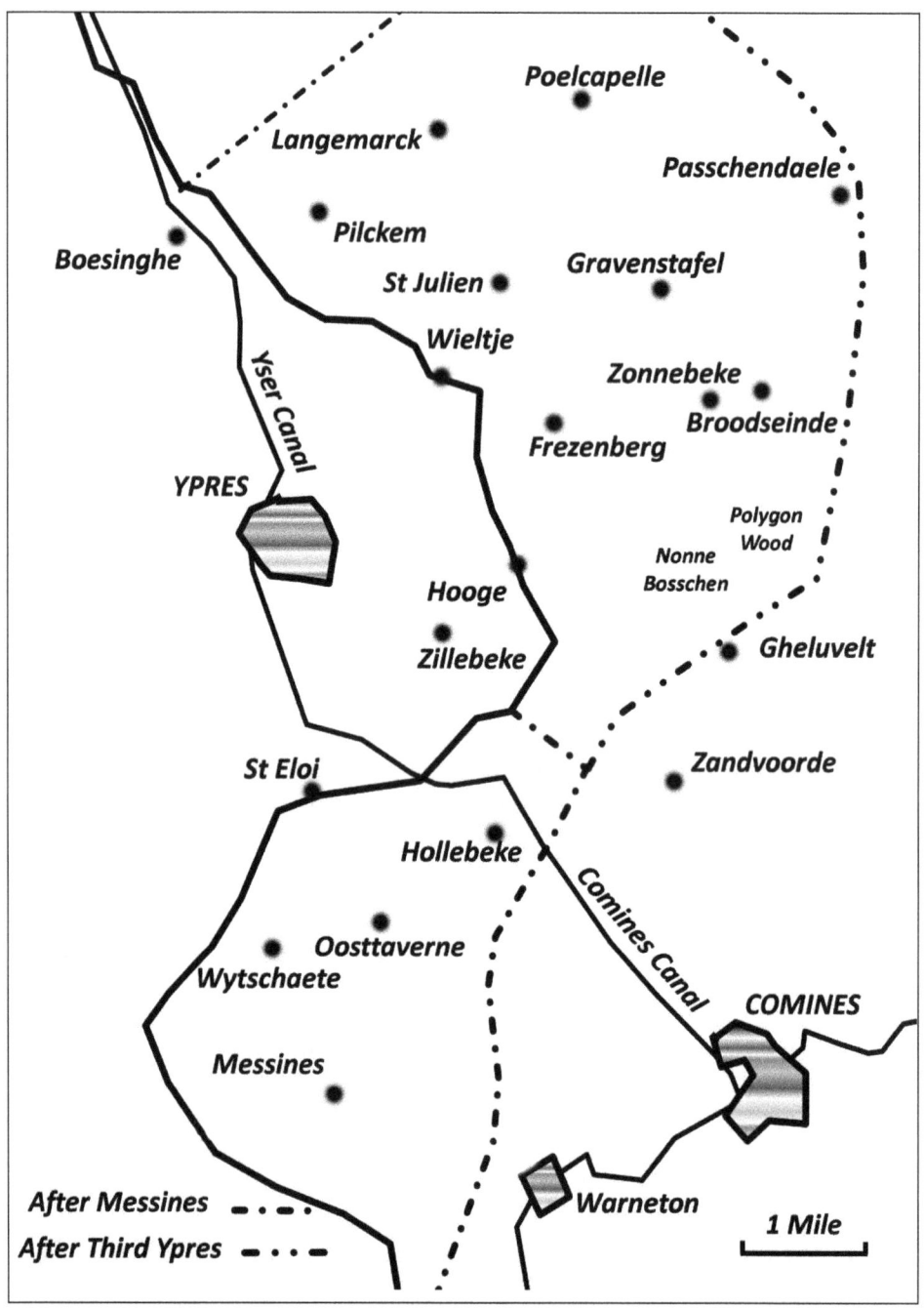

Map 5. Messines and Third Ypres Campaigns, 7 June-2 December 1917: A dependence on artillery combined with poor weather brought the advance east of Ypres to a halt.

The engineers supervised many other underground schemes for headquarters, communications centres and medical facilities.[5] Around 3 miles of tunnels were dug, along with beds and shelters for 16,000 men. They also opened twenty railheads, each dedicated to a different type of stores, making it easier to organise deliveries to the front. They were all connected by 115 miles of broad-gauge and 58 miles of narrow-gauge tracks.

Preparations

Second Army had stockpiled 144,000 tons of shells for the 1,500 field guns and howitzers and they were organised into forty groups. The barrage began on 21 May, but the guns fired at different times, to make them harder to spot, while others stayed silent.[6] Again, groups targeted the wire, trenches, strongpoints and enemy batteries. High explosive and gas shells hit Wytschaete and Messines while the heavy howitzers shelled distant targets. Machine-gun teams stayed hidden in dug outs big enough to hold 'spare personnel, reserve ammunition and belt-filling machines' during daylight hours.[7] They were given daily charts which noted new targets for their night time barrages.[8]

The 300 planes of the Royal Flying Corps had a two-to-one advantage over the German air force. Messines Ridge had been divided into two sectors (or beats) and patrols of four or six planes flew high patrols during the bombardments.[9] Battery positions were photographed every second day, while the rest of the targets were checked every day by larger low-flying patrols. Bombers attacked the rail junctions in Menin, Wervicq and Comines.

The shelling intensified on 31 May and the observers' reports, photographs, captured documents and prisoners' statements were used to monitor damage.[10] A fake creeping barrage was fired on 3 June and dozens of German batteries had answered the SOS signals before they realised it was only a practice. A second fake barrage on 5 June confirmed that many had shifted north or south, in case the ridge was lost. Altogether, 3.5 million shells silenced many of the 200 enemy batteries.

Second Army had based its training on four GHQ pamphlets which covered the infantry, the artillery, engineering tasks and communications. Between them, they consolidated the lessons drawn from the Somme and Arras campaigns. 'Message

---

5   Ibid., the extensive engineering works carried out for Messines are detailed on pp. 39-41.
6   Ibid., artillery preparation is covered on pp. 41-2.
7   Stewart, *The New Zealand Division 1916-1919, Vol. II*, p. 174.
8   Edmonds, *Military Operations: France and Belgium, 1917, Vol. II*, p. 44. The machine-gun teams aimed where repair parties were likely to be working and tracks used by supply parties.
9   Ibid., *the Royal Flying Corps'* part is chronicled on pp. 42-3.
10   Ibid. Details of the final stages of the barrage are explained on pp. 46-9.

Maps' had also been introduced to improve how progress was reported.[11] A common complaint was that it was hard to explain a tactical situation in a written message, it was difficult to get the map coordinates right and it was almost impossible to draw an accurate map. Sending large numbers of maps into enemy territory was a security risk, so all the officers and NCOs were issued with a postcard which had the map section covering their objective on one side and map symbols on the other side. The snippets of information were easily transferred to a large map at a battalion headquarters, so the overall picture could be seen.

The infantry would use Watson fans (a pleated canvas disc marked black on one side and white on the other) to report their progress to ground observers but smoke and dust often limited visibility. Contact planes would have more success, sounding their Klaxon horns and firing Very lights at set times, so the infantry could reply by lighting flares. They were lit in bundles of three, so they were easier to see from the air and often burned in the bottom of trenches so enemy ground observers could not see them. The pilots then flew over the report centre and dropped a marked-up map in a weighted bag onto a target. The information was written up and the evaluation was forwarded to corps headquarters. It meant the artillery batteries could keep track of the Second Army's advance.

Tanks had been on the Western Front for nine months by June 1917 and the Germans had developed a range of anti-tank tactics. They dug wider trenches and felled trees to block roads. They had also mounted field guns on small wheels (so they were harder to spot) and given them armour-piercing shells; anti-tank rifles which fired armour-piercing bullets were also starting to appear.

The new Mark IV tank was deployed for the first time at Messines, and there had been many improvements based on the experiences at Arras. The engine was more reliable, and the larger fuel tank meant it could travel further between refuelling stops. The body had been made with hardened steel, which improved the protection the crew was given without increasing the weight.[12]

The Male still had two 6-pounder guns to tackle strongpoints while three extra Lewis machine guns kept the enemy infantry at bay. The Female now had five Lewis guns and one Hotchkiss gun, and they all used flexible ammunition belts, which were easier to use inside the cramped hull. The driver had improved steering while the rest of the crew had been given escape hatches. They could use them to access the beam on the roof stowed on the roof. It was reinforced with sheet metal and could be chained to the tracks if the tank became bogged down.

The Heavy Branch, Machine Gun Corps[13] had also expanded its maintenance facilities, so tanks could be repaired quicker. It also had improved its logistics, so

---

11   *Cyril Falls, The History of the 36th (Ulster) Division (Belfast: McCaw, Stevenson & Orr, 1922), pp. 82-84.*

12   Ibid. Edmonds, *Military Operations: France and Belgium, 1917, Vol II*, pp. 50-1.

13   Ibid. The expansion of the Heavy Branch, Machine Gun Corps is covered on p. 50.

that the crews were kept supplied with fuel and ammunition. There had also been attempts to improve cooperation with the infantry by studying tactics and improving communications. Second Army had been given seventy-two tanks and while senior tank officers wanted to see how the new model performed, GHQ was still sceptical about them.

Documents captured at Arras said the Germans planned to create fortified zones and there were many on Messines Ridge.[14] They would be based around concrete pillboxes, built every 200 yards, and shelters for the men, built at 50-yard intervals. The plan was for the men to deploy into shell holes and slit trenches at zero hour, so they could delay the assault troops until the counter-attack troops turned up. However, they did not know that they were about to be rocked by several hundred tons of explosives.

The Attack Against Messines Ridge

General Plumer set zero hour for 3.10 am on 7 June only three days before. The timing was chosen so that men could only see 100 yards, which was light enough to carry out an organised advance but dark enough to stop the machine-gun teams and artillery observers seeing their targets until it was too late. The guns fired their usual barrages during the night and the planes flew low over the German area, to hide the sound of the tanks moving forward.

A prisoner had given away the date of the Messines offensive, but he did not know how early it was going to be. Then at zero, the nineteen mines exploded, killing or stunning many of the Germans in the front line. The sky was lit by flames followed by clouds of smoke billowing into the sky while the 'effect on the troops was overpowering and crushing.'[15]

The barrage then crashed down before starting to creep up the slope at 100 yards every two minutes. Two out of three of Second Army's guns fired the creeping barrage, while the rest hit targets in front of the first objective.[16] The 18-pounder guns fired three rounds a minute while the 4.5-inch howitzers fired one round a minute. All guns reduced to one round a minute during pauses in the advance. The increase in the rate of fire told the infantry to start moving again at 100 yards every three minutes. Around 450 machine guns fired ahead of the artillery, deepening the barrage to 700 yards. Some howitzers fired gas and high-explosive shells at the German batteries while the rest fired high-explosive at strongpoints. Both the howitzer crews and the machine-gun teams were aware they could be asked to disperse counter-attacks.

The smoke screen and dust hid the SOS flares while the German gunners were able to do little, because they were being hit by counter-barrage fire. Officers led the

---

14   Ibid. See p. 45 for an insight in the German defence system.
15   Ibid., p. 61. Taken from a report by the German 204th Division.
16   Ibid., see p. 48 and p. 67.

waves of men forward on compass bearings but 'there was little resistance from the Germans, who either ran forward to surrender or, if they could do so, ran away; very few of them put up a fight.'[17]

Three mines, totalling fifty-six tons, exploded around Mount Sorrel and 23rd Division captured everything but Battle Wood.[18] The largest mine on the whole Messines front (at forty-three tons) exploded next to the Comines Canal but 47th Division could not take the Spoil Bank embankment, while it took several hours to capture the White Chateau.[19] Major General Morland later wrote that to begin with, 'everything went like clockwork and the various objectives were taken according to programme' on 41st Division's front.[20] There was a tough fight to clear Damm Strasse but the Germans eventually ran.

Two mines killed or stunned many of the Germans in front of 19th Division, while the rest surrendered or ran away.[21] There was no one in Grand Bois, because blazing oil drums and high explosive shells had made it uninhabitable by the early hours of 4 June. The main problem was keeping direction and cohesion, as they moved through the smoke and dust covering the ridge north of Wytschaete. Some of the mines on 16th Division's front exploded a little late and men were hit by falling debris.[22] However, the Irishmen encountered little resistance in Bois de Wytschaete because it had also been hit by blazing oil and high explosive early on 4 June. High-explosive and gas shells had also been used to make Wytschaete's cellars uninhabitable but machine-gun teams inside the houses gave supporting fire for the men holding the trench on the west side of the village. Eventually, a tank caught up and helped to clear the ruins before heading down the slope beyond. Five mines demoralised the Germans across 36th Division's front and the infantry advanced towards the south end of Wytschaete.[23] Orange flags marked captured pillboxes while two tanks helped the infantry clear the trenches on the summit.[24] Lewis guns, rifle grenades and trench mortars supressed the garrison, while riflemen and bombers moved from shell hole to shell hole to outflank the pillboxes. Sufficient mopping up teams had been deployed to clear all the dug outs, while the forty-eight tanks helped the support battalions silence any centres of resistance.[25]

Three mines detonated on 25th Division's left flank and a fourth in front of it.[26] The infantry made good progress up the slope, but the tanks struggled to cross the ridge

---

17   Ibid., p. 59. Gleaned from 19th Division's War Diary.
18   Ibid., p. 61, 66, 69-70.
19   Ibid., pp. 60-1, 65-6, 69.
20   Ibid., p. 60, 65, 69.
21   Ibid., p. 59, 65, 69.
22   Ibid., pp. 58-9, 65, 68-9.
23   Ibid., pp. 57-8, 64-5, 69.
24   *Falls, The History of the 36th (Ulster) Division, pp. 94-8.*
25   Edmonds, *Military Operations: France and Belgium, 1917, Vol. II,* p. 62.
26   Ibid., pp. 57, 64 and 68.

north of Messines. The New Zealand Division entered the north side of the village, taking the perimeter trench from the rear as the barrage moved across the ruins.[27] The gunners slowed the creep down, to give the infantry time to move through the ruins, using Stokes mortars to target the strongpoints. The infantry moved through the houses when possible, using smoke bombs to hide any movement in the streets.

Gas shells had incapacitated 500 men of 3rd Australian Division as they headed to the front and the rest had to march though Ploegsteert Wood in their gas masks. Four mines shocked the Germans and they 'made many fruitless attempts to embrace us, I have never seen men so demoralised.' But the Australians moved too close to the barrage, resulting in more casualties from friendly fire than from enemy fire.[28]

The smoke cleared and the sun rose while the men waited on the Black Line (or observation line) for the reserve brigades and tanks to move up.[29] The batteries responsible for the creeping barrage continued to fire at targets beyond while batteries which had fired the standing barrages waited for SOS calls; few were made. There was, however, plenty of enemy artillery fire and a lack of discipline meant there were unnecessary casualties due to overcrowding.[30]

Plumer expected a counter-attack around mid-morning, so the batteries of the three reserve divisions fired a standing barrage. However, there were delays while the German commanders tried to assess the extent of Second Army's advance. British aerial observers spotted advancing columns around midday and the large calibre artillery made sure no one reached Second Army's line.[31]

Plumer set 3.10 pm as the time to complete the advance, because he was sure the ridge was secure. That gave the 200 machine-guns teams time to set up on the crest, while the reserve of twenty-four tanks crawled over the ridge. Forty batteries also moved forward and while some set up next to camouflaged ammunition dumps which had been stockpiled close to the old front line, the rest deployed in the original No Man's Land.[32]

Requests to delay 19th Division's and 11th Division's advance, following a late change in orders, were denied by IX Corps.[33] Battalion commanders just had to advance on a compass bearing behind the barrage and some of the companies were late. Fortunately, there were few Germans in the Oosttaverne Line and the bunkers were soon cleared. A British SOS barrage landed short during the evening, forcing 11th Division to withdraw. Rumours of a breakthrough were telephoned to the rear,

27   Stewart, *The New Zealand Division 1916-1919, Vol. II*, pp. 192-7.
28   Edmonds, *Military Operations: France and Belgium, 1917, Vol. II*, p. 56 and 64.
29   Ibid., p. 68. Divisional commanders were granted permission to decide their own deployment, according to the width of the objective and the distance to the advance.
30   Ibid., p. 71.
31   Ibid. The counter-attacks, and the reason behind their delays, are covered on pp. 72-4.
32   Ibid. Preparations for the resumption of the advance are covered on pp. 76-7.
33   Ibid. IX Corps rushed advance is detailed on pp. 77-8, 80-1.

causing the gunners to shorten their range even more. Fortunately, the Germans had no idea what was happening, and the Oosttaverne Line was soon reoccupied.

Both the New Zealand Division and the 3rd Australian Division reached their objective without a hitch but one of 4th Australian Division's brigades was spotted by a German aerial observer because it crossed the ridge too early.[34] Two hours of being shelled was followed by a tough fight for the Oosttaverne Line. Some of Australians moved too far north, leaving a large gap in their line and then an SOS barrage made some of 4th Australian Division's men retire. More artillery fire onto the abandoned area, caused even more to fall back. Again, the Germans did not realise what was happening and the Oosttaverne Line was reoccupied.[35]

A lack of coordination during a relief the following day led the artillery observers to think an attack was underway. An unnecessary SOS barrage triggered a German bombardment and the planned attack was postponed. The observers on Messines soon found the range of the enemy trenches, so the German withdrew to a safe distance on 10 and 11 June.[36]

A short advance by 25th Division on 13 June left part of its line under observation, so two battalions spent all day deploying, sending just a few men forward at a time. The creeping barrage at 7.30 pm took the Germans by surprise and Gapaard was cleared. The capture of the Spoil Bank on 14 June brought the offensive to an end.

Second Army's advance had been a complete success except for the fact that the German gunners had been able to save most of their guns.[37] The new Mark IV tanks had proved to be reliable, even if they had not been able to keep up with the infantry. But it had been noted that the creeping barrage had knocked out most of the anti-tank guns and machine-gun teams which had deployed in the open under camouflage.[38]

Operation Hush

The Admiralty was concerned how easy it was for German ships and submarines to attack British shipping in the English Channel. There had been talk of landing troops on the Flanders coast as early as January 1917. The commander of the Dover Patrol, Admiral Sir Reginald Bacon, wanted to capture the German trenches east of Nieuport, so the Belgians could advance from Dixmude.[39] They could seize the coastal

34   Ibid. II Anzac Corps' advance is covered on p. 77, 78-9.
35   Ibid. The mix up on IX Corps' and II Anzac Corps' fronts are covered on pp. 82-5
36   Ibid., p. 86. The Germans had fallen back to an obsolete trench which was overlooked and continuous, making it easy to target.
37   Ibid., Second Army had hoped to seize 120 field guns, but it had only taken 48, and most had were damaged and abandoned.
38   They deployed away from obvious targets, such as bunkers and buildings. However, the creeping barrage was so deep and intense, that they had suffered for choosing to deploy in the open.
39   Ibid. The proposed landings are discussed on pp. 116-7.

batteries west of Ostend, and then heavy howitzers could be moved forward to shell Zeebrugge.

On 6 June, General Gough asked how long his corps commanders needed to prepare for an attack east of Ypres and while two said six weeks, the third wanted eight weeks. So, the date for the offensive was set for 25 July; three landings would take advantage of the high tide on 7-8 August. Monitors would sail up to the shore, pushing piers onto the beach. They would shell the enemy positions along coast, while a smoke screen hid the men as they ran onto the beach. Half the men would climb the sea wall while the rest unloaded stores from pontoons. The gunners would manhandle their weapons onto the beach while three tanks dragged sledges loaded with equipment ashore.

The units of 1st Division were put under fake quarantine conditions at the beginning of July due to an alleged outbreak of a contagious condition. The men stayed in 'Camp Hush' west of Dunkirk for three months, where they practised climbing a replica of the sea wall and getting into and out of rafts.[40]

Part of the plan was for Fourth Army to take over the Nieuport sector, where the French were holding the sand dunes on the east bank of the Yser. The first British troops to enter the trenches were dressed in French uniforms, but the German observers realised a relief was underway when they spotted that the guns being replaced. So, they organised Operation *Strandfest* (Beach Party), to capture the vulnerable bridgehead.

Only one third of XV Corps guns were in place by the time the German bombardment began on 6 July. Most of the British contact planes had been damaged in bombing raid and the few that were able to fly were unable to do much when the shelling intensified on 10 July. To make matters worse, the Germans used two new types of gas for the first time. Sneezing gas (codename Blue Cross) made it difficult to wear a gas mask while mustard gas (codename Yellow Cross) blistered lungs and damps areas of skin.

Flame thrower teams led the five waves of infantry at dusk, pushing deep into the British position while mopping up teams cleared up behind them. Only a few men escaped by swimming the river.[41] Rawlinson wanted to retake the area, but Lieutenant General Du Cane's warned that hastily organised counter-attacks usually failed, so no attack was made.[42]

Planning for 31 July

GHQ's final instructions for the Flanders offensive were issued on 22 May but the Cabinet Committee on War Policy took their time to consider it. Plumer's Second

---

40   Ibid., p. 116.
41   Ibid. The attack is covered on pp. 118-21. The first wave pushed deep; the second established a defensive line; the third set up outposts; the fourth carried consolidating material and tools; the fifth set up a second defensive line.
42   Ibid., pp.121-2.

Army had handed the Ypres Salient over to Haig's favourite, Gough, and his Fifth Army, on 10 June. The Committee would not authorise the attack until 20 July, two days after the bombardment started.

Haig had promised that he would plan the advance in small steps. Gough was happy to do so but Plumer said they should push deep.[43] Haig agreed and the first day called for Fifth Army to make a 3-mile advance, in the hope it would trigger a general withdrawal. It would be supported by 752 large calibre pieces and 1,422 field guns.[44] A lot of deception was used, with batteries moving between emplacements at regular intervals. Sometimes a single gun would fire from a position, to entice the German gunners to give away their position by shelling.[45]

Rawlinson's Fourth Army had five divisions and over 580 artillery pieces, ready to advance along the coast. The Belgian Army was ready to cross the flooded Yser while First French Army was on Fifth Army's left flank. Second Army had handed over most its tanks and more than half its medium and heavy artillery to Fifth Army. Its role was to demonstrate east of the Messines Ridge, to divert German attention from the Gheluvelt plateau.

The bombardment started on 18 July and it sparked a counter-barrage. The area around Ypres was crammed with units that the Germans gunners could hardly fail to miss. They would use so much mustard gas, that it became known as *Yprerite*.[46] At the same time, the German divisions reduced the number of men in the front line to form counter-attack units. The batteries also pulled back, so they would not have to if the infantry lost any ground. It meant the British aerial observers needed another three days to find them, and then haze pushed Z Day back to 31 July.

The Machine Gun Corps' Heavy Branch was renamed the Tank Corps just before the attack. Most infantry battalions were used to fighting alongside tanks by now, but officers and NCOs were billeted together to improve relationships. Their crews spent three nights driving to their assembly points and only two broke down.[47] The artillery was detailed to silence the strongpoints across the crater field, in front of the first objective. Around forty-five tanks would then clear strongpoints covering the second objective while a similar number did the same en route to the third objective.

Again, each corps headquarters built a large model to study and companies practiced across taped out courses. Objectives were calculated on requiring one man for every three yards of front. Extra men were detailed for each farm in the area.[48] There were dozens of pillboxes to tackle but platoons had been training according to the recently

43   Ibid. Fifth Army's scheme is explained on pp. 126-31.
44   Ibid. The bombardment is covered on pp. 135-8. They fired over 4.28 million shells were fired; three times as many as for 1 July 1916.
45   Ibid., p. 136.
46   Ibid. The effects of mustard gas (codenamed Yellow Cross) are explained on pp. 138-9.
47   Ibid. The deployment of the tanks and their employment is covered on p. 148. It was correctly estimated that only half of the tanks would reach their objective.
48   Ibid., p. 147.

issued SS 143; 'Instructions for the Training of the British Armies in France'. The Lewis gunners and rifle grenadiers had learnt how to put down suppressive fire while riflemen and bombers moved in for the kill behind a smoke screen.[49]

The gunners stepped up the bombardment on 28 July, hitting enemy battery positions with high-explosive, shrapnel and gas. It meant the assault battalions were able to enter the assembly trenches late on 30 July, without too many problems.[50] They were all ready to move when over 3,000 guns opened fire at 3.50 am.

Two-thirds of the 18-pounders hit the enemy front line for seven minutes while the infantry deployed in No Man's Land and advanced to the German trenches.[51] It then crept forward at 100 yards every four minutes and the gunners fired four rounds a minute; they reduced to two rounds a minute during pauses. A mixture of graze and standard fuses created ground bursts and air bursts while more than 250 machine-guns fired an overhead barrage. The rest of the 18-pounders and all the 4.5-inch howitzers targeted the pillboxes, the 6-inch howitzers and 60-pounder guns hit distant targets and the larger guns were employed on counter-battery fire.

The tanks were detailed to follow the infantry across the first line of trenches. One third of the tanks would then help the mopping up teams to clear the many strongpoints between the first and second trench systems. Another third would join the infantry in the advance to the third trench system. The final third would go as far as the final objective.[52]

The Attack, 31 July

Tanks could not cross the Yser Canal, but aerial observers had reported empty trenches east of the waterway before the attack. The Guards Division had occupied them, so it advanced thirty-eight minutes after zero hour, to keep in line with 38th Division to its right.[53] The Guardsmen cleared many pillboxes and they sometimes zig-zagged through gaps in the German barrage to get to the Steen stream. The support battalions followed, crossing the canal on rafts constructed of chicken wire, canvas and wood frame or duckboards tied to petrol tins.[54]

Hundreds of thermite shells and blazing oil drums exploded on the German trenches opposite 38th Division's front. Some companies lost the creeping barrage

49 *Australian Army* <https://www.army.gov.au/sites/g/files/net1846/f/instructions_for_the_ training_of_the_british_armies_in_france_1917_uk_0.pdf> (Accessed 13 February 2019).
50 Edmonds, *Military Operations: France and Belgium, 1917, Vol. II.* Typically, only two-thirds of a battalion went into the trenches, so there was a cadre of men to train replacements. This meant approximately 675 officers and men went into action.
51 Ibid. The creeping barrage is explained in detail on pp. 150-1.
52 Ibid., p. 148.
53 Ibid., pp. 161-2.
54 Ibid., p. 161. The Guards Division had practiced crossing on a canal before hiding the equipment in tunnels under the canal bank, ready for zero hour.

after British smoke shells landed amongst them, while others were delayed clearing the many fortified craters. The Welshmen still crossed Pilckem Ridge and reached the Steen stream, having advanced over two miles.[55]

A prisoner had reported the date of attack to the Germans but not the time in XVIII Corps' sector. It meant the front-line units were begin relieved when burning oil and thermite shells exploded across their trenches. Eight tanks ditched crossing the Pilckem Ridge but 51st Division kept moving forward, 'not by wild frontal, expensive charges, but by the skilful use of ground and their weapons.'[56] Many Germans were caught in their dug outs during 39th Division's advance towards Kitchener's Wood.[57] Four tanks then helped clear St Julien, where many more were found hiding in the cellars. Enemy planes flew low to mark the Scots line once they were on the objective, so they chose to dig slit trenches to avoid the counter-barrage.

'The Germans surrendered or ran when the tanks appeared across XIX Corps' front, but the barrage was lost because it took too long to clear all the pillboxes. But both 55th Division and 15th Division still crossed the Steen stream, in touch with the troops to their flanks.[58]

Thermite shells exploded along the banks of Bellewaarde Lake and many Germans were 'too dazed to put up a fight'. Eight tanks followed 8th Division but it was slow going and the barrage was lost in Chateau Wood.[59] The troops then discovered that the objective was exposed to cross fire from the Hanebeek valley and Glencorse Wood, so they had to pull back.

There were problems on 30th Division's front before zero hour because twenty-nine tanks bogged down before they reached No Man's Land, while the counter-barrage delayed the deployment of the right brigade. A request to slow the creeping barrage down through Sanctuary Wood had been made too late to change the barrage plan and the infantry could not keep up with it.[60] The shells landed amongst the right brigade and it was delayed even more when 24th Division drifted across its front, as they tried to avoid Lower Star Post.[61] Finally, most of the nineteen tanks which went into action were knocked out by a single anti-tank gun along the Menin Road. The limit of the advance proved too exposed to hold, so there was a withdrawal into Sanctuary Wood and Shrewsbury Forest, while some of the reserves formed a line around the 'tank graveyard'.[62]

55   Ibid., p. 161.
56   F. W. Bewsher, *The History of the 51st (Highland) Division 1914-1918* (London: Blackwood, 1921), p. 205.
57   Edmonds, *Military Operations: France and Belgium, 1917, Vol. II*, p. 159.
58   Ibid., pp. 157-8.
59   Ibid., pp. 156-7.
60   Ibid., pp. 154-6.
61   Ibid., p. 153.
62   Ibid., p. 157.

31 July Continued

The reserve brigades on Fifth Army's left and centre kept advancing, getting weaker the further they went, while the right was struggling on the Gheluvelt plateau. The field artillery had moved forward but they had no time to register their guns, while only nine tanks made it across the Steen stream and they were too late to help the infantry.[63]

On the left, 39th Division lost many men crossing the Steen stream and then discovered that St Julien was a shell trap. The barrage moved on too fast as 39th, 55th and 15th Divisions fought through the Langemarck – Gheluvelt Line. Most of the tanks could not cross the Steen and Hane streams while the few that did never caught up with the advance. Once on the objective, German planes flew low, directing artillery fire onto the advancing troops, while the British guns overshot their targets. Enfilade fire from Glencorse Wood and Nonne Bosschen, where 30th Division should have been, caused 8th Division to lose the barrage.[64]

By noon, Fifth Army had advanced 2½ miles in places but the divisions had reached their limit; and past it in places. Battalions were weak, divisions had used their reserves and corps reserves were too far away. The artillery had little idea were the front line was and the few tanks still running were struggling to find their way back for fuel.

Corps squadrons were reporting progress and army squadrons were locating targets, but an oversight meant that no planes had been allocated to watch for counter-attacks. The first was spotted near Zonnebeke before midday but it took the runners two hours to reach the signal centres. Heavy rain then grounded all spotter planes and interfered with ground signalling. It meant that the forward observers could not report back while the rear observers could not see through the rain.[65]

The artillery did not see SOS flares through the rain, so 38th and 51st Divisions had to fall back across the Steen stream, because it was flooding. A counter-attack drove 39th Division back into the shell trap that was St Julien and it too withdrew across the Steen stream.[66] The artillery stopped firing, leaving 'a very weak and disorganised' 55th Division exposed, just as waves of German infantry came over the Zonnebeke spur, using flares to control their own batteries. They charged the Lancashire men as they redeployed to cover the flank, left exposed by 39th Division's retirement. The survivors found themselves fighting for their lives along the east bank of the flooded Steen stream. The same happened to both 15th Division and 8th Division as they were driven from the Frezenberg Ridge and the Bellewaarde ridge. There was no

63   Ibid., pp. 164-66 considers the challenges faced during the later advance.
64   Ibid. The advance is covered on pp. 166-8.
65   Ibid. The communications breakdown is explained on p. 170. Fifth Army had no contingency plan to detect for counter-attacks in heavy rain.
66   Ibid. The counter-attack is described on pp. 171-4.

counter-attack astride the Menin Road but the Germans did abandon Lower Star Post, allowing 30th Division to move forward.

Fifth Army may have advanced over 2 miles in the morning but the counter-attack had driven it back over half that distance in the afternoon. The rain forced all wheeled transport onto the roads while the streams began overflowing. Gough's left and centre were astride the flooded Steen stream while its right flank was engaged on the Gheluvelt plateau. Fifth Army had lost a lot of men and two thirds of its tanks; its artillery now needed time to find new targets and then register the guns. A barrage was followed by a counter-attack against the Frezenberg Ridge late on 1 August and 15th Division had to call a SOS barrage onto its own position, to halt the onslaught.

The attack of 31 July was discussed by senior commanders on 7 August. They concluded that choosing objectives according to maximum artillery ranges was too optimistic and they had to match the infantry's ability to capture and hold ground instead. The plan was to use short attacks in quick succession in the future; just as soon as the ground had dried out and enough ammunition had been stockpiled.

Plumer's memorandum on infantry tactics on 12 August[67] called for a radical change in infantry tactics to deal with the belts of pillboxes stretching across the Ypres Salient. A line of skirmishers would find routes across the crater field and trigger fire from enemy positions. The platoons could then follow the safest route to their next objectives in worm or diamond shaped formations. Moppers up would clear the pillboxes while support troops would fortify them.

A new bite and hold method would involve three steps; each shorter than the previous. The first involved one battalion clearing the outpost zone of around 800 yards and then waiting forty-five minutes for the mopping up to finish. A second battalion moved through the battle zone, around 500 yards deep, and then waited two hours so all the pillboxes could be cleared. Two battalions then advanced 300 yards to the final objective and dug in, ready to meet the counter-attack.[68]

Fifth Army, 10-16 August

The rain continued for three days and nights, turning the battlefield into a bog, and an attack to clear the Menin Road for the tanks had to be postponed to 4.35 am on 10 August.[69] Westhoek Ridge was taken by 25th Division and the flooded Hane stream stopped the Germans counter-attacking. But 18th Division suffered inside Glencorse Wood and Inverness Copse until Major General Richard Lee refused to

67   Ibid., pp. 240-2 and Appendix XXIV cover the new battle drill which would be used for the rest of the campaign.
68   Ibid., p. 241.
69   Ibid., p. 183. Brigadier General Elles and Lieutenant Colonel Swinton were considering attacks on other fronts, more suitable for tank operations. One was Cambrai and their plan would be used on 20 November 1917.

send any more reinforcements forward, because he was expecting counter-attacks.[70] When they came, batteries responded late to the SOS flares, if they replied at all. One battery extended its range ninety seconds late, disorganising 24th Division, giving the Germans in Shrewsbury Forest time to man their trenches.

Three days later, 18th Division cleared Glencorse Wood, 'without any artillery preparation and entirely on the initiative of the commanders on the spot. The assaulting troops advanced by rushes, under the cover of fire from Lewis guns and rifles.' It shows that the artillery sometimes caused more problems than it solved.

Fifth Army gave its divisions time to form bridgeheads across Steen stream but a thunderstorm late on 14 August meant that Gough had to postpone the next attack to 4.45 am on the 16th. No replacements had arrived, leaving battalions at half strength, so Gough had to halve frontages, to maintain the troop density. Even so, one observer said the advance 'looked more like a big raiding party than anything else.'

Some Germans surrendered and others ran around Langemarck, as their angry comrades shot at them. Afternoon counter-attacks recaptured some pillboxes but the Langemarck – Gheluvelt Line was cleared by the following afternoon.[71] A plane flew low as machine guns targeted Au Bon Gîte pillbox, allowing infantry to creep close and throw smoke bombs. The important position was then rushed by specially trained troops.[72] The British barrage passed over 11th Division, south-east of the village while contradictory orders caused a withdrawal, while tanks were unable to help 48th Division clear St Julien.

There were too few men to take all the pillboxes south-east of St Julien, while calls for reinforcements went unanswered.[73] The men of 36th Division were then shot down as they passed through the gaps in a new entanglement. A request to use gas shells on the pillboxes had been ignored and there were too few moppers up, so the Germans inside fired into the backs of 16th Division's men. The advance was going well onto ANZAC spur but both of 8th Division's flanks were under enfilade fire because the rest of the divisions were struggling.

The orders for 56th Division were complicated and late while requests for reinforcements had been ignored.[74] The marshy Hane stream disorganised the infantry and stopped the tanks on the left, while the infantry could not keep up with the barrage through Glencorse Wood and Polygon Wood. The support troops were pinned down, the mopping up was incomplete, and smoke meant the aerial observers could not see the Germans approaching the Londoners position. Nonne Bosschen and Glencorse Wood were abandoned after the ammunition ran out, while no one

70   Ibid. The attack is covered on pp. 184-9.
71   Ibid. The northern part of Fifth Army's attack is covered on pp. 198-201.
72   Ibid., p. 200.
73   Ibid. The southern part of Fifth Army's attack is covered on pp. 190-7.
74   Ibid. The 56th Division attack is covered on p. 192

returned from Polygon Wood. One pigeon message said; 'ammunition and bombs exhausted. Completely surrounded. Regret no course but to surrender.'

Smoke also prevented aerial observers spotting the counter-attack developing against Fifth Army's centre. The ground observers saw it coming but the artillery could not see their SOS signals and there was a fierce battle between St Julien and ANZAC Spur. Lieutenant General Herbert Watts eventually had to pull the barrage back, to stop XIX Corps being driven back across the Steen stream, in the knowledge that many wounded men had to be left behind. The counter-attack left both of his divisions too weak to attack again.

Operations 19-22 August

Platoon tactics were in place to take individual pillboxes, but the men were having to clear belts of them and it was causing problems. They had been built to create interlocking fields of fire, making it difficult, if not impossible, to outflank individual strongpoints. Everyone agreed 'not try and penetrate too deeply', while extra troops had to be allocated to mopping up and consolidating captured ground. An extra aerial observer was also added to each division, so one was always in the air to watch for counter-attacks.

Soft ground caused five tanks to ditch before the 4.45 am attack on 20 August and the remaining seven had to stay on the roads.[75] The advance to Keerselaere Crossroads by 11th Division was proof that the tanks could dominate ground but the infantry had to secure it, before they withdrew for fuel.

The orders were late and so the deployment was rushed for another 4.45 am attack two days later.[76] Two tanks helped the advance east of Langemarck but anti-tank guns put six out of nine tanks out of action north-east of St Julien; another eight were ditched. Men struggled through the mud beyond the Steen stream and no one came back from the Langemarck – Gheluvelt Line. The infantry who reached Inverness Copse came under fire from three sides, after the tanks turned back. German flamethrower teams entered the shattered wood early on 24 August and it was lost after the SOS barrage landed short.

The battlefield was a muddy mess by 27 August and men were forced to shelter in shell holes that filled with water as zero hour approached. They then 'found great difficulty in getting out and keeping up with the barrage' when it was time to advance.[77] Seven tanks would either break down or get bogged down along the Menin Road. In some places the Germans intended to surrender until they saw the British soldiers floundering in the mud, so they carried on fighting.[78]

---

75   Ibid., p. 202.
76   Ibid., pp. 201-4.
77   J. E. Munby, *A History of the 38th (Welsh) Division* (London: H. Rees, 1920), p. 27.
78   Edmonds, *Military Operations: France and Belgium, 1917, Vol. II*, pp. 207-8.

The men of 38th Division could not reach Eagle Trench and White Trench, but three tanks helped 11th and 48th Divisions advance east of St Julien. Neither 61st nor 15th Divisions could not capture the strongpoints along the Steen stream, while 23rd Division lost the creeping barrage as they moved through Glencorse Wood and Inverness Copse.

Haig had asked Gough and Plumer how long they needed to prepare for step-by-step advances on 25 August. Plumer's request was the longest at three weeks and while it was granted, further wet weather meant more postponements. The War Cabinet refused to send any more replacements because they were concerned about casualties and a lack of a breakthrough, so Haig had support units checked for men who could be transformed to the infantry.[79] The long postponement then prompted Prime Minister David Lloyd George to suggest ending the offensive, so that divisions could be sent to the Italian front; his idea was rejected.[80]

Delivering 54,500 tons of ammunition to the front in just two weeks involved thousands of men building and repairing roads while hundreds of horses hauled wagons to the front. There was never enough crushed stone to make foundations for new roads, while surfaces were made from beech slabs and sleepers; split logs were found to give a better grip on gradients.[81] The infantry followed pairs of duckboards through the crater field, one for going forward and the other for returning. They were quick to lay, easy to mend and could be moved from dangerous areas. Mats of wire netting and canvas stretched around wooden frames were used to cross boggy areas. Mules were often used, and they were skilled at following their leader across the crater field.

As much material as possible was moved at night and timetables made sure the wagons which faced the longest journeys left first.[82] Light railways were quick to build and they could carry huge quantities, but it was a complicated task getting the wagons loaded correctly and the trains sent off in the right order. As Fifth Army hauled ammunition and equipment forward, the Germans were baffled by the lack of offensive action and they eventually concluded that the Ypres offensive had been called off. It had not; Gough was just waiting for better weather. Sunny weather eventually dried up the ground except where water spilled across the fields around blocked streams.

Hill 70, 15-25 August

During the delay on Fifth Army's front, General Sir Henry Horne was asked to attack to keep German reserves opposite First Army's front. He chose to do so by

---

79   Ibid., pp. 234-5.
80   Ibid. Details of the London conference where this was discussed are on pp. 233-4.
81   Ibid. The problems associated with building and maintaining adequate roads in the Ypres Salient are covered on pp. 213-6 and 245-7.
82   Ibid. Issues with building and running the light railways behind Fifth and Second Armies' fronts are detailed on pp. 216-8.

attacking Hill 70, 2 miles north of Lens. Lieutenant General Sir Arthur Currie was the Canadian Corps' new commander, but the attack was delayed until 4.25 am on 15 August because of the rain which had started on 31 July.[83]

The attack would have been 'a killing by the artillery' but the Canadians were short of heavy howitzers, because most of them had been sent to Flanders. Fortunately, the spotter planes had been fitted with improved wirelesses, so their sightings could be rapidly relayed via corps headquarters to the batteries. The gunners were using predicted fire for the first time, a combination of precisely locating both the Canadian and German battery positions, calibrating the guns and assessing the weather conditions. Mathematics meant the guns could fire accurately with their first salvo; it both shortened registration times and reduced ammunition expenditure. One squadron of planes had also been trained in strafing targets and it would attack targets as soon as they were spotted.

The artillery fired 900 gas shells into Lens while Lieven projectors shot over 3,500 gas drums filled at the German trenches. Dummy tanks were used (because all the real ones were in Flanders) while drums of burning oil created a smokescreen. The infantry then advanced behind a creeping barrage which moved forward 'with beautiful accuracy.'[84]

The attack by 1st Canadian Division against Hill 70 was going well until the smoke cleared.[85] The Canadians then advanced by rushes to an objective which had been kept in range of the guns, and the men then prepared to meet any counter-attacks. The advance into the Lens' northern suburbs was also a success and the aerial spotters were able warned 2nd Canadian Division about the German movements. A Chinese attack the previous day had merely alerted the Germans, so they emerged from their cellars as 4th Canadian Division dug into the rubble on the outskirts of Lens.

The following day, 1st Canadian Division waited until 4 pm to attack but the men eventually had to fall back after running out of ammunition.[86] Bombers cleared the objective the following evening only for flamethrower teams to drive them back. Two bombing parties from 4th Canadian Division struggled on 21 August because their barrage missed the target. The Germans withdrew into their tunnels early on 23 August, until their heavy artillery to drive the Canadians from St Louis colliery and Green Crassier slagheap.

The Canadian Corps made its final attack during the early hours of 25 August, having stopped five German divisions moving north to Flanders for ten days. 'It was altogether the hardest battle in which the Corps has participated... There were no

---

83   Nicholson, *Canadian Expeditionary Force.* The preparations for the attack are explained on pp. 286-7.
84   Ibid. The bombardment is discussed on pp. 287-8. The Canadian Corps was short of heavy guns and those it did have were worn.
85   Ibid. The assault is covered on pp. 288-90.
86   Ibid. Subsequent fighting is covered on pp. 290-2.

fewer than twenty-one counter-attacks delivered, many with very large forces and all with great determination and dash...'[87]

Menin Road Ridge, 20 September

Fifth Army and Second Army organised their heavy and medium guns into three groups for the attack; counter-battery, long distance stationary targets, and targets of opportunity.[88] Success was reported by the corps squadron dedicated to reporting damage while two squadrons of fast-moving fighters were ready to drop messages, to the warn the troops of counter-attack. Batteries worked their way down target lists, according to the progress recorded by regular aerial photographs. The field artillery batteries were organised into groups, which hit targets closer to the front.[89]

Around 3.2 million shells had been stockpiled, four times as many collected for the 31 July attack. The two armies fired different barrages, because they faced different types of terrain. Gough faced the open countryside east of the Steen stream and Fifth Army's guns remained silent under camouflage until twenty-four hours before zero hour.[90] They then fired a 'really intense and hurricane bombardment' which boosted the troops' morale.[91]

Plumer wanted to destroy the pillboxes in the woods astride the Menin Road and knock out the batteries facing Second Army, so the bombardment started on 31 August.[92] The gunners then switched to hitting the tracks, to cut off the ammunition supply, before targeting battery positions. Double the amount of shells were fired at night because most movement in the dark was above ground. Each corps had a squadron to look for targets, while two fighter reconnaissance squadrons carried out long range missions. They photographed targets before and after they had been shelled.[93] The prolonged shelling also gave the sound-ranging sections time to locate batteries, so the medium and heavy guns could start targeting them on 13 September. The field guns then started practicing different types of creeping barrages, to test the German reaction and to fool their batteries into firing.[94]

---

87 Ibid., from General Currie's diary and repeated on p. 292.
88 Edmonds, *Military Operations: France and Belgium, 1917, Vol. II*. The organisation of the artillery is explained on p. 238.
89 Ibid. The ratio of heavy to field guns had tripled from 1:4.5 in March 1915 to 1:1.5 in September 1917.
90 Ibid., p. 249. The front-line areas were too exposed to provoke a reaction, but Fifth Army still suffered 3,500 casualties a week.
91 Ibid., p. 248.
92 Ibid., pp. 247-8.
93 Ibid., p. 248.
94 A creeping barrage would fool the German infantry into thinking an attack was underway. Their SOS flares would provoke the German gunners to open fire, making them vulnerable to counter-battery fire.

The creeping barrage had five parts which passed over the enemy trenches in 200-yard belts.[95] Heavy calibre high explosive shells were followed by medium calibre high explosive shells and they drove the Germans underground. A machine-gun barrage followed, enticing them to man their trenches. Then some of the field guns fired more high explosive shells. The troops followed the final curtain of shrapnel shells fired by the rest of the field guns and a mixture of graze and delay fuses created a deadly mixture of ground and air bursts.

The first wave deployed in No Man's Land, while the shrapnel barrage exploded only 150 yards ahead of the deployment tapes, keeping stationary for three minutes. The second wave deployed quickly at zero hour, to avoid the counter-barrage, while the third wave waited over ½ mile back for the same reason.[96]

The gunners fired four rounds a minute, extending their range by 50 yards every two minutes, while smoke shells were fired to tell the infantry they had completed the 800 yards to the first objective.[97] The heavy howitzers switched to specific targets while the rest of the barrage crept forward, the gunners firing only one round a minute to hide the fact that the advance had paused.[98]

The 300 oil drums fired on the left flank overshot Eagle Trench, and the flames illuminated 20th Division's attack (a second attempt using smoke shells succeeded during the evening).[99] Elsewhere along the line, the first wave of battalions overran the Germans sheltering in shell holes in No Man's Land, where they were hiding to avoid the barrage, before clearing the trenches beyond.

Forty-five minutes later the five-layer barrage reformed, and a second line of smoke shells warned the infantry that the barrage was about to move. The rate of fire was now only two rounds a minute while the creep had been reduced to 100 yards every six minutes, to give the infantry time to deal with the many pillboxes. The barrage plan was repeated on the second objective after 500 yards and on the final objective after a final 300 yards.

The barrage had to be accurate because many casualties occurred if the gunners overshot a camouflaged pillbox, as happened to 23rd Division in Dumbarton Wood.[100] Lewis gunners often used suppressive fire as they advanced, shooting blindly into the mist from the hip. Smoke grenades were used to cover the final approach to pillboxes while the Lewis gunners waited to shoot at anyone who ran. The Germans sometimes mounted their machine guns on the top of their pillboxes to get a better field of fire, but the infantry soon learnt they were then vulnerable to rifle grenades.

---

95 Edmonds, *Military Operations: France and Belgium, 1917, Vol. II.* The five-layer barrage is covered on p. 253-4.

96 Ibid., p.251. I Anzac Corps deployed battalions for all three battalions well forward, to avoid the counter-barrage.

97 Ibid., p. 254.

98 Ibid., p. 290.

99 Ibid., pp. 270-1.

100 Ibid., pp. 255-6.

The mist hid the assault troops, but it also made it difficult to locate the dugouts, and the Germans often climbed out to shoot at the support waves. Such an occurrence made 55th Division's first wave hesitate, and it lost the creeping barrage.[101] None of the runners made it back, so the gunners stuck to their timetable, leaving the infantry pinned down.

The artillery fired a special bombardment against the many pillboxes on 9th Division's front. High explosive shells suppressed the garrisons while smoke screens hid the fact that lanes had been left in the barrage. The infantry followed the smoke and the nearest sections outflanked the bunkers, while the rest continued to the objective.[102]

The troops lost the barrage crossing the muddy area around the Basseville stream and the Germans holding Tower Hamlets and the Quadrilateral were preparing to surrender when they realised that 41st Division was too weak to take the ridge.[103] The tanks were late, leaving 58th Division to tackle London Ridge on its own. Instead they were used to carry ammunition and equipment to the infantry.[104]

The short advance meant that the artillery could continue to give support without having to redeploy. The 1,200-yard advance was a success in most places and a solid defence was created across a 9-mile front. New trenches were dug because the existing ones had been dug to benefit the enemy; they were also on the German artillery target lists. However, the infantry preferred to hold pillboxes and shell holes because new trenches became targets as soon as they were spotted.[105]

The final objective became the new British outpost line while the second objective became the main line of defence. Two battalions then went forward to stop a counter-attack taking it and while each company commander held one platoon in reserve, each battalion commander held one company back.[106] Each division kept one brigade in reserve while each corps had a fresh division ready to take over the captured position during the night.

Communications were difficult to maintain[107] because cables could not be dug deep enough while the noise of battle interfered with the power buzzers. Visual signalling relied on clear weather, runners were also slow and vulnerable, and pigeons only flew one way. Second Army even tried mounting wirelesses in tanks.

Great steps had been made in watching for counter-attacks, since the catastrophe on 31 July. One wireless equipped plane watched each corps' front line while a second

---

101 Ibid., p. 266.
102 TNA WO 95/1795/2: 4th South African Regiment's War Diary.
103 Edmonds, *Military Operations: France and Belgium, 1917, Vol. II,* pp. 261-2.
104 Ibid., pp. 268-9.
105 Ibid., p. 271.
106 Ibid., pp. 241-2. Plumer's memorandum of 7 August detailed the organisation and deployment of reserves, in light of the disaster caused by the German counter-attack on 31 July.
107 Ibid., pp. 271-2.

watched for movement behind the German lines.[108] A unique SOS flare was introduced which would not be confused with any other; it showed three colours and hung in the air for several minutes.[109] The measures worked and each attack was broken up by the artillery, while the German artillery often missed their targets.[110]

Supplying the divisions across the broken ground was difficult because each one 'needed about 1,000 tons of supplies every day - equivalent to two supply trains each of 50 wagons.'[111] A lot was carried forward in Canadian designed Yukon packs, which used a strap around the forehead so the weight could be increased.[112] Unfortunately, they were so heavy that men often became bogged down in the mud or toppled over.

Polygon Wood, 26 September

Batteries moved forward as soon as the new defensive line had been established, ready for the next short advance, starting at 5.30 am on 26 September. Only this time the batteries had to deploy where they could be seen and casualties amongst the gunners doubled and there would be fewer practice barrages, because the field artillery had to cut the Flanders I Line wire. The successful five-layer barrage would be used again and over 1.7 million shells would still be fired at an area only 1,350 yards deep. False barrages were fired against the Zandvoorde and Warneton sectors, to the south, even though they were not going to be attacked.

Commanders made sure their troops moved quickly at zero, to avoid the counter-barrage. For example, 5th Australian Division deployed all twelve waves of men in a narrow strip, just 60 yards deep. They spread out at zero hour into 'worm columns, each led by an NCO' as their officers counted paces along compass bearings en route to their objectives in Polygon Wood. But the rapid deployment caused problems for another Australian Brigade which been lent two fresh battalions. The two assault battalions knew to wait for three minutes, to avoid walking into the creeping barrage but no one told the new arrivals to wait and they all merged together.[113]

The barrage threw up dust, which thickened the morning mist, but there would be many were casualties if a machine-gun team was overlooked.[114] The troops struggled to walk across or dig in the boggy areas around the streams, while those who sheltered

---

108 Ibid., pp. 274.
109 Ibid., pp. 275.
110 Ibid., pp. 274-6.
111 *Imperial War Museum* <https://www.iwm.org.uk/history/transport-and-supply-during-the-first-world-war> (Accessed 13 February 2019). Estimated at around three million rounds of ammunition, 35,000 grenades and 15,000 rifle grenades.
112 Edmonds, *Military Operations: France and Belgium, 1917, Vol. II*, p. 67. Each division was equipped with 250 Yukon packs and they could carry up to 65 lbs in weight.
113 Ibid., pp. 283-4. Replacements for two struck by a counter-attack on 25 September.
114 Ibid., pp. 284-9.

in pillboxes had to endure accurate artillery fire because the German gunners knew where they were.

The 20 September defensive formation was deployed but the machine-gun teams were divided into three groups this time. One in four were deployed along the final objective; a same number were placed in strongpoints and the rest were deployed further back, ready to fire overhead barrages.[115] Aerial spotters saw the counter-attack in time and artillery and machine-gun fire dispersed it, as the Germans discovered that the British and Australian troops were 'settled down' (*Eingenistete*).[116]

Broodseinde, 4 October

After the success of the two bite and hold attacks, Ludendorff decided to create 'one line and a strong one'. There would be more counter-barrages, to disrupt the enemy artillery and more raids to upset the infantry deployment. Most of the machine-gun teams would be deployed in the outpost zone, to break up the next attack, so that local reserves could strike before the captured ground was consolidated. Observation had to be improved, to help the artillery during the battle, while patrols had to locate the new enemy line, so it could be shelled when the attack ended. All counter-preparations had to be complete before the *Eingreif* divisions attacked the following morning.[117]

There had been a seven-day barrage before 20 September and a twenty-four-hour bombardment before 26 September. The five-layer barrage was defeating the Germans but there was insufficient time to extend the tracks, deliver ammunition to the new battery positions and register the guns. A few fake creeping barrages were fired, to trigger counter-battery fire, but there would be no preliminary barrage. Instead 2,300 guns would open fire in support of Second Army alone at 6 am on 4 October.[118] This time, it was hoped the Germans would be overwhelmed by a surprise attack, rather than by a heavy bombardment.

So, it seems that the increasingly difficult logistical situation dictated Second Army's style of attacks. A prolonged, methodical bombardment had preceded the 20 September attack. A short, intense bombardment had preceded the 26 September attack but no bombardment would precede the surprise attack on 4 October.

Assault teams armed with pistols, grenades and flamethrowers counter-attacked around Polygon Wood and the Menin Road before dawn on 30 September.[119] Most were driven back and the only problem occurred because the artillery could not see 23rd Division's SOS flares through the mist. The Germans decided to try again early

---

115 Ibid., p. 290.
116 Ibid., pp. 289-92.
117 Ibid., pp. 294-5.
118 Ibid. The creeping barrage is discussed on pp. 300-1.
119 Ibid., pp. 301-2.

on 4 October and by chance, they chose to attack a few minutes after Second Army's zero hour.

It had been noted that German patrols were looking for jumping off tapes, so string lines were used to mark out the line of departure while tapes were added just before zero. Drizzle created a mist as the troops moved into No Man's Land, but the Australians thought they had been spotted when flares called down artillery fire on their trenches at 5.30 am. It was in fact the start of the German barrage and their infantry were deploying on the opposite side of No Man's Land, ready to advance at 6.10 am.[120]

The British and Australian guns opened fire at 6 am and high explosive and gas shells exploded amongst the German batteries while they fired their preliminary bombardment. Shrapnel simultaneously showered the German infantry deploying in No Man's Land. Three minutes later Fifth Army and Second Army advanced, as the barrage crept forward and there were a few moments of disbelief as everyone 'blazed at once' in a bloody encounter which the British and Australian soldiers won.[121]

The main objectives had been reached, over 4,600 prisoners had been taken and many dead were counted. Each company sent one platoon forward with the barrage, two cleared the strongpoints and the fourth was held in reserve. Support companies formed an outpost line along the objective until the assault troops deployed and then withdrew, ready to follow the advance.

The 4 October was referred to as a 'black day' for the German Army because 'an overwhelming blow had been struck and both sides knew it.'[122] The Germans had suffered 'enormous losses' and the 'idea of holding the front line more densely... was not the remedy.' The question was, could it be repeated?

Poelcappelle, 9 October

The Germans had been driven back three times in just two weeks and spirits were high across the BEF. The high ground around Broodseinde had been taken, giving views across the green fields beyond, and the plan was to capture the high ground around Passchendaele. We all know now what happened at the end of the Third Ypres campaign, but that is with the benefit of hindsight. GHQ did not know and, as Charles Bean, the Australian Official Historian said; 'in view of the results of three step by step blows, what will be the result of three more in the next fortnight?'[123]

The plan for 9 October was the same as before but the drizzle soon turned to heavy rain. The wet weather made the longer logistics route more difficult to maintain, as the

120 Ibid., pp. 303-4.
121 Ibid., pp. 304-15.
122 Erich Ludendorff, *My War Memories* (London: Hutchinson & Co,) p. 490 quoted in Edmonds, *Military Operations: France and Belgium, 1917, Vol. II*, p. 316.
123 Bean, *Australian Official History, Vol. IV*, p. 881.

rain turn the mud into 'a porridge of mud'.[124] It turned the battlefield into a marsh, as streams overflowed, filling ditches and craters with water. Fascines now had to be used for foundations (because hardcore just disappeared into the mud) and then topped with stone and beech planks. Wagons slid off the muddy roads, wheels broke through the planks, while mules and pack horses crowded around them, looking for firmer footing. There was only time to build gun platforms alongside the roads, creating dense linear targets that were easy to spot. It was difficult to get shells to the guns or remove the wounded laying in the mud around the aid posts; as many as sixteen men were needed to carry a casualty back.[125]

The gunners were having a particularly bad time because their gun platforms were easy to see and they were sinking.[126] They had to work for prolonged periods in the rain (gunners stayed in the line longer than the infantry) and many were falling ill. Some batteries had not reached their platforms, others had to fire at their extreme range and the rest had not had time to register. It was difficult to get shells to the gun lines and even more difficult to keep them clean in the mud.

There was a brief dry spell in the weather, but the rain returned on the afternoon of 8 October, with more predicted for the next few days. Men faced a long walk through the night in the rain to reach the front line, leaving them 'so done they could hardly stand up and hold a rifle.' Appointed guides had no landmarks to help them, just lines of stakes topped with lamps to follow. It meant a relief that was supposed to take five hours took up to eleven hours to complete. Zero hour was postponed by two hours, but companies were still late, and officers had to spread out their men, to fill gaps in the line for the 5.15 am zero.[127]

Despite the problems, the battle became one of two halves, with success on the left and defeat in the centre and on the right. Fifth Army's advance was at a rate of 100 yards every six minutes and the gunners fired a solid barrage astride the Staden railway; the machine-gun barrage was described as 'superlative'. Both the Guards Division and 29th Division crossed the Broem stream, where patrols had marked it was safe, and advanced over one mile towards Houthulst Forest, as the Germans surrendered en mass.[128]

Meanwhile, 11th, 48th and 4th Divisions had all struggled to get into position around Poelcappelle in time and the exhausted men came under machine-gun fire from the Flanders I Line, on the high ground to the east.[129] Many were pinned down in front of pillboxes while those who made any progress were never seen again. Rubble

---

124 Edmonds, *Military Operations: France and Belgium, 1917, Vol. II*, p. 327.
125 Ibid. The impossible task faced by the engineers, gunners and supply trains are described on p. 327-9.
126 Ibid., p. 328-9.
127 Ibid., p. 330.
128 Ibid., the success on Fifth Army's left is detailed on pp. 335-7.
129 Edmonds, *Military Operations: France and Belgium, 1917, Vol. II*. The failure on Fifth Army's right is explained on p. 335.

stopped the few tanks getting through Poelcappelle, while the creeping barrage 'was very ill-defined' and the 'heavy batteries fired very short'.[130] The Germans then retook the ruins from 11th Division.

Second Army's barrage was weak and ragged, and the men could barely see the exploding shells through the rain. Most buried themselves deep in the soft ground before exploding, sending up plumes of mud. Five minutes later the barrage crept forward at only 100 yards every eight minutes, but the infantry could still not keep up, as they waded through the mud.[131]

There were no messages from 49th Division's front line and while some commanders refused to send their men forward, the rest did, and they suffered the same fate. The men of 66th Division had to advance as soon as they reached the jumping off line, resulting in an uncoordinated attack.[132] The pillboxes on Bellevue spur poured fire into their flank when the rain stopped, and a localised withdrawal was mistaken for a general retirement. The withdrawal by 66th Division left part of the 2nd Australian Division in danger of being surrounded, so it had to withdraw from the Keiburg spur.

The first report to reach Major General Perceval came from an aerial spotter. It said that 49th Division was on Bellevue spur and he ordered his reserve brigade forward, despite protests from his staff. It turned out the observer had misread the map, but the advance went ahead and it too failed; Percival was relieved.

There were mixed results on X Corps front, where 7th Division took Reutel village. However, poorly planned orders had omitted Gheluvelt, the main German defensive position, from the artillery and infantry orders. It meant that 5th Division could not hold any ground.[133]

First Battle of Passchendaele, 12 October

Gough wanted to stop sending men across the crater field around Poelcappelle but Plumer wanted to clear the rest of the Passchendaele ridge. Neither realised that the logistics chain had broken down, leaving the living short of supplies while the wounded were left to die. They were both still waiting for feedback from the 9 October attack, so Plumer did not understand that two deep belts of wire had stopped the advance onto the ridge, rather than mud. Then II Anzac Corps said it had not advanced as far as originally reported and there was no time to change the artillery plan. It meant the

---

130 TNA WO 95/2329/3: 6th Green Howards War Diary.
131 This slow creeping speed gave the Germans enough time to prepare themselves and shoulder their weapons.
132 Edmonds, *Military Operations: France and Belgium, 1917, Vol. II*, pp. 330-3 covers the impossible conditions faced by the three divisions.
133 Ibid., p. 334.

creeping barrage had to move at double the speed from the new front line to the first objective.[134]

Field Marshal Haig's chief intelligence officer, Brigadier General John Charteris, said 'my God, did we send men to fight in this?' during a visit to the battlefield on 9 October. He returned to GHQ believing 'there is now no chance of complete success here this year.' But only two days later, Haig told the war correspondents that the BEF was 'almost through the enemy defences, the enemy only has flesh and blood against us, not blockhouses and they take a month to make.'[135] He believed a couple more successes could break them and set the next zero hour for 5.25 am on 12 October. Most of Gough's artillery did not have to relocate but he still considered calling off the attack, however, Plumer persisted.

More rain just made everything worse and Crown Prince Rupprecht said it was his 'most effective ally.'[136] He had again given instructions to deploy more troops in the outpost zone because of weakness of the barrage and the poor state of the ground. After the experience on 9 October, it was believed they could stop the attack in its tracks.

The BEF's problems were many; the guns were worn, weapons jammed in mud, the battalions and batteries were short of men and the survivors were wet and exhausted. A sweep of the BEF had found some replacements but they were 'reclassified owing to the adoption of a less rigorous physical standard: their military training was therefore less than perfect.'

The Guards Division advanced to the edge of Houthulst Forest, but Gough did not want them to enter the maze of tree stumps, craters and bunkers.[137] Both 17th and 4th Divisions crossed 'a vast sea of malignant mud and water' at zero. They cleared strongpoints around the Staden railway, and an SOS barrage then stopped the German reinforcements wading through the mud.

A late change in 18th Division's orders did not reach everyone in the shell holes in front of Poelcappelle in time. The creeping barrage then started 30 seconds late and landed amongst the advancing troops. The companies which chose to wait or advanced late were cut down because they 'could not swim nor fight, only drown or stay where they were'; a counter-attack retook the village.[138] Machine-gun fire upset 9th Division's advance astride the Lekkerboter stream and 'only men with webbed feet could fight with comfort' on Wallemolen spur.[139]

134 Ibid., The late disclosure of these two problems are covered on pp. 337-8. The problem was attacks were being carried out too close together, so there was no time to incorporate all the information into the planning.
135 Ibid., p. 339.
136 Ibid., p. 341.
137 Ibid. Fifth Army's advance is described on p. 343-4.
138 TNA WO 95/2049/1: 7th Buffs (East Kent) Regiment War Diary.
139 TNA WO 95/ 1772/2: 6th King's Own Scottish Borderers War Diary.

The Germans around Bellevue spur were nervous, so their artillery hit II Anzac Corps' assembly area before zero hour. The Anzac artillery had been unable to cut the wire on Wallemolen and Bellevue spurs while the New Zealanders lost the creeping barrage while cutting through the first belt.[140] The Germans mounted their machine-guns on top the bunkers and trained them on the gap left astride the s'Gravenstafel road.[141]

The 3rd Australian Division found that the front line was not where it was supposed to be after a nightmare march across the crater field. It meant their artillery was inaccurate while the German gunners were on target. The barrage was so ragged that the infantry 'made no attempt to conform to it. There was really nothing to conform to.' There was a 'terrible mix-up' and 'great confusion' while the men looked for firm ground north of the Roulers railway but one small group moved up the Rave stream gully into a deserted Passchendaele. However, the main problem was the enfilade fire from Bellevue spur, where the New Zealanders should have been. That led to 4th Australian Division abandoning Nieuwmolen.

Fifth Army, 22 October

The bombardment started on 21 October and Fifth Army attacked at 5.35 am the following morning, to draw attention away from the Canadian Corps' deployment in front of Passchendaele. The creeping barrage had been slowed right down, but the men still could not keep up in the mud.[142]

There had been a mix up over which battalion would capture several pillboxes on 35th Division's front, so everyone in range was pinned down. The rest of its attack was pinned because of enfilade fire from the right flank where the creeping barrage had landed behind 34th Division, stopping it taking the shelters either side of the Watervliet stream.[143] A Chinese attack focused the enemy's attention south of Poelcappelle while 18th Division captured the brewery; the men had to withdraw when they came under fire from British howitzers.

The Germans had used a different type of defence on 22 October, in which machine-gun teams held the 800-yard-deep outpost zone. Most withdrew as soon as the attack began, leaving a few behind in the pillboxes, while an artillery and machine-gun barrage hit the advancing troops. The problem was the 'men attacked so closely upon the barrage, that they seemed mixed up with their own shell fire.'[144]

140 Edmonds, *Military Operations: France and Belgium, 1917, Vol. II,* Second Army's attack is covered on p. 341-3.

141 Stewart, *The New Zealand Division 1916-1919, Vol. II,* pp. 262-70.

142 Edmonds, *Military Operations: France and Belgium, 1917, Vol. II,* p. 348. The British Official History dismisses the attack as an 'artillery action'.

143 J. Shakespear, *The Thirty-Fourth Division, 1915-1919* (London: Witherby, 1921), p. 158-60.

144 Edmonds, *Military Operations: France and Belgium, 1917, Vol. II,* p. 348.

Fifth Army, 26 October

Zero was at 5.40 am on 26 October and the barrage creep was again as slow as possible, at 100 years every 8 minutes. The men crowded around the water filled craters either side of the Stadendreve and Watervliet streams, while the wounded drowned in the mud. Snipers targeted the officers until their men stopped cutting the wire blocking the Staden railway, the only dry land in the area.

It was 57th Division's first action and they too floundered in the mud astride the Stadendreve and Watervliet streams. The only consolation was that the Germans fared no better when they counter-attacked. The Flanders I Line pillboxes fired down from Wallemolen spur as 58th and 63rd Divisions struggled to advance astride the Lekkerboter stream. It left a ragged front line and one battalion commander eventually took his artillery officer on a tour of the front line, so he could plan an accurate SOS barrage.[145]

Second Army, 26 October

Lieutenant General Arthur Currie had been against using the Canadian Corps to take Passchendaele, believing it should be saved for a more decisive role.[146] His command had been given to Second Army 'because the Canadians [did] not work kindly' with Gough, a problem which dated back to Somme campaign the previous autumn.[147] The Canadian engineers and pioneers had started work on 17 October but they faced an uphill battle to keep the tracks open. But they also worked to complete 1 mile of double plank road and over 1 mile of light railways.[148]

Currie was 'convinced that this reconnaissance and close liaison between the artillery, the infantry units, and the staff is vital to the success of any operation.'[149] He wanted set piece actions, supported by planned bombardments and good logistics. However, the conditions were so bad that over half of the 550 howitzers and guns were either knocked out or stuck in the mud.[150] Many others fired from where they could find an area of dry land, providing the ammunition wagons could reach them.

The Germans once again defended an 800-yard-deep outpost line with sniper rifles and light machine-guns, the only weapons a man could carry in the mud.[151] They had

145 TNA WO 95/3115/1: Hood Battalion War Diary.
146 Edmonds, *Military Operations: France and Belgium, 1917, Vol. II*. The arrival of the Canadian Corps is covered on pp. 346-8.
147 Nicholson, *Canadian Official History*, p. 312.
148 Ibid., p. 312. Drainage trenches were dug either and birch or elm planks then were laid across runners. They were spiked in position and protected with curbs of half round pine logs.
149 Ibid., p. 314.
150 Ibid. Control of the Canadian Corps' artillery is given on p. 315.
151 Ibid. The change in defensive tactics is further explained on p. 316-8.

endured four days of bombardments by the time the assault troops advanced through the mist at 5.40 am on 26 October.[152] The barrage moved as slow as 100 yards every eight minutes but it was too fast for the four divisions of Fifth Army advancing astride Lekkerboter stream. The 'mud, knee-deep, checked progress to a crawl of less than a yard a minute. The barrage was lost, rifles became quickly clogged and the men fell back or were cut off.'[153]

The 3rd Canadian Division suffered heavy casualties advancing up the Wallemolen and Bellevue spurs. Some men were in danger of being cut off, and had to withdraw, while a battalion commander fetched reinforcements to hold onto some of the Flanders I pillboxes. Meanwhile, the 4th Canadian Division could not advance any closer to Passchendaele until the following morning.[154]

The attack on Gheluvelt Chateau started badly because 5th Division had to pull back, so the artillery could fire a straight barrage. The Germans occupied the abandoned trenches, leaving the troops having to clear their own trenches before wading across the muddy Scherria stream. Some were unable to cross the Reutel stream, while others were cut off when 7th Division withdrew on the right flank. A battalion commander had to rally every man he could find and then called down an SOS barrage, believing only Germans were left alive in front of his position.[155]

The slow creeping barrage meant 7th Division became disorientated moving through Gheluvelt, while others were hit by the pillboxes along the Menin Road. The rest could not cross the Kroome stream nor take the Tower Hamlets strongpoint. Officers rallied the stragglers, got them to clean their weapons and strip ammunition from the casualties, so they could hold the position. However, no reinforcements came because the runners had all been killed, so they had to fall back.

Second Battle of Passchendaele, 30 October to 10 November

On 26 October, Haig was informed that the Italian front had collapsed, in the battle of Caporetto, and he to send troops south to help. Zero had been set for 5.50 am on 30 October but fog had replaced the rain, making it impossible to register the guns. Some guns fired two minutes early, alerting the Germans and a counter-barrage caught 58th and 63rd Divisions as they deployed.[156] They then lost the creeping barrage trudging through the knee-deep mud and Lieutenant General Ivor Maxse summarised that 'nothing but the impossibility of crossing the mud prevented their usual complete success.'

---

152 Ibid. The Canadian summary of the attack is detailed on 319-20.
153 Edmonds, *Military Operations: France and Belgium, 1917, Vol. II*, p. 351. The four divisions made no progress and suffered over 5,400 casualties.
154 Ibid. The British version is covered on pp. 349-351.
155 Ibid. The disastrous attack is described on p. 351.
156 Ibid., pp. 353-4.

The Canadians moved faster, but they were still hit by the German barrage.[157] Too few guns had deployed to create an effective barrage and some fired short because they had not had time to register their targets. It again crept forward at 100 yards every eight minutes up Bellevue and Passchendaele spurs but it was still too fast. It meant 3rd Canadian Division and 4th Canadian Division suffered heavy casualties clearing the outpost zone covering Passchendaele.[158]

GHQ had abandoned the idea of crossing the flooded area west of Poelcappelle, but it did want to extend its hold on Passchendaele ridge. Every night, the Canadian gunners fired at random points and then fired a full bombardment on 5 November, revealing new targets. The attack began at 6 am on 6 November and the Canadians used continuous wave wireless sets for the first time. There were teething problems, but they were far better than the spark-based wireless set and they would transform how battles were fought in the future.[159]

Again, 1st Canadian Division moved fast through the shell holes and pillboxes on Goudberg and Bellevue spurs to the west of Passchendaele.[160] But 2nd Canadian Division was slower moving up the Rave stream gully, which was 'knee deep and in places waist deep in mud and water', and into Passchendaele.[161] They then spread out into shell holes beyond, before the German artillery hit the ruins.

The Germans had no intention of recapturing the village but another effort to secure the area in heavy rain ended in disaster for 1st Canadian Division, because the barrage landed on the assault troops at 6.45 am on 10 November.[162] One battalion went the wrong way and the Germans counter-attacked through the gap, causing many casualties, but 2nd Canadian Division had better luck around Vindictive Crossroads.[163] The Canadians Corps started leaving the Ypres Salient on 14 November, having suffered over 15,600 casualties; many more men were ill.

There was one final attack on the Passchendaele ridge. The infantry was supposed to rush the German outpost line at 1.55 am on 2 December whilst the guns targeted the main trenches eight minutes later. However, the Germans detected movement across the snow under bright moonlight and there were many casualties prior to the

157 Nicholson, *Canadian Expeditionary Force*. The Canadian attack is explained on pp. 321-3.
158 Edmonds, *Military Operations: France and Belgium, 1917, Vol. II*, the British version of events is on pp. 353.
159 Nicholson, *Canadian Expeditionary Force*, pp. 325. From now on commanders would be 'willing to consider wireless as an integral part of the general scheme of communication.'
160 Edmonds, *Military Operations: France and Belgium, 1917, Vol. II*, the British version of events is on pp. 355-8.
161 Nicholson, *Canadian Expeditionary Force*, pp. 324-5.
162 Ibid., pp. 326.
163 Edmonds, *Military Operations: France and Belgium, 1917, Vol. II*. The British version of events is on pp. 358-9.

scheduled British bombardment. The survivors were, with some exceptions, back in their trenches the following morning.[164]

The Messines and Third Ypres Campaigns Summary

The artillery used fake barrages to trigger counter-battery fire south of Ypres, making it possible to silence many of the enemy guns before 7 June 1917. The Germans may have built extra pillboxes to defend Messines Ridge but the mines stunned the German into submission. It did, however, mark the last time the tunnellers contributed to an offensive.

The attack drew on the many lessons learned from the Somme and Arras campaigns and the upgraded Mark IV tanks proved their worth in clearing the ridge. The Royal Flying Corps also found new ways to effectively report the advance, so the gunners could provide valuable support at all times.

The creeping barrage used a mixture of air and ground bursts to devastate the Germans east of Ypres on 31 July 1917. The gunners also used various methods, including smoke and different rates of fire to keep in touch with the infantry. Riflemen, grenadiers, Lewis gunners all knew how to work together to silence pillboxes but the poor ground meant that the tanks could only play a limited role. Wet weather then interfered with operations for several weeks.

The five-belt barrage was effective at supporting a bite and hold strategy in the autumn and for a time it looked as the Germans had no answer to it. However, the lengthening logistics route made it increasingly difficult to advance the guns, while bad weather made it impossible to advance the infantry. Only superhuman efforts made it possible to edge forward onto the Passchendaele Ridge in appalling conditions.

164 See Michael LoCicero, *A Moonlight Massacre. The Night Operation on the Passchendaele Ridge, 2 December 1917: The Forgotten Last Act of the Third Battle of Ypres* (Solihull: Helion & Company, 2014).

6

The Cambrai Campaign
30 November – 7 December 1917

Planning

Brigadier General Hugh Elles had been pushing for the Tank Corps to play a bigger part in operations and on 4 October 1917, he produced a series of notes based on recent experiences.[1] The tanks were unable to cross wet, broken ground and could only move slowly across dry, broken ground. They were unable to keep up with the infantry until they had crossed the shelled zone.[2] They were vulnerable to barrages, while smoke, mist and dust limited their movement. Tank commanders had to be able to see their objectives from the start line and routes had to be both passable and direct.

Elles wanted to use the tanks en mass, so they could concentrate their power and provide mutual support, otherwise they would be destroyed one-by-one. They also had to work closely with the infantry, taking instructions from platoon commanders to help them achieve their objectives. The infantry had to be made aware of what the tanks were able to do, never to bunch behind them and to be prepared to press on, if the tanks were delayed.[3]

Haig had discussed the plan with Third Army's General Byng on 13 October and he was looking 'to gain a local success at a point where the enemy did not expect it' when the Flanders campaign ended.[4]

The plan for Cambrai came about due to several factors. The tanks would cut the wire, so there was no need for a preliminary bombardment. The gunners would pre-plot their fire, so again there was no need for a bombardment, leaving the gunners

---

1   Falls, *Military Operations: France and Belgium, 1917, Vol. II*, pp. 319-22.
2   This was usually 2 miles deep.
3   Practical ideas, such as painting crew numbers on the backs of tanks, for identification, and SOS panels to notify aerial observers they were broken down, were recommended.
4   Everard Wyrall, *The History of the Second Division, 1914-1918, Vol. 2* (London: Thomas Nelson, 1921). p. 478.

able to concentrate more firepower on the enemy artillery. This in turn meant that less shells were needed, reducing the amount of traffic on the roads. It also meant the ground would be less churned up, which was better for the tanks. This way of combining the arms did, however, mean that the tanks were again back in front of the infantry.

Battery positions were surveyed, gun pits were camouflaged and then dug, while screens were erected to stop enemy observers spotting the flashes. Battery boards marked with targets were prepared and signal communications were installed before the guns were towed to the position during the hours of darkness. Only established batteries were allowed to fire routine barrages before zero, to keep the build-up of artillery a secret. It meant the new batteries could deploy closer to the front line if they kept quiet, meaning they could fire deeper into enemy territory during the attack. All the time, batteries were slowly cutting wire all along the rest of Third Army's front, to draw attention away from the area to be attacked.

Brigadier General Henry Tudor, 9th Division's artillery officer, had been considering a surprise attack in the Cambrai sector, to divert attention away from Flanders.[5] He wanted to used predictive fire rather than the usual observe, fire and check for damage method. Every gun was being tested on a calibration range while friendly and enemy batteries were being surveyed. It meant the gunners could calculate angles and ranges to targets, even aiming the field guns so they would fire their creeping barrage in a parallel line.[6] The tanks would cut the wire, so there was no need for preliminary bombardment, nor masses of shells and the ground would not be churned up. It also meant most of the crews manning the one thousand guns behind Third Army's front would be fresh at zero hour.

The Tank Corps assembled three tank brigades and they each had three battalions.[7] Each battalion had forty-two tanks and around two-thirds were new. The Hindenburg Line trenches had been dug wider than a tank's maximum crossing span, so crews practiced using two arms to lower a fascine into the trench as a bridge.[8] Training started during the first week in November, leaving each battalion just two days to train with the tanks. The men watched a tank crush a section wire and cross a trench with its fascine, to give them confidence. They practised following them as a team and then practiced advancing over a taped version of their sector.[9]

5   Captain Wilfrid Miles, *Military Operations: France and Belgium, 1917, Vol. III: The Battle of Cambrai* (London, HMSO, 1948), the decisions leading up to Cambrai are outlined on pp. 6-8.

6   Miles, *Military Operations: France and Belgium, 1917, Vol. III.* Unregistered shooting is detailed on pp. 10-2.

7   Ibid. The deployment of the Tank Corps is given on pp. 27-8.

8   Ibid., pp. 14-5.

9   Ibid., p. 33 and Bewsher, *The History of the 51st (Highland) Division 1914–1918*, p. 236.

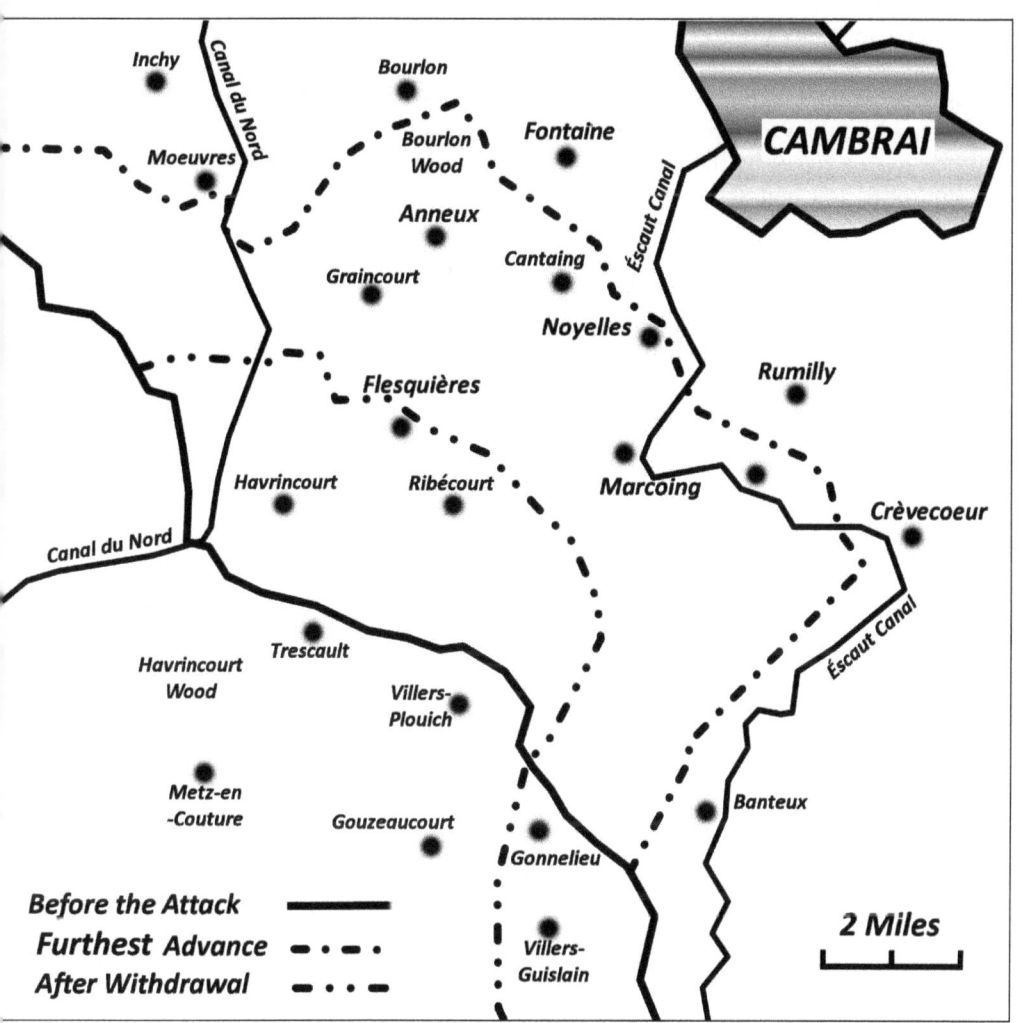

Map 6. Battle of Cambrai, 20 November to 6 December 1917: The use of tanks and predicted artillery fire presented a brief opportunity to breakthrough at Cambrai before the German struck back.

Around 200 tanks would cross the trenches while another 135 crossed the 'bridges' and joined those still running, for the advance beyond.[10] Tanks hauling batteries, loaded with supplies and dragging sleds of supplies (700 tonnes) followed. Another thirty-two tanks would be busy dragging the rest the wire aside with grappling hooks, so wheeled transport could get forward. Two tanks would carry timber to cross streams while bridging companies would help the tanks cross the St Quentin Canal. Over 40 would wait in reserve.

A deep advance by the tanks was expected and two days' worth of supplies were stockpiled at a central depot, ready to be sent forward. The plan was to connect the roads and trench railways across No Man's Land, so they could be carried forward as quickly as possible.

The need for secrecy and a lack of time and manpower, meant that armoured ground cables and overhead cables were used, to reduce the amount of digging. Radio sets (albeit unreliable ones) were given to each infantry brigade headquarters. Nine tanks were also equipped with a radio while a tenth would lay a telephone cable, so the Tank Corps could speak directly to Third Army. The usual network of amplifiers, power buzzers, observation posts, signal stations, pigeons and runners were established while an advanced report centre was on standby to support a Cavalry Corps break out.

Deploying in Secret

There were hundreds of things to build and most of the work had to be done at night. Lorries only showed their lights when they heading back, making it look as if the line was being thinned out.[11] Mist hid most of the work after 10 November but Third Army's rear area was still divided into three areas; where ground observers could see, where balloon observers could see and where spotter planes could see. Different rules applied to each area and spotter planes flew when the weather allowed, checking that camouflage was sufficient.[12]

Around one hundred guns deployed in silence every night for ten nights. The Germans had cut down all the trees in Havrincourt Wood and so a 2-mile-long screen of bushes was erected to screen twenty battery positions.[13] Divisions moved to the front over the course of three nights, and the men only realised an offensive was afoot when they saw the camouflaged tanks and guns. The original divisions held the front trench while the assault divisions checked the ground. Officers were made to dress as other ranks, so as not to arouse suspicion if they captured, while 51st Division's

---

10   Miles, *Military Operations: France and Belgium, 1917, Vol. III*, the deployment of tanks is covered on p. 28.
11   Bewsher, *The History of the 51st (Highland) Division 1914–1918*, p. 237.
12   Everard Wyrall, *The History of the 62nd (West Riding) Division 1914–1919* (London: The Bodley Head, 1924). Steps taken to maintain secrecy are explained on pp. 75-7.
13   Wyrall, *The History of the 62nd (West Riding) Division 1914–1919*, pp. 73-4.

officers had to wear trousers instead of kilts, so as not to give away the fact that Scots were in the line.[14]

Trains carried 476 tanks to Third Army's assembly area near Bray-sur-Somme and then delivered them within 5 miles of the front line. They drove slowly during the hours of darkness, reaching their positions before dawn on 19 November. The Cavalry Corps had gathered in the Péronne area by 9 November and then started moving towards the battle front the day before the battle. It put around 20,000 mounted men and their artillery and supply trains on the roads and it required plenty of staff work to keep them moving.

Rumours that other parts of the line were going to be attacked were started while there was talk of a new training school, to account for the number of tank officers in Albert. They were also taken to see the front line dressed as other ranks, so as not to arouse suspicion. Secrecy was paramount and even senior officers at GHQ were kept in the dark until it was absolutely necessary.

The few prisoners which fell into enemy hands knew nothing of importance but German aerial spotters saw something on 19 November. Messages suggested a possible tank attack around Havrincourt but it gave no indication that Third Army had assembled around 90,000 men, 1,000 guns and over 300 tanks in secret.[15]

Royal Flying Corps[16]

Seven fighter squadrons controlled the skies, with the help of twenty-eight anti-aircraft guns deployed in a chequerboard pattern across Third Army's rear. Six squadrons looked for German infantry and reported troop movements while intelligence sections made sure the information was assessed and forwarded to the infantry and artillery. Six kite balloon sections also looked for movement behind the German line while more squadrons looked for artillery targets. Eighteen planes would watch the Cavalry Corps' progress while one squadron was on standby to carry out dangerous observation missions. Twelve armed bombers were also ready to carry out long-range missions.

The Attack Begins

During the hours before zero, the drivers followed tapes to their start position behind the support trench.[17] Few broke down or ditched en route. They then drove forward at 6.10 am, crossing Third Army's front trench as the artillery opened fire ten minutes

---

14 Ibid., p. 74
15 Miles, *Military Operations: France and Belgium, 1917, Vol. III*. The German reaction before the battle is covered on pp. 47-8.
16 Ibid. The Royal Flying Corps' role is detailed on pp. 30.
17 Wyrall, *The History of the 62nd (West Riding) Division 1914–1919*, p. 77.

later. The pre-dawn light allowed the tank drivers to see where they were going while the infantry officers could see their platoons and the tanks. However, the German machine-gun teams would not be able to see far enough to cause many casualties.

Trench mortars and field guns fired a standing barrage at the outpost line and the Hindenburg trenches for the first five minutes, while the heavy artillery targeted likely anti-tank gun positions. A mixture of shrapnel and high explosive then crept forward. Delay action fuses were used against the outpost line and first trench, because the below ground explosions would stun the Germans in their dug outs. Meanwhile, impact fuses were used against the support trenches because the ground bursts would hit them as they manned their trenches.[18]

On 30 October, Third Army had issued two papers; one called 'Tank and Infantry Operations without Methodical Artillery Preparation'[19] and 'Notes on Infantry and Tank Operations'.[20] However, each corps interpreted them in different ways to get their tanks and infantry through the Hindenburg Line.[21] Each division then altered the scheme to suit their objectives.[22]

Four tanks led each infantry company across IV Corps' sector.[23] Tank A crushed the wire, planting flags to mark the gap, and used its fascine to cross the fire trench. It then made a gap in the support trench wire and turned right. Tank B employed its fascine to cross the support trench and then both A and B headed for the rendezvous point. Tanks C and D also crossed the fire trench and turned right to shoot into it as the infantry approached; they too then headed for the rendezvous point. The first wave of infantry followed 150 yards behind the tanks, while the rest followed in section columns. The remaining twelve tanks crossed the support trench, helping the infantry clear pockets of resistance.

In III Corps' sector, Tank A crushed the wire and turned left to shoot into the fire trench. Tank B crossed the fire trench with its fascine and then turned left to shoot into the same trench. It then crushed the second belt of wire before shooting into the support trench. Tank C crossed the support trench with its fascine and turned left to shoot into it. All three tanks then headed for the rendezvous point.

The infantry followed in files and they had been split into three groups. The 'trench cleaners' checked the dug outs, the 'trench stops' guarded the fascines (now serving as trench blocks) and the 'trench supports' garrisoned the trench.[24] A simple series of

---

18   Miles, *Military Operations: France and Belgium, 1917, Vol. III.* The creeping barrage is detailed on pp. 26-7 and 30.
19   Ibid. Appendix 9A printed in full on pp. 348-354.
20   Ibid. Appendix 9B printed in full on pp 355-8.
21   Ibid. A partial explanation of the different tactics is given on pp. 34-5.
22   For example, 20th Division faced the fortified village of La Vacquerie. For a detailed summary, see *Landships Homepage* <https://sites.google.com/site/landships/home/narratives/1917/cambrainarratives/tank-tactics-at-cambrai> (Accessed 18 February 2019).
23   Bewsher, *The History of the 51st (Highland) Division 1914–1918*, pp. 238-9.
24   Ibid. Infantry tactics are explained on pp. 232-3.

signals had been devised so the infantry and tank commanders could communicate. The tanks used a green disc to show the wire had been crushed and a red disc to show it was still uncut. Red and green displayed together meant the tank had reached its objective. The infantry waved their rifle above their head when they had reached their objective and placed a helmet on one when they required assistance.[25]

IV Corps, 20 November

The dog-leg nature of No Man's Land on IV Corps' front meant two divisions advanced at 6.20 am on the right bank of the dry Canal du Nord. A third division would move along the left bank at 8.35 am, while a fourth would advance towards Moeuvres during the evening.

Some of tanks were late across 62nd Division's front, so the infantry followed the creeping barrage.[26] They eventually joined the infantry around Havrincourt village and then led the advance across the west end of Grand Ravin and the Hindenburg Support Line. The reserve brigade was to 'keep moving forward and directly the leading brigades had gained their initial success' along the Hindenburg Support Line, next to Canal du Nord.[27] Thermite bombs were used to 'smoke' the Germans out of their dug outs.

The left flank reached the Bapaume-Cambrai road but six tanks were knocked out on the right flank because 51st Division was having problems around Flesquières. Major General Braithwaite's suggestion to move the Scots through his area, to outflank the village, was rejected. His order to stop the advance was not received either and the infantry continued towards Graincourt, while the tanks returned for fuel and ammunition.[28]

Over sixty tanks accompanied 51st Division's advance through Havrincourt Wood towards Flesquières.[29] Field guns knocked out some, others became disorientated and a few ran out of petrol. The infantry then found that the entanglement included V shapes which protruded 200 yards in front of the trench.[30] There was insufficient coordination between the infantry and the tanks and it was hardly surprising. There was no artillery support and there were few officers still standing to make a plan.[31] The Germans knew to scatter whenever a tank approached, only to return to shoot at

---

25   Miles, *Military Operations: France and Belgium, 1917, Vol. III*, p. 357.

26   Wyrall, *The History of the 62nd (West Riding) Division 1914–1919*, pp. 79-82.

27   Miles, *Military Operations: France and Belgium, 1917, Vol. III*, pp. 84-7. The brigade was led by Brigadier Bradford VC, the youngest brigadier in the army at 25 years of age.

28   Wyrall, *The History of the 62nd (West Riding) Division 1914–1919*, pp. 86-9.

29   Bewsher, *The History of the 51st (Highland) Division 1914–1918*. The initial advance is covered on pp. 241-4.

30   Ibid., pp. 244-8.

31   Miles, *Military Operations: France and Belgium, 1917, Vol. III*. The repeated attacks against Flesquières are explained on pp. 57-59.

the infantry when they tried to move forward. A few infantry entered the village, only to be driven out before six tanks crawled down the main street around dusk, but the Germans just hid until they left.[32]

IV Corps headquarters had heard about Flesquières at 2 pm but it was still in German hands at nightfall, six hours after it should have been taken.[33] The division to the left offered to let the Scots pass through its area, to outflank the village, but the suggestion was turned down because 51st Division did not have sufficient reserves. A plan for using the reserve brigade of the division to the right involved talks at corps command level and it took too long to find out if it was feasible.[34]

Around thirty tanks had been knocked out in 51st Division's zone and the infantry was pinned down in front of Flesquières. The traffic was cutting the communication cables faster than the engineers could lay them, while various factors had made visual signalling difficult. No one had told the artillery about the hold up and the gunners had packed up and were waiting to move forward.

On IV Corps' left flank, Stokes mortars fired thermite bombs at the Spoil Heap at 8.35 am, as 62nd Division drew level with it. Four minutes later the men of 36th Division overran it and advanced up the Hindenburg Line.[35] The brigadier had said 'no bombing until other methods failed', so the Lewis gunners 'had a sling over the left shoulder, the gun resting on the right hip' as they sprayed the wide trenches with bullets.[36] The Germans hid in their dug outs and guards stopped them leaving until the moppers up arrived; platoons waved the battalion colours above the trench to report progress.[37]

The 56th Division had staged a 'Chinese attack' around Boursies when the offensive began.[38] Around 250 figures of infantry and a dozen models of tanks were displayed behind a thin smoke screen. Motorbikes in the front trench were revved up to simulate the sound of engines, to complete the charade.[39] The Londoners then waited for the battle to develop.

III Corps, 20 November

Three divisions had to break the Hindenburg Line on III Corps' front, so a fourth could cross the St Quentin Canal between Marcoing and Masnières. Thirty-six tanks

---

32 Bewsher, *The History of the 51st (Highland) Division 1914–1918*, p. 249.

33 Miles, *Military Operations: France and Belgium, 1917, Vol. III*. The deadlock about Flesquières is detailed on p. 84.

34 Ibid. The failure to resolve the situation at Flesquières is covered on pp. 82-4.

35 Ibid., p. 61-2.

36 *Falls, The History of the 36th (Ulster) Division)*, pp. 149-51.

37 Miles, *Military Operations: France and Belgium, 1917, Vol. III*, pp. 84-7.

38 Ibid., p. 88.

39 C. Dudley Ward, *The Fifty Sixth Division 1914–1918 (1st London Territorial Division)* (London, Murray, 1921), pp. 174-5.

led 6th Division forward but some men preferred to stay close to the creeping barrage, rather than wait for them.[40] The Hindenburg Support Line was cleared and then seventeen tanks headed north-west of Marcoing; only four had been knocked out by the time III Corps' left flank was secure around Nine Wood.[41] Another fourteen tanks helped the infantry clear Marcoing and cross the St Quentin Canal.[42]

Eighteen tanks led 20th Division across Couillet valley and several were knocked out crossing Welsh Ridge.[43] The infantry lagged behind past La Vacquerie, as more were knocked out en route to Marcoing. The railway bridge was made safe, so eight tanks could cross the canal but three encountered boggy ground, east of the village. The reserve brigade was unable to capture the Crèvecoeur bridge, while a nearby bridge was too weak for tanks.[44] Seventy-two tanks led 12th Division across the Bonvais Ridge and the only resistance came from the farms the artillery had missed.[45] Less than twenty tanks had been put out of action and the rest led the infantry towards the St Quentin Canal.

Third Army had broken into the German position across a 7-mile-wide front. The number of infantry casualties were low but over one hundred of the tanks were out of action, while the 'runners' needed fuel and ammunition. So far, there had been a 4-mile advance and around 4,200 prisoners and 100 hundred guns had been taken for the cost of approximately 4,000 casualties.

Around 10.30 am, twelve tanks led the 15,000 men and seventy-six artillery teams of 29th Division forward. Battalions and companies were deployed ready to engage any resistance with 'not a single battalion being kept in reserve; but organised opposition was not expected, the operation being regarded as in the nature of a pursuit.'[46] Information was sketchy but Byng was expecting to be across the St Quentin Canal and through the Beaurevoir-Masnières Line by early afternoon. His main concern was that the men were tired after being on the move for over ten hours.

Fourteen tanks waited to help clear the area, north of Marcoing, before turning back for fuel.[47] Only two crossed the canal at Marcoing and they found the infantry pinned down in front of the Beaurevoir-Masnières Line.[48] The infantry saw one tank break down on the Masnières bridge while the damaged bridge collapsed under the weight of a second.[49] Several battalions crossed the canal via nearby footbridges and

40   Ibid. The 6th Division's attack is covered on 54-6.
41   Major General T. Marden (ed.) *A Short History of the 6th Division 1914 to 1919* (London: Hugh Rees, 1920), p. 38.
42   Miles, *Military Operations: France and Belgium, 1917, Vol. III*. The 6th Division's advance to the St Quentin Canal is detailed on pp. 65-7.
43   Ibid., 20th Division's initial advance is covered on pp. 53-4.
44   Ibid., 20th Division's problems along the St Quentin Canal are detailed on pp. 64-5.
45   Ibid., pp. 51-2.
46   Ibid., p. 67. The formation was around 2 miles wide and over 1 mile deep.
47   Ibid. The clearing of the area north of Marcoing is explained on pp. 75-7.
48   Ibid. Attempts to get beyond Marcoing are detailed on pp. 73-5.
49   Ibid. The fight around Masnières is covered on pp. 68-70, 72-3.

lock gates, only to be pinned down in front of the Beaurevoir-Masnières Line. The rest of the tanks had been knocked out or had broken down.

Major General Richard Mullens received orders to move before midday but it was soon clear to 1st Cavalry Division that Flesquières had not been taken. It left thousands of horses and dozens of artillery batteries blocking an 8-mile stretch of road. Two regiments were sent towards Marcoing but neither could cross the canal north of the village.[50] Major General Henry Macandrew received his orders to move after midday and 5th Cavalry Division advanced over 10 miles to reach the action. A couple of squadrons crossed the canal around Marcoing during the early afternoon[51] but the rest jammed the roads back to La Vacquerie, where they were joined by 2nd Cavalry Division. It meant that over 30,000 troopers were backed up, blocking the roads behind Third Army's front. Byng considered sending the cavalry back, because there was insufficient water, but he changed his mind after issuing the orders for the morning attack.[52]

There had been bombardments along the front either side of Third Army. Shrapnel, high-explosives and burning oil made the Germans believe they were under attack, while smoke hid the fact that they were not. Both 55th and 24th Divisions attacked tactical points whilst there were Chinese attacks elsewhere.

21 November

The long advance presented many challenges. The infantry had to dig trenches and erect wire, the engineers had to open roads and the signallers had to extend their communications. The batteries waited until dawn before redeploying and then their observers struggled to find targets in the rain. General Byng wanted IV Corps to capture the wooded Bourlon ridge and push towards Cambrai, while III Corps would go on the defensive along the St Quentin Canal.

Overcrowded roads made all the tanks late, so the infantry advanced alone after a twenty-minute bombardment. All eighteen caught 62nd Division up, only to find the Cantaing Line did not exist,[53] so the infantry fell back to a sunken road.[54] Six tanks helped capture Anneux, but they then had to withdrew because their supply tanks could not get through the traffic.[55]

A machine-gun barrage had been fired at Flesquières throughout the night, resulting in seventeen German crews abandoning their guns. There was no sign of

50   Ibid., pp. 75 and 77-8.
51   Ibid., pp. 69-71. Attempts to stop the cavalry crossing the St Quentin Canal failed and they returned after dark.
52   Ibid., pp. 80-2.
53   The line had only been marked out and the turf cut, a process known as spit-locking. The trenches would have looked deep enough to defend on aerial photographs.
54   Miles, *Military Operations: France and Belgium, 1917, Vol. III*, pp. 111-3.
55   Wyrall, *The History of the 62nd (West Riding) Division 1914–1919*, pp. 102-3.

the tanks when the thirty-minute bombardment ended at dawn and 51st Division waited another thirty before advancing through the deserted village.[56] Again, the Scots discovered that most of the Cantaing Line did not exist but they were pinned down in front of the section protecting Cantaing village. The tanks eventually turned up at midday[57] and cavalry joined them, as they led the infantry through the village. Civilians believed the Germans had fled, but the Scots had orders to wait until 62nd Division had captured Bourlon Wood. Two battalions and several tanks were later told to clear Fontaine, but it left them holding a vulnerable position.

An attack against the Beaurevoir-Masnières Line was delayed until 11 am because it took the artillery time work out where 29th Division's front line was. Seventeen tanks crossed the Marcoing railway bridge but the Germans hid in their dug outs when they approached, emerging to engage the infantry who were lagging behind. The tanks drove parallel with the enemy trenches, 'a change in tactics which prevented the infantry from following close enough...'[58] They remained pinned down and several tanks had been knocked out by the time the survivors withdrew two hours later.

The Germans attacked first east of Masnières and while they were stopped, it meant 29th Division was unable to advance at 11 am.[59] The tanks were left waiting for petrol and orders as 20th Division advanced towards Crèvecoeur, unaware that 29th Division would not be on their left flank. The Germans pulled back when the tanks eventually arrived and then returned when they withdrew for more fuel.[60] It left III Corps straddling the canal. All the infantry could do was to dig in, knowing that Cambrai was only a short distance away.

Third Army's plan for a breakthrough in forty-eight hours had failed but Byng's flawed assessment gave Haig hope.[61] His plan was to regroup on 22 November and then IV Corps would use fresh troops to capture Bourlon ridge, while III Corps' took the Beaurevoir-Masnières Line around Rumilly. Unfortunately, the Germans attacked first, and the British artillery never saw the SOS signals through the mist.[62] By nightfall, 62nd Division had been pushed away from Bourlon Wood, while 51st Division had been driven out of Fontaine.[63]

Only ninety-two tanks were still running, and it was difficult getting fuel and ammunition to them along the crowded roads.[64] The Germans were also getting better at countering them, hiding when they approached, emerging to engage the infantry as soon as they withdrew.

56 Miles, *Military Operations: France and Belgium, 1917, Vol. III*, pp. 108-11.
57 Their orders had arrived late.
58 Miles, *Military Operations: France and Belgium, 1917, Vol. III*, pp. 104-5.
59 Ibid., pp. 102-3.
60 Ibid., pp. 103-4.
61 Ibid. The decision to continue the offensive is discussed on pp. 115-8.
62 Ibid., pp. 121-2.
63 Ibid., pp. 120-1
64 Compared to the 372 fighting tanks engaged only forty-eight hours before.

The artillery focused on hitting targets the left bank of the Canal du Nord on 23 November, where the ground was too soft for tanks.[65] Communications were difficult, so a pigeon was sent back every time a machine-gun post was spotted around Moeuvres and the coordinates were relayed to the heavy artillery. Eleven tanks led 36th Division's attack along the east bank but the decision to group all the guns west of the canal meant the creeping barrage was too weak.[66] It meant the machine-gun teams were able to pin down the Ulstermen, leaving the tanks vulnerable and most were knocked out.

Thirty-three tanks had been allocated to clear Bourlon Wood but the men of 40th Division 'had never seen [them] before and there was no time for much explanation concerning combined tactics.'[67] All the battalion commanders could do, was to tell their officers to follow them as they drove past at 10.10 am. Nineteen had to wait for their petrol to be delivered but the rest helped clear Bourlon. The Germans retook the village when they turned back for fuel. The infantry had cleared half of Bourlon Wood by the time the rest of the tanks caught up, and they reached the north edge. A fierce bombardment and counter-attack drove them back to the centre. A probing attack before midnight made 40th Division give its position away and it spent the rest of the night under accurate artillery fire.

Tanks helped 51st Division clear the east edge of Bourlon Wood, but smoke failed to hide the tanks as they crawled along the tracks around Fontaine.[68] Barricades and tank traps forced them drive in front of hidden anti-tank guns in the village and nineteen had been lost by the end of the day.

Early reports were optimistic but incorrect and both the Cavalry Corps and the Guards Division were put on standby. Later information was more accurate and the cavalry were stood down but the Guardsmen had to endure a 15-mile march to reach the front line. After 'a day full of orders, countermanded orders, new orders and lack of orders' they relieved 51st Division around Fontaine rather than advancing beyond it.[69]

Bourlon Wood, 24-26 November

IV Corps' attack against Bourlon village was postponed to 3 pm after a wet and windy night, so the reliefs could be completed. Unfortunately, the Germans attacked first, driving 40th Division off the two ends of Bourlon ridge by 9 am.[70] Eventually,

65   *Falls, The History of the 36th (Ulster) Division), pp. 163-4.*
66   Miles, *Military Operations: France and Belgium, 1917, Vol. III*, 36th Division's action astride the canal is explained on pp. 132-3.
67   Ibid. The 40th Division's epic fight for Bourlon Wood is covered on pp. 129-32.
68   Ibid. The 51st Division's battle for Fontaine is detailed on pp. 126-9.
69   Cuthbert Headlam, *History of the Guards Division, 1915-18: Vol. II* (London: John Murray, 1924), p. 296.
70   Miles, *Military Operations: France and Belgium, 1917, Vol. III*, pp. 137-8.

a support battalion sent its officers forward to help the forward battalions organise a counter-attack which captured all of the wood.

A late decision not to enter Bourlon failed to reach the front line, and an uncoordinated attack was made against the village.[71] The German infantry hid while anti-tank guns knocked out eight tanks and the survivors were withdrawing by the time the infantry caught up. The Germans emerged to drive half the infantry back, leaving the rest cut off in the north half of the village.

After another stormy night, 6.15 am had been chosen for zero hour on 25 November, to surprise the Germans, but it left 40th Division advancing over unknown ground in the dark.[72] The tanks were late and the artillery dare not shell Bourlon, for fear of hitting their own men, so trench mortars were used as close support in the street fighting. The south half of the village was cleared but the men in the north end ran out of ammunition before they could be rescued. A hailstorm blinded the Germans south-east of Bourlon Wood, but the Guards Division discovered there was no trench on the objective, so they withdrew.

Byng had his lost patience and while he took personal control of the Bourlon front, he was so short of reserves that the 62nd Division had to return to the line. It endured a long night of reliefs in blizzard conditions after having only forty-eight hours rest. The heavy artillery was running short of shells while the late decision to attack at 6.20 am on 27 November meant the plans were rushed. The barrage crept slowly through Bourlon village and wood at 100 yards every five minutes, but it was still too fast for the infantry.[73] Four tanks were knocked out clearing the Marquion line west of Bourlon while another six were hit negotiating barricades, tank traps, rubble and wounded men in Bourlon. Four led the advance through Bourlon Wood only for artillery fire and a counter-attack to push them back.[74]

Major General Feilding thought the Guards Division's order to attack Fontaine was 'a dangerous and impracticable undertaking for which there could no kind of justification'.[75] His men had been 'brought up in the dark through utterly unknown surroundings; given a compass bearing and despatched at dawn into a dense wood.' He also thought the objective was too wide and overlooked by the German position. Feilding was promised all the support Third Army could muster, but the tanks were late and there was no heavy artillery barrage.

There was only time to distribute verbal orders to follow the 'feeble and erratic' barrage and the Guardsmen were pinned down east of Bourlon Wood until four tanks drove past.[76] Another group of tanks cleared Fontaine but there were insufficient men

71   Ibid., pp. 138-9. The infantry had been ordered to remain 200 yards behind the tanks, meaning there was little cooperation between them.
72   Ibid., pp. 144-6.
73   Wyrall, *The History of the 62nd (West Riding) Division 1914-1919, Vol. I*, pp. 116-8.
74   Miles, *Military Operations: France and Belgium, 1917, Vol. III*, pp. 156-8.
75   Headlam, *History of the Guards Division: Vol. II*, p. 306.
76   Miles, *Military Operations: France and Belgium, 1917, Vol. III*, pp. 153-4.

to continue the advance, search the village and guard the prisoners. The remaining eight tanks bogged down in soft ground south of the village.

Feilding's prediction proved to be correct because his men were left in a vulnerable position after the surviving eleven tanks turned back for fuel. A counter-attack prompted some of the prisoners to escape, while more Germans emerged from the cellars.[77] All the reinforcements could do was form a rally line, as their comrades abandoned Fontaine. It was the last offensive operation of the Cambrai campaign.

German Counter-Attack, 30 November-1 December

Some thought the Germans were preparing to counter-attack as the fighting around Bourlon Wood came to a close. Large numbers of troops were reported around Cambrai, smoke was being used to hide activity along the St Quentin Canal, aerial spotters were registering the artillery and a new wireless group had been detected.[78] However, both Byng and Pulteney dismissed the reports as rumours.

VII Corps' line was stretched thin and General Snow had told his divisional commanders on 25 November that Banteux ravine was the danger point.[79] Byng's chief of staff, Major General Louis Vaughan, and Snow's chief of staff, Brigadier General Burnett-Stuart, drew the same conclusion three days later.[80] But both GHQ and Third Army remained convinced that the Germans were too exhausted to attack and no warning orders were issued.

Lieutenant General Snow received no reinforcements and he had to make his own arrangements with III Corps for extra artillery support.[81] It left 55th Division stretched out across a 7-mile front[82] and the instruction to the 1/5th South Lancashires in Banteux ravine summarises the situation: 'In case of enemy attack, all posts and trenches will be held to the last at all costs and there will be no retirement from any line to another line.'[83] The Germans were indeed preparing to attack Third Army at several points.[84] The Arras Group had taken over the line opposite IV Corps, the Caudry Group faced III Corps and Busigny Group moved into position opposite VII Corps. On 27 November, Crown Prince of Bavaria, Rupprecht, set the date for 30 November.

---

77   Ibid., pp. 154-6.
78   Major General J Latter, *The History of the Lancashire Fusiliers, 1914-1918, Vol. I* (Aldershot: Gale and Polden, 1949), p. 271
79   Miles, *Military Operations: France and Belgium, 1917, Vol. III.* VII Corps precarious situation is explained pp. 166-7.
80   Ibid. The conversation is recorded on p. 169.
81   Ibid., pp. 171-2. Local arrangements had to be made at divisional level as well.
82   Rev. J Coop, *The Story of the 55th Lancashire Division, 1916-1919* (Liverpool: Daily Post Printers, , 1919), pp. 72-3.
83   TNA WO 95/2929/2: 1/5th South Lancashires War Diary.
84   Miles, *Military Operations: France and Belgium, 1917, Vol. III.* Details of Crown Prince Rupprecht's plans are given on pp. 173-5.

Busigny Group Attacks, VII Corps, 30 November

Everyone stood to before dawn and the German gunners opened fire at 6.05 am, slowly intensifying their bombardment to a crescendo as the minutes ticked by. Gas and high explosive shells hit the artillery while more gas shells thickened the morning mist. The gunners were firing as fast as they could when the German infantry attacked 55th Division's line at 7.05 am.[85] It only consisted 'of platoon posts connected by travel trenches' and there were 'few men left alive in the front line to offer much resistance after the barrage lifted.'[86]

The advance then followed a formula which would become familiar over the next six months. Scouts located the British strongpoints in the morning, so assault teams armed with light machine guns and flamethrowers could follow Banteux ravine and sunken roads without being noticed, before fanning out behind them.[87] The infantry regularly fired flares to indicate progress to the heavy artillery, while the field guns followed the advance. The Lancashire men did indeed hold to the last, leaving their commanders wondering what had happened.[88]

Flares soon indicated that the Germans had reached Villers Guislain, forcing the British gunners to disable and abandon their guns.[89] The reserve 'companies were quickly in position, fire was opened and great execution was done',[90] as they fought on in the support line into the afternoon. Lewis gun teams gave covering fire while flares coordinated the withdrawals when it was dark. The fight had cost 55th Division dearly but the 'attack had been held and checked.'[91]

The reserves were joined by infantry and cavalry about Peizière, Epéhy and Lempire, while squadrons from 5th Cavalry Division tried to capture Gauche Wood.[92] Snow was told to fortify all the villages behind VII Corps' line while three cavalry divisions moved closer. Byng expected the Germans would advance towards Metz, across the base of Third Army's salient, and he was planning to counter-attack their flank around Gouzeaucourt and Villers Guislain.

Busigny and Caudry Groups Attack, III Corps, 30 November

German infantry followed Banteux ravine into 12th Division's rear and the survivors fell back through Gauche Wood.[93] A mixed group of stragglers then withdrew, moving

---

85   Ibid., pp. 176-7. The advance started while it was still dark.
86   TNA WO 95/2926/2: 1/6th King's (Liverpool) Regiment War Diary.
87   Miles, *Military Operations: France and Belgium, 1917, Vol. III*, pp. 177.
88   Ibid., pp. 177-9.
89   Ibid., pp. 179-82.
90   TNA WO 95/2924/1: 1/4th Loyal North Lancashire War Diary.
91   Coop, *The Story of the 55th Lancashire Division, 1916-1919*, pp. 74-82.
92   Miles, *Military Operations: France and Belgium, 1917, Vol. III*, pp. 191-2.
93   Ibid., pp. 185-6.

one platoon at a time back to Chapel Hill, where they were joined by the division's reserves. Some of the Germans headed for Gonnelieu and no one saw the SOS signals through the mist. The field guns continued firing until the last minute next to the infantry along the Péronne-Cambrai road. However, the heavy batteries could not engage targets at short range while it took their transport too long to reach them.[94]

Assault parties infiltrated 12th Division's thin line along Bonvais Ridge during a relief, while the supports dealt with the strongpoints.[95] Some men made suicidal counter-attacks while the rest fell back, trying to keep order by combining fire and movement. The Germans were more reckless, often overtaking the British and the support troops sometimes hesitated before they too were overrun. Stragglers helped the Lewis gun teams protect the batteries and some British gunners hauled their guns out of the pits to open direct fire. They would disable their guns and make their escape after they ran out of ammunition. All the heavy machine-guns had been deployed as anti-aircraft guns and every one was lost.[96] A few brave officers held on in the Hindenburg trenches until dusk, stopping the Germans crossing La Vacquerie valley.

Sentries had been unable to see the St Quentin Canal around Crèvecoeur on a clear day, while smoke, gas and mist blinded them even more. The trenches had been shelled when 55th Division and then 12th Division had been attacked, while a third barrage kept 20th Division under cover until the Caudry Group attacked at 8 am.[97] German infantry then 'advanced in a succession of from eight to twelve waves, preceded by a great number of low-flying aeroplanes which rained machine-gun fire on the troops and dropped smoke bombs to screen the assaulting lines.' The defensive measures organised between VII Corps and III Corps failed because the artillery could not see the SOS flares and many batteries only realised what was happening when stragglers moved past their positions.

Major General Douglas Smith decided to use 20th Division's reserves to cover La Vacquerie, after hearing that siege batteries were withdrawing through Villers Plouich, 2 miles behind his front line. He could also see that Gonnelieu had been lost, so stragglers were made to extend the line along Cemetery Ridge and Fusilier Ridge.

Two of 29th Division's brigades were covering Masnières, on the far bank of the St Quentin Canal.[98] The German guns extended their range at 7 am and one officer reported he had 'never seen so many Germans in his life before'. The line around Masnières held but the men holding La Vacquerie were pushing the Germans towards the battery positions and les Rues Vertes behind 29th Division's right flank. The reserve brigade was 2 miles away and it was down to a handful of signallers and

94   Ibid., the loss of Gonnelieu is covered on pp. 192-4.
95   Ibid., pp. 198-201.
96   No Man's Land was too wide for them to be any use.
97   Miles, *Military Operations: France and Belgium, 1917, Vol. III*, pp. 201-5.
98   Ibid. The 29th Division's defence is chronicled on pp. 205-9.

orderlies to stop them taking the canal bridges. They held on until two companies crossed the canal, to help them drive the Germans out the village.

Major General Beauvoir De Lisle heard that one brigade was 'fighting for its life' near Marcoing, so he ordered his reserve brigade to counter-attack around 9 am.[99] The 'platoons combined fire and movement' and 'helped each other... keeping line and direction admirably and maintaining the advance steadily'. The brigade also covered the divisional artillery while it fired until the last minute before escaping from Couillet Wood.

The single attack against Cantaing was stopped by 6th Division's artillery.[100] It meant that Major General Thomas Marden was able to redeploy his batteries to support 12th Division and send one brigade to reinforce the line to the south.

Arras Group Attacks IV Corps

The Germans had been told there was little to stop them but they were late and it was light by the time observers spotted them assembling in the open. A slow barrage built up to a crescendo by 10.15 am and the guns then extended their range while 56th Division watched as 'a most extraordinary sight followed. Mounted officers led the masses of German infantry' west of the Canal du Nord.[101]

Each man had a specific task, according to the weapon he carried. The rifle grenadiers fired volleys of grenades at the German trench,[102] while the Lewis gun teams swept No Man's Land. The riflemen waited until the Germans were close, while the bombers waited out of sight, ready to drive out anyone who entered the trenches. Time after time, the Germans came forward and they were stopped each time.[103] Runners and pigeons took back messages but the message was always 'I am holding on – but hard pressed'.

There was a similar successful defence by 2nd Division around the canal.[104] The German 'front ranks were cut to pieces, caught in the concentrated fire from artillery, Lewis and machine guns and rifles. But as one wave was swept away another took its place: all were bloodily repulsed.' The Germans east of the canal did not extend into open order, choosing to advance 'in full marching order with packs and evidently thought they would break right through.'

A 'box barrage' cut the men holding Lock 5 off but a council of war agreed they were 'unanimously determined to fight to the last' when they were running low on

---

99   Ibid. The 29th Division's counter-attack is detailed on 209-10.
100   Ibid., pp. 210-1.
101   Ibid., pp. 218-21.
102   The trench was a fixed range target where the Germans had to assemble to deploy.
103   Everard Wyrall, *The History of Second Division 1914-18, Vol. 2* (London: Thomas Nelson & Sons, 1921), pp. 485-94. Five attacks were made.
104   Miles, *Military Operations: France and Belgium, 1917, Vol. III*, pp. 215-8.

ammunition.[105] They refused to surrender and were overrun during the night. The Germans reached the Bapaume-Cambrai road after the rearguards 'fell fighting to the last'. 'When night fell it was found that certain small posts had been swamped, each one dying to a man and with a full toll of the enemy in front.'[106]

Bourlon Wood was hit by gas and high explosive shells since before dawn and it made the 'air became heavy with gas and there was no wind to scatter it. It was a crowded area, extremely inconvenient and poisonous' and many men had to be evacuated. Just before 9 am the guns switched targets, low flying aeroplanes strafed the trenches west of the ridge, and the attack was made against 47th Division.[107]

Guards Division Counter-Attack

Gouzeaucourt was the danger point but it was also a shell trap. Every available man was sent to the Revelon ridge to the south-west with orders 'to hold on to the last man and cover the retirement of the others.' They were met by 'gunners carrying their dial-sights, infantry in stray groups, some throwing away their Lewis guns and others without rifles, all wearing a hunted look and all hurrying back...' The sights were 'enough to dishearten the stoutest'.[108] They could see the 'Germans advancing in the most perfect order, entirely unopposed' through Gouzeaucourt when the mist cleared. They had captured dozens of supply wagons and five batteries of heavy howitzers but the Guards Division was about to meet them head on.

Twenty-seven tanks drove towards Gouzeaucourt only to withdraw when they saw the Germans had already taken it.[109] Three Guards battalions and a regiment of cavalry then advanced towards the village without any artillery or tank support and drove the Germans back, while 20th Division's line fired into their flank. It meant the rest of the Guards battalions and two tank battalions could move up to reinforce the line along the Quentin ridge. Twenty-two tanks counter-attacked at 3.15 pm but they withdrew to reinforce the Guards because there was no smoke to cover them.

30 November Summary

Byng's headquarters told GHQ about the German offensive at 10 am and Haig headed to Albert to speak to him. He confirmed reinforcements would be sent and the schedule of their arrival was telephoned through during the evening. A brief

---

105 Wyrall, *The History of Second Division 1914-18, Vol. 2*, pp. 495-6.
106 Ibid., p. 221. The IV Corps' successful defence was written up in a GHQ pamphlet called *The Story of a Great Fight*.
107 Ibid., pp. 214-5.
108 TNA WO 95/721/1: 1/4th Royal Welsh Fusiliers War Diary.
109 Miles, *Military Operations: France and Belgium, 1917, Vol. III*. The advance onto the Quentin Ridge is covered on pp. 189-91.

summary illustrates how fast the BEF could react.[110] Three divisions which had just left the area were sent back to the battlefield. Trains were organised to deliver an infantry brigade to Third Army every hour and three divisions would arrive over the next forty-eight hours. The first field batteries would arrive on 2 December and the larger guns would follow two days later.[111] Haig had also arranged French support and two infantry divisions were put on standby 10 miles south of Third Army while two cavalry divisions deployed along the Somme River.

Counter-Attack, 1 December

Pulteney and Snow only had a few infantry reserves left but batteries were redeploying ready to meet the next attack. The gunners knew exactly where the British trenches were as well as the roads the Germans were using, so they had plenty of targets. Their limbers were now kept close to the batteries, ready to pull the guns out of the line if they were threatened.

A counter-attack was planned for 6.30 am but it was difficult to deploy in the dark. One brigadier did not hear about the dawn zero hour and so he made his own surprise attack with men from 20th and 6th Divisions at 1 am. Some were stopped by fire around Gonnelieu while others became disorientated in the dark. Pulteney only heard of the attempt just before the Guards advanced.

IV Corps, Moeuvres to Bourlon

Lieutenant General Sir Edward Fanshawe and V Corps replaced Lieutenant General Charles Woollcombe and IV Corps staff.[112] The fighting along the Canal du Nord continued throughout the night and day, with 2nd Division refusing to give up any ground. The rest of IV Corps thinned out its front line, to create a reserve, which could build a support line south of the Bourlon ridge.[113] But Byng was still concerned that the Germans would push III Corps further back and destabilise both lines.

The Congreve Caudry Group's attack had left 29th Division in a vulnerable salient astride the St Quentin Canal.[114] The Germans shelled and attacked the head of the salient, rather than the flanks, throughout 1 December but Major General De Lisle had no reserves to reinforce it. Two brigadiers recommended abandoning the area but the Germans decided the issue before the third was asked for his opinion. They rushed the line south of the canal but the men in Rues Vertes hung on. The fighting died down at dusk and Lewis gun teams gave covering fire while the men carried their

---

110 Ibid. The full schedule is detailed on pp. 220-2.
111 Third Army lost sixty guns on 30 November.
112 Woollcombe and Pulteney were subsequently relieved of command; Snow was sent home at his own request.
113 Miles, *Military Operations: France and Belgium, 1917, Vol. III*, pp. 246-7.
114 Ibid., pp. 244-6.

wounded and ammunition through Masnières under bright moonlight; any spare ammunition was buried or thrown into the canal.

Both 12th Division and 20th Division held on around La Vacquerie and Gonnelieu[115] but the Guards Division had found it difficult to assemble for a dawn attack because its orders were issued late. Major General Feilding had no artillery support, some of the forty promised tanks got lost in the dark, while the rest had to wait for their petrol. None joined the attack, while the barrage missed Gonnelieu, leaving the Guardsmen to fight a desperate battle they could not win.[116] A single tank would save the day when it turned up late. Eight tanks led the advance across Quentin ridge but another twelve were late and they eventually reinforced the attack on Gauche Wood. The Guards Division may have only gained a little ground, but it had stopped the German advance towards Metz.

The tanks also arrived late on 5th Cavalry Division's front and then headed the wrong direction in the mist.[117] The cavalrymen reinforced the Guardsmen in Gauche Wood but the tanks headed for Villers Guislain when they eventually turned up. They came under heavy fire and headed to their assembly point, short of petrol, leaving it to Guards and the cavalry to secure Gauche Wood.

The 4th Cavalry Division was to secure the area south of Villers Guislain, to help 55th Division hold its line on 1 December. However, the squadrons found it difficult to deploy in the dark, because one assembly point was changed just before zero.[118] There was no time to redeploy nor tell the artillery to change targets, while the six tanks could not find the start line. One commander held his regiment back, because he thought it was suicidal to advance, but the rest of the two brigades went forward, even though they had no idea where the front line was.

The third brigade was late because one regiment had to retrieve their lancers and their brigadier protested that it was pointless sending his men forward where twice the number had just failed. Major General Alfred Kennedy insisted and most of the squadrons came under heavy fire from Villers Guislain and headed back to Peizière. Several squadrons went on a wild charge along Catelet Valley and while they reached trenches overlooking Targelle Ravine, they were cut off. Troopers were sent forward on foot to help but they were unable to rescue them. Another attack at 3 pm scattered the Germans around Chapel Crossing and Gauche Wood but it was impossible to reach Villers Guislain, so a new line was formed west of the village.

The two cavalry divisions had been unable to recapture the ground lost by 55th Division; they had been too few in numbers and they had insufficient artillery or tank support. They spent the night digging in while the cut off troopers made a difficult withdrawal along Catelet Valley. The cavalry not taken any ground but they had

---

115 Ibid., pp. 242-4.
116 Ibid., pp. 240-2.
117 Ibid., pp. 236-7.
118 Ibid., pp. 235-6.

stopped the German attack against VII Corps. Snow was later pleased to hear that 21st Division was about to relieve the weakened 55th Division.

Withdrawing to a New Line

Third Army was holding Bourlon ridge but the slightest setback would allow German observers to see across its rear. However, the first to withdraw was 29th Division from astride the St Quentin Canal.[119] Masnières was abandoned in time and then 6th Division took over but two battalions were cut off and the men had to swim to escape. The canal bridges around Marcoing were blown early on 4 December while the river bridges were prepared for demolition. The Germans attacked 61st Division's position around La Vacquerie on 2 December and they secured an observation point on Welsh Ridge over the following twenty-four hours.[120]

Haig and Byng agreed to pull back to the Flesquières Ridge, a withdrawal of around 2 miles, and the order was issued on 4 December.[121] The engineers spent the day setting explosives and booby traps while the infantry removed or burnt everything they could. Batteries fired random barrages while the 'withdrawal was made from the left by platoons: one platoon remained behind in the centre company's frontage to cover the withdrawal.' The troops stopped at the 'Covering Position', code named the Yellow Line, about 1 mile to the rear. Some work had been done on it but labourers had found that the 'ground was frozen solid for about a foot or more'. The rear guards followed an hour later, as the engineers detonated their explosives.

There was no interference and it was late afternoon before the Germans realised and they dug in some 600 yards from the new line during the night. The whole operation was then repeated taking IV Corps back to Boursies and Flesquières and V Corps back to the Hindenburg Support line, where they had a good view of No Man's Land. Work then started on three defensive zones; the forward area, the battle area and the rear area.[122]

The Germans wanted more of Welsh Ridge, so they bombarded 63rd Division's position with gas shells all night and then targeted it with high explosive shells at dawn. Flamethrower teams and pioneers dressed in white infiltrated the line in the mist at 6.45 am on 30 December but they could not take the position.[123]

119 Ibid., pp. 250-1, 253-5.
120 Ibid., pp. 249-50.
121 Ibid. The decision to withdraw is discussed on pp. 257-9.
122 Ibid. The withdrawal process is chronicled on pp. 262-7.
123 Ibid., pp. 269-71.

The Cambrai Campaign Summary

The Tank Corps needed good ground to try out its tactics en mass and the opportunity came near Cambrai on 20 November 1917. The artillery used firing ranges to calibrate their guns and weather reports to make sure their guns could fire accurately at targets without registering. That meant less ammunition had to be stockpiled and the ground would not be churned up. Complex deception plans also meant the infantry, artillery and tanks could deploy in secret. The assault troops were given time to practice with the tanks but they also developed their own tactics for clearing and consolidated the captured trenches.

The attack went well in most sectors but German anti-tank tactics, such as those used around Flesquières, illustrated that the tanks were still vulnerable if the infantry did not stay with them. They also suffered from a lack of repair, maintenance and fuelling facilities, which reduced their effectiveness on the second and subsequent days.

The tanks could break in but they could not break out and while there was plenty of cavalry on stand-by, they could not get forward quick enough. If anything, they made the situation worse by blocking the roads, stopping other troops getting forward. The long advance also presented problems for the artillery because they had to re-deploy and establish contact with the front line, before they could give supporting fire. Disorganised attacks then followed as the tanks and infantry failed to work together, allowing the Germans to deal with each in turn.

The later stages of the battle deteriorated into an infantry battle for Bourlon Wood in awful weather. Then the Germans struck back, after Third Army had ignored all the signs that a counter-offensive was due. The belated attack against the north flank of the Cambrai salient failed in the face of a well-organised defence but the one to the south succeeded in the fog. Success was short-lived in the face of brave last stands and impromptu counter-attacks and the situation was quickly stabilised with the help of reinforcements. A well-organised withdrawal left Third Army holding a strong front, but had abandoned most of the ground it had taken on 20 November.

7

The German Somme Offensive
21 March-5 April 1918

Vladimir Lenin signed the Decree of Peace on 26 October 1917, while the Bolsheviks rebelled on 7 November; the White Army then counter-attacked in a Russian Civil War. Lenin's new Russian Soviet Federative Socialist Republic signed an armistice with the Central Powers on 15 December and a peace treaty was signed on 3 March 1918.

Germany began moving divisions from the Eastern Front, at a rate of ten divisions a month, until there were 195 on the Western Front by the end of March.[1] Allied strategy was now in the hands of the Supreme War Council and Haig told his army commanders to make their defensive plans once the battle of Cambrai ended at the beginning of December.

The BEF was under-strength after a demanding 1917 and while the men were tired, morale was good. Haig announced on 3 December that 'Army commanders should give their immediate and personal attention to the organisation of the zones for defensive purposes and to the rest and training of the troops.'[2] However, they were short of 100,000 men and there was a lot of work to be done before the inevitable German attacks began. On 14 December GHQ announced it wanted three defensive zones; the Forward Zone, the Battle Zone and the Rear Zone, each 1 to 2 miles deep.[3] Each army, corps and divisions had to draw up defensive plans covering a range of issues including trench layouts, artillery barrages, and the deployment of reserves and reinforcements. Administrative issues included the allocation of labour, management of railheads, distribution of supplies, casualty and refugee evacuation and the control of traffic. Staff also had to consider how their position might be attacked and how

---

1   Sir James E. Edmonds, *Military Operations: France and Belgium, 1918, Vol. I: The German March Offensive and its Preliminaries* (London: HMSO, 1935). The transfer of divisions is outlined on p. 49.
2   Ibid., p. 37.
3   Ibid. Defensive preparations are discussed on pp. 38-9.

to defend against each scenario. Instructions were written up and maps were drawn ready to be handed over to the next division.

It was all relevant but there were too many tasks and too few men.[4] The front trenches were often poorly sited, and it was difficult to improve them under fire. It was easier to improve the Battle Zone but there were few men available to work on the Rear Zone.[5] The problem was there was hardly anyone left by the time all the essential tasks had been carried out.

The BEF's problems were intensified when Haig was forced to extend the BEF's sector as far south as St Quentin by mid-January and then to the River Oise by the end of the month. Soldiers reported the French trenches were in a poor state and there was no one left to improve them.[6]

Reorganising the BEF

The War Office reported it could not keep sending men to the Western Front at the beginning of November 1917, because every able-bodied man was needed for the nation's industry, for shipping and in other theatres. Haig warned he would have to break up a quarter of his divisions if he did not receive 600,000 men to replace the casualties.[7] The Ministry of National Service only had 100,000 available and so the BEF faced having to reduce the number of infantry battalions in each division from twelve down to nine; other arms had to be reduced as well.[8] The BEF was reorganised in February and many Territorial battalions were merged while many New Army battalions were disbanded; 150 battalions would cease to exist. Only the colonial divisions stayed at twelve battalions.[9]

German Offensive, 21 March

The Germans were going on the offensive against the British for the first time in three years. By dawn on 21 March, sixty-two divisions were poised to attack Third and Fifth Armies. GHQ knew a large attack was imminent and knew the limits of it, as detailed in its Weekly Summary of Intelligence on 10 March. Aerial observers had seen many new ammunition dumps and light railways, while deserters and prisoners reported plenty of activity. The summary a week later reported the many signs that were 'definite indications that the Germans are completing their preparations for an

---

4   Ibid. Fifth Army's shortage of labour units is detailed on p. 99.
5   Ibid. Further discussion about the three defensive preparations is on pp. 41-3.
6   Ibid., pp. 47-8.
7   Ibid. General Jan Smuts' report on the BEF's morale, its shortage of men and its defences at the end of January 1918 is on pp. 40-1.
8   Ibid. Manpower issues and decisions are explained in detail on pp. 49-53.
9   Ibid. Reorganisation of the BEF is detailed on pp. 53-5.

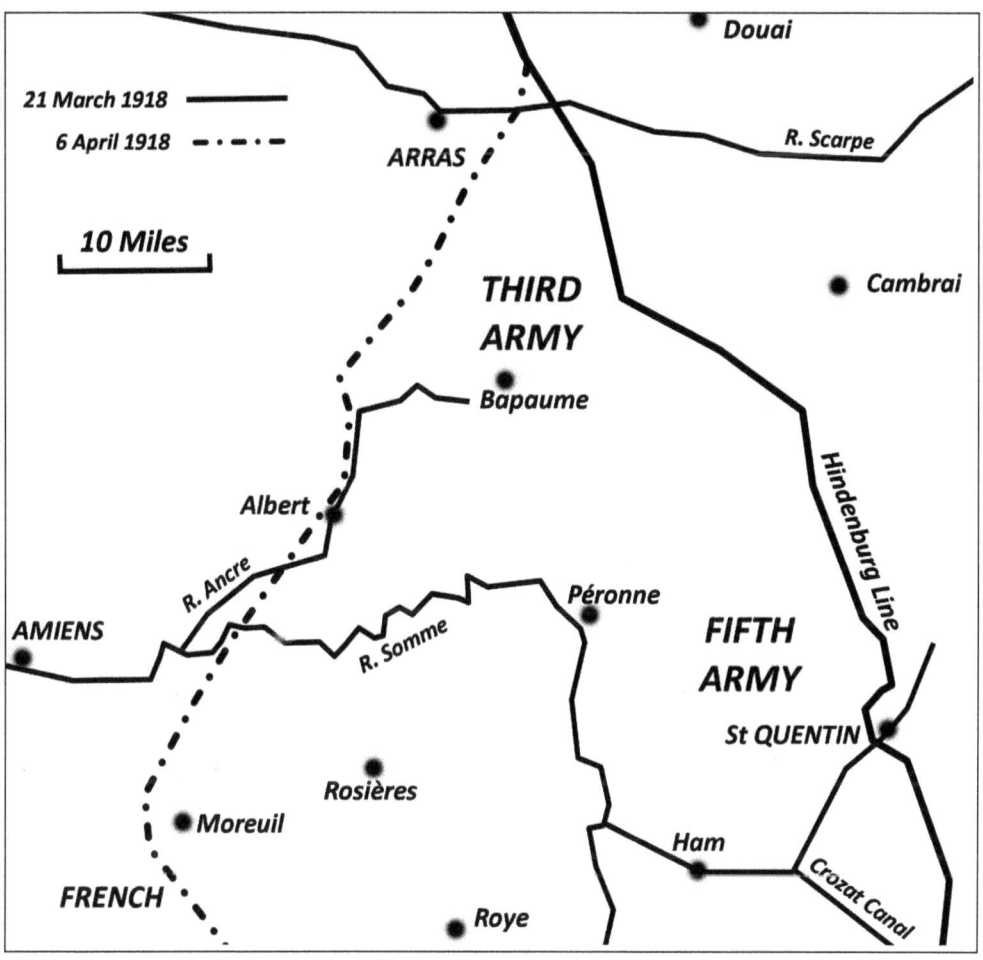

Map 7. German Somme Offensive: 21 March to 6 April: Repeated attacks forced Third Army to give up the 1916 Somme battlefield while Fifth Army was forced back towards Amiens.

attack.'[10] On 21 March Fifth Army's Intelligence Summary ended with the words, the 'enemy's preparations are practically complete.'[11]

Oberst Georg Bruchmüller had been given the task of designing the barrage and he had divided the guns into three groups.[12] The rapid firing guns of the Counter Artillery Groups would smother the British batteries with gas. The long-range guns of the Deep Battle Artillery Groups would neutralise the British communications system. The Infantry Artillery Groups were divided into four sub-groups; two armed with howitzers and super howitzers and two with field guns. They would hit the trenches and wire before zero hour and then provide the creeping barrage.

The guns opened fire across a 70-mile front at 4.40 am[13] with a mixture of two high explosive shells to every nine gas shells, mixing tear gas and mustard gas. At the same time, mortars fire equal number of gas and high explosive shells at the trenches.[14] The trench mortars halted after twenty minutes but the field guns and howitzers continued firing for another one hundred minutes. There was a ten-minute burst of high explosive shells against the Forward Zone at 5.30 am, while gas shells hit the second position. The counter-battery crews then rested for ten minutes, to rest, before resuming fire. The guns selected to create the creeping barrage checked their ranges in three groups of ten minutes, starting at 6.40 am. All the Infantry Artillery Groups then fired two short, but intense bombardments of high explosive and gas, against strongpoints and targets behind the first position.

A final crescendo of fire by all guns at 7.35 am told the infantry to deploy in No Man's Land. The Infantry Artillery Groups then created six belts of fire; howitzers, trench mortars, field guns, super heavy howitzers, deep battle batteries and heavy trench mortars. The rest of the guns switched to hitting the second line of trenches. Five minutes later, the barrage jumped 300 yards and then stopped for three minutes while scouts led the assault troops across No Man's Land. It was an 'assault without hurrahs', leaving the British guessing what was happening, and the men had orders to 'keep close behind the barrage regardless of shell splinters', to avoid the worst of the British machine-gun fire.[15]

The field artillery, 5.9-inch howitzers and light mortars extended their range by 200 yards every four minutes while the heavy guns jumped forward 400 yards every eight minutes. The infantry followed, firing green flares every 200 metres if they were delayed, so the gunners could adjust their range.[16] Flame thrower teams would also shoot squirts of flames so the aerial observers could follow progress. Scouts located

---

10   Ibid. The relevant sections of the two intelligence summaries are given on pp. 107-8.
11   Ibid., p. 110.
12   Ibid., The organisation of the German artillery is covered on p. 159.
13   Ibid. The seven stages of the preliminary bombardment are detailed on pp. 159-60.
14   Ibid. The mixed shelling of targets is explained on p. 158.
15   Ibid., p. 160.
16   Ibid. The creeping barrage is described on p. 160.

centres of resistance, the lightly armed assault teams bypassed them, and heavy armed support teams surrounded them.[17]

The bombardment had wrecked the Forward Zone and there was little resistance, so the German 'Storm Troops' moved fast through the fog, to reach the fortified zones before the garrisons knew what was happening. Communications with battalion and brigade headquarters had been cut and the German storm troops were moving faster than the British runners. Reserves discovered that the Battle Zone trenches were battered and reeked of gas. The gunners knew something was afoot but they had no information and their observers were blinded by the mist. All they could do was fire at pre-determined targets, unaware that the enemy batteries had relocated during the night.[18]

Smoke and mist cleared from the ridges mid-morning, but it did not clear from the valleys until after midday. The aerial observers were supposed to report the enemy batteries using target zone codes, because they were easier to transmit than map references.[19] However, most battery commanders were busy responding to calls for help from the nearest infantry units. It meant that the few zone codes transmitted were ignored in the chaos. The spotters were also supposed to track the enemy infantry, but they often found it difficult to distinguish between British and German troops. Spare squadrons were sent to strafe and bomb targets behind the lines but it was soon found that it was easier to shoot up the crowded roads, rather than trying to find targets off a map.[20]

Third Army, 21 March

The attack against Third Army's left started two hours after the main attack.[21] Smoke was used to thicken up the mist, as the assault troops overran 59th Division's line, and 'what happened to these companies is not known as they were never seen again'.[22] Some followed the Hirondelle stream while others turned north towards Bullecourt, planning to wheel north behind 34th Division's flank. They captured Ecoust ridge and then turned against the British line to the left and right. Those who fell back to the Battle Zone found nothing more than a 'spit-locked' line of cut turf and had to search for entrenching tools to dig with. The reserves found themselves having to fight

17 Ibid. Quotes obtained from a series of pamphlets titled; 'The preparation of the German army for the Great Battle of France in the spring of 1918' provided on pp. 156-7.
18 Ibid. The problems, particularly the cutting of communications, experienced during the first few hours are detailed on pp. 166-8.
19 Ibid., p. 168.
20 Ibid. A summary of the Royal Flying Corps' contribution is on p. 169.
21 Ibid. The VI Corps' early fight is covered on pp. 228-40.
22 Editor: Major General CR Simpson: *The History of the Lincolnshire Regiment 1914-1918* (London: Medici Society, 1931) p. 299.

off 'wave after wave of grey figures advancing over the Hog's Back, undismayed by the heavy losses inflicted on them.'[23]

A feint attack drew 34th Division's reserves from the left flank before the main attack hit the right flank, where 59th Division had been forced back. Many were captured in fighting 'of a ding-dong nature' as the survivors were driven back to the Battle Zone.[24] An afternoon attack failed to take Hénin Hill from 3rd Division after the Germans 'were shaken and scattered by the mad-minute practice' but a flank had to be formed, where 34th Division had fallen back.[25]

VI Corps had ordered 40th Division forward to hold the Battle Zone at midday but there was little news from the front, apart from that the Germans had broken.'[26] The line was secured but the incomplete Green Line was the only defensive line and it was only a short distance behind.

Both the Forward and Battle Zones across IV Corps sector were on forward slopes and they were 'wholly unsuitable both in construction and siting for the purpose for which they were now required.' Redoubts were connected by short lengths of narrow crumbling ditches, which, partly owing to the rank growth of thistles and other weeds, and partly to their siting, had practically no field of fire.'[27]

The Germans followed three valleys, hidden by the mist, driving 6th and 51st Divisions back towards Lagnicourt.[28] Late in the day, Lieutenant General Harper instructed both commanding officers to break contact and withdraw to the back to Battle Zone when it was dark. They were met by 25th Division as it deployed astride the Cambrai road.[29]

The Germans had no intention of attacking the Flesquières salient and instead planned to push past its flanks, to trap V Corps in a pincer movement. Astride the Canal du Nord, the 'impression that evening was that things were going well' for 17th Division, although there were concerns that 51st Division had been driven back on its left flank. Elsewhere across the salient, the Germans staged raids and shelled it with so much mustard gas that it was the 'density of a London fog'.[30] Byng obtained Haig's approval to abandon the area but it would be dawn before the battalions received their orders and they then had to move across the gas saturated ground.[31]

23   J. Shakespear, *The Thirty-Fourth Division, 1915–1919*, p. 186.
24   Edmonds, *Military Operations: France and Belgium, 1918, Vol. I.* The later battle on VI Corps' front is covered on pp. 240-4.
25   TNA WO 95/1423/5: 2nd Royal Scots War Diary.
26   TNA WO 95/2614/2: 121 Brigade War Diary.
27   Bewsher, *The History of the 51st (Highland) Division 1914-18*; both quotes are on p. 265.
28   Edmonds, *Military Operations: France and Belgium, 1918, Vol. I.* The attack against IV Corps is described on pp. 220-7.
29   Ibid. The latter fighting on IV Corps' front is covered on pp. 244-8.
30   Ibid., p. 219.
31   Ibid., p. 49. The consensus of officers present, was 'that it would have been wise, if a retirement from the salient had been ordered directly the signs of a German offensive became mistakeable.'

Fifth Army, 21 March

Lieutenant General Gough was responsible for 42 miles of front and his divisions were stretched thin. His Forward Zone was well developed, and the Battle Zone was half built but hardly anything had been done to the Rear Zone.

The north end of VII Corps' line was not attacked because it was part of the Flesquières salient while 9th Division's right flank was holding on.[32] The Forward Zone and Battle Zone almost touched around Peizière and Epéhy and the Germans were soon through 21st Division's line. Many were caught in the open when the mist lifted from the Heudicourt valley, but those who turned north reported that the 'Leicester Brigade at Epéhy gave us the most trouble'.[33]

The real trouble occurred when the Germans overran 16th Division's Forward Zone, astride the St Quentin Canal. They pushed through the Battle Zone in the mist and continued to advance down the Cologne valley. They then turned north, heading for Ronssoy, at the back of the Battle Zone. A counter-attack against Ronssoy ended in disaster because two out of three battalions were held back. It left Lieutenant General Walter Congreve having to send 39th Division to hold the back of the Battle Zone. So, 'it came as a huge surprise to General Tudor when he was ordered to withdraw [9th Division] to the Battle Zone during the night' because of the breakthrough to the south.

Mist hid the troops moving along the Cologne and Omignon valleys but it had cleared by the time the Germans reached redoubts across 66th and 24th Divisions' Battle Zone.[34] A brave stand gave the garrison of Le Verguier time to deploy but XIX Corps had to send 1st Cavalry Division to the back of the Battle Zone when Vermand was threatened.

Lieutenant General Ivor Maxse's plan had been for the troops to withdraw into XVIII Corps' redoubts, so the field batteries could cover the gaps between them. But the Germans were on top of most of the redoubts and batteries before the mist had cleared.

The men holding 61st Division's Forward Zone had 'simply fought it out on the spot and their heroism will live for ever in the annals of their regiments...' The redoubts held on, but a flank had to be thrown back until a counter-attack stalled the German advance along the Omignon stream.[35] Again, the Forward Zone was overrun but 30th Division's redoubts, like Manchester Hill, held on until the mist had cleared. The strongpoints across the Battle Zone then targeted the columns of German troops advancing towards them. The assault teams broke through 36th Division's east flank

32   Ibid. The early part of the attack against VII Corps is covered on pp. 180-2, 190-193, 203-5 and 214-5.
33   As reported in the German Communiqué of the day.
34   Ibid. The XIX Corps' defence is covered on pp. 178-9, 187-90, 202-3, 213-4.
35   Ibid. The XVIII Corps' situation is covered on pp. 176-7, 185-7 and 199-202.

and then turned west, moving behind the front line. They then moved deep into XVIII Corps' territory, leaving the redoubts for the support troops to deal with.

The Ulstermen also encountered the first German tank, the *Sturmpanzerwagen*, or A7V tank, was 7.3 metres long, 3.1 metres wide and 3.3 metres high and it weighed in at 33 tons.[36] Fourteen men manned the 5.7 cm Maxim-Nordfelt cannon mounted in the front and the six MG08 machine guns. Another four drove the tank. It had a top speed of 9 miles an hour on roads, which was faster than the British tank, but it ran on twenty-four wheels, making it unstable on the battlefield. It was a very different beast to the British Mark IV tank.[37]

III Corps had to cover a 20-mile sector, on Fifth Army's right. Lieutenant General Richard Butler doubted the Germans would attack where the Oise river and canal ran along No Man's Land and he was sure that they would not cross the marshes surrounding the River Oise. They did, however, breakthrough 14th Division's line between Urvillers and Essigny.[38] Butler deployed his reserves to hold the Battle Zone, but they could not stop the Germans taking the Essigny plateau, an important area for the German artillery observers.

The Oise river and canal were both shallow enough to wade across and patrols engaged 18th Division's outposts while columns of troops crossed.[39] The mist lingered longer along the waterways, giving the Germans time to get amongst the redoubts and batteries before it cleared, so Butler had to deploy all his reserves to hold the line. A later attack overran 58th Division's Forward Zone, north of the Oise. The Germans then pushed the Londoners all the way back on the Crozat Canal, at the back of the Battle Zone, using the river to cover their flank.[40]

21 March Summary

Byng knew that both VI and IV Corps had suffered heavy casualties and he had committed three of his five reserve divisions to hold the Battle Zone. However, Gough's optimistic report had led him to believe that all was well south of V Corps and the Flesquières Salient.[41]

Gough had expected to lose the Forward Zone but the loss of the Essigny plateau had compromised XVIII and III Corps' line and he had no reserves to take it. So, he allowed Maxse and Butler to abandon the Battle Zone, and withdraw behind the

36   Maxwell Hundleby and Strasheim, Rainer, *The German A7V Tank and the Captured British Mark IV Tanks of World War I* (Sparkford: Haynes Foulis, 1990), pp. 23, 34, 61, 79.
37   Only four A7V tanks and five British Mark IV tanks were deployed to engage with strongpoints bypassed by the storm troops
38   Edmonds, *Military Operations: France and Belgium, 1918, Vol. I*, pp. 173-4, 183-4, 198.
39   Ibid., pp. 172-3 and p. 198. The river was lower than expected while the Germans had partially drained the canal.
40   Ibid. The 58th Division's situation is covered on pp. 196-8.
41   Ibid. Gough's round trip to his corps commanders is detailed on 195-6.

canal, where they could await French reinforcements.[42] The heavy guns and as many men as possible crossed the waterway before dusk before everyone else withdrew during the night. The engineers blew up the bridges, but the rubble could often be crossed, while the railway bridge east of Jussy was still standing because 'old French charges were faulty'.[43]

General Philippe Pétain was warning that a wide spread bombardment of the Reims front could be the start of a new attack against the French front, but Gough knew he was wrong when he returned to his headquarters. Afternoon aerial reports spoke of columns of troops opposite Fifth Army and some were stretching back 10 miles.

Reports on the German side varied.[44] The Kaiser announced 'a complete victory' while Crown Prince Rupprecht's Chief of Staff, General Hermann von Kuhl said the 'hoped for objectives were not reached'.[45] The official communiqué gave a pragmatic assessment; 'After a heavy bombardment of artillery and trench mortars our infantry assaulted on a wide front and everywhere captured the enemy's first lines.' Ludendorff decided the best way forward was to deploy all OHL's reserve divisions against Fifth Army, to drive a wedge between the British and the French.

Third Army, 22 March

British artillery fire made Hénin Hill untenable during the evening and then an enemy spotter plane directed the German guns as the troops ran to safety.[46] The Germans secured the position before turning on the rest of 34th Division.[47] Battalions escaped to the back of the Battle Zone when they could, sometimes waiting until the Germans were quiet before running to safety as Lewis gun teams gave covering fire. The loss of Hénin Hill required 3rd Division[48] to withdraw across the Cojeul stream during the night but no one dare say 'retirement' over the telephone in case the Germans were listening. But it took so long to find everyone in the dark, that one battalion received its order over the phone in Hindustani. Sections stayed behind in perfectly good trenches to make 'war noises' while the rest discovered that they had been directed to shallow, unconnected ditches.

42   Ibid. Overnight withdrawals of XVIII Corps and III Corps are described on pp. 208-13.
43   G. Nicholls, *The 18th Division in the Great War* (Edinburgh, William Blackwood and Sons, 1922), p. 277.
44   Edmonds, *Military Operations: France and Belgium, 1918, Vol. I*. A summary of prisoner reports on the attack is provided on pp. 259-60.
45   Ibid. The German reaction to the first day of the attack and plans for the second day are covered on p. 260-1.
46   TNA WO 95/2456/3: 101 Brigade War Diary.
47   Edmonds, *Military Operations: France and Belgium, 1918, Vol. I*, pp. 315-7.
48   Ibid., pp. 318-9.

Meanwhile, 40th Division's men had revealed their positions when they fired on the Germans advancing along the Hirondelle stream and spotter planes directed artillery fire until they retired.[49] Again, they found that the Green Line was just a shallow ditch. Later attacks forced a withdrawal behind Mory, while a plan to counter-attack was foiled, because the orders did not get through in time. It was the only part of the Green Line lost along Third Army's front.

Across IV Corps' front, the reports concerned 'losses everywhere and asking for reinforcements' but the men continued to 'contest every foot of ground, conform as far as possible with the movement of other troops and only retire fighting.' They only fell back when they were in danger of being surrounded or when they had to go in search of the ammunition wagons waiting along the Green Line.

Twenty-five tanks crawled up the Cambrai road but the infantry commander thought the 'information was scant, orders were many and contradictory, rumour was wild and they knew nothing of what was taking place on their left' to join them.[50] So, the tanks advanced alone from 19th Division's front, hidden by smoke from grass fires. Sixteen were knocked out by artillery fire and while the survivors returned having 'done their duty',[51] there was still a large gap in the line north of the Cambrai road.[52]

Meanwhile, the 'Jocks were at the top of their form, [they] were inflicting great losses on the enemy and were complete masters of the situation'.[53] That was until 6th Division's right flank gave way at dusk, forcing 51st Division's adjacent flank to fall back to abandoned battery positions. The rest had to retire when it was dark, because they were running out of ammunition.

A feint attack east of the Canal du Nord was a distraction from the real threat to the west but the clearing mist meant that 17th Division 'caught [the Germans] with enfilade fire and mowed them down'. However, 51st Division was retiring to the north-west, so V Corps needed to form a defensive flank.[54] The Germans were also pushing through Gouzeaucourt Wood, on the south side of the salient, along the army boundary. Third Army had 47th Division deploy a brigade to cover the gap, only to find the Germans had reached Equancourt, increasing it to 3-miles.[55]

Byng waited until the afternoon before giving the order to withdraw from the salient into Havrincourt Wood, and it was far too late for 63rd Division. The orders took several hours to reach the battalions and it was dawn by the time some men

49   Ibid., pp. 317-8.
50   TNA WO 95/2092/2: 9th Welsh Regiment War Diary.
51   TNA WO 95/2079/1: 9th Cheshires War Diary.
52   Edmonds, *Military Operations: France and Belgium, 1918, Vol. I,* the tank attack is covered on pp. 309-10.
53   Ibid., pp. 308-9.
54   Ibid., pp. 310-1.
55   Ibid., pp. 306.

caught up with the rest of V Corps; they then received another order to head for the Green Line.[56]

Fifth Army, 22 March

Gough believed Fifth Army might be destroyed if it stood and fought, so he decided to hold the Green Line for a short time, while the Somme and Crozat Canals were prepared for defence. A longer stand could then be made, giving time for French reinforcements to arrive behind his right flank.

Again, the mist only lasted until mid-morning on the high ground, but it lingered longer in the valleys, so the Germans attacked different parts of the line at different times. A lot had happened by the time the instructions to retire to the Green Line reached the corps commanders, around midday.[57] For example, the Germans seized Chapel Hill and then Heudicourt, forcing 9th Division to make a desperate dash through Fins.[58] It increased the gap along the army boundary and there was 'a most awkward contretemps' between Generals Tudor and Gorringe, over who should cover it. As we have seen, an attempt to sort the issue was made after Gough paid a visit to Byng.

Two of 21st Division's brigades had been overrun around Epéhy and Peizière when the order to retire reached the front line.[59] Few men made it back to the Battle Zone, by which time General Congreve was worried about his right flank as well. Again, the enemy intervened before the orders to continue the withdrawal reached the front line. Those who heard in time had a lucky escape in the dark, their path to the Green Line lit by burning stores. The order to withdraw to the Green Line came too late for 16th Division as well, because the Germans had forced their way along the Cologne stream, in the mist.[60] They had then turned north towards Ste Emilie, cutting behind the Battle Zone, leaving 39th Division to hold the Green Line. It left Congreve with no reserves and large gaps on his flanks; VII Corps had also lost 120 guns.

Gough's instruction to withdraw reached XIX Corps headquarters around midday.[61] Lieutenant General Watts' told his divisional commanders to prepare for an afternoon move behind the Green Line but again events moved on apace. For example, the Germans were behind 66th Division's flank, where VII Corps' was being driven back along the Cologne stream, and driving the rest from the back of the Battle Zone by the time the order arrived.[62] All that could be done was to instruct 'every officer to take command of any of his own battalion he could find and make his way towards Roisel'.

56   Ibid., pp. 371.
57   Ibid., pp. Gough's order and the communications difficulties are detailed on 265-7
58   Ibid., p. 295
59   Ibid., pp. 293-4.
60   Ibid. The VII Corps' difficult situation is covered on pp. 292-3.
61   Ibid. The XIX Corps' fight and retirement are described on pp. 281-90.
62   Ibid., pp. 284-5.

Six tanks were knocked out helping some cavalry squadrons restore the line, while the few units that did make it back found that the Green Line was in a poor state.

The German artillery pounded the garrison of Le Verguier into submission when the mist cleared but the rest of 24th Division was holding its own. So, the men were surprised to receive the midday order to retire to the Green Line. Many were hit breaking contact in broad daylight before the survivors discovered that the Green Line was not fit for purpose.

After a long night on the road, 50th Division deployed between the Cologne and Omignon streams, forming a rally line for XIX Corps to fall back on. The Green Line was 'only in a spit-locked condition but a good belt of wire protected the position', leaving the Northumbrian men only a few hours to dig in before they were in action. Both 66th and 24th Divisions soon fell back through the weak line with the Germans close behind.[63] General Watts was worried that the Germans were pushing along the Cologne stream, around the north end of his line, but the withdrawal started after the divisional guns started firing short. XIX Corps ended the day behind the Somme, but it had lost nearly ninety guns and its headquarters was bombed, putting it out of action for several hours.[64]

The clearing mist mid-morning revealed large gaps in XVIII Corps' front.[65] General Maxse ordered his divisions to retire early in the afternoon, even though the officers wanted to wait a few hours and escape under cover of darkness. The guns were sent back immediately but the Germans had infiltrated the line in many places by the time 61st and 30th Division broke contact in small groups. XVIII Corps' retirement to the Crozat Canal had exposed XIX Corps' right flank and Germans troops got behind 36th Division despite the engineers' efforts to blow up the Somme Canal bridges.

Two brigades of 20th Division were waiting for them (one brigade had been committed to a counter-attack) in the Green Line[66] but the 'incomplete trenches were shallow and meagrely wired'. The Germans were so close, that Maxse decided to withdraw behind the River Somme, involving another 10 miles of marching for some men.[67] There were rear-guard actions, men were cut off and some even encountered German transport, during a night. The rapid retreat meant that the Royal Garrison Artillery had to abandon many batteries, bringing the total of howitzers lost to forty-three in just two days.

The Germans spent the morning moving towards III Corps' line, under cover of the morning mist.[68] Enfilade fire raked the towpath, where there was a bend on the Crozat Canal, but 18th Division held on. However, the Germans crossed the damaged bridges at Quessy and Tergnier, pushing 58th Division back from the Crozat Canal.

63   Ibid., pp. 286-7.
64   Ibid., p. 289.
65   Ibid. XVIII Corps' battle and withdrawal are covered on pp. 271-6.
66   Ibid., pp. 279-80.
67   Ibid. The overnight withdrawal is covered on pp. 276-81.
68   Ibid. III Corps' fight along St Quentin and Crozat Canals is detailed on pp. 267-71.

The only good news was that French troops were starting to deploy behind III Corps' line.

Summary, 22 March

Byng and Haig's chief of staff, Lieutenant General Herbert Lawrence, agreed a new defensive line, called the Red Line, would be prepared a couple of miles behind the Green Line. Third Army's left was holding on but Fifth Army's left was withdrawing faster than Third Army's right, opening a gap along their boundary. So, Gough and Byng agreed that V Corps had to withdraw to the Green Line, to cover it. The artillery left at dusk but General Fanshawe did not issue orders to the infantry until 1.30 am, too late for a pre-dawn move. It meant the front-line units had to break contact in daylight and then withdraw 3 miles to an incomplete line of defences.[69]

It was clear that the timing of withdrawals was problematic and that some generals were underestimating how long it took to convert an order from Army headquarters into a message for the commanders in the front line. It was dangerous to expect men to break contact and withdraw during daylight and it would have been far safer to withdraw quietly at night, giving the men time to dig in and rest. The Germans would then fire their shells at empty trenches the following morning, leaving the infantry needing to locate the new British line. The Germans would then have to relocate the British line, leaving only a few hours to attack before nightfall.

It was also clear that it was unwise to defend a canal because units could not patrol ahead of their front line. The Germans could check the towpaths for the best place to cross, while the assault troops gathered in nearby woods. The long straight waterways were also easy targets for the artillery to register, whatever the weather.

Third Army, 23 March

Byng had received GHQ's order to withdraw across to the Green Line after midnight but it was 5 am before the divisions knew. The front-line battalions heard at 10 am and the plan was to start withdrawing after midday. It had taken twelve hours for the message to be acted on and a lot could and did happen in that time.

Both XVII Corps and VI Corps had been forced to abandon good trenches to prepare a new defensive position. The men watched as the German artillery shelled the abandoned trenches only to encounter 'strong, wired trenches in which the brave defenders, unshaken and not disheartened, were standing firm'. The main pressure was against around Mory and 40th Division eventually had to withdraw because the shallow Green Line trenches had been levelled by shell fire.[70]

---

69   Ibid., pp. 371-2.
70   Ibid., pp. 388-9.

IV Corps issued an early order to withdraw, to keep in line with V Corps on its right flank, but parts of 41st and 19th Divisions had been overrun astride the Cambrai Road before it could be carried out.[71] The survivors made it back to the Green Line but 'had it not been for the gallant defence of Beugny by the 9th Welsh, the whole line must have been driven back.'[72] The Germans then moved behind 51st Division's flank and while some of the Scots fell back 'in perfect order, fighting both to their front and to their flanks', others fought until they were overrun. Meanwhile, 2nd Division was forced to hold onto Bertincourt while the supply dumps were emptied.[73] The field guns always stayed in line until the infantry had passed through, while traction engines hauled the heavy guns back in relays, leaving them close to the roads so they could be moved quickly.

V Corps still had to extricate itself from a salient. It left 17th Division facing a difficult withdrawal, at right angles to the fighting line, while the Germans pushed 51st Division back behind its flank.[74] The infantry and the guns took it in turns to withdraw but they were 'quite happy and were not worrying', even after fighting off Germans dressed in British uniforms and helmets.[75] The 63rd Division fell back across the Battle Zone and the Canal du Nord Tunnel, reaching the Green Line at dusk. Only they found 'a group of trenches about 2-feet deep with no field of fire and no dug-outs. There was no cover and no communication. There was no water, no transport and little ammunition.'[76]

Meantime, 47th Division found the Germans enlarging the gap along the army boundary. It too crossed the Canal du Nord but it 'was disintegrating' and the Germans were close behind.[77] Some men found that the Green Line did not exist, so they found better positions to hold and 'just lay down and started to throw up a light cover of earth'. The gunners struggled to locate the correct ammunition for their guns or forage for their horses in the dark.

Across V Corps' area, 'huts, camps, wagon parks and even horse lines were abandoned, whilst various bodies of troops moved about in apparently aimless fashion.'[78] The Londoners would have been overrun except that the Germans found stocks of alcohol in Ytres. They drank their fill, set fire to dumps and then cheered and shouted as they charged; they were shot down.

71   Ibid., pp. 385-6.
72   Ibid., p. 385.
73   Ibid., p. 380.
74   Ibid., p. 380.
75   A.H. Atteridge, *The History of the 17th (Northern) Division* (Glasgow: Robert Maclehose & Co, 1929), p. 310.
76   Edmonds, *Military Operations: France and Belgium, 1918, Vol. I*, pp. 390-1. The confident tone in Third Army's report to GHQ conflicts with the gloomy mood at the front-line.
77   Ibid. The problems faced by the 47th Division are detailed on pp. 377-9.
78   TNA WO 95/1372/2: 23rd Royal Fusiliers War Diary.

It appears that neither Byng nor Fanshawe realised how serious the problem was and while 47th Division had been made responsible for closing the 3-mile gap, no one had told Major General Gorringe. Even if he had known, he did not have the troops to cover the gap. His officers were busy rounding up the stragglers, making sure they were fed and given ammunition before they were allowed to sleep for a few hours.

Fifth Army, 23 March

Gough's tired divisions were spread across 40-miles and gaps were opening in Fifth Army's line. The Germans were pushing through the gap on VII Corps left but they were unaware of the one along the Cologne stream yet. It would grow larger, because Gough had to let XIX Corps withdraw another 6 miles to the Somme, to stay in contact with XVIII Corps.

The Germans were pushing past 9th Division's south flank before the withdrawal order could be acted on, so a counter-attack had to be made to facilitate the escape across the Canal du Nord.[79] Congreve ordered another withdrawal at dusk and while some battalions fell back earlier because they were short of ammunition, the South African Brigade was told to 'hold at all costs.'

The withdrawal order came too late to save 21st Division.[80] It had been shelled out its shallow trenches and then the mist cleared as they fell back across the Canal du Nord, exposing them to machine-gun fire. The engineers blew some of the bridges early, leaving men to scramble across on fallen trees, only for them to hear they had to keep retiring because Mont St Quentin had been abandoned.

It was important to hold Péronne as long as possible because all roads led through the town. The Germans kept pressing forward until Major General Edward Feetham had to tell his brigadiers to make good their escape. It resulted in 39th Division's brigades becoming split up as they looked for crossings over the Somme and the Tortille.[81]

There was a dash to the Somme across XIX Corps front and both 66th and 50th Divisions crossed south of Péronne.[82] It was a race against time and the divisional commanders had been given authority to order the engineers to destroy the bridges, as soon as all their troops had crossed. Sometimes they were blown when the main bodies were across, leaving the rearguards to swim across the river. British and German soldiers reached Pargny on the Somme at the same time, so the bridge was blown without orders, leaving many men of 24th Division having to swim across.[83] Meanwhile, some crossed in 8th Division's sector and the infantry had to drive them

79   Edmonds, *Military Operations: France and Belgium, 1918, Vol. I*, pp. 362-5.
80   Ibid., pp. 361-2.
81   Ibid., pp. 359-61.
82   Ibid., pp. 348-52.
83   Ibid., pp. 346-7.

back across the canal. The 1st Cavalry Division came under artillery fire after a spotter plane saw it, stampeding many horses. Some troopers escaped across the Somme, but the rest had to abandon their horses and swim for it.[84]

Dawn found XVIII Corps' battalions mixed up and holding shallow trenches along the Somme, a fordable watercourse. XVIII Corps was across the river by dawn and most of the road bridges had been blown, but the rapid withdrawal had left many problems. It had stretched the corps front to 12 miles, leaving a gap on the left flank, next to XIX Corps, which the Germans were passing through.

The centre was weak because 30th Division had left one brigade to guard the canal bridges until everyone had passed through Ham and across the canal.[85] The Germans infiltrated along the wooded river bank in the morning fog and overran the rest of the bridgehead. They then crossed the canal and turned east, to roll up XVIII Corps' line. They aimed to link with troops crossing a railway bridge, left standing east of the town because the French railway engineers did not have enough explosives to demolish it.[86]

A despatch rider warned 36th Division that the Germans were crossing at Ham, as it fought off the attack over the railway bridge. It was also under attack from the east, where III Corps' line had been broken at Jussy, on its right flank. Every spare man was deployed as 36th Division was squeezed into a narrow salient by nightfall.[87] To the west of Ham, 20th Division only had 200 men to counter-attack with and they were given no artillery or machine-gun support.[88] The attack was a failure but the flank was safe because the Germans were intent on pushing east.

Dawn found III Corps deployed along the Crozat in the mist. Again, battalions were mixed up and short of officers and the only good news was that French units were deployed in support. The Germans crossed the canal as several points around Jussy, causing 14th Division to fall back through the French to a railway embankment.[89] The breakthrough brought 18th Division under enfilade fire, and it too fell back through the French. On several occasions, the French were unable to engage the Germans, because they were close behind the retiring British.

Spotter planes took to the air when the mist cleared, directing the artillery to support the railway embankment position, but it was too little, too late because everybody was falling back. French cavalry regiments were sent forward and while they failed to clear the Germans from Bois de Frières, they did give the infantry time to rally.[90]

Meanwhile, 58th Division had been unable to drive the Germans back to the Crozat Canal at Tergnier. French troops also tried but had not had time to reconnoitre

84   Ibid., pp. 347-8.
85   Ibid., pp. 340-2.
86   Ibid., p. 277.
87   Ibid., pp. 340-2.
88   Ibid., pp. 344-5.
89   Ibid., pp. 332-3.
90   Ibid., pp. 331-2.

the ground, before engaging a stronger force. So, they fell back, taking the Londoners with them, all the way to Bois de Frières.

Summary, 23 March

Pétain wanted Fifth Army to hold on until his own troops had taken over. That would allow Gough to send his divisions north, to reinforce Third Army. The safest way to make this happen was to break contact with the enemy and Haig told Byng and Gough of his plan on 23 March. They had to retire quickly which would both shorten their lines of communication and place the former 1916 battlefield behind the advancing Germans. Byng had to organise a line between Arras and the old trenches along the Ancre; it would be called the Purple Line. Meanwhile, Gough had to 'hold the River Somme at all costs. There will be no withdrawal from this line.'[91]

The engineers would mark out another defensive line, some 8-miles west of the Purple Line and the Ancre; it would be called the GHQ Line.[92] Every spare man across the BEF would be sent to erect wire and dig ditches, which could be turned into trenches. They would prepare 5,000 miles of trenches and erect 23,500 tons of wire over the next two weeks.

Third Army's withdrawal to the Purple Line was quite straightforward. However, both XVIII Corps and III Corps were being pushed back on Fifth Army's front, leaving the British and French troops mixed up behind the Somme, Crozat and Oise Canals. Ludendorff, meanwhile, had to decide what to do now the British were retiring in the wrong place. Was he to reinforce the failure south of Arras or reinforce the success astride the Somme? He chose the second course, hoping a push south of the Somme would reach the rail centre of Amiens, separating the British and the French armies.[93]

Third Army, 24 March

By dawn, 40th Division had been forced out of Mory but enfilade fire and a fresh line formed by 42nd Division stopped the Germans going far.[94] Byng told IV Corps to abandon Bapaume in the afternoon but most battalions were already retiring before the order got through.[95] The German refused to follow them through the town because their own heavy guns were shelling it. The Scots helped themselves to ammunition dumped for them on the Albert road but their transport found it difficult. They had little artillery support because the guns were stuck in traffic jams around Achiet-le-Grand

91   Ibid., p. 368.
92   Ibid. The resources allocated to the GHQ Line are detailed on pp. 394-5.
93   Ibid. Ludendorff's choices and decision is covered on pp. 395-8.
94   Ibid. The desperate battle for Mory is detailed on pp. 442-3.
95   Ibid., pp. 439-41.

and Bucquoy, because of the poor road network. The solution was to divert the 'lightest and best horsed vehicles, such as field batteries and empty ammunition wagons, off the roads and across country ...'[96]

The gap next to Fifth Army continued to grow by the hour but part of V Corps held onto Bertincourt well into the night, while a huge dump was evacuated. The rest faced a nightmare march across the 1916 battlefield and while some battalions found the Germans across their line of retreat, others became scattered and out of touch with their headquarters.[97]

Byng's plan was to make a long march to break contact, leaving Third Army facing a difficult night negotiating the old battlefield.[98] The Albert road was jammed with traffic because no one dare drive their horses into the maze of trenches, wire and shell holes. It meant the soldiers had to negotiate the crater field in the dark, and hopefully find the rest of their unit. Those who did not were rounded up by staff officers who directed them to rally points, so they could be sent in the right direction.

The Germans also struggled to cross the battlefield, but they were always close behind, and in some cases ahead of, Third Army's scattered battalions. They used flares to mark their progress and to keep in touch with adjacent units, as they moved forward. Different types of flares indicate gaps in the British line, so reinforcements could be sent forward to exploit them. They were, however, always cautious because they expected to encounter British machine-guns at each and every trench line. They were puzzled by the lack of resistance but Byng's men were anxious to get clear of the crater field before dawn.

Fifth Army, 24 March

General Gough had a 2-mile gap on his left flank, while his right had been driven back across the Somme; he also had the 1916 battlefield to his rear. Most of 9th Division's battalions were falling back before the order to hold reached them and they withdrew 'as though at an old fashioned field day, with mounted officers conveying orders.'[99] Only the South African Brigade received the stand instruction and they made a heroic last stand near Bouchavesnes which lasted seven hours. The survivors marched past 'a continuous double line of transport and guns', as they were led into captivity; evidence of the lengthy delay they had caused.[100]

The Germans drove 21st Division along the north bank of the Somme in the morning mist and only a few of Major General Campbell's men assembled around Maricourt later in the day. All day long 39th Division fired across the river at the advancing

96   Ibid., pp. 508.
97   Ibid., see pp 426 and 429-31 for examples of the confused night march.
98   Ibid. The challenges of traversing the 1916 battlefield are explained on pp. 433-4.
99   TNA WO 95/1772/2: 6th King's Own Scottish Borderers War Diary.
100 Anon. *Union of South Africa and the Great War 1914-1918* (Uckfield: Naval and Military Press, 2015), p.154.

columns and 16th Division eventually had to deploy to extend Fifth Army's flank.[101] The only good news for Major General Walter Congreve was that 35th Division and the 1st Cavalry Division were approaching his rear, having been delayed on roads full of transport columns and refugees. Several of the infantry battalions were overrun around Maurepas ridge but they stemmed the German advance long enough for the rest to escape.

XIX Corps held the Somme canal between Biaches and Béthencourt but the Germans were able cross the river and marshes, infiltrating through the trees and undergrowth. They eventually crossed at Béthencourt and drove 8th Division back, compromising the entire corps' line.[102]

South of Ham, 36th Division bore the brunt of 'two thin lines of men, literally back to back, with 1 mile between them.'[103] They were expecting to be relieved by the French when the salient 'suddenly caved. From all sides the semi-circle fell back...'[104] Those cut off fought to the death when their ammunition ran out. Around 150 troopers of 3rd Cavalry Division immediately countered by charging and the 'Germans were caught in the open, a considerable number cut down or shot and over a hundred prisoners taken.'[105] The Ulstermen followed up the charge before falling back to Buchoire and Guiscard.

The Germans then focused on widening the Somme bridgehead, using pontoons to cross the Somme west of Ham. They first forced 30th Division and then 20th Division to fall back to the Canal du Nord. A mistake during the night left Dreslincourt unoccupied and the Germans were able to move past 61st Division.

Problems had occurred on Fifth Army's right flank when the Germans advanced out of the Bois de Frieres in the dawn mist. The French soon fell back 'for want of ammunition', leaving III Corps' thin line to stop the attack.[106] Meanwhile, 58th Division became isolated as French fell back along the Oise Canal. It would be several days before it re-joined the BEF.

Third Army, 25 March

Byng's left was secure, but IV Corps had withdrawn up to 5 miles while V Corps had fallen back double that distance. He ordered a retirement beyond the 1916 battlefield during the evening, so IV Corps could occupy the old British trenches while V Corps crossed the River Ancre. It meant the men faced another long, wet day marching along crowded roads.

101 Edmonds, *Military Operations: France and Belgium, 1918, Vol. I,* pp. 413.
102 Ibid., p. 411.
103 Falls, Cyril, *The History of the 36th (Ulster) Division* (M'Caw, Stephenson and Orr, London 1922), p.214.
104 Ibid., p. 215.
105 Ibid., p. 217.
106 Edmonds, *Military Operations: France and Belgium, 1918, Vol. I,* pp. 402.

VI Corps' problems began when 59th Division fell back south of Ervillers and then 42nd and 40th Divisions were forced to retire through Béhagnies and Sapignies, enduring 'a very gruelling time, fighting many ding-dong battles'.[107] They were 'very scattered and communications between battalion headquarters and their companies broke down, so they were at the mercy of rumours of cancelled orders and reports of retirements on their flanks.' It left 31st Division having to throw its right flank back to Bucquoy.[108]

Both 41st and 25th Divisions held on with the help of tanks but the Germans moved past their flanks. They then withdrew towards Biefvillers and Bihucourt as 62nd Division marched up to fill the 4-mile gap between Puisieux and Beaumont Hamel, on IV Corps left.[109] The same happened to 19th Division because the Germans were pushing around its flanks.[110] One brigade had to evacuate Grévillers when it ran out of ammunition and Major General Jeffreys then heard that the Germans were in Courcelette, 2 miles to his south-west. He sent every spare man back to dig trenches along the Ancre and the rest of his men headed back at dusk. They were 'split into small parties, separated, lost, they plodded on, by chance in the same direction and then came together again.' The problem was that the divisions were having to retire before Byng's withdrawal order reached them or be overrun. It meant 51st Division was left holding on while 19th and 2nd Divisions retired past its flanks, with Germans following.[111] The Scots were then chased through Irles and one group had to hold back the onslaught, while the rest escaped across the Ancre. An even bigger problem was that the premature demolition of the Miraumont bridge forced V Corps to cross the Ancre at Beaucourt.[112] It forced troops to find other crossings, resulting in a 3-mile gap opening in Third Army's line between Bucquoy and Beaumont Hamel.

Four battered divisions were scattered across V Corps' front, between the Butte du Warlencourt and Bazentin-le-Petit, early on 25 March. Battalions were constantly falling back along busy roads and it was a struggle to keep the chain of command operating. Logistics were also a problem and staff officers had to direct units to ammunition dumps along the Albert road. V Corps' order to withdraw reached the divisions around 9.30 am and the Lewis gunners had to keep the Germans at bay until everyone escaped.[113]

Most of 2nd Division had withdrawn too far during the night and it took time to locate them and organise them as a rearguard around Pys and Courcelette.[114] They

---

107 TNA WO 95/2655/1: 1/7th Lancashire Fusiliers' War Diary.
108 Edmonds, *Military Operations: France and Belgium, 1918, Vol. I.* The battles for Béhagnies and Sapignies are chronicled on pp. 483-4.
109 Ibid., p. 486.
110 Ibid., pp. 483-5.
111 Ibid., pp. 484-5.
112 Ibid., p. 480.
113 Ibid. The V Corps' tired and disorganised state is detailed in a personal account on p. 470.
114 Ibid., pp. 478-9.

then withdrew to Miraumont, only to find the bridge had been blown up. So, they crossed the Ancre at Beaucourt instead and staff officers then directed them onto the Beaumont Hamel ridge.

Men of the 63rd Division withdrew after seeing 2nd and 47th Divisions falling back on their flanks.[115] They stopped in the old German trenches around Thiepval, before heading to the Ancre around Mesnil and Authuille when it was dark. The men of 47th Division held La Boisselle until 12th Division arrived, after a long 15-mile march along busy roads.[116] They both then headed back to Albert, taking a shattered 17th Division with them. A major collected around one thousand stragglers along the main Bapaume road and made the officers organise them into three battalions. They all then marched through Albert and joined the new line to the west of the town.

Major General George Franks of 35th Division had been given control of VII Corps' front and while his right flank was anchored the Somme, his left was in the air. Both 9th and 35th Divisions endured attacks north of the river until their line collapsed, 'overwhelmed by the sheer weight of numbers.' The brigade staff eventually stopped the retreat and had launched a counter-attack before they were instructed to withdraw at dusk.

Fifth Army, 25 March

Third Army was 4-miles behind Fifth Army's left flank along the Somme and then there was another 4-mile gap to the French on the right. Lieutenant General Watts wanted XIX Corps to hold on but he told his divisional commanders to fall back if they thought they were in danger. All 39th and 16th Divisions could do was watch as the Germans advanced past their flank, along the north bank of the Somme.[117] Meanwhile, 66th Division had stopped the Germans leaving Péronne but they did cross the La Chapellette railway bridge, initiating a retreat from the river.[118] Orders to fall back did not reach all of 8th Division after the Germans crossed north of Eterpigny, so the Brie and St Christ bridges were held for too long.[119] A plan to counter-attack never took place because the Germans struck first. A counter-attack towards Dreslincourt was made by 24th Division but the French did not join in and the Germans were around the flanks before the order to retire was received.[120]

The Germans had discovered the gap in XVIII Corps' line along the Canal du Nord and they were pushing past 20th and 61st Divisions, heading for Dreslincourt.[121] To make matters worse, the French withdrew from the canal when German cavalry

115 Ibid., pp. 477-9.
116 Ibid., pp. 480-1.
117 Ibid., pp. 469.
118 Ibid., pp. 466, 468.
119 Ibid., pp. 464-6.
120 Ibid., pp. 463-4.
121 Ibid., pp. 458-63.

approached and it needed a heroic last stand at Buverchy bridge, so 30th Division could withdraw to Roye.

III Corps was disintegrating on Fifth Army's right flank and the infantry was out of the touch with the artillery as they fell back across the Canal du Nord to the west or the Oise Canal to the south.[122] The French were short of artillery and the Germans pushed through a large gap in their line, capturing Noyon at the junction of the two canals. Both Haig and the Chief of the Imperial General Staff, General Henry Wilson, were concerned about Fifth Army's situation and they were looking to the French for more help.

Third Army, 26 March

The early demolition of the Miraumont bridge had resulted in a 4-mile gap in Third Army's line between Puisieux and Serre. Byng intended to withdraw to a new trench line, so reinforcements could plug it quicker. The corps commanders were told not to mention the plan because it might undermine morale and precipitate a retirement before the reinforcements arrived.[123]

Advances towards Rossignol Wood were stopped by 62nd Division with the help of one hundred machine gunners from the Machine Gun School.[124] However, various rumours that IV Corps line was in danger took some time to dispel.[125] German cavalry units were only mounted patrols; sightings of German tanks were actually new Whippet tanks reinforcing the line while German armoured cars turned out to be escaping French agricultural vehicles. Lieutenant General Haldane sent out staff officers to check the stories while his corps reinforcements deployed on the roads to manage the traffic and organise the stragglers.[126]

The day ended with a senior staff officer reporting that the Germans had captured Hébuterne but he too was wrong; only a few had entered. A brigadier rounded up 250 men of 19th Division and they 'fixed bayonets and doubled in fours down the main streets', driving the enemy before them. The rumours made 4th Australian Division deploy prematurely, and mounted officers were sent forward to learn that the Germans has not broken through.[127]

The four divisions of V Corps had crossed the Ancre between Hamel and Albert but the Germans were close behind, following old trenches down to the river bank.[128]

---

122 Ibid., pp. 455-8.
123 Ibid. The message is given on pp. 508. Only Lieutenant General Congreve mentioned it in his morning orders.
124 Ibid., pp. 522, 524.
125 Ibid., pp. 530-1.
126 Ibid., p. 530.
127 Ibid., pp. 524.
128 Major General Sir Arthur Scott, *History of the 12th Division in the Great War, 1914-1918* (London: Nisbet, 1923), p. 172.

Lieutenant General Edward Fanshawe's men found few trenches waiting for them on the far bank while they had little ammunition to fight with and no tools to dig with. The bridges were under fire and the engineers had no explosives to blow them up.[129]

On the left, 2nd Division had formed a defensive flank along Hawthorn Ridge, which faced a 4-mile gap the Germans were pushing through. The only good news was the New Zealand Division was soon deploying on their flank, having marched 10 miles through the night to the sound of guns.[130] The sight of twelve Whippet tanks driving out of Colincamps made the Germans run and the crisis was averted.

Both 63rd Division and 12th Division stopped the Germans crossing the Ancre around Aveluy but Albert proved to be a shell trap, so the men had to deploy west of the ruins. The Ancre ran through tunnels under the town, so the two divisions were able to pass through it with ease.[131] A mass attack was stopped during the evening and the Germans then decided to help themselves to the abandoned stocks of food and drink in the town.[132]

As 9th Division shortened its sector behind the Ancre, Lieutenant General Congreve was looking to Major General Franks to continue VII Corps' line south-east to the River Somme, to allow the reserve divisions time to deploy. Unfortunately, the British bombardment drove 35th Division out of Bray earlier than desired, triggering a withdrawal.[133] Both Byng and Congreve wanted to restore the line, but the artillery was powerless to help when the Germans attacked at dusk, because it did not know where the new front line was.[134] The timely arrival of 1st Cavalry Division blocked the road to Amiens but Franks was sacked because he 'had misinterpreted the verbal instructions and orders issued'.[135]

Fifth Army, 26 March

XIX Corps was holding a 13-mile sector south of Somme, with large gaps on both flanks. Watts had ordered a withdrawal and the engineers demolished the bridges along the river because Third Army was withdrawing along the north bank. However, the loss of high ground around Herbécourt in the morning mist pre-empted the order.[136]

129 Scott, *History of the 12th Division in the Great War*, p. 171.
130 Stewart, *The New Zealand Division 1916-1919, Vol. II*. The arrival of the New Zealanders and the Whippets is covered on pp. 343-7.
131 Scott, *History of the 12th Division in the Great War*, p. 171.
132 Edmonds, *Military Operations: France and Belgium, 1918, Vol. I*, the attacks on Aveluy and Albert are covered on pp. 519.
133 Ibid. The misunderstanding over 35th Division's withdrawal is covered on pp. 511 and 513-4,
134 Ibid. The attempt to restore 35th Division's line is explained pp. 515-6.
135 H. M. Davson, *The History of the 35th Division in the Great War* (London: Sifton and Praed, 1926), p. 211.
136 Edmonds, *Military Operations: France and Belgium, 1918, Vol. I*, The collapse of XIX Corps' left is detailed on pp. 503-4

Enfilade fire forced both 39th and 66th Division to fall back on the rear guards along the Amiens road. It was then the turn of 50th Division and 8th Division to retire but they headed south-west rather than west. The retreat upset 24th Division's plan to retire in echelon from right to left around Chaulnes. Instead it was forced to retreat from left to right, leaving some battalions having to fight their way back to Fransart.[137]

Gough sent forward the four battered divisions of XVIII Corps north of the Avre, to cover the gap on XIX Corps' right.[138] His plan had been for two of them occupy le Quesnoy and Andechy but the Germans already held them and some battalions were 'entirely surrounded and only knew hazily what direction to make for...'[139] A rearguard covered 30th Division's retreat to Folies, while part of 36th Division ended up defending an old trench. The abortive attack had left a large gap in the line and several staff officers were captured before the line stabilised.

Summary, 26 March

So far, GHQ's plan for Third Army was working because it had reached the 1916 trenches and the River Ancre. Eight of the nine divisions sent to the Somme had been given to Byng, to make sure the line between Arras and Albert was secure. However, it was a completely different matter on Fifth Army's front. Gough had no natural or man-made feature to defend, so he had rounded up 3,000 rear area men to create a new defence line, only 12 miles from Amiens. Major General George Carey was given every spare machine-gun team, while a line of posts directed every straggler to reinforce the position.[140]

Road control was lacking, and it was a struggle to evacuate the wounded along the busy roads, especially when the casualty clearing stations started relocating. The Army Service Corps did its best to stock up dumps, but the lorry and wagon drivers found it difficult to find the fast-moving front line. It left soldiers scrounging for food and ammunition in abandoned canteens and stores, but it was always hard to find water. Refugees added to the traffic chaos, so cross-country tracks controlled by traffic police were set up for military traffic.[141]

The Germans had found it difficult to traverse the 1916 battlefield, but they were also struggling to come to terms with the amount of material the British were leaving behind. The ate and drank and then wondered if the U-Boat campaign against Allied shipping was as successful as their politicians were telling them.

As the fighting grew ever closer to Amiens, the British and French high command were meeting in the town of Doullens. The outcome of the conference was that they

---

137 Ibid. The fighting withdrawal of XIX Corps' right is detailed on pp. 502-3.
138 Ibid. The confusing situation caused by XVIII Corps' advance is covered on pp. 500-1.
139 *Falls, The History of the 36th (Ulster) Division*, p. 226.
140 Edmonds, *Military Operations: France and Belgium, 1918, Vol. I.* The composition of Carey's Force is given on p. 507.
141 Ibid. Road control and the evacuation of facilities and stores is detailed on pp. 534-5.

pledged to work close together under new management. Maréchal Ferdinand Foch would be in overall command Western Front.[142]

Third Army, 27 March

Third Army was holding a relatively intact line and it had plenty of reserves, so Byng's midday order banned corps headquarters from withdrawing because it had a negative effect on morale. Artillery fire stopped early massed attacks against VI Corps, so the Germans sent forward men in ones and twos, so they could attack in small groups. However, the men were reaching the limit of their endurance and an intense barrage stopped them in their tracks.[143] Battalion commanders were eventually allowed to retire around Ayette when the evening mist descended; it would be dangerous to hold the vulnerable position because it impossible to see the SOS flares.

Rossignol Wood was lost when 62nd Division ran out of bombs and the Germans knocked out two of the tanks sent to retake it; a misinterpreted order led to two more withdrawing. The 4th Australian Division had marched through the night to reach Hébuterne as the Germans probed the New Zealand Division, north of Beaumont Hamel. Enfilade fire by the Australians and SOS barrages dispersed all attacks and the Australians and New Zealanders closed the gap in IV Corps line, after forty-eight nerve-racking hours.[144]

There was desperate fighting along the Ancre, where 12th Division was driven out of Hamel and Mesnil. Reserves were sent from two locations and 'quite a lively fight raged, each under the impression that the other force was German'. North of Albert, 63rd Division had to abandon the low-lying river bank and withdraw onto the high ground.

Both 9th and 35th Divisions 'repulsed the massed attacks with great slaughter' south of Albert, before evacuating the shell trap called Dernancourt. Meanwhile 1st Cavalry Division held off the Germans between the Ancre and the Somme, while 4th and 3rd Australian Divisions deployed behind VII Corps. Lieutenant General Congreve's staff explained the situation and the current German tactics to the Australian staff, before handing over control.

Fifth Army, 27 March

Fifth Army still had a 6-mile gap to Third Army on its left and an equally dangerous gap to the French on its the right. Some of 16th Division's battalions did not get the order to join the chaotic withdrawal as the Germans crossed the Somme at Cérisy and

---

142 The Doullens conference is covered in detail on pp. 538-42.
143 Frederick Ponsonby, *The Grenadier Guards in the Great War of 1914-1918* (London; Macmillan, 1920) p. 14.
144 Stewart, *The New Zealand Division 1916-1919, Vol. I*, pp. 352-5.

Morcourt.[145] They continued pushing behind XIX Corps' flank but 39th Division had orders to prepare to counter-attack at dawn. Both 66th and 50th Divisions retired when they received the order but a few units fell back earlier than expected, either because they misinterpreted their orders or because they ran out of ammunition.[146] They were helped by 8th Division, which had sent reinforcements to drive the Germans back across Amiens road. Meanwhile, 24th Division had to abandon Warvillers when their ammunition ran out and it then withdrew to Vrély because the divisions to its flanks were withdrawing.[147]

Problems all along the line prompted Watts to tell his divisional commanders to withdraw onto Carey's line at 4 am. The men struggled to summon up enough strength to make one last march, but the Germans did not follow them. XIX Corps had escaped one more time.[148]

The remnants of 30th Division and 36th Division were scattered around Erches and Andechy. The first attack nearly captured 108 Brigade headquarters, so many units did not get General Maxse's message to retire. Some men were taken prisoner but the rest rallied round Folies, while the Germans focused on pushing south-west of XVIII Corps, towards Montdidier in the French sector.

During the fighting the Military Secretary, Major General Harold Ruggles-Brise, visited Gough.[149] It was clear that Fifth Army had not developed the Battle Zone but the fact he had too few troops and had too little to do so was required was ignored. That had led to the fast withdrawal to the Somme and Crozat Canals, where it proved impossible to hold on for long. The rapid retirements had left the French no time to deploy, resulting in further withdrawals and a loss of face in front of the French. Haig's offer to resign was ignored by the War Cabinet and instead, Gough was replaced by General Rawlinson. Fourth Army staff only had a little time to take over from Fifth Army's long-suffering team.

Third Army, 28 March

Ludendorff's plan was to extend the attack front by another 17 miles on 28 March, in the hope it would kick-start the advance elsewhere. But preparations for Operation Mars were so hurried, that men were seen working in the open, while batteries were spotted deploying.[150] The bombardment was similar to that fired on 21 March,

---

145 Sir James E. Edmonds, *Military Operations: France and Belgium, 1918, Vol. II: March and April: Continuation of the German Offensives* (London, HMSO, 1937), pp. 20-1 and 24-5.
146 Edmonds, *Military Operations: France and Belgium, 1918, Vol. II*, pp. 21-2.
147 Ibid., p. 23.
148 Ibid., pp. 26-7. The Chief of the Imperial General Staff, Sir Henry Wilson, 'had chosen to regard General Gough as responsible for the British retirement...'
149 Ibid., pp. 27-8.
150 Ibid. The problems the Germans faced in preparing and launching Operation Mars are covered on pp. 74-5.

however, the registration was rushed, and the preliminary bombardment missed many British trenches. The British artillery retaliated, causing havoc among the troops assembling for 7.30 am zero hour.

The British gunners reduced their range when they heard the sound of the barrage change, indicating the creeping barrage was moving forward. It meant many assault troops were hit crossing No Man's Land and this time, there was no fog to hide them. They soon discovered that the defences were much stronger than they had on 21 March because they had been held by the British for the past twelve months.[151]

First Army, 28 March

The outposts were overrun but the assault teams lost the creeping barrage crossing 56th Division's trenches between Arleux and Gavrelle. The artillery SOS barrage dispersed the assault troops while machine-gun teams pinned the survivors down. The Londoners fought from shell holes and communication trenches, withdrawing to the Battle Zone when the smoke cleared.[152]

Third Army, 28 March

Along the Scarpe, 4th Division had been keeping men out of the front line by day to reduce casualties but the early bombardment caught them before they could evacuate the front line.[153] Two battalions were overrun but the supports made a fighting withdrawal to the Battle Zone, as the mist cleared. Attacks hit 15th Division in succession from right to left, starting at 6 am. Green flares told the Germans gunners where to fire while the infantry advanced after a pre-arranged bombardment. XVII Corps ordered the artillery to fall back but the infantry misinterpreted the order and followed.[154]

VI Corps' artillery did not see the SOS signals in the mist, so 3rd Division fought along the Cojeul stream until their ammunition ran out.[155] One battalion commander took over the front line while another controlled the support line and they coordinated the withdrawal to the back of the Battle Zone between them. Flares signalled a new bombardment and the infantry advanced at a pre-agreed time but a message about holding the Green Line around Neuville Vitasse was again misinterpreted, so the Battle Zone was abandoned.

Ayette was also lost but 31st Division found it safer to keep the Germans at bay with machine-gun and artillery fire, rather than counter-attack. Both 42nd Division

151 Ibid. The German bombardment and the reaction to it are examined on p. 64
152 Ibid., pp. 69-71.
153 Ibid., p. 71.
154 Ibid., pp. 65-7.
155 Ibid., pp. 65-6.

and 62nd Division stopped many attacks, but Rossignol Wood was still entered.[156] The Australians stopped 'several half-hearted attempts' to take Hébuterne while the New Zealand Division stopped all attacks east of Colincamps.[157]

Along the Ancre, 12th Division, held on to Hamel and Aveluy Wood, even though the Germans attacked wearing helmets taken from the British dead, as a disguise.[158] But in Albert, 17th Division saw that the Germans were more interested in getting drunk than attacking: 'It is practically certain that the reason [they] did not reach Amiens was the looting in Albert.' The town which had been 'captured fairly easily, contained so much wine that the divisions, which ought properly to have marched through them lay about unfit to fight in the rooms and cellars.'

Fifth Army, 28 March

Rawlinson had seven battered divisions in a line south of the Somme, with only stragglers and support troops in support. The Germans had expanded the bridgehead across the river at Cérisy and 39th and 66th Divisions were under attack by the time the orders were issued. Some runners were hit while others could not find their destination, so the planned withdrawal turned into a chaotic retreat.[159] The two divisions broke contact and escaped across the Luce stream when it rained heavy during in the afternoon and they then withdrew behind Carey's Force when it was dark.

A plan to counter-attack towards the Amiens road, to secure XIX Corps left flank, was postponed to give the men time to rest. But there was still no artillery or machine-gun support for 61st Division when it advanced at midday and the attack ended in disaster.[160]

On XIX Corps' left, 50th Division was driven back towards Guillaucourt, resulting in 8th Division being outflanked.[161] One brigade major was wounded before the withdrawal order could be issued, so two battalions were overrun and the third had to fight its way out. Meanwhile, the Germans were driving 24th Division's flanks back around Vrély and Warvillers.[162] Again, the afternoon rain allowed all three divisions to break contact. On Fifth Army's right flank, the French relief of XVIII Corps took longer than expected and the Germans drove 30th and 20th Divisions from Arvillers before it was complete.[163]

156 Ibid. The fight for Rossignol Wood is chronicled on pp. 56-8.
157 Stewart, *The New Zealand Division 1916-1919, Vol. II*, pp. 358-9.
158 Edmonds, *Military Operations: France and Belgium, 1918, Vol. II*. The battle for Aveluy and Albert is detailed on pp. 55-6.
159 Ibid., pp. 49-50. Both divisional commanders were hit during the retreat.
160 Ibid., p. 48.
161 Ibid., pp. 21-2.
162 Ibid., p. 23.
163 Ibid., pp. 45-6.

A Lull in the Fighting, 29 March

Ludendorff halted Operation Mars and cancelled Operation Valkyrie, north of Arras. He then told Fourth and Sixth Armies to prepare Operation Georgette in Flanders. It meant 29 March was the quietest day across the Somme since the offensive had begun.

Third Army, 30 March to 3 April

An attack against the Guards Division, along the Cojeul stream on 30 March, was 'raked by the fiercest machine-gun, Lewis gun and rifle fire, while the gunners, working on their SOS lines, poured shells into them with relentless persistency.' The Germans got nowhere and there was no other action against Third Army.

On Fifth Army's front, enfilade fire was driving 66th and 39th Divisions back around Démuin until Australian troops counter-attacked.[164] But the main problem occurred when the French abandoned Mezières, allowing the Germans to infiltrate XIX Corps' line in Moreuil Wood in the mist. Both Rifle Wood and Little Wood were abandoned for a time and 20th Division could do little because its counter-attack orders arrived too late to act on. But the Canadian Cavalry Brigade recaptured Moreuil Wood while 8th Division secured the nearby bridges across the Avre stream.[165]

The only attack made on 31 March failed to take Moreuil Wood, again thanks to a timely cavalry charge.[166] The only action over the next three days involved dismounted cavalry clearing Rifle Wood, to secure Fifth Army's boundary with the French.

As the fighting died down, it was time to consider whether the Germans would attack the British around Villers Bretonneux or the French around Montdidier. The BEF was very understrength but Haig had to place his few reserves in the Arras area, so they could deploy north or south.[167] Foch wanted Fifth Army to advance astride the Somme, to secure Amiens while his own troops secure the railway south of the town. It was unlikely because Fifth Army was unable to go over the offensive. GHQ also wanted to pool their aerial resources because the German Air Force outnumbered the newly renamed Royal Air Force[168] 4:3 in planes while the French air force outnumbered the Germans by 8:1.[169]

---

164 Ibid., pp. 91-2.
165 Ibid. The fight for Moreuil Wood is explained on pp. 89-91.
166 Ibid., pp. 103-4.
167 One third of the BEF's divisions had just received replacements for casualties suffered while another third were waiting for theirs to arrive. It left them both short of experienced officers and men.
168 The Royal Flying Corps was renamed Royal Air Force on 1 April 1918.
169 Edmonds, *Military Operations: France and Belgium, 1918, Vol. II*, pp. 117-8.

Fourth Army, 4 and 5 April

Prisoners talked about a new offensive to capture ground on 4 April, so heavy howitzers could move close enough to shell Amiens. Panic in the city would make it difficult to supply Fourth Army during subsequent attacks. It was aimed at XIX Corps and all its battalions were exhausted, under strength and short of experienced officers and men.[170]

The attack north of the Amiens Road drove one brigade back and then turned behind the rest of 14th Division. Brigadier General Forster stayed as long as possible, so as not to cause alarm, only to be captured with many of his men. The Germans then advanced south, pushing 9 Australian Brigade out of Villers Bretonneux. A mixed group of cavalry, armoured cars and motor machine-gun batteries held the line, but it left 18th Division's flank exposed. Mud jammed their weapons and Germans surged forward through Lancer Wood when the rate of fire slackened. They may have moved closer to Amiens, but they were not close enough.

The attack the following morning was only carried out by a few assault teams. It was a shadow of what had happened on morning of 21 March because it was proving difficult to carry ammunition across the 1916 crater field. Bucquoy was lost and then regained while Chinese attacks disguised the real attack against Rossignol Wood. Ten out of eleven Mark IV tanks ditched crossing the rough ground, most of the infantry lost the barrage and the rest were pinned down in a sunken road.[171]

A portion of Aveluy Wood was lost but the Germans could not leave Albert. The biggest problem befell 4th Australian Division along the railway embankment south of the town, where the Germans used hedges for cover in the mist.[172] The artillery did not see the SOS flares, while the message asking for support arrived too late to stop the assault troops breaching the defensive position. The afternoon barrage was on time and the infantry retook the position without waiting for the tanks. These few minor attacks brought the battle of the Somme to an end on 5 April; Operation Georgette would start in Flanders only four days later.

The German Somme Offensive Summary

The BEF faced three difficulties at the start of 1918. It was short of men and had to reorganise its divisions down from nine to twelve battalions; something it did efficiently in a short space of time. It also had to take over a sizeable section of the French line, reducing the reserve below a safe limit. Meanwhile, the end of the war on the Eastern Front had allowed the Germans to move huge numbers of troops to the Western Front.

170 Ibid., pp. 121-2.
171 Ibid., pp. 134-5.
172 Ibid., pp. 131-2.

The BEF issued orders to create three layers of defence to resist a large attack but Fifth Army had too few troops to fulfil them. There was no one left to build new defensive systems by the time all the necessary tasks, such as manning the line and maintaining the logistics system, had been carried out.

The BEF's intelligence services warned of an attack, correctly guessing both its location and timing, but there was little Fifth Army could do to stop it. Many parts of the line endured the barrage and then stopped the initial attacks but the German storm troops infiltrated in enough places in the fog to warrant extensive withdrawals. It meant that troops often had to give up good defensive positions to man poor ones.

Communications were frequently compromised because the front line was moving so fast, however, few generals appreciated how long it took for orders to reach the front and they often arrived too late to be effective. Mistakes were made by ordering troops to withdraw in daylight to begin with, resulting in unnecessary casualties, however, movements were later confined to the hours of darkness.

The decision to abandon the 1916 Somme battlefield was a risky one but it proved to be the correct one. It shortened the BEF's supply line while placing the vast crater field behind the Germans. After just a week, the attack was spent and the failure of Operation Mars brought the offensive to an end.

8

The German Lys and Aisne Offensives
9 April-6 June 1918

Operation Georgette

Operation Michael may have been the main German offensive, but five others were planned to follow in quick succession in Flanders. Following the failure of Operation Mars around Arras on 28 March, Sixth Army scaled Operation Georgette down to an attack across the Lys plain with twenty-two divisions. Operation Flanders III involved Fourth Army crossing the Messines Ridge with fifteen divisions. The two attacks would seize Hazebrouck rail junction and the Flanders hills, forcing the BEF to abandon Ypres and fall back towards the Channel ports.[1]

By 6 April, both GHQ intelligence and the Royal Air Force observers were warning that the Portuguese Corps was threatened.[2] The German artillery then started shelling the British and Portuguese batteries with mustard gas but GHQ still thought the main attack would be made against Vimy Ridge.

The BEF's problems were many because Operation Michael had exhausted its reserves and First Army only had one spare exhausted division, even though it was holding a 40-mile long sector. GHQ was worried about the fighting qualities of the Portuguese Corps, because it was short of men and its morale was low.[3] The Lys area was usually too wet for operations until the end of the spring but the plan was to defend the Rivers Lys and Lawe, if it was driven back. Reserve troops would man the Battle Zone while engineers prepared the bridges for demolition. First Army even

---

1   Sir James E. Edmonds, *Military Operations: France and Belgium, 1918, Vol. II: March and April: Continuation of the German Offensives* (London, HMSO, 1937), the evolution of the German plan, and the scaling down of the Lys attack, is covered on pp. 149-55.
2   Edmonds, *Military Operations: France and Belgium, 1918, Vol. II*, pp. 140-1.
3   Ibid. The Portuguese Corps' problems are explained on p. 147-8.

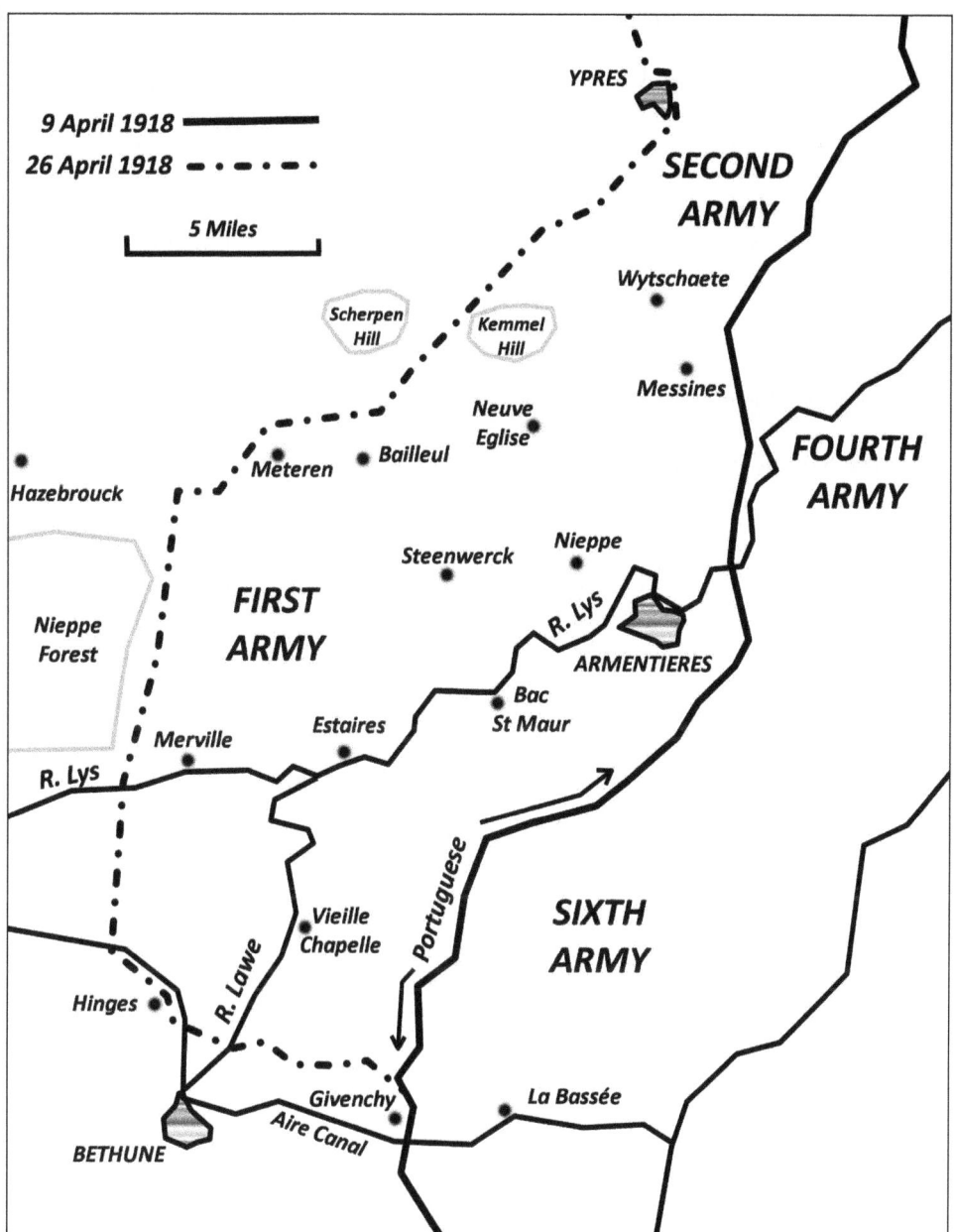

Map 8. Lys Offensive: 9 April-26 April 1918: A second great offensive threatened to capture Hazebrouck and destabilise the BEF line in Flanders.

talked about giving the Portuguese a rest on 8 April and the plan was to carry out the relief the following evening.[4] Unfortunately, the Germans attacked first.

First Army had developed the typical three-zone defence across the Lys area, with a Forward Zone and a Battle Zone 2 miles behind. The Army Line (or Green Line) was another 2 miles to the rear but little work had been done on it. Infantry would man bridgeheads along the River Lys and Lawe stream, while the engineers demolished the permanent bridges and burnt the temporary bridges.[5]

The German Air Force had built new airfields but squadrons did not move to the area until just before the attack. It kept the build-up of aircraft secret but it also gave the crews little time to familiarise themselves with the area. Fighters would keep the skies clear and make ground attacks; reconnaissance planes would find targets for the artillery and bombers and then assess damage. Sixth Army managed to keep Z-Day a secret and 250,000 men made their deployment march (*Aufmarsch*) over several nights.

The Bombardment and Zero Hour

Again, *Oberst* Georg Bruchmüller had designed Sixth Army's bombardment and it started with 35,000 mustard gas shells exploding in Armentières late on 7 April. The 425 German batteries were then divided into three groups which waited until 4.15 am on 9 April.[6] The field guns of the Counter Artillery Groups hit the Allied batteries with mustard gas and high explosive while the heavy guns of the Deep Battle Artillery Groups began a one hundred-minute-barrage against First Army's lines of communications. At the same time, the field guns and trench mortars of the Infantry Artillery Groups hit the trenches with tear gas, phosgene gas and high explosive shells with three short bombardments.[7] A crescendo of shelling at 8.20 am warned the troops to deploy and then the Infantry Artillery Groups switched to firing the protective barrage which crept across No Man's Land after a few minutes.

The advance used the same tactics as Operation Michael, with scouts guiding the shock troops to weak points in the Portuguese line with flares.[8] Progress was reported with flares or flame throwers discharging fire every 200 yards intervals. It meant the aerial observers could adjust the artillery barrage, so it was just ahead of the infantry. The support troops would then surround and silence any strongpoints with bombers, flamethrowers, mortars and field guns.

---

4   Ibid., p. 148.
5   Ibid. First Army's defensive schemes are described on pp. 160-2.
6   Ibid. The bombardment is covered in detail on pp. 164-
7   Mustard gas was not used on the trenches because it would have affected the advancing German troops.
8   The *Stossentruppen* were armed with light machine guns, light trench mortars and flame throwers.

Sixth Army Attacks First Army, 9 April

Some officers in 40th Division's sector thought the German bombardment was retaliation for a raid but part of the line was soon overrun. Many troops found it difficult to distinguish between the Portuguese and German uniforms in the mist.[9] Some of the Germans headed for Fleurbaix but the rest turned on 40th Division's flank.[10] Major General John Ponsonby eventually issued an order to stand fast at 9 am; 'as the troops were not thoroughly familiar with the defences of the sector, there was to be no retrograde movement; units were to fight it out where they stood'. In other words, he recognised that a withdrawal could easily turn into a rout. Instead he directed his reserve brigade to the Battle Zone covering Laventie but the Germans had reached it first, so they deployed in the shallow trench called the Green Line. They were soon overrun in the mist and the survivors then faced a running battle to get back to Sailly-sur-Lys, on the river.

The bombardment proved too much for the men of the 2nd Portuguese Division and the survivors either surrendered or fled, leaving a huge gap in First Army's line between Neuve Chapelle and Richebourg l'Avoué.[11] All communications were cut and stragglers had given the reserve brigade tales of woe before the mounted messenger reached it. The commander later reported that the 'whole division was either lost or scattered.'[12]

The left flank of Sixth Army's attack hit Givenchy and the Germans had a low opinion of 55th Division because it had been overrun at Cambrai, the previous November. The division had been holding the sector for three months and it had been busy building a 'series of well-concealed breastworks, loop-holed walls and buildings. Cross fire from the various posts covered the ground in front and excellent enfilade machine-gun fire was possible from concrete emplacements.'

Most of the line held on but again, the similarity between the Portuguese and German uniforms caused problems. 'Owing to the thick fog and a large amount of wire, the fighting consisted of isolated combats carried on all over the area by small parties of officer and men'. Route A Keep was lost because most of the garrison were hit en route but the reserves extended the flank back to the Lawe stream.[13]

Hundreds of refugees joined the Portuguese soldiers squeezing past the wagons queuing to escape across the Lys. XV Corps' reserves deployed along the river, protecting the engineers preparing the charges on the bridges. But only a few men reached Bac St Maur and the bridge was only damaged because some of the leads had

---

9   Edmonds, *Military Operations: France and Belgium, 1918, Vol. II*, p. 170. The uniforms were similar shades of field grey. 'Fire was withheld until the shape of helmets could be distinguished in the fog'.
10   Ibid., pp. 171-3.
11   Ibid. The German reports on p. 168 talk of 'feeble resistance'.
12   Ibid., p. 168.
13   Ibid. 55th Division's heroic stand is covered on pp. 169-71.

been cut. So, the Germans were across as soon as it was dark and lorries delivered material to build their own temporary bridge. It left XV Corps with a big dent in the middle of its line and the brigade sent forward to make a counter-attack found the enemy in Croix du Bac.[14]

The only troops moving forward across the Lawe on IX Corps' front were two small corps' units and they were met by a tide of stragglers and refugees as they tried to get to the Battle Zone.[15] They took rifles and ammunition from the fleeing Portuguese and would use them to defend the bridgeheads along the canal.

Over 6,000 Portuguese were taken prisoner and another 13,650 would eventually assemble behind First Army's line, creating a 10-mile wide breach and First Army only had two divisions to cover it. The 50th Division deployed along the Lys and the Lawe, only to come under fire from field guns which had been man-handled up to shoot at the bridgeheads at point blank range. Most of the bridges were demolished but the Germans had crossed at Bac St Maur and were poised to seize Pont Levis as well.[16] It took until evening for 51st Division to reach the Lawe because the 'roads were so congested with Portuguese troops and refugees moving westwards'.[17]

There they were joined by the corps troops. The Germans had not had it all their own way. The morning mist may have blinded the British machine gun and artillery teams and the bombardment had cut communications to the front but it had also disorientated some of the assault troops and they had lost contact with their creeping barrage. The bombardment had then slackened off around dawn while batteries moved forward, and the infantry marked their new front line. The bombardment restarted at 8 am and trench mortars joined in at the end of the forty-five-minute barrage, to cover the assault troops as they deployed.

Ditches and streams were slowing the advance down, leaving gun limbers and supply wagons queuing up at the bridges.[18] Ten captured Mark IV British tanks were supposed to have supported the attack but the ground was too soft to deploy and some stopped the traffic after breaking down on the roads.[19] RAF fighter planes were able to strafe the traffic jams as soon as the mist cleared.

Fourth Army Attacks Second Army, 10 April

The original plan had been for Fourth Army to wait until Sixth Army had crossed the River Lys. However, Crown Prince Rupprecht decided to let it attack twenty-four hours afterwards, to give General Sixt von Armin a date to work towards. Fourth Army would attack Second Army's right flank, on the Messines ridge while Sixth

14   Ibid. The loss of Bac St Maur and the fight for Croix du Maur are detailed on pp. 182-3.
15   Ibid. The fight to hold the Lawe is covered on pp. 176-7.
16   Ibid., pp. 179-81 covers 50th Division's deployment.
17   Ibid., pp. 177-8.
18   Ibid., pp. 190-2 explains the German view of the events of the day.
19   Ibid., p. 189.

Army kept advancing across the River Lys. The two advances would force First Army to evacuate Armentières.

It was obvious to IX Corps that an attack was being planned, in fact the preparations were so obvious that some though they were a diversion. Everything had been quiet on 9 April, but Second Army's batteries were subjected to a gas bombardment at 5.15 am the following morning. A barrage of high explosive shells then hit communications centres, switching to the British Forward Zone at 7.30 am. The assault troops advanced through the mist fifteen minutes later.[20]

All three of IX Corps' divisions had just received replacements to replace casualties from the Somme battle and 'many brigadiers saw their reformed brigades for the first time on the march up to the battle'.[21] Messines ridge was a crater field, so the troops held outposts and strongpoints on the east side rather than trenches.[22] The reserves used the old trenches on the west side where the heavy artillery relied on deep signal cables which dated back to the previous year's offensive. Again, the morning mist meant the machine-gun teams had to shoot along pre-determined lines while batteries could only hit pre-registered targets, providing they saw the SOS flares.

Assault troops overran 9th and 19th Divisions' outposts around Wytschaete, Messines and the Comines Canal in the morning mist and then pushed beyond the strongpoints. The support troops then surrounded them with flamethrowers, machine guns and field guns.[23] Artillery helped hold the centre of the ridge but the villages at either end were lost. There were protests when the South African Brigade was told to recapture Messines, because every man was a replacement for those killed or captured only three weeks earlier, on the Somme. They still recaptured the village.[24]

Major General Guy Bainbridge had been warned that 34th Division was due to withdraw from Armentières, so he deployed troops to cover his right flank. But he did not know that the German engineers had secretly bridged the Lys, leaving the duckboards just below the water surface. They launched pontoons during the night, ready for the troops to run across at zero hour and infiltrate the British line. The main force then deployed into the bridgehead and forced 25th Division back 2 miles into a salient covering Hill 63, north of Ploegsteert Wood.[25]

20   Ibid. Fourth Army's preparations and bombardment are covered on pp. 206-7.
21   Ibid., p. 160 covers the challenges faced in bringing divisions back up to strength in only a few days after the Somme. For example, 50th Division only had three days to accomplish many tasks.
22   Ibid., p. 205 describes Second Army's position on the Messines ridge.
23   Ibid. The fight for the ridge is covered on pp. 209-12.
24   Ibid. The South African Brigade's attack is detailed on pp. 211-2.
25   Ibid. The loss of Ploegsteert Wood is covered on 207-9.

First Army Defends the River Lys, 10 April

The two German attacks placed 34th Division in 'a truly precarious situation',[26] particularly from the Bac St Maur bridgehead, to the west, so, Lieutenant General John DuCane issued the order to evacuate Armentières at 10 am. It meant that 15,000 men and fifty guns had get through the gas filled streets and across the Lys before the engineers could demolish all the bridges. It was relatively easy to escape from the east side of the town but the runners had to 'run as hard as God would let them' to get the message to the battalions south-east of the town.[27] One escaped through the town around 3 pm but three other commanders decided to wait until 4.30 pm, to give their men time to organise. However, the line began to crumble earlier, and it soon became every man for himself. Improvised rearguards allowed most to escape but a few had to build makeshift bridges or swim across the Lys. One battalion made a last stand around Erquinghem for eight hours, allowing hundreds to escape across the river.[28] The engineers waited until the last few men were across before the bridges were blown and they then joined the salient around Pont de Nieppe and along the Bailleul railway.

Brigadier General Freyberg VC advanced towards Bac St Maur during the afternoon, only to find the Germans were already in Steenwerck, so he dug in alongside the gun batteries to await the next attack.[29] Another attack towards the Lys was driven back in the mist, taking several other battalions with them. Fortunately, the Germans had stayed in the village and they ate and drank as 'duty was forgotten.' They had been told that Allies were starving but it was, in fact, they who were short of food and drink.

Major General Henry Jackson had deployed 50th Division along an 8-mile sector of the River Lys and the Lawe stream but he faced three problems. The Germans who had crossed at Bac St Maur were pushing past his left flank while a mix-up had left Pont Levis unmanned. But another misunderstanding led to Estaires being lost and it sparked a withdrawal from the Lys.[30] Again, the Germans preferred to loot and drink alcohol rather than follow up their success.[31]

Meanwhile, repeated attacks were pushing 51st Division back around Fosse and Vieille Chapelle and they crossed the Lawe during the night.[32] But Major General George Carter-Campbell could not fall back to a better line, because he had to hold

26   Shakespear, *The Thirty-Fourth Division, 1915–1919*, p. 218.
27   Ibid. The evacuation of Armentières is detailed on pp. 218-20.
28   Edmonds, *Military Operations: France and Belgium, 1918, Vol. II*. The 1/4th Duke of Wellington's heroic defence is covered on pp. 201-2.
29   Shakespear, *The Thirty-Fourth Division*, p. 199. Freyberg had been awarded for leadership during the 1916 Somme campaign.
30   Edmonds, *Military Operations: France and Belgium, 1918, Vol. II*, pp. 196-8.
31   Ibid., p. 228.
32   Ibid., pp. 194-5.

on until 61st Division arrived. He was comforted to hear that 55th Division was able to hold on around Le Touret, Festubert and Givenchy.[33]

Backs to the Wall, 11 April

Both 9th Division and 19th Division opened fire at the last minute when the Germans advanced across the Messines Ridge, driving them back in disorder.[34] Wytschaete was held but a serious problem occurred south of Messines during the afternoon. The Germans had outflanked Hill 63, so Major General Bainbridge ordered a withdrawal of everyone but the outposts during the morning, however, three of 25th Division's battalion commanders misinterpreted the instructions and decided to hold on until dusk. The next attack overran their line and many men were taken prisoner in the tunnels under Hill 63. 'Interference by divisional headquarters with the men on the spot had brought about an unnecessary disaster.'[35]

All day long, 34th Division fought to reduce the salient it was holding, withdrawing first to the Nieppe Switch and then to Pont d'Achelles during the night.[36] Men were supposed to follow the Bailleul road and railway but the 'night was very dark, detailed maps were scarce, the positions alike of friend and foe were very uncertain and were constantly changing.'[37] Artillery fire were also hitting the two routes, so the men moved in small groups across country, only to find the Germans at the rendezvous point. Major General Nicholson's men had to escape capture for the second night in a row.

Two of 29th Division's brigades contained the Bac St Maur bridgehead until they withdrew behind the Stil Becque stream during the night.[38] However, an early attack drove 40th Division back, south-west of the Steenwerck, before 31st Division could reinforce it.[39] The decision to withdraw from the Lys had left 50th Division spread thinly, with no one on its flanks. The German gunners man-handled their weapons forward to add to the weight of fire and while some battalions withdrew north, others fell back to the west.[40] Officers could only control the men in sight, without any direction or maps, in a running battle which became a fight for survival.[41]

---

33   Ibid., p. 194.
34   Ibid., pp. 243.
35   Ibid., pp. 240-2, 244.
36   Ibid., pp. 235-7.
37   Shakespear, *The Thirty-Fourth Division*, p. 228.
38   Edmonds, *Military Operations: France and Belgium, 1918, Vol. II*, pp. 229-30.
39   Ibid., pp. 231-2.
40   Ibid. The 50th Division's battle is detailed on pp. 227-9, 233-4.
41   This was outstanding behaviour considering that many of the officers and men were replacements for casualties suffered only a couple of weeks earlier. Some officers had barely got to know their companies and platoons before going into battle.

Dawn found 51st Division sheltering in ditches or shell scrapes along the Lawe stream; not only 'platoons and companies but also men from different battalions, becoming intermingled.'[42] A brave stand at Vieille Chapelle helped many men to escape but battery commanders were forced to send their guns back one at a time, while the rest kept firing, as the Germans pushed the infantry back.[43]

The situation was eased a little by 55th Division extending its left flank as far as the Lawe Canal.[44] The Aire Canal was held by 'a succession of men of mixed units strung out at wide intervals, who had scratched themselves into the ground with their entrenching tools under heavy rifle and machine-gun fire.' They held their position despite 'shelling of our front, support and reserve lines by our own artillery.'[45]

Fourth Army had advanced 8 miles in just three days, almost to the edge of the Nieppe Forest. It meant their heavy artillery were nearly in range of Hazebrouck's rail junction, which GHQ relied on to supply both First and Second Army. The second attack on 10 April had miss-footed the BEF, because Second Army's reserves had been sent south to First Army's area. Foch refused to send any infantry divisions to Flanders while his offer of a cavalry corps had been refused because it would obstruct the roads behind the British line. Instead a promise was made to assemble a French reserve around Arras, but that would take time.[46] All Haig could do was to issue a special Order of the Day, stating the situation and telling everyone to hold on; it would become known as the 'Backs to the Wall' order.[47]

Marching to the Sound of Guns, 12 April

Brigades were down to the size of battalions, while battalions were reduced to the size of a companies, after just three days in action, and First Army had few reserves left. The clear weather meant that the RAF pilots dropped more bombs and took more photographs than any day since the war.[48] It meant the artillery knew where the front line was for the first time but the confused nature of the fighting meant that batteries were often supporting divisions other than their own, making communications difficult. For example, IX Corps had organised its artillery into four sector groups, each containing field guns and heavy howitzers.

---

42   Edmonds, *Military Operations: France and Belgium, 1918, Vol. II.* The 51st Division's fight is covered on pp. 224-6, 232.
43   Again, remarkable discipline, considering 51st Division had 'scarcely reconstituted after the March fighting [and] had entered the battle with less than half its establishment of officers. Edmonds, *Military Operations: France and Belgium, 1918, Vol. II*, pp. 224.
44   Edmonds, *Military Operations: France and Belgium, 1918, Vol. II*, pp. 222-3.
45   TNAWO 95/2928/5: 166 Brigade's War Diary.
46   Edmonds, *Military Operations: France and Belgium, 1918, Vol. II.* The discussions with Foch are covered on pp. 247-8.
47   Ibid. The text of the message is given on p. 249.
48   H. A. Jones, *The Air in the War, Vol. IV* (Oxford: Clarendon Press, 1934) p. 381.

Gun batteries withdrew from the Ypres Salient, one at a time, during the day and the infantry battalions followed at dusk, creating the reserve Second Army needed. Supply wagons had removed everything before dawn while outposts made it seem that the Forward Zone was still being held in strength.[49]

Elsewhere artillery observers were using church towers to establish a rudimentary flash spotting system, to find the German guns which were being manhandled forward. Mist meant they could not see far most of the time, so the heavy guns focused on hitting the congested roads with map fire. The field batteries had no time to dig in, so they had to hide their guns behind buildings or hedges. It was easier for the machine-gun teams and infantry to hide and they built camouflaged positions in ditches and behind hedges. All the time, engineers were marking out the next defensive line to fall back on and putting men to work on fortifying farms and cottages.

German observers on Hill 63 directed artillery fire onto 25th Division and it had to fall back to the Green Line, east of Neuve Eglise, during the night. XV Corps was attacked at 7.30 am in thick mist. One of 34th Division's battalions was cut off at Pont-d'Achelles but the support battalions blocked the Bailleul road. However, the Germans were pushing through gaps in 31st and 29th Divisions' line and enfilading the troops to the flanks. An orderly withdrawal in stages followed but groups of men were often cut off by ditches and streams as 'thick clouds of skirmishers supported closely by mobile trench mortars and light batteries' followed close behind.[50] Some German flares told the artillery where to fire while others guided reinforcements to weak points in the British line. By nightfall, the two battered divisions had fallen back 3 miles to the south-west of Bailleul.

The good news was that reinforcements had arrived. The 33rd Division rounded up stragglers, reinforced 31st Division on Hoegenacker Ridge and then dug in as supply wagons cantered along the line, dropping off boxes of ammunition and food. A different tactic was used in front of Strazeele, where the 1st Australian Division formed a new line, ready for 29th Division to fall back through, rather than trying to fill the gaps in the line.

The men of 50th Division fought on, 'taking up and falling back from one position to another, incurring many casualties, but causing great loss to the enemy' between Vieux Berquin and the River Lys.[51] Meanwhile, 5th Division encountered disorder as it marched through the Nieppe Forest, 'where all was chaos; no one knew what was happening or where any troops were.' Major General Reginald Stephens 'urged that the line should be in front of the forest and not through it.'[52] They met 3,000 refugees

49   Edmonds, *Military Operations: France and Belgium, 1918, Vol. II.* The withdrawal is detailed on pp.274-5.

50   TNA WO 95/2358/1: 11th East Lancashire Regiment's War Diary.

51   Edmonds, *Military Operations: France and Belgium, 1918, Vol. II.* The 50th Division's fighting withdrawal is explained on pp. 262-4.

52   A.H. Hussey and D.S. Inman, *The Fifth Division in the Great War* (London: Nisbet and Co.,1921) p. 210

from Merville but very few soldiers; British or German. They deployed on the far side of the trees with ease but they could not retake the town.[53]

On XI Corps front, the German trench mortars hit the men holding 51st Division's line, who were sheltering in a line of shell scrapes and ditches, but the British guns overshot their target. The German infantry advanced through the mist, as the Scots tried to 'improvise [their] lines of defence but, in the absence of officers, these all broke down'.[54] There was no time to blow up the bridges along the Clarence stream, so the German troops were soon amongst the field batteries.[55]

The line was only saved because 61st Division had marched to the sound of guns and it arrived as the Scots fell back across the Clarence stream. The battalions were at full strength but the men had never been in action before.[56] The 1/5th DCLIs (Pioneers) had 420 drafts and the 'change from the barrack square to the firing line against a well-trained, war bitten enemy was a terrible experience.'[57] It was just as well that one hundred machine-gun teams from a machine-gun battalion and a tank battalion were deployed along the Clarence stream between the infantry posts.[58]

Along the Aire Canal to the south, artillery officers used their guns to cover the bridges, using stragglers to cover their position. Major General Cyril Deverell studied 3rd Division's chaotic situation from the top of Mont Bernenchon, uncertain where his men were.'[59] The Germans had decided against advancing beyond Locon and tried to cross the Aire Canal instead; they failed. They also failed to dislodge 55th Division around Festubert and Givenchy for the fourth day running.

Fourth Army's Attacks, 13-16 April

Fourth German Army's plan was to capture Neuve Eglise on 13 April and a surprise attack overran 25th Division's line in the early morning mist, creating a gap between Neuve Eglise and Crucifix Corner.[60] Some Germans turned west behind 34th Division, only to be scattered by their own supporting barrage.[61] The rest became involved in a confused fight around Neuve Eglise which lasted into the following day. Lieutenant General Alexander Hamilton-Gordon decided against making a costly

---

53   Edmonds, *Military Operations: France and Belgium, 1918, Vol. II*. 5th Division's deployment is covered on pp. 264-5.
54   Bewsher, *The History of the 51st (Highland) Division 1914–1918*, p. 313.
55   Edmonds, *Military Operations: France and Belgium, 1918, Vol. II*, 51st Division's difficult situation is detailed on pp. 258-61.
56   Ibid. The 61st Division's timely arrival is covered on pp. 261-2.
57   TNAWO 95/3050/3: 1st Duke of Cornwall's Light Infantry.
58   Edmonds, *Military Operations: France and Belgium, 1918, Vol. II*, p. 261. There were no tanks in Flanders. The Tank Corps had lost around 60 per cent of its strength during the recent Somme offensive.
59   Ibid., p. 259.
60   Ibid. The breakthrough to Neuve Eglise is detailed on pp. 295-7.
61   Ibid., pp. 292-4.

counter-attack and instead ordered Major General Lothian Nicholson to hold onto until dusk, to give reinforcements time to reach on Ravelsberg Ridge. 'During the night they slipped away' one company at a time, while Lewis-gun teams gave covering fire.[62] The highest point on the ridge, Crucifix Corner, was lost the following morning until a counter-attack 'drove off the Boche, deceiving them as to their numbers by their loud shouts'.[63] There was heavy fighting along the crest throughout the day, but the line still held.

It took 59th Division all night to take over Ravelsberg Ridge because it had just received a lot of replacements who had never been in action. They then discovered that their shallow trenches were 'clearly visible and no attempt at camouflage had been possible' when the German bombardment started at dawn on 15 April.[64] Crucifix Corner was soon lost and the Germans then rolled up the line, taking Mont de Lille which overlooked Bailleul. A general retreat to and beyond the Kemmel-Meteren Line followed.

It meant 34th Division's weary men had to be sent back into the line after just sixteen hours rest. 'The strength and position of the enemy, as well as the lines on which he was advancing, were not known and there had been no time to form an organised outpost line.'[65] Major General Nicholson had to take command of six depleted brigades but this time they were supported by forty-eight Lewis gun teams taken from a tank battalion.[66] Observers thought the Germans would assemble around the asylum north-east of Bailleul, ready for a dawn attack and they were right; a barrage by heavy howitzers caused many casualties.

To the west, the Germans had edged forward to locate 33rd Division's line along Hoegenacker Ridge for their artillery on 14 April.[67] Fortunately, the line had been reinforced by forty Lewis gun teams handed over by a nearby tank battalion. The Germans exploited a gap 33rd Division left in its line by accident the following day and Meteren was lost.[68] The 2nd New Zealand Entrenching Battalion struggled to contain the breakthrough, resulting in the largest number of New Zealand prisoners seized during the war.

Fourth Army's attack on 16 April was made west of Wytschaete, where XXII Corps had just taken over 9th Division's line. The heavy artillery had not had time to add the Scots front line to their target list when two battalions were overrun

---

62   Shakespear, *The Thirty-Fourth Division, 1915–1919*, p. 234.
63   Ibid., p. 236.
64   Edmonds, *Military Operations: France and Belgium, 1918, Vol. II*, p. 322. They had been dug in the dark by inexperienced men.
65   Shakespear, *The Thirty-Fourth Division, 1915–1919*, p.240.
66   Tanks were of little use in defence because they could not hide from the enemy artillery, but their machine guns were very valuable.
67   Edmonds, *Military Operations: France and Belgium, 1918, Vol. II*, p. 308.
68   Ibid., p. 331.

around Spanbroekmolen crater. The counter-attack set off late and missed its creeping barrage.[69]

Sixth Army's Attacks 13 to 16 April

Repeated attacks finally drove 31st Division and 29th Division back around Vieux Berquin late on 13 April, but they had done what had been asked of them. They had given 1st Australian Division and 5th Division time to establish a line without interference. There was little wire, while the high-water table made it unwise for 5th Division's men to dig deep in front of the Nieppe Forest. The crops in the fields made it difficult to see, so the tired gunners had to resort to map fire and target roads and villages. Supplies were few and far between, so scroungers were sent out to find abandoned stores and ammunition dumps; they then used stolen lorries to distribute supplies.[70] Fortunately, the Germans were too busy 'ransacking the cellars in Merville and had not pressed their advantage home.'[71]

The Germans had not realised that the tired men of 31st Division and 29th Division had withdrawn, leaving them facing the fresh 1st Australian Division and 5th Division covering Strazeele and the Nieppe Forest. At dawn on 14 April, they saw 'miles of infantry, slowly but surely goose-stepping towards them. Officers on grey horses were riding up and down the column.'[72] The Australian officers allowed 'them to come close before giving the order to fire, then meeting them with intense bursts which had demoralising effects.'[73]

The Germans were so tired and harassed that there had been little action along west and south sides of the Lys salient. Men from 55th Division had recaptured Keep A following a three-minute hurricane bombardment on 13 April.[74] Then 4th and 3rd Divisions prepared a counter-attack across the Aire Canal the following day. The assault companies ran across the bridges in small groups, assembling in ditches on the far bank.[75] A thirty-minute barrage covered the support companies as they crossed and then the attack went in. The north bank of the canal was secured but an extra artillery barrage was required to drive the Germans out of Pacaut Wood. A counter-attack at dawn on 15 April failed to establish a foothold across the Aire Canal. German

69 Simpson (ed.), *The History of the Lincolnshire Regiment 1914-1918*, p. 323.
70 Hussey and Inman, *The Fifth Division in the Great War*, pp. 210-2. The artillery teams had covered 65 miles in just twenty-four hours.
71 Hussey and Inman, *The Fifth Division in the Great War*, p. 211.
72 Charles E.W. Bean, *The Official History of Australia in the War, Vol. V: The Australian Imperial Force in France during the Main German Offensive, 1918* (Sydney: Angus and Robertson, 1941) p. 466.
73 Ibid., p. 469.
74 TNA WO 95/1429/2: 13th King's War Diary.
75 TNA WO 95/1495/5: 1st Hampshire Regiment War Diary. Also, TNA WO 95/1609/4: 1st Somerset Regiment War Diary.

General Lothian

on

engineers launched a pontoon bridge during the night, but the morning attack just created a narrow bridgehead.[76]

Operation Tannenberg, 17 to 19 April

Mist hid the preparations for Operation Tannenberg, and it had three ambitious objectives. Firstly, to hit the Belgians north of Ypres; secondly, capture the Flanders hills; thirdly, advance either side of the Nieppe Forest. The bombardment began before dawn on 17 April.

The German observers had spent two days locating 19th Division's new line north of Wulverghem[77] but the bombardment still missed its targets and the attack two hours later did not go far. It did mean that Major General George Jeffreys' men had given away their position, so the German observers could direct a second, more accurate, barrage while the infantry crept closer. Both Aircraft Farm and Donegal Farm were taken but the German troops then decided to withdraw to a safe distance, so they could dig in.[78]

The German artillery also hit both Mont Rouge and Mont Noir at dawn on 17 April, 'shifting the barrage backwards and forwards' but the counter-barrage disorganised the assault troops. 'The attacking waves were cut down by furious machine-gun fire… The foremost waves were compelled to return to their jumping-off trenches, suffering severe losses. There the troops lay the whole day under the heaviest fire and the British aeroplanes swooped low, their bombs tore great gaps in the ranks.'[79]

On XV Corps' front, 1st Australian Division had hidden its artillery in the Nieppe Forest, while their camouflaged machine guns had created interlocking fields of fire. The German gunners eventually opened fire at 9 am on 17 April but the aerial spotters had failed to locate the Australian front line and they 'shot at pretty well everything marked on the map, farms, cross-roads, villages, even some hedges.'[80] The German infantry advanced in short rushes an hour later but heavy fire made sure they did not go far. The German artillery soon ran short of ammunition, but the Australians had plenty. 'German officers could be seen leaping out of the trenches and trying to induce

76   Edmonds, *Military Operations: France and Belgium, 1918, Vol. II*, pp. 361-2.
77   The division had withdrawn after the loss of Neuve Eglise hill because German observers could look over its line.
78   Ibid., p. 346.
79   Ibid., p. 341. Taken from German regimental histories (96 and 163rd Regiments).
80   Bean, *Australian Official History, Vol. V*, pp. 483-4.

their men to follow, but the barrage of artillery and the fire of small arms was so intense that the infantry standing along the trenches would not leave shelter.'[81]

The Germans were in an even bigger dilemma opposite 61st Division, south of the Nieppe Forest. The ground was flat, and they were forced to live in shell scrapes and ditches. It was hard to get ammunition to the front line and even harder to get their field guns forward because there was so little cover.

The Final Attacks on the Lys, 18 to 29 April

The BEF was short of men because it had lost 210,000 casualties in just twenty-five days and 90 per cent of them were infantry. It had only received 114,000 and while some of the conscripts were young, they were all inexperienced.[82]

Haig wanted to open the sea locks around Dunkirk and St Omer, to create a last stand position if the Flanders hills were lost. Foch was reluctant to do so, because the saltwater would ruin the farmland and he was confident the British and French troops would hold their line.[83] Plumer was considering how to withdraw back to St Omer if the hills were lost because he had no manpower to build any new defensive lines behind Second Army. But the Germans were having their own problems as they prepared to attack Kemmel hill. They were struggling to get guns and ammunition across the River Lys, because they were under continuous artillery fire, while it was difficult to hide them from the British observers.

Several attacks were made at different times around the Lys salient on 18 April. Fourth Army planned a pre-dawn attack against 59th Division. However, the bombardment landed short, hitting the assembling assault troops. The observers could not see the SOS signals through the mist, and no one was in a fit state to advance at zero hour.[84]

On Sixth Army's front, the preliminary bombardment struck XI Corps' batteries for four hours while the infantry assembled close to the Clarence stream.[85] A three-hour pause followed, while the mist cleared, and then an intense barrage at 8 am was the signal for the assault troops to deploy. No one reached the Clarence stream when the attack began ten minutes later.

The bombardment hit trenches, villages and road junctions for two hours before the infantry advanced towards 4th and 3rd Divisions' positions along the Aire Canal at 5 am. Pontoons and footbridges were launched onto the water but everyone was pinned down along the canal bank and they surrendered at dawn.[86]

81   Ibid., pp. 484-5.
82   Edmonds, *Military Operations: France and Belgium, 1918, Vol. II*, The statistics are given on pp. 326-7.
83   Ibid., pp. 338.
84   Ibid., p. 363.
85   Ibid., pp. 362-3.
86   Ibid., pp. 361-2.

A gas barrage kept 1st Division's reserves underground for too long and wounded men then delayed them deploying out of the dug outs, so they were all captured. Route Keep A was lost because the garrison was hit as it deployed but orderlies, cooks and signallers helped to hold the Tuning Fork. The rest of the attack faltered in the mist and a counter-attack drove the Germans back.[87]

The failure on 18 April resulted in a pause in the fighting for several days. Haig's staff thought the Germans wanted to capture Hazebrouck in Flanders but Pétain's staff were adamant that Amiens on the Somme was the target. The start of a five-day bombardment of Kemmel hill signified the British were right. The Germans planned to advance through the Nieppe Forest, and a gas bombardment of the area began late on 21 April. Steps to make the area safe included roaming teams neutralising gas concentrations, men posted along the roads and rides to warn of problem areas and teams of stretcher bearers who could evacuate the affected.[88]

Men ran across the Aire Canal in ones and twos to form a bridgehead and then three pontoons were launched on 22 April, so 4th Division could secure Pacaut Wood. The 1st Australian Division captured Meteren by stealth early the following morning, reporting the success with green flares. However, a similar attack the following night ended in disaster because the men were spotted in the bright moonlight and the gunners did not see the SOS signals.[89]

The front then went quiet, so the British artillery fired a bombardment every morning, hoping to catch German troops deploying, and the observers then spent the rest of the day looking for targets. Evening raids were used to capture documents or prisoners and they soon learnt that the elite Alpine Corps had taken over the line and it had orders to capture Kemmel hill.[90]

Foch had eventually sent reinforcements north to help the BEF and Fifth French Army deployed north of Amiens. The Tenth French Army moved to Flanders and had been named the *Détachement de l'Armée du Nord* (the Army Detachment of the North or DAN) when it took over the Kemmel hill sector on 21 April.[91] British batteries stayed behind to give support while a handover team remained on the hill to show the new arrivals the trenches and tunnels. The French were unimpressed with the British trenches and they were concerned that they were on the forward slopes of Kemmel him but there was little they could do.[92] Foch and Haig were still worried about the Flanders situation and both Plumer and the Belgian Chief of Staff had to make contingency plans, in case Ypres was lost. The sea locks were eventually opened, to speed up the flooding around St Omer.

87   Ibid., pp. 358-60.
88   Hussey and Inman, *The Fifth Division in the Great War*, p. 220.
89   Edmonds, *Military Operations: France and Belgium, 1918, Vol. II*, p. 373.
90   Ibid., p. 293.
91   Ibid. The French arrival on the Lys is covered on pp. 374.
92   Ibid., p. 411.

The German bombardment began late on 24 April and then the French batteries and communication centres were hit by short, intense barrages of high-explosive and gas, starting at 2.30 am. The shelling stopped at 4.30 am, to rest the gunners, and then restarted thirty minutes later. Zero had been set for 6 am and the infantry advanced through thick mist.[93]

The line south of Ypres was driven back as far as Dickebusch Lake and troops from 39th Division had to help 21st Division form a flank around Voormezeele after Vierstraat was lost.[94] There was 'stone wall defence' around St Eloi and Spanbroekmolen but flamethrowers forced 9th Division back to the Vierstraat Line.[95] The clearing mist revealed that the French had been driven back and the Germans were 'pouring down towards Kemmel and turning north'. A mixture of cavalry, cyclists and motorbikes armed with machine-guns had to hold the Cheapside Line, while one of 49th Division's brigades formed a flank back to the French.[96]

The Détachement de l'Armée du Nord advanced their line south of Kemmel hill, late on 24 April and it led to their undoing.[97] The German barrage caught the French reserves moving in the open while the SOS barrage fell behind the German assault troops. The Alpine Corps advanced 2 miles in just a few hours, taking over 2,500 prisoners, many of them in the tunnels beneath Kemmel hill.[98] The only consolation was that Kemmel's summit did not give the Germans the view they wanted over the BEF's rear; they would have to take Scherpen hill as well. Machine-gun fire from Kemmel hill confirmed the situation was bad but neither British nor French guns shelled the hill until late in the afternoon, because no one knew who held it.

Many batteries on the north slopes had been abandoned, whilst other crews fired over open sights before escaping. The British troops sent to find out what was happening on Kemmel hill were shot down. Instead, a thin line of troops deployed between Locre and La Clytte and they were reinforced by stragglers, cavalry and all sorts of rear area troops. It gave the generals time to formulate a plan.[99]

Two divisions were to recapture Kemmel hill at 3.30 am the following morning but bad weather resulted in chaos on 49th Division's front.[100] Two battalions never got their orders; two battalions only advanced a short distance before they were forced back; two battalions advanced at the wrong time and found no one their flanks. The failure was attributed to 'bad staff arrangements, poor artillery support and the lack of drive exhibited by the French infantry.'[101]

93   Ibid. The barrage is detailed on pp. 412 and 428.
94   Ibid., pp. 420-1.
95   Ibid., pp. 419-20.
96   Ibid., pp. 420.
97   Ibid. The French attack is described on pp. 411-2.
98   Ibid. The attack by the Alpine Corps is detailed on pp. 413-5.
99   Ibid. The French defence of the area is covered on pp. 416-7.
100 Ibid. The counter-attack is described on pp. 431-4.
101 Ibid., p. 434.

Across 25th Division's front, some men were hit by enfilade fire as they crossed the Kemmel stream but the rest captured Kemmel village. The French advanced late and so the Germans were waiting for them; no one went beyond the front line in what was described as a 'discreditable affair'.[102] The only positive outcome of the attack was that it had upset the German plans to capture the Scherpen hill at 8 am.

The only German success occurred at St Eloi, where the British artillery had not seen the SOS flares through the mist. The loss of the observation point prompted Plumer to abandon the rest of the Ypres Salient during the night. A withdrawal to the town ramparts and the Cheapside Line, to the south-west, meant that Second Army was preparing to make a last stand.[103]

It took the Germans two days to locate the new line. Their guns then smothered the British batteries with gas shells at 3 am on 29 April before targeting the front line with high explosive shells two hours later.[104] The infantry infiltrated what remained of 30th and 9th Divisions forty minutes later, forcing them to fall back to the Voormezeele Switch. However, the German barrage missed the Lewis gun teams covering Ridge Wood and Cheapside, hitting the assault troops advancing towards 49th Division instead.[105] Second Army had survived the final attack in Flanders. It brought the battle of the Lys to an end and once again, OHL looked to capture Amiens, on the Somme.

Fourth Army, Villers Bretonneux, 7 to 27 April 1918

The Australian Official Historian, Charles Bean, explained the absurdity of senior officers drawing lines on map compared to junior officers trying to reach the line on the ground a few hours later.[106] The 'operation, readily sketched with a sweep of the pencil by higher authority and formulated in a fluent order... came to the test of all military operation orders with some harassed company commander standing in the dawn among the bullets on the actual country and wondering how he could fulfil the designs implied in his instructions.' Operations which looked feasible on a map spread out on a table, looked very different when viewed through binoculars under fire.

There was no barrage at dawn on 7 April but 2nd Australian Division cleared Hangard Wood, only to find that the objective was covered in scrub, so it pulled back to a safer line.[107] Fighting continued for the high ground south of Hangard until a prisoner warned that Villers Bretonneux was going to be attacked. The village was hit by thousands of gas shells, starting on 17 April, and 5th Australian Division's

---

102 Ibid.
103 Edmonds, *Military Operations: France and Belgium, 1918, Vol. II*. Second Army's withdrawal from the Ypres Salient is covered on pp 438-9.
104 The new line was called the 'GHQ Number 1 Line'.
105 Edmonds, *Military Operations: France and Belgium, 1918, Vol. II*, pp. 448-52.
106 Bean, *Australian Official History, Vol. V*, p. 503.
107 Ibid., pp. 506-11.

casualty count rose to over one thousand in just a week.[108] Aerial observers spotted the build-up of troops while the ground observers reported that the German batteries were registering their guns. Deserters said the final reliefs had been made and there were rumours that Germans planned to use their A7V tanks again.[109]

High-explosive and gas shells hit batteries, roads and rear areas at 3.45 am, and also forced the evacuation of Villers Bretonneux. Thirteen A7V tanks (another one had broken down) moved forward in three groups, with two heading for Cachy and Villers Bretonneux while six tanks moved between them. The Germans guns switched to the front lines just before zero hour, but many fired short, hitting the advancing infantry.

Tanks and flamethrowers overran two of 8th Division's battalions, entering Villers Bretonneux and Bois d'Aquenne. The support line held on for several hours, but counter-attack battalion did not know anything had happened until the tanks drove through their position. The tanks reached Cachy Switch to the south, taking Hangard Wood from 58th Division. Mark IV and Whippet tanks helped contain the breakthrough around Villers Bretonneux, in the first tank on tank engagement. An aerial observer dropped a message to seven Whippet tanks, and they raced forward to stop the advance towards Cachy.[110]

The artillery had no time to silence the machine-gun teams, so Major General William Heneker agreed to the brigadiers' suggestion to make a surprise night attack. But Heneker had to coordinate three brigades from three divisions; none of them from his own.[111] The plans were issued late, so zero hour was delayed by nearly two hours but there was still no time to plan a creeping barrage, so the gunners hit specific targets before lifting beyond the objective.

Two Australian brigades advanced to their objective either side of Villers Bretonneux at 10 pm but the British brigade and three tanks entered the village late, due to the change in orders.[112] Meanwhile, the barrage had overshot the German line in Hangard Wood, and so 18th Division was unable to take Hangard Wood. The Germans eventually withdrew from Villers Bretonneux, only to be gunned down in a railway cutting. Three tanks helped the Australians clear Bois d'Aquenne at first light and then three Whippet tanks helped secure the gap in the line.[113]

An attack by French troops was planned for 5.15 am on 26 April, because the Germans were thought to be planning their own attack. Whippet tanks joined the Moroccans but the deployment was rushed and the Australian guides 'were of no help whatever, being completely ignorant as to the position of the elements to be

---

108 Ibid., pp. 532-4. Affected men had to be stripped and washed, their eyes bathed, and their throats gargled. Tender skin was dusted with sodium bicarbonate and starch.
109 Ibid., p. 537.
110 Ibid., p. 565.
111 Ibid. The organisation of the counter-attack and the delay until it was dark are covered on pp. 569-75. Heneker's own brigades were exhausted.
112 Ibid., p. 397.
113 Edmonds, *Military Operations: France and Belgium, 1918, Vol. II*, pp. 398, 403.

relieved'.[114] There had been no time to arrange a preliminary bombardment while the creeping barrage landed beyond the German line, because it was further west than expected.[115] The French were cut down in an operation which was 'plainly suicidal'.[116]

Operation Blücher-Yorck on the Aisne, 27 May to 6 June

General Plumer issued the following message to Second Army as the battle for Villers Bretonneux came to an end. It illustrates the seriousness of the situation along the BEF's front:

> Every yard of ground must be contested and all ranks must understand this: successive rear lines were in the course of construction, but every opportunity must be taken to strengthen and improve the front lines: local counter-attacks should be made freely, if possible, from a flank, strongly supported by machine guns: the artillery policy of counter-battery, harassing and annihilating fire must be vigorously maintained.[117]

GHQ then instructed Plumer to consider building fortifications to protect the Channel ports.

The BEF had suffered around 260,000 casualties and had lost many guns in one month. It had only received 133,000 replacements; the majority were teenagers and eight divisions had to be reduced to cadre. Many officers and NCOs were away training, leaving the rest struggling to carry out the most basic of tasks. Major General Guy Bainbridge[118] explained the problem:

> These reinforcements, largely composed of the nineteen-year-old class, who had been training for the last nine months in England, were most excellent material, but the absence of older men suitable for promotion to NCOs rank was, in some units, a serious disadvantage: their presence in the ranks rendered them a danger to their units.[119]

The good news was that the remaining guns had plenty of ammunition, while the Tank Corps had amassed nearly 600 tanks.

114 Bean, *Australian Official History, Vol. V,* p. 630.
115 Ibid. The disastrous attack is detailed on p. 631-2.
116 Ibid., p. 632.
117 Edmonds, *Military Operations: France and Belgium, 1918, Vol. II,* p. 443-4.
118 General officer commanding 25th Division.
119 David Blanchard, *Aisne 1918* (Barnsley: Pen and Sword, 2015), p. 21.

A 'Roulement', or exchange, of five tired British divisions for five fresh French divisions was arranged.[120] IX Corps' headquarters reached the Aisne on 26 April, to find a quiet sector where the men could recover. Three British divisions had taken over the Chemin des Dames, a narrow ridge overlooking the Rivers Aisne and Ailette by 15 May. Unfortunately, IX Corps had taken over the line where Ludendorff planned to attack next.

General Philippe Pétain preferred to deploy only a few troops in the Forward Zone, to break up the German attack before it reached the Battle Zone. However, General Denis Duchêne positioned more forward, with Foch's agreement, to secure the important Chemin des Dames ridge.[121] Major General Heneker[122] said the deployment 'was contrary to what all the British divisional commanders had learnt up north …'[123] Duchêne's reply was that 'you English have learnt up north how to retreat, I will teach you to stand' when challenged by Lieutenant General Hamilton-Gordon.[124]

The men were not impressed with the French trenches for several reasons.[125] The Forward Zone had too many trenches, making it easy to infiltrate, while the German artillery knew where all the battery positions were. The Battle Zone was a line of 'Centres de Résistance', which required machine guns and field guns to cover the gaps, while the Rear Zone consisted of abandoned trenches and unfinished strongpoints.[126] IX Corps' also had the River Aisne behind its line and many of its reserves had to be billeted on the south bank.

The German Build-up

Operation Blücher-Yorck would cross the River Aisne and the River Marne, forcing the French to pull reserves south from Flanders to protect Paris. But the attack had to be delayed until replacement soldiers and horses arrived and then forty-one divisions could make their *Aufmarsch*[127] over several nights towards the Chemin des Dames. They faced only twelve weak French and British divisions.

The sound of preparations at the front and the dust columns to the rear made it obvious that an offensive was evident but steps were taken to hide the size of the

---

120 Sir James E. Edmonds, *Military Operations: France and Belgium, 1918, Vol. III: May to July: The German Diversion Offensives and the First Allied Counter-Offensive* (London: HMSO, 1939), pp. 30-1.
121 Edmonds, *Military Operations: France and Belgium, 1918, Vol. III, pp. 39–41*. It would have been a serious blow to French morale to give up the ridge without a fight.
122 8th Division's commanding officer at the corps commanders' conference on 15 May.
123 Blanchard, *Aisne 1918*, p. 29.
124 Ibid., p. 29.
125 Edmonds, *Military Operations: France and Belgium, 1918, Vol. III*. The state of IX Corps' new position is described on pp. 37-8.
126 Ibid., pp. 37-8.
127 Deployment march.

attack.[128] The German air force stopped Allied planes crossing No Man's Land on 24 May while men on the ground stopped patrols crossing No Man's Land. The guns started registering on 25 May while wireless traffic stopped, and radio jammers were turned on the following day. Two prisoners also reported a pre-dawn attack would be made on 27 or 28 May.

Bruchmüller had again been chosen to plan the bombardment plan for 5,200 guns. They started with ten minutes of mustard gas at 1 am, enough to force the British and French troops to put their masks.[129] However, it would have cleared by the time the assault troops advanced through the morning mist. Trench mortars hit the Forward Zone while some of the artillery hit the communications for sixty-five minutes. The rest hit the Allied batteries with gas and high explosive, so the engineers could bridge the Ailette stream with the minimum interference.[130]

At 2.15 am, the long-range guns targeted the Vesle and Aisne crossings, to catch the French and British reserves moving over the river. The rest of the guns continued to hit the Forward Zone and the batteries until zero hour, switching to form a barrage across No Man's Land at 3.40 am. Troops from twenty divisions then followed the line of exploding high explosive shells through the dusk and smoke. Tear gas preceded the explosions, forcing the French and British soldiers to put on their masks, increasing the surprise.[131] Twenty captured British tanks also went forward but they could not keep up with the assault troops and instead helped clear the few pockets of resistance.

Launching the Attack, 27 May

The bombardment had levelled the trenches and knocked out communications along the 5-mile part of the Californie Plateau held by 50th Division.[132] It had also blasted gun emplacements apart while the gas choked the crews, as they fired at set targets in the absence of instructions. The storm troops moved between the redoubts, while the supports silenced them with field guns, flamethrowers and tanks. Many were taken prisoner in the Forward Zone and the assault teams reached the Battle Zone before the British reserves. It proved impossible to hold on along the River Aisne crossings and so the engineers blew up most of the bridges while under fire. Altogether, 50th Division lost around one thousand men killed and all forty-eighty of field guns and

128 Edmonds, *Military Operations: France and Belgium, 1918, Vol. III*, p. 43-4.
129 The whiff of mustard gas was enough to make the Allied troops put on their masks, slowing them down.
130 Edmonds, *Military Operations: France and Belgium, 1918, Vol. III*, the German bombardment is detailed on pp. 47-50.
131 Ibid., p. 50.
132 Edmonds, *Military Operations: France and Belgium, 1918, Vol. III*, pp. 51-5.

howitzers. Another 4,000 men 'were surrounded and forced to surrender before they could come into action.'[133]

There was a similar story across 8th Division's front. It held a 4-mile-wide vulnerable salient between Juvincourt and Berry-au-Bac, which was covered in old trenches, shell holes and wire, and split by the Miette stream.[134] The assault troops moved rapidly, catching the reserves deploying in the Battle Zone off their guard. Meanwhile, the support troops surrounded and silenced points of resistance in the Forward Zone. The gunners were deployed in well-known battery positions and so 8th Division lost all of its guns, either smashed or captured.

On IX Corps' right, 21st Division was holding even more difficult 5-mile long sector along the Aisne Canal. The Front Zone was east of the Aisne-Marne Canal while the Battle Zone was on the west bank.[135] Major General David Campbell had asked if he could deploy everyone behind the drained canal, but General Duchêne had refused. All he could do was deploy the minimum number of men in the Forward Zone and reinforce the Battle Zone strong points.

Attacks from the flanks quickly isolated the Forward Zone and the clearing many targets for the German machine-gun teams. 'There were hundreds of our fellows running along it, like a football crowd running for the trams. Jerry's machine guns were going, and they were dropping, a score at a time and lying in heaps, khaki heaps.'[136] The canal bridges were blown up but there no time to remove the spare building material around the sites, so the Germans were able to cross.

The assault troops used abandoned trenches to get past the strongpoints, leaving them to the support troops to deal with them. Confusion over a message led to part of the Battle Zone being abandoned, allowing the Germans to exploit the gap. It proved impossible to retake position and the responsible officer (Lieutenant Colonel Alexander) would be sacked.

By the evening, all of the Battle Zone had been lost but most of 21st Division's guns had been saved. The infantry would later complain about the lack of artillery support, unaware that the gunners had no idea what to fire at. Meanwhile, the gunners criticised the infantry for abandoning them, unaware that most of them had been killed or captured.[137]

Lieutenant General Hamilton-Gordon had sent 25th Division forward to hold the Green Line.[138] In many places it allowed the engineers time to demolish the bridges, once the stragglers had crossed the River Aisne. By nightfall, the 'new line, thin and

133 Everard Wyrall, *The History of the Fiftieth Division, 1914-1919* (London: P. Lund, 1939) p. 345.
134 Edmonds, *Military Operations: France and Belgium, 1918, Vol. III*, pp. 55-61.
135 Ibid., pp. 61-3.
136 Dominick Graham, *Against Odds: Reflections on the Experiences of the British Army, 1914-45* (London: Palgrave McMillan, 1999) p. 62.
137 Edmonds, *Military Operations: France and Belgium, 1918, Vol. III*, pp. 79-81.
138 Ibid., pp. 75-9.

disjointed, with several gaps, was manned by tired troops with little or no artillery support.'[139]

Stemming the Tide, IX Corps, 28 May-6 June

There was little news from the front early on 28 May, because so many battalion and brigade headquarters had been captured. But it was clear that the Germans had broken through across a 40-mile sector between Soissons and Reims and they had penetrated over 12 miles in places. Nine out of the seventeen Allied divisions engaged had been decimated and it would take the French several days to move reserves to the River Marne. IX Corps' units were short of ammunition because the dumps had been abandoned or blown up.[140]

The men along the Breuil stream could see columns of German troops heading towards them when the mist cleared but there were no batteries to tell. There were no orders either and it was down to individual officers, like Brigadier General George Grogan, to use their initiative and make sure they 'established a good line along the railway embankment, which here runs parallel to the river [Vesle].'[141] Survivors of 50th and 8th Divisions made a stand along the Vesle but the position was lost after the engineers failed to demolish the Jonchery bridge and hard fighting for Montazin Hill and along the River Ardre followed.[142] Some troops were cut off as 21st Division crossed the Prouilly stream and then the River Vesle.

Pétain's orders were out of date by the time they reached the front, so he decided to let the Germans keep pushing into large salient. He toured the front, making sure four divisions assembled on each flank, ready to counter-attack. Meanwhile, General Duchêne summarised the situation to Prime Minister Georges Clemenceau, telling him he faced around twenty German divisions and 'he had nothing to oppose them but mere dust'.

The Germans advanced another 7 miles towards the Marne on 29 May, but the Allied flanks around Soissons or Reims were holding. Lieutenant General Hamilton-Gordon had deployed 25th Division across his front and he was expecting to receive 19th Division. His right flank was secure but the Germans pushed through a 4-mile gap on his left and 8th and 50th Divisions were forced to abandon Montazin Hill. They fell back across the Treslon valley, to find 19th Division waiting on the last ridge north of the River Ardre. Gun batteries had also arrived, giving IX Corps its first artillery support since the battle began.[143]

---

139 Ibid., p. 81.
140 Ibid., p. 82.
141 Ibid., p. 107.
142 Ibid. The fighting on 28 May is covered on pp. 106-7.
143 Ibid. The arrival of is detailed on pp. 126-7.

Attacks across the River Vesle were stopped until the French were driven back, forcing 21st Division to retire before it was relieved during the night.[144] Major Generals Heneker and Jeffreys then took responsibility for each side of the Ardre; both were concerned that Senegalese troops were defending the valley between them.

The Fifth French Army took over the east side of the salient on 29 May, including IX Corps, but Pétain had decided to change tactics. He wanted to attack the head of the salient and drive the Germans back across the Vesle and the Aisne, starting on 31 May. However, the Germans struck first, crossing the Marne between Chartéves and Dormans, compromising IX Corps position.[145] The loss of Romigny and the disappearance of the Senegalese troops left 19th Division having 'to run the gauntlet of heavy machine gun-fire, which was directed at them from all sorts of unexpected points' across the Ardre valley.[146] Many were cut off and while some fought on until they ran out of ammunition, others made a break for it and the rest joined French units.

Heavy fighting continued around Montagne de Bligny on 31 May and 19th Division had to deploy all its reserves to hold on, while the French were driven back on the flanks. The summit was lost for a time the following day, compromising the whole line, but a counter-attack retook it. The line had been saved but it had cost 19th Division dearly and Lieutenant General Hamilton-Gordon was asked if it could be relieved.

The French armies had been driven had advanced 20 miles over the past four days and the politicians were looking for scapegoats; they chose Pétain and Duchêne.[147] The Germans were only 40 miles from Paris but OHL was also reconsidering its situation. It planned to wait for the French to move their reserves to the area, to protect the shortest route to their capital. It would use the Marne as a defensive line, so divisions could be taken from the line ready to strike the British at Amiens again.

Further German attacks along the Marne on 2 and 3 June made the salient deeper and more vulnerable. And then there was a final attack against IX Corps on 6 June.[148] Battery positions were smothered with a mixture of phosgene and chlorine gas[149] but the high explosive barrage missed the trenches 'as the standing corn masked the position considerably.' Once again, the summit of Montagne de Bligny was lost and then recaptured 'at the point of the bayonet' but the barrage started late, 'owing to an error in timing and the rapidity with which the attack went forward.'[150]

The divisions which had been sent south for a rest in a quiet sector were heading north by 19 June.[151] All four divisions would be rebuilt (two after a time as cadres) and return to the line, in time for the final campaigns.

---

144 Ibid., pp. 120-1.
145 Ibid., pp. 137.
146 TNA WO 95/2093/1: 2nd Wiltshire Regiment War Diary.
147 Edmonds, *Military Operations: France and Belgium, 1918, Vol. III*, p. 141 and 171.
148 Ibid., pp. 158-9.
149 Code named Green Cross gas.
150 TNA WO 95/2078/2: 1/4th Shropshire Regiment's War Diary.
151 Edmonds, *Military Operations: France and Belgium, 1918, Vol. III*, pp. 159.

The German Lys and Aisne Offensives Summary

The failure to spot the build-up of troops across the Lys plain resulted in the Portuguese Corps being overrun, leaving First Army struggling to plug the gap. The attack against Messines Ridge the following day was also missed, leaving Second Army in a difficult position south of Ypres. A combination of desperate defensive actions and challenging withdrawals limited the success of the offensive during the first forty-eight hours. It then became clear that the German plan was flawed because it involved fighting across the River Lys and the Lawe stream. Infantry units were able to cross but it proved difficult to get the guns and supplies over the bridges.

The performance of the BEF's reinforcements is remarkable, considering that many had never been in action before; they all fulfilled Haig's 'Back's to the Wall' plea to hold on. The deployment of reserves behind the line, so they could dig a defensive line to fall back through, proved very effective in front of Hazebrouck. Coordinating counter-attacks between the British and French would later prove difficult to achieve, resulting in further loss of ground.

For a second time in less than a month, a German offensive ground to a halt after just a few days and it was again due to the German inability to manage their logistics, as much as it was down to the BEF's ability to defend its line.

A failure to deploy in depth on the Aisne front resulted in disaster for the British troops sent there to rest. The French desire to hold onto ground led to unnecessary casualties and a desperate fight to fill the breach followed. For a third time, the German advance slowed down as Allied reinforcements moved to the Aisne area and it came to halt after just a few days.

9

The Allies Strike Back
18 July to 11 September 1918

The Attack at La Becque, 28 June

The attack was made at 6 am without a preliminary bombardment, surprising the Germans who had 'stood down when daylight came'. The men ran across No Man's Land and took 450 prisoners in the first successful British offensive operation of the year. It meant the German artillery observers would not be able to target Hazebrouck station in future.[1]

The Capture of Le Hamel, 4 July

The Australians used 'peaceful penetration' tactics to discover that the enemy defences were patchy, with the main centres of resistance in the village and woods. This involved carrying out 'reconnaissance by day and then advance by night, in bounds of 500 yards,' to test the reactions of the Germans.[2]

The original plan was that the 'tanks, in accordance with Tank Corps' theory, would advance in three lines.'[3] The first line moved independently beyond the first German position, to cut off the garrison and stop reinforcements. The second line accompanied the infantry, starting alongside to avoid the counter-barrage, moving ahead as they advanced towards the objective. The third line was a small reserve which

---

1 Sir James E. Edmonds, *Military Operations: France and Belgium, 1918, Vol. III, May to July: The German Diversion Offensives and the First Allied Counter-Offensive* (London, HMSO, 1939), pp. 195-7.
2 Charles E.W. Bean, *The Official History of Australia in the War, Vol. V: The Australian Imperial Force in France during the Main German Offensive, 1918* (Angus and Robertson, Sydney, 8th edition, 1941), p. 567.
3 Bean, *The Official History of Australia in the War, Vol. VI*, p. 247.

could deal with any strongpoints or replace lost tanks.[4] The plan to dispense with a creeping barrage and rely solely on the tanks for protection was rejected because of the problems at Bullecourt in May 1917 and because the infantry trusted the artillery to deliver. It meant the first two waves would operate together. Great emphasis was placed on practising and 'set-piece manoeuvre exercises on the scale of a battalion were designed and rehearsed over and over again...' During the breaks in the training, platoon and company leaders met dozens of tank officers face to face and they argued each other to a standstill upon every aspect that arose.'[5]

Over 625 artillery pieces moved into position over five nights, while targets were registered during routine bombardments, so the Germans did not spot the extra guns. Gas was used each time, to get the Germans used to putting their masks on; it would be replaced by smoke on the day of the attack. Around 150 machine guns were deployed, most of them on the flanks, so they would avoid the counter-barrage.[6]

Zero was set for 3.10 am, when it was light enough to identify a uniform at 20 yards, and the barrage had three layers. The first was fired by 6-inch howitzers while the second was formed by 4.5-inch howitzers shooting high-explosive shelled armed with instantaneous fuses which exploded at ground level, to drive the Germans underground. Enough smoke was included to make the Germans put their gas masks on. The creeping barrage had 60 per cent shrapnel, 30 per cent high explosive shells armed with delay action fuses and 10 per cent smoke shell. The high explosive stunned the men underground while the smoke blinded the German machine gunners.[7] Up ahead, three smoke screens made sure the Germans on the high ground could not see what was happening. Extra smoke was also used to warn the infantry that the barrage was about to move and about to stop.[8]

The operation would confirm that tanks could be brought within 4,000 yards of the front line at full speed before stopping to load up with ammunition and fuel.[9] Sixty tank drivers then took twelve minutes to drive 1,000 yards to the infantry at half speed, being careful not to rev their engines as planes flew low overhead, bombing Hamel to hide the noise and randomly dropping flares to confuse the Germans.[10] The guns opened fire at eight minutes before zero, drowning out the sound of the tanks' final approach.[11]

4   Ibid., pp. 253-4.
5   Ibid., pp. 267-8. Gleaned from Monash's *The Australian Victories in France in 1918*, pp. 49-50.
6   Edmonds, *Military Operations: France and Belgium, 1918, Vol. IV*, pp. 199-200.
7   Ibid., p. 202. Bean, *The Official History of Australia in the War, Vol. VI*, pp. 247-8.
8   Bean, *Australian Official History, Vol. VI*, p. 270.
9   Ibid., pp. 245-8 explains how Brigadier General Elles took steps to ease Monash's concerns over fighting alongside tanks.
10   Ibid., p. 283. Old planes with noisy engines were employed.
11   Ibid., p. 249.

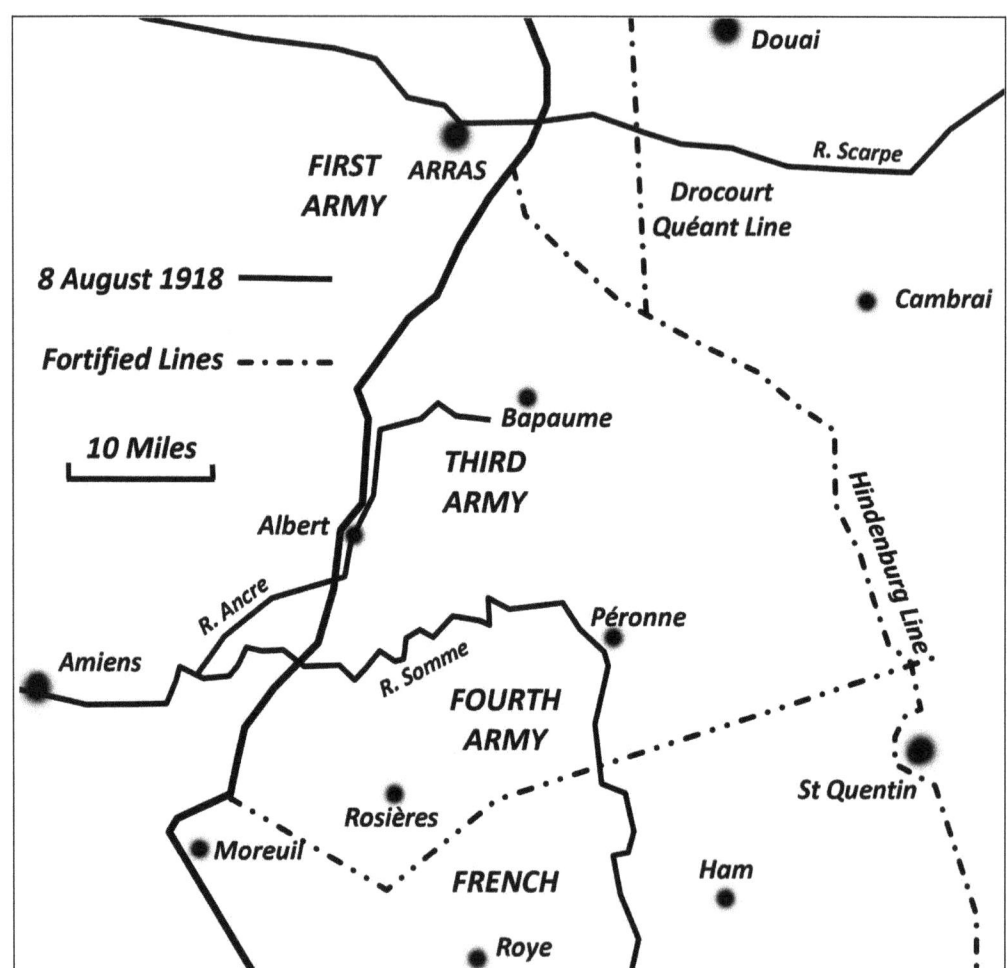

Map 9. The BEF Strikes Back, 8 August–11 September 1918: The successful offensive east of Amiens on 8 August was followed up with further advanced south of Arras.

The infantry had deployed along the tapes in silence and then moved back 50 yards to create a safety zone, because the guns had not registered.[12] The start of the bombardment warned 4th Australian Division to 'edge up close behind the line of shell bursts', ready to advance as the tanks drove past.[13] Four waves squeezed together until they were sure they were clear of the counter-barrage. The second wave then let the first get 50 yards ahead, while the rest followed in artillery formation.[14]

Some tanks cut the wire, some stopped on the front line and fired along the trenches and the rest drove towards the objective.[15] Patrols fired into village and the woods, to pin the Germans down, while the rest of the assault troops followed the tanks onto the high ground beyond. The support troops cleared Hamel, catching the garrison in their dug outs. Tanks also followed tracks through the woods while the infantry went around the edges.[16]

Two squadrons of planes dealt with anti-tank guns during the advance and then kept a look for counter-attacks as the infantry consolidated the objective.[17] One squadron dropped ammunition at pre-arranged points or when the machine-gun teams asked for some. Twelve supply tanks carried the same amount of ammunition and tools that 1,250 men could and the fighting tanks waited until the infantry had dug in before withdrawing. Only five had been hit and they were all salvaged.[18]

The capture of le Hamel was the BEF's first set piece attack, involving all arms, for nearly a year and it was a useful reminder of what could be achieved when the ground was suitable for tanks. Lieutenant General John Monash had planned it and 'an account of the operation, giving technical details, was speedily issued to the Armies.'[19]

Capture of Meteren, 18 July

First Army wanted Meteren ridge because it gave a good view over the Lys plain. Artillery hit the area every day with smoke and gas shells for two weeks, so the Germans always put their gas masks when the guns fired. The barrage started at 7.54 am and a smoke screen landed 150 yards in front of the field artillery barrage, as the centre crept forward in line with the flanks. The men of 9th Division climbed out of

---

12 Ibid., p. 281.
13 Ibid., pp. 198-201. Also, Bean, *The Official History of Australia in the War, Vol. VI*, pp. 256.
14 Ibid., p. 204.
15 Ibid. The deployment of the tanks is detailed on pp. 202-3.
16 Ibid., the account of the attack is given on pp. 204-8.
17 Bean, *The Official History of Australia in the War, Vol. VI*, p. 249.
18 Edmonds, *Military Operations: France and Belgium, 1918, Vol. IV*. A summary of the capture of le Hamel is detailed on p. 208.
19 Bean, *The Official History of Australia in the War, Vol. VI*, p. 332. SS Number 218, Operations of the Australian Corps against Hamel, Bois de Hamel and Bois de Vaire.

their trenches one minute later and then 425 barrels of burning oil exploded across the German support trench three minutes later.[20]

The Scots were in the German trenches before they knew what was happening and most had just put their gas masks on. However, wind dispersed the smoke as the 8th Black Watch cut through an unexpected piece of wire and they suffered many casualties.[21]

The Attack and Counter-Attack on the Marne, 15 July-1 August

Prisoners and deserters had given away the time and date of final German offensive of the war, as well as details of the bombardment.[22] The French gunners opened fire as soon as their aerial observers spotted troops marching towards the Chemin des Dames, early on 15 July. The attack still drove the French from the ridge, across the Aisne and as far south as the Marne, for the second time in just seven weeks. Foch believed the Germans would be vulnerable after seventy-two hours on the offensive and he was right.[23] Their advance had stalled by the time a counter-attack with four British divisions was made on 18 July.

Deployment for the eastern attack was rushed and there was no time to plan a barrage, so artillery was just told to fire 1,000 yards ahead of the start line. Both 51st and 62nd British Divisions were delayed moving through the woods and were then pinned down because the barrage had overshot the machine-gun teams hidden in the fields and woods either side the Ardre stream.[24] The jumping off line was set behind the German front line the following morning and the troops had to run to catch up the barrage. They were repeatedly ambushed in the woods and then pinned when they emerged from the trees.[25]

The first successful operation started at 12.15 pm on 22 July. Men of 62nd Division formed a cordon around Bois de Reims while artillery fire drove the Germans out of the centre.[26] But an attempt by 51st Division to 'dribble forward by individual rushes' late on 23 July failed and then the supporting barrage fell short.[27]

The Germans withdrew late on 27 July and one of the few prisoners taken had been left behind to report the British progress by telephone. Early the following morning, the troops moved silently up the slopes of Mont de Bligny and then drove the Germans

---

20   Edmonds, *Military Operations: France and Belgium, 1918, Vol. IV*, p. 211.
21   Ibid., pp. 209-12.
22   Sir James E. Edmonds, *Military Operations: France and Belgium, 1918, Vol. III, May to July: The German Diversion Offensives and the First Allied Counter-Offensive* (London, HMSO, 1939), pp. 231-2.
23   Ibid., pp. 232-4.
24   Ibid. The assault on 20 July is covered on pp. 247-9.
25   Ibid., pp. 255-7.
26   Ibid., pp. 257-8.
27   Ibid., pp. 263.

from the summit. Advances by section rushes through the cornfields then cleared the west side of the hill.[28]

Meanwhile, the French Tenth Army had been unable to advance south of Soissons, so 15th and 34th British Divisions were sent to force the issue around Buzancy and Hartennes. The reliefs were delayed and then the troops were spotted, drawing artillery fire. The men found themselves holding nothing more than shallow ditches, while their officers tried to work out where they were on the small-scale maps. No one knew where the front line was or that the German machine-gun teams were waiting in the long grass not far away. No one observed the signal flares; the telephone lines had been cut and all the runners were hit. The first the troops knew they were to attack was when the creeping barrage landed too far ahead; the attack was a disaster.[29]

For several days, 15th and 34th Divisions tried to advance, and the most successful attempt was made at 12.30 pm on 28 July.[30] A two-minute barrage caught the Germans resting after lunch and teams armed with flamethrowers and explosive charges cleared Buzancy. An attack by 34th Division at 4.10 am the following morning started well in fog, but it was difficult to keep in touch with the heavy artillery. A pause on the first objective was needed to let the field artillery to move up but it also gave the Germans time to counter the attack against Hill 158.[31]

Early on 1 August 15th Division awaited a robust sequence of signals that meant it was to support a French attack. Contact planes and balloons fired rockets while 155mm batteries fired shells which exploded in black smoke at 8.25 am. That warned the Scots to prepare to advance on the hour, but a 'ragged and desultory' barrage meant the attack on Bois d'Hartennes failed.[32] Later that night, officers of 34th Division led their men on compass bearings through smoke and mist onto Hill 203 and Point 194. It meant they could see the Germans withdrawing across the Vesle valley to the River Aisne the following morning. The battle of the Marne was over, and it was time to launch an offensive on the Somme.

Preparations for Amiens, 26 July to 7 August

Haig and General Marie-Eugène Debeney had met to discuss an offensive on 26 July; they would not meet again to maintain secrecy.[33] Officers were only told what they needed to know when they needed to know it. GHQ's operation order was circulated

---

28   Ibid., pp. 272-5, 278-9.
29   Ibid., pp. 259.
30   Ibid., pp. 275-8.
31   Ibid., pp. 283-5.
32   Ibid., pp. 296-8.
33   Bean, *The Official History of Australia in the War, Vol. VI*, p. 467. There had been discussions about a combined attack east of Amiens since May. Foch planned a French attack towards Montdidier, so the two would hit the shoulders of the German salient. They were shelved when the Germans attacked on the Aisne on 27 May.

on 29 July and Rawlinson issued brief orders on 31 July but detailed instructions only appeared on 6 August; less than forty-eight hours before zero.[34] All correspondence only discussed an upcoming raid, while troop movements were referred to as a relief of the French. All civilians had been moved out of Amiens during the German spring offensive, while the villagers living east of the city were subjected to curfews and cordons.[35]

The plan was for three objectives. The troops would follow the tanks and a creeping barrage to the Red Line. A pause long enough to allow the artillery to move up was then made before the advance to the Blue Line. Mark V* supply tanks would drive to the Green Line and 'drop machine-gun crews at eighty yards' intervals to hold out until infantry came up to garrison it'.[36] Experience had shown that the fighting troops moved faster, so the reserves had to set off at zero hour to be ready to take over the advance.[37] Monash chose to leap frog his divisions after the first objectives but Currie preferred to deploy his on narrower fronts and let them go all the way to the final objective.[38] It meant the leading Australian division had to control the whole advance, to avoid handing over control of a sector during the battle.[39]

Buses carried troops to camouflaged billets during the hours of darkness while troops had to stay under cover during daylight hours. Meanwhile, plenty of troop movements were made behind other parts of the line, while a large amount of dust was created near St Pol and reported as a tank training exercise. New batteries deployed under camouflage at night and stayed silent while existing batteries relocated hours before zero, to avoid the inevitable counter-battery fire.[40] The movement of large numbers of troops and stockpiling of ammunition made it clear something was planned but printed instructions in each man's pay book were summarised with the words – *Keep Your Mouth Shut.*[41]

Many diversionary reliefs were made, to confuse the Germans. The Australian Corps took over all the front first, leading the Germans to believe that they were relieving French divisions for operations on the Marne.[42] Two Canadian battalions and two casualty clearing stations were sent to Flanders, to make it look like the

---

34   Sir James E. Edmonds, *Military Operations: France and Belgium, 1918, Vol. IV: 8 August to 26 September: The Franco-British Offensive* (London, HMSO, 1947), p. 16.
35   Edmonds, *Military Operations: France and Belgium, 1918, Vol. IV,* p. 17.
36   Bean, *The Official History of Australia in the War, Vol. VI,* p. 467. The Mark V tanks had lengthened by six feet to accommodate two machine-gun crews as passengers.
37   Ibid., p. 491-2.
38   Ibid., p. 492.
39   Ibid., p. 493. Problems had arisen during the Messines June 1917 offensive when 4th Australian Division passed through 3rd Australian Division.
40   Edmonds, *Military Operations: France and Belgium, 1918, Vol. IV.* The deployment of infantry and artillery to Fourth Army is explained on p. 36.
41   Ibid. The full text of the instructions to soldiers to maintain secrecy is given on p. 16. It also gave instructions on what to say if taken prisoner and to watch out for spies in captivity.
42   Ibid., p. 19.

Corps was heading north. Meanwhile, the rest of the Canadian Corps entered Fourth Army's trenches in secret, only a few hours before zero.[43] Both Second and First Army broadcast attack plans and a Canadian signal unit 'began a flow of dummy wireless traffic, while the rest of the corps moved into Fourth Army's area under radio silence.[44]

The Tank Corps deployed 342 fighting tanks and 120 supply tanks to carry ammunition and machine-gun teams.[45] Extra Mark V* tanks could also carry huge amounts of ammunition and equipment while two Whippet battalions and a company of armoured cars would work with the cavalry during the exploitation phase. They all drove through Amiens on a road covered in sand, to muffle the sound of their tracks on the cobbles, while planes flew overhead, to hide the sound of engines.[46] The crews waited under camouflage during daylight hours, while their commanders checked the routes to the front line. They started moving late on 7 August, ready to drive across No Man's Land at zero hour.

The Royal Air Force discreetly assembled 800 planes around Amiens, while increasing air activity over other areas.[47] Around 375 fighters would make the skies safe, so aerial observers could find targets, report progress and warn of counter-attacks. Around 250 bombers would attack a variety of targets deep in enemy territory, trying to hit the German Air Force while it was still on the ground.

Amiens, 8 August

Aircraft dropped phosphorus bombs to thicken up the mist, while their engines drowned out the noise of the tanks. They drove to within 3,000 yards of the German line and then throttled down for the next 2,000 yards. The last half hour was spent crawling carefully through the waiting assault troops while planes bombed the German positions, to drown out the noise.[48] They passed the first wave at 4.20 am, just as Fourth Army's 2,000 guns opened fire; infantry, tanks, planes and artillery were working in perfect unison.[49] The time had been chosen so the front line could be broken while it was dark, yet it would be light enough to see as the advance progressed. One in three batteries hit assembly points and approach routes while one in three

43 Bean, *The Official History of Australia in the War, Vol. V,* p. 492. Also, Bean, *Australian Official History, Vol. V,* pp. 506-9.

44 Nicholson, *Official History of the Canadian Army in the First World War.* The move is covered on pp. 389-90.

45 Edmonds, *Military Operations: France and Belgium, 1918, Vol. IV,* the composition of the tanks units is given on pp. 24-5.

46 Ibid., pp. 21-2. The sand also made it easier for the horses of three cavalry divisions to walk on the cobbles. The number of horses in Fourth Army rose to nearly 100,000.

47 Ibid. The breakdown of the Royal Air Force's squadrons is given on pp. 25-6 and its orders are on p. 34-5.

48 Bean, *The Official History of Australia in the War, Vol. V,* p. 496. The same plan which had proved to work at Le Hamel on 4 July.

49 Edmonds, *Military Operations: France and Belgium, 1918, Vol. IV,* p. 34.

silenced the enemy guns with high explosive and gas shells. The rest of the guns fired a creeping barrage of shrapnel and smoke shells, which landed just 200 yards in front of the first wave, before creeping across No Man's Land and over the German trenches.[50]

All three corps used two lines of skirmishers to locate the enemy machine-gun teams for the tank crews, with some walking close by and others riding on top.[51] Across the Australian Corps, the 'main bodies of the leading battalions [were] strung out in successive lines of tiny columns, in single file …'[52] Another three waves followed in columns, accompanied by the machine guns and trench mortar teams. Carrying parties brought up the rear. The support battalions moved forward in a diamond pattern, so they could deploy to the front or the flank.

Some officers followed white tapes which pointed the right way across No Man's Land and then either followed the nearest tank or navigated by compass through the mist and smoke. Many just followed the shell flashes of the creeping barrage until the air cleared around ninety minutes after zero hour.

III Corps, 8 August

The three divisions slated to cross the plateau between the Ancre and the Somme had recently received many conscripts, replacements for the heavy casualties suffered during the March retreat.[53] The infantry had been forced to dig new assembly trenches and the artillery had to alter their barrage plan, due to trenches lost near Morlancourt on 6 August.[54] A fresh brigade had to be given to 18th Division because of casualties suffered trying to recover the ground, while the officers had no time to check the ground.[55] It all meant that Lieutenant General Butler had been given approval to stop the first day's advance short of the Amiens Outer Defence Line.[56]

The men of 18th Division soon became separated from the barrage, as they fought their way through the lost trenches. Tanks helped 58th Division make a pincer attack on Malard Wood but the infantry went the wrong way in the mist because they were following the contours.[57] The support battalions following trampled corn, to keep

50   Bean, *The Official History of Australia in the War, Vol. V,* no smoke would have been fired if it had been dry, because dust created a screen. The wet weather meant that 5 per cent smoke shells were included.

51   Nicholson, *Official History of the Canadian Army in the First World War.* The Corps' attack plan is detailed on p. 398.

52   Bean, *The Official History of Australia in the War, Vol. V,* p. 549.

53   Edmonds, *Military Operations: France and Belgium, 1918, Vol. IV,* p. 75.

54   Bean, *The Official History of Australia in the War, Vol. V,* Australian troops had captured enemy trenches on 28/29 July. They then left the area and the German counter-attack retook some of them from III Corps. It left the front line in a confused state.

55   Edmonds, *Military Operations: France and Belgium, 1918, Vol. IV,* p. 76. Gas bombardments interfered with the deployment.

56   Ibid., p. 74.

57   Ibid. The III Corps' main attack is covered on p. 79-82.

direction, and the infantry and tanks found themselves deep in the enemy position when the mist lifted. Nineteen tanks had been lost by the time the seventeen survivors were heading back for fuel. Few men could cross the Chipilly spur, but a contact plane reported it was in British hands, so the barrage was cancelled, and the infantry were pinned down. A second bombardment landed too far ahead to help a later attempt. Two hours after zero, 12th Division cleared Morlancourt on III Corps' left flank.[58]

The Australian Corps, 8 August

The Australian soldiers were proud that their five divisions were fighting together under their new commander, Lieutenant General John Monash, for the first time.[59] Over 1,000 field guns fired the creeping barrage as far as the first objective, while nearly 100 heavy calibre guns shelled distant targets.

Scouts directed tanks towards machine-gun nests along the Somme while columns of men struggled to keep up with the barrage, as they navigated the river's reed beds. The rest of 3rd Australian Division advanced along the high ground against 'hardly any stubborn resistance; the fog had rendered it most difficult and where the tanks appeared most of the Germans were terrified.'[60] Thirty-eight guns were captured whilst eighteen out of twenty-four tanks rallied.

Many of 2nd Australian Division followed the main St Quentin road, which ran at an angle to front, but they still captured thirty-six guns around the Inner Amiens Defence Line. Men had to withdraw because the barrage was falling short in the mist, but the advance was corrected when it 'lifted like a curtain'.[61]

Twenty-four batteries moved forward but there was no creeping barrage, because it was impossible to register guns in such a short time. So, the guns shelled the second objective while planes dropped smoke bombs in front of villages and likely strongpoints, to blind the German machine-gun teams.[62] The lack of mist meant the German artillery were able to target the tanks, but forty-eight Mark IV and Mark V tanks still joined the advance to the Outer Amiens Defence Line. Many were knocked out by anti-tank guns while the infantry had been taught to fire at the observation slits or run up to them, 'throwing bundles of bombs on to their backs.'[63]

The 4th Australian Division came under fire from across the Somme and the artillery could not see through the morning haze to help. The tanks struggled to cross the gullies and ridges and all but one were knocked out. The leading companies

58   Ibid. The flank attack is detailed on p. 82.
59   Bean, *The Official History of Australia in the War, Vol. V.* Monash's message of encouragement is given on p. 525.
60   Ibid., p. 543.
61   Ibid., p. 545.
62   Ibid., p. 496. A screen created by 50 per cent smoke shells had covered the troops during the pause at the first objective.
63   Ibid., p. 567.

continued to skirt the woods and advance east, while the support companies mopped them up, capturing 'canteens, stores, transport lines, and shelters, teeming with unresisting Germans.'[64]

One enterprising German officer had placed his observers in the trees and his field guns had knocked out seven of the tanks supporting 5th Australian Division, before his two field guns were knocked out. It demonstrated how vulnerable they were to anti-tank tactics, when there was no smoke or mist to hide them. Another seventeen tanks cleared the area while the German gunners cantered past the infantry running down the Roman Road. Cavalry and Whippets took over the advance, moving fast to seize the Amiens Outer Defence Line around Harbonnières.

Many more Whippets and a dozen armoured cars accompanied the cavalry beyond the Amiens Outer Defence Line. The armoured cars followed the Roman Road, fired on 'a camping ground for German reserves' in Morcourt valley and then went exploring.[65] The cavalry and Whippets raced to the Outer Defence Line and had cleared it before thirty-six Mark V* tanks arrived, loaded with machine-gun teams and supplies. Altogether, the Australian Corps had advanced around 7 miles and captured nearly 8,000 men and 173 guns.

Canadian Corps, 8 August

Australian troops held the sector while the Canadian Corps moved behind Fourth Army's right. They completed their deployment across a 4-mile-front only twenty minutes before zero. Four tank battalions would support three divisions as they advanced 3 miles to the first objective and two more battalions would support the advance to the Amiens Outer Defence Line, another 4 miles away.[66]

The tanks struggled to find 2nd Canadian Division's front line, as it advanced towards Marcelcave.[67] The field batteries then moved forward to support the advance on Guillaucourt. Many tanks were hit when the mist lifted, bringing the total lost to twenty. Cavalry and Whippet tanks took over the final stage of the advance, reaching the Amiens Outer Defence Line ahead of the infantry.

The creeping barrage landed short in front of 1st Canadian Division.[68] The infantry had to clear the dense woods along the Luce stream on their own, but twenty-one tanks led the advance past Hangard Wood and Morgemont Wood, in the mist. Only eleven reached the second objective, around Cayeux, and the infantry often had to rely on the Lewis gun teams for support. As the mist cleared, contact planes could see the Germans withdrawing and the reserve company of tanks joined the final advance.

---

64   Ibid., p. 569.
65   Ibid., p. 558.
66   Nicholson, *Official History of the Canadian Army in the First World War*. The Corps attack plan is detailed on pp. 396-8.
67   Ibid. The 2nd Division's advance is covered on pp. 402-3.
68   Ibid. The 1st Division's advance is covered on pp. 400-2.

However, some anti-tank gun teams stayed behind, knocking out more tanks as they headed for the Amiens Outer Defence Line.

The bombardment started twelve minutes early across 3rd Canadian Division's front, to cover the three tank companies crawling down the Roye road.[69] Fourteen followed the north bank of the Luce, before crossing on a fascine. Six tanks were knocked out, but the rest encouraged the Germans to run from Démuin. The infantry rushed the German trench where the Roye road crossed the high ground, but the counter-barrage hit the company of tanks queuing to cross the bridge; several bogged down when they drove off the road to escape the shelling. The rest of the tanks had crossed the stream at Thennes, in the French sector, before turning north to outflank the German line. The advance was then 'more or less a route march enlivened by the sight of the panic-stricken enemy running in every direction.'[70]

Artillery crossed the Luce bridge and the infantry filed across footbridges, to discover that only thirteen tanks had survived the fighting. Another six joined the advance from Hamon Wood at 8.20 am while Brutinel's Independent Force co-operated with the French along the Roye road. The mixed force of armoured cars and motorcycles armed with machine guns were supported by lorry mounted mortars.

The advance to the final objective was to be carried out by 4th Canadian Division but only eight tanks were still running; the other thirty-four were out of action. So, zero had to be postponed an hour, to allow another thirty fighting tanks to catch up. Mark V* supply tanks were supposed to carry machine-gun teams to the final objective, but many men chose to make the journey on foot because they 'suffered severely from the unaccustomed heat and fumes from the engines.'[71]

Both 1st and 3rd Cavalry Divisions moved through the Canadian infantry, as they waited for the tanks. Twenty-five Whippet tanks had been attached to the squadrons, to give them extra firepower, but they had been given no time to practice tactics together. It turned out that the cavalry were too fast for the tanks, so the troopers had to chase down the Germans on their own and the 'German machine-guns had shown their superiority over Canadian sabres.'[72] A contact plane later reported the enemy was abandoning the Amiens Outer Defence Line but it had failed to spot a few field guns around Beaucourt and Le Quesnel. Seventeen Whippets were knocked in quick succession and the rest had to withdraw and wait for the infantry to catch up.[73]

The Canadian Corps had advanced 8 miles across the Santerre plateau, taking over 5,000 men and 161 guns. Its casualties had been as low as 3,500 but the Tank Corps had suffered grievous losses; only five tanks would be able to deploy with the Canadians the following morning.[74]

69   Ibid. the 3rd Division's advance is covered on pp. 399-400.
70   Ibid., p 400.
71   Ibid. The 1st Division advance is covered on pp. 405.
72   Ibid. The 1st Division advance is covered on pp. 405.
73   Ibid.
74   Ibid.

8 August Summary

Fourth Army's divisions had suffered less than 9,000 casualties and Rawlinson issued instructions to continue the advance the following day.[75] The infantry and cavalry had done well but the Tank Corps had lost one in four of its tanks and many more were in the workshops; only 145 out of 415 were still running.[76] The RAF had also had a bad day because Major General John Salmond had decided to attack the Somme bridges with over 200 planes as soon as the mist cleared, to stop reserves reaching the front. Unfortunately, many German planes flew to the area and the low cloud forced the pilots into a limited amount of air space. Nearly one hundred RAF planes had been hit by nightfall and not one bridge had been demolished.[77] The 8 August was an unlucky day for the RAF.[78]

The attack had taken both Ludendorff and his new Army Group commander, General Max von Böhn, by surprise. The frontline had been driven back over 7 miles while Second Army and Eighteenth Army reserves had been hit by air attacks as they moved up. The number of men killed, wounded or captured would top over 27,000, the majority of them captured.[79] Ludendorff would later refer to 8 August as a 'black day' for the German Army.[80]

Fourth Army, 9-20 August

There would be no surprise attack on 9 August, there had been no time to register the guns and there were far fewer tanks. To make matters worse, Fourth Army now faced an area of old wire and trenches dating from the 1916 battle. The Germans were moving several divisions to the area and Rawlinson only had one in reserve. Rawlinson gave his corps commanders the freedom to choose their zero hour for 9 August, so they would advance when they were ready but it caused delays in some cases. In many cases it was because messages had to be taken by officers mounted on horseback or motorcycles. 'The difficulties of communications due to a sudden change from trench warfare to open warfare had been great.'[81]

75   Edmonds, *Military Operations: France and Belgium, 1918, Vol. IV*, p. 85.
76   Ibid., p. 87.
77   Nicholson, *Official History of the Canadian Army in the First World War*, p. 421.
78   Edmonds, *Military Operations: France and Belgium, 1918, Vol. IV*, p. 84.
79   Ibid., p. 89. This included approximately 15,000 prisoners.
80   Ludendorff, *My War Memories, Vol. 2* (London: Hutchinson and Co., 1919), p. 679.
81   Edmonds, *Military Operations: France and Belgium, 1918, Vol. IV*, p. 102.

III Corps, 9-10 August

The attack had to be postponed until 5.30 pm, to give an American regiment time to take over 12th Division's front.[82] One tank advanced too early and the noise alerted the Germans who had reinforced Morlancourt. Most of the infantry then advanced late but they still cleared the village. The late change in orders meant that 58th Division's barrage was cancelled but some battalions advanced behind three tanks onto Chipilly spur at the original time.[83] The British gunners then opened fire to give support, only to pin down the Londoners until the rest of the battalions followed five tanks across Hill 105 at 5.30 pm. This time, the Americans received their orders late, but they too were pinned down because the smoke screen failed to cover them.

The barrage missed the machine-guns around Chipilly when another attempt was made at dusk.[84] The gunners then switched to smoke, while Australian troops led the Londoners behind the enemy position. The Germans fell back during the night, abandoning Hill 105 and seventy guns in Gressaire Wood. An advance at 6 pm on 10 August was stopped by a counter-attack but Méaulte was captured at dawn the following morning.

The Australian Corps, 9-12 August

The 4th Australian Division took over both banks of the Somme on 9 August, so that operations could be coordinated across the river, and it then held its position. A lack of telephone lines meant that the 10 am zero had to be delayed.[85] But the tanks were still late, the artillery had not had time to organise a barrage and some units were delayed by a counter-barrage. So, 5th Australian Division struggled; even more so when six out of seven tanks were knocked out east of Harbonnières by a single anti-tank gun.

The Corps' right flank expanded, because the boundary with the Canadians followed the Roye road, so 2nd and 1st Australian Divisions passed through 5th Australian Division, en route to the second objective.[86] Again, the artillery had no time to organise a creeping barrage for 2nd Australian Division, while the infantry received 'hurried verbal instructions' before they advanced three hours late.[87] Fifteen tanks led the advance but more were knocked out thirteen around Vauvillers.[88] The Germans had not realised that most were unarmed supply tanks before they withdrew.[89]

---

82   Ibid., pp. 107-8.
83   Ibid. The 58th Division's initial advance is detailed on pp. 108-9.
84   Ibid., the later attack is covered on p. 110.
85   Bean, *The Official History of Australia in the War, Vol. VI*, p. 621.
86   Ibid., p. 632. One observer stated, 'it was butchery for the tanks.'
87   Ibid., p. 644.
88   Ibid., p. 635.
89   Ibid., p. 625. This illustrated the 'extreme helplessness of even the Mark V tank, when unprotected by smoke-shell from supporting field-guns.'

Motorcars, motorcyclists and runners rushed orders out to 1st Australian Division's units as they marched forward. A counter-barrage delayed the deployment for so long that the creeping barrage had finished, and the smoke screen had dispersed by the time the advance started. Eleven tanks were hit around Framerville but most of the resistance came from the left flank, where 2nd Australian Division was delayed even longer.[90] The infantry resorted to bombing forward along old trenches. Cavalry squadrons cantered towards Lihons, only to withdraw when the Whippets failed to turn up, leaving the Germans to reoccupy their trenches.

After only forty-eight hours in battle, the Australian Corps had very few tanks left, but it still had plenty of artillery and shells. The Germans carried out a controlled withdrawal in the mist, as 2nd Australian Division, pushed past Framerville on 10 August. But their machine-gun teams stopped the advance towards Raincourt as soon as it cleared.

'Through very defective liaison, no word of the movement had reached' the 1st Australian Division about the Canadian Corps' delay to zero hour.[91] Major General Hobbs assumed a copy had been sent to every division and so he did not forward them. It meant 1st Australian Division was stopped by enfilade fire from the Canadian zone, when it advanced towards Lihons at 8 am.

Monash's plan for the night of 10 August involved driving the few remaining tanks[92] behind the infantry, so the sound of their engines scared the Germans. The plan worked for 4th Australian Division, north of the Somme, but it was a different matter south of the river. The tank officers 'thought the job was mad', while 3rd Australian Division's officers considered that 'someone's confidence had overreached itself'; the other ranks believed the 'enterprise was ridiculous and stupid.'[93] The Germans were alerted by 'several armoured cars dashing eastward along the Roman road with headlights full on' and they lit up the sky with flares.[94] They saw tanks leading, rather than following the infantry, and all kinds of fire scattered the infantry, while the tanks turned back.

Hardly any of the nine tanks allocated to 1st Australian Division's joined the 4 am attack on 11 August. The infantry only advanced a short distance towards Lihons because the Canadians did not move on their right flank. Monash wanted to cut off the Germans dug in along the south bank of the Somme but the artillery observers could not see them behind Méricourt spur. So, 3rd Australian Division had spent the day moving a battalion into position under a smoke screen, 'dribbling men forward' in ones and twos. At dusk, machine-gun barrages covered the flanks, while Proyart was shelled as a diversion. The real attack followed a creeping barrage though Méricourt.

---

90 Ibid., p. 646.
91 Ibid. They had been vaguely addressed to the 'Australian Division on our flank' and had ended up with 5th Australian Division, in reserve.
92 Both fighting and supply tanks, to increase the volume of engine noise.
93 Bean, *The Official History of Australia in the War, Vol. V*, p. 687.
94 Ibid., p. 687.

Artillery supported the advance east of Méricourt the following day, but there was no barrage as troops crossed the Étinehem spur and the Proyart heights when it was dark. The two-pronged advance, either side of the Somme, brought the Australian Corps' advance to an end; it had captured 8,767 prisoners and over one hundred guns.

The Canadian Corps, 9 to 14 August

By dawn on 9 August, 3rd Canadian Division only had one brigade and seven tanks capable of offensive action, so General Currie ordered 4th Canadian Division to clear Le Quesnel at 4.30 am.[95] The rest of the Canadian Corps had to distribute messages by hand, because the telephone lines were insecure, resulting in delays to zero hour. Changes in plans eventually lengthened the delay to five hours but some batteries still fired several minutes late while the infantry battalions advanced at different times; some up to an hour late.[96] The mist had cleared by 10 am but the uncoordinated attack confused the Germans and Le Quesnel was taken when five tanks caught up with the infantry.

The enfilade fire grew heavier as 2nd Canadian Division advanced parallel to the Nesle railway, because no one was advancing to their flanks.[97] The infantry followed sunken roads and ditches to outflank the enemy positions around Rosières and then directed the Lewis gun teams to fire on them. The tanks were late because they had nowhere safe to assemble until smoke grenades could be found to create a screen where they could deploy. They had soon caught up but all seven were knocked out as they 'took out one machine-gun nest after another.'[98]

It took 1st Canadian Division longer than expected to side-slip south of the Luce stream and the gunners did not hear of the change in zero hour while the tanks were late.[99] Some of the infantry battalions waited until the artillery were ready but the rest advanced without any support and they became involved in heavy fighting around Vrély and Warvillers. One squadron of cavalry fell foul of the wire fences beyond the two villages, but they had been cleared by the time the support brigade was ready to advance. This time there was artillery support and seven Whippets led the infantry into Rouvroy.

It took 4th Canadian Division until after midday to clear Le Quesnoy and 3rd Canadian Division had to continue the advance because Currie had no more reserves. It took a long time to tell everyone, so the advance through Folies to Bouchoir did not

95   Edmonds, *Military Operations: France and Belgium, 1918, Vol. IV*, p. 89.
96   Nicholson, *Official History of the Canadian Army in the First World War*. These delays are discussed in detail on p. 411.
97   Ibid. The 2nd Canadian Division's advance is covered on pp. 411-2.
98   Ibid., p. 411.
99   Ibid. The 1st Division's attack is explained on pp. 412-3.

start until 4.30 pm.[100] A cavalry regiment and seven Whippets reinforced the line, covering the flank along the Roye road, until the French caught up.

The Canadian Corps' left held its position, but enemy action and late tanks meant that centre and right advanced at different times on 10 August, starting at 4.20 am.[101] Four out of eight tanks were knocked out helping 3rd Canadian Division clear Parvillers and Le Quesnoy. The twelve tanks allocated to 4th Canadian Division were late, so zero was delayed by two hours. The advance past Maucourt was cautious because the Canadians had no maps of the old trenches. However, they still reached Chilly and Fouquescourt once the tanks turned up.[102]

The plan was for 32nd Division to continue the advance on 10 August but German bombers hit the division's field artillery during the night, so zero was delayed. The Mark IV and V tanks did not turn up for the 10.30 am attack on Rouvroy while the seven Whippets stood no chance during the fight for the old trenches. Nearly all the sixteen heavy tanks which joined the attack around Parvillers were knocked out. Another four were sent forward to crush the entanglements around Fouquescourt and Parvillers but the artillery was short of ammunition, while the infantry were too disorganised to pursue the retreating Germans.

By this stage of the battle, it was difficult to locate the enemy positions, so the artillery focused on three types of targets; the heavy guns hit the villages and woods; some of the field batteries fired creeping barrages in support of the infantry; the rest of the field batteries were on standby to shoot at fleeting targets, as directed by the infantry. The tanks and infantry were finding it difficult to advance across the 1916 battlefield, while the cavalry was finding it too dangerous. Late on 10 August, Currie sent his senior staff officer to Fourth Army headquarters to 'remonstrate that the enemy's resistance was now very strong and that the ground over which the proposed advance was to be made was quite impassable for cavalry.'[103] Rawlinson, nevertheless, persisted.

The Germans struck back on 11 August and their barrage delayed 4th Canadian Division's deployment while the artillery did not see the SOS signals through the mist when the counter-attack began.[104] A decision was taken not to try and retake Hallu, to conserve troops, so the Canadian artillery made it untenable instead. Eight Whippets would help recapture some of the lost ground later.

Currie's plan for 32nd Division was for the gunners and machine-gun teams to target Parvillers and Damery. Sixteen tanks would lead the infantry past them before turning, to take them in the rear. At least that was the plan; zero had to be delayed until 9.30 am and then the artillery overshot their targets. The German machine-gun

100 Ibid. The 4th Division's advance is covered on pp. 413-4.
101 Germans reinforcements were shoring up the line and counter-attacking.
102 Nicholson, *Official History of the Canadian Army in the First World War*, p. 415.
103 Ibid., p. 417.
104 Ibid., p. 418.

teams had hidden well forward in ditches and shell holes, so they were able to pin down the infantry. Fourteen tanks had soon been knocked out and the two survivors had to turn back; the infantry followed because they could not cut the wire.

General Currie ordered 2nd and 3rd Cavalry Divisions to seize the high ground opposite his right flank, hoping the Germans would abandon Roye when the squadrons appeared. However, machine-gun fire stopped them getting far and further probes were called off.

The 3rd Canadian Division eventually cleared the 1916 trenches around Parvillers and Damery, while 1st Canadian Division secured Fransart and La Chavatte over the days that followed. Damery fell without a fight on the 14th but it had been abandoned on purpose because a 'German ruse, which materialized in the afternoon with a violent shelling [was] followed by an attack from two battalions.'[105]

The Canadian Corps had advanced over 15 miles, captured 9,200 prisoners and taken nearly 200 guns. It had suffered 11,000 casualties but Currie told the survivors that 'This magnificent victory has been won because your training was good, your discipline was good and your leadership was good.'[106] They would have no time to rest because they were about to move north to the attack east of Arras.

Summary 9-11 August

Foch had made an accurate prediction before the Amiens offensive; 'Go as far as you can the first day, go on again on the second, and again on the third, before the enemy can concentrate his reserves. After that you will certainly have to pause...'[107] He considered continuing the advance after the third day, convinced that the Germans were demoralised, but Haig objected because Rawlinson was reporting several problems.[108]

Fourth Army's divisions were tired, and it had used up all its reserves. The Tank Corps had lost over half its number on 8 August alone, while the rest were being repaired or serviced. The BEF would miss them over the weeks that followed. It would have been better to deploy fewer tanks on the first day, saving the rest for the later breakout phase. Rawlinson's engineers and labour units had to build roads and railways across the old battlefield, before it was wise to advance again. He also knew the Germans were reinforcing the Somme and they had plenty of old 1916 trench systems to defend.[109]

It was time for Fourth Army to regroup and rest while another army attacked. The plan was for Third Army to attack between Arras and Albert instead, while the

---

105 Ibid., p. 418.
106 Ibid., p. 419.
107 Edmonds, *Military Operations: France and Belgium, 1918, Vol. IV,* p. 133.
108 Ibid. The discussions with Foch are covered on p. 133-5.
109 Ibid. Details of Rawlinson's corps commanders' meeting is on pp. 152-3.

French First Army attacked further to the south. That would pull reserves away from the area south of the Somme. Fourth British Army and First French Army could then renew the offensive, creating one huge attack front.[110]

Ludendorff welcomed the lull in the fighting, and he took the opportunity to put the Ninth, Second and Eighteenth Armies together into a new army group. General Max von Böhn considered how he could withdraw them to the Hindenburg Line, a sensible plan on paper, but there was too little time to repair after nearly 18 months of neglect. Ludendorff did not want to carry out a such a withdrawal because it would also have a negative effect on morale.[111]

Widening the Attack, 21-26 August

On 19 August, Haig and Byng agreed Third Army's centre would start crossing the Ancre two days later while First Army drew the Germans' attention to the Arras area.[112] Third Army's left flank would advance the following day, while Fourth Army helped its right flank clear the Thiepval heights. The Australian Corps would extend the attack south of the river the following day. The French would be carrying out a similar extension of its front, starting on 20 August, again working from the outside for the attack towards the centre.

Third Army, 21-26 August

Several hundred artillery pieces opened fire at 4.55 am on 21 August. They focused on hitting the villages across a 10-mile-wide front between Arras and Albert rather than trying to create a creeping barrage in the morning mist. General Byng's plan was for the worn-out Mark IV tanks to stop at the first objective, while the newer Mark V tanks continued to the second objective;[113] the Whippets and armoured cars would head for the exploitation line.[114] Several tank chassis carrying 6-inch howitzers and ammunition also deployed as the world's first self-propelled gun. They all found it hard to reach the start line on time in the mist.

Eight divisions had deployed and there had been many casualties from the mustard gas shells which hit the assembly areas. There were also concerns about the replacements because '50 per cent of the infantry were said to be boys, who would do well if the first action in which they took part was a success.'[115]

---

110 Ibid. The reasoning behind and the plans for a wider attack are covered on pp. 153-4.
111 Ibid. The German defensive plans are discussed on p. 161.
112 Ibid., p. 172.
113 The older Mark IV tanks were less likely to survive a long drive.
114 Edmonds, *Military Operations: France and Belgium, 1918, Vol. IV.* Byng's full orders are provided on pp. 183-4.
115 Ibid., p. 181.

Third Army faced a 2-mile-deep outpost zone dotted with machine-gun posts and anti-tank guns and it was very different to the attack on 8 August. The area was so sparsely held that the guns formed three standing bombardments instead of the traditional creeping barrage. A shortage of experienced officers meant the assault troops followed the 'barrage in groups at very wide intervals but not in great depth'.[116] But the thick mist meant they navigated by compass bearing while the Germans struggled to spot any targets until it had cleared.[117]

Prisoners taken from the Guards Division had given away zero hour on 21 August, so the assembly areas were hit by a gas bombardment. The outposts around Hénin were cleared by 59th Division but five tanks were unable to help the Guardsmen clear Moyenneville and Hamelincourt because the crews had been gassed.[118] Meanwhile, twelve tanks helped 2nd Division's advance towards Courcelles before machine-gun teams deployed to kept watch during the later stages of the advance.[119] The tanks allocated to 3rd Division were also late whilst a cavalry brigade suffered many casualties probing Ervillers and Gomiécourt.

The creeping barrage across IV Corps' front could only cover the advance as far as the first objective but the plan to move two brigades of artillery forward had to be cancelled because the enemy artillery and planes were targeting the roads. Nearly ninety tanks had been allocated to IV Corps' attack but twenty-two tanks lost their way in the fog. It left twenty-four Mark V tanks and twenty-four Whippets to join the advance towards Achiet-le-Petit, while twelve Whippets, six armoured cars and a cavalry Brigade went beyond it.[120]

The Germans around Ablainzevelle and Bucquoy 'fought [37th Division] with great determination and continued to fire until their guns were run over by the tanks'. There was a late change in the order of 63rd Division's battalions, so the advance was delayed, and they then bypassed several German positions in the mist. There was hard fighting to cross the railway line, south of Achiet-le-Petit where 'twenty-three machine guns were captured on a 50-yard-front, each with a great heap of empty cartridges by its side.' They delayed 5th Division's advance and many of IV Corps' tanks were knocked out when the mist cleared.

The New Zealand Division had an easier time and the 'surprise so studiously aimed at was completely realised' in the fog.[121] In fact, they advanced too far around Puisieux and had to withdraw to a safer line as soon as the mist lifted. However, 42nd Division had taken all day and night to clear the high ground overlooking the Ancre only to

116 Ibid., p. 183.
117 Ibid., pp. 185-6.
118 Ibid., VI Corps' attack is covered on pp. 186-7.
119 The machine-gun teams were called 'guns of opportunity' and they looked out for counter-attacks.
120 Edmonds, *Military Operations: France and Belgium, 1918, Vol. IV.* The IV Corps' advance is covered on pp. 188-92.
121 Stewart, *The New Zealand Division 1916-1919, Vol. II*, p. 421.

abandon it due to counter-attacks and machine-gun fire across the valley. The final counter-attack was broken up because the German barrage fell short.

Lieutenant General Cameron Shute's plan was for V Corps' left flank to cross the Ancre around Beaucourt and Hamel while his right flank waited until III Corps, on Fourth Army's front, was on the Thiepval heights to his right.[122] But 21st Division had a difficult time crossing the river, which consisted of deep-water channels, over flowing shell holes and marsh land. Even so, the men found ways across and fought their way up the slope, so the engineers could build bridges.

The fog had both helped and hindered the attack. It had delayed the tanks, but it had let the infantry outflank the German outposts. The tanks may have found it hard to navigate in the mist but 'when it lifted many were knocked by enemy fire.'[123] It was also impossible to send the Whippets and cavalry forward because the Germans still held a strong line along the Arras – Albert railway.

Byng's plan was for VI Corps to push its right flank beyond the railway crossing its front at 4 am on 22 August, while the rest of Third Army 'was to stand fast whilst guns and troops got into position for the continuation of the advance the next day.'[124] The tanks struggled to cross the railway because anti-tank guns were covering the few places where they could cross.[125] They knocked out six tanks supporting 3rd Division's advance beyond Courcelles. The six Whippets were unable to subdue the machine guns waiting for them on the far side, when the mist cleared. It was then 2nd Division's turn but the creeping barrage was too slow for the Whippets and too fast for the infantry. The artillery paused for a time, to let the infantry catch up, but most of the tanks were knocked by anti-tank guns around Ervillers. 'The guns were often placed in depth and as soon as the foremost gun was either captured or put out of action, a retirement was made to the next gun.'

The Germans were waiting for Third Army to attack again, so their artillery hit its rear areas and assembly areas with gas shells early on 23 August, making the infantry and tanks late. VI Corps' artillery had not had time to register targets around Hénin Hill. either[126] Meanwhile, the guides got lost leading 52nd Division's battalions forward, leaving them no time to reconnoitre the ground before the 5.07 am advance. The tanks were late, so 56th Division advanced 'by working forward and then to a flank, [which] evidently much demoralised the enemy.'[127] Only three tanks reached the Guards Division in time, but many prisoners were still rounded up around

---

122 Edmonds, *Military Operations: France and Belgium, 1918, Vol. IV.* The V Corps passage of the Ancre is explained on pp. 192-3.

123 Ibid., p. 194.

124 Ibid., p. 204.

125 The railway passed though and over many cuttings and embankments, where the slopes were too steep for the tanks.

126 Edmonds, *Military Operations: France and Belgium, 1918, Vol. IV.* The VI Corps' attack is detailed on pp. 221-8.

127 Ward, *The Fifty Sixth Division 1914–1918*, p. 265.

Hamelincourt. It did raise the question, though 'what as to be done if the tanks were late... it was difficult for the infantry to know whether to wait for the tanks or obey the order fixing the hour of advance.'[128]

The New Zealand and 42nd Divisions carried out a preliminary attack at 2.30 am on 23 August, seizing the high ground overlooking Miraumont on IV Corps' right.[129] They then joined the general advance at 11 am, which proved to be a mistake because the mist had cleared. The Germans were waiting for them, so Lewis guns and trench mortars had to put down suppressive fire on Bihucourt brickworks, while another group outflanked it and took 400 prisoners.

However, no one knew how far 37th Division had advanced, so the evening barrage landed beyond many of the German machine-gun teams. In the centre, 5th Division lost the barrage fighting across the railway cutting. The artillery then had no idea if the infantry had taken Irles, so they refused to shell it, while an evening attack on Loupart Wood failed.[130] However, both New Zealand and 42nd Divisions followed up their early success and advanced closer towards Miraumont.

On V Corps' front, 17th Division had crossed the Ancre by being 'dribbled over in small parties in single file and under continual fire' before climbing the slope towards Thiepval.[131] Men from the 38th (Welsh) Division had also waded across the Ancre at Aveluy, so two tanks could cross the causeway early on 23 August. V Corps' two crossings convinced the Germans to abandon the Thiepval heights.[132]

Bright moonlight foiled 2nd Division's plan to advance towards Sapignies, on VI Corps' right, at 1 am on 24 August. A pincer attack against Thiepval ridge then started badly because some of 21st Division's battalions lost their way while others did not receive their orders. However, they persevered until the Germans abandoned Grandcourt, in the Ancre valley.

Third Army's main attack on 24 August started at 4.30 am but there were problems telling the artillery what time zero hour was.[133] The heavy British guns stopped 52nd Division climbing Hénin Hill for a time and the Scots were then pinned down by machine-gun fire. Meanwhile, ten tanks helped 56th Division reach Croisilles Trench, only to find it was 'only 2 feet deep and quite useless as a reorganising point'.[134] The Guards Division had crossed the Sensée valley, pausing only when they were hit by

128 F. Loraine Petre and Major General Sir H. Cecil Lowther, *The Scots Guards in the Great War, 1914-18* (London: John Murray, London, 1925).

129 Edmonds, *Military Operations: France and Belgium, 1918, Vol. IV.* The IV Corps advance is covered on pp. 228-32.

130 It appears communications broke down after the initial attack, leaving the artillery unable to help the infantry.

131 Atteridge, *The History of the 17th (Northern) Division*, p. 379.

132 Edmonds, *Military Operations: France and Belgium, 1918, Vol. IV.* The V Corps crossing is explained on p. 193 and 233.

133 Edmonds, *Military Operations: France and Belgium, 1918, Vol. IV*, p. 252.

134 Dudley Ward, *The Fifty Sixth Division 1914–1918*, p. 183.

the British guns while 2nd Division was again pinned down, even though six tanks tried to outflank the position.

IV Corps' artillery had not been told zero hour was 4.30 am, so 37th Division and New Zealand Division took the garrisons of Favreuil and Grévillers by surprise in the pre-dawn mist.[135] The loss of Thiepval ridge had caused the Germans to abandon Miraumont and Loupart Wood in front of 42nd Division but the tanks sent to assist 63rd Division's pursuit were late. Brigadier General DePree called off the advance as soon as his men encountered the German rearguards and Major General Charles Lawrie sacked him for letting the opportunity slip by.[136]

Meantime, 17th Division had crossed the Thiepval Ridge, south of the Ancre, only for the leading brigade to advance in the wrong direction. The brigade staff could see the error but there was no way of communicating with them, so they crossed the river, only to lose contact with everyone. Fortunately, the second brigade headed in the right direction, towards Courcelette. The 38th Division had crossed the Ancre before the Germans realised and their advance triggered a withdrawal from the La Boisselle area.

Third Army's left did not move on 25 August because all the tanks were being serviced. Instead, the artillery hit the villages with high-explosive shells by day and gas shells by night. VI Corps planned a two-phase attack, with the first being made at 4.30 am and the second at 9 am. However, there was a mix up over the start times and most of the infantry advanced before down, without any artillery or tank support.[137] Both Béhagnies and Sapignies were cleared by 2nd Division before dawn, as planned. Major General Feilding mistakenly ordered the Guards Division to advance at the earlier time, surprising the Germans. The Guardsmen were unable to cut the wire covering St Léger Wood and two out of three tanks were knocked out because the mist had cleared. One of 62nd Division's battalions advanced towards Mory at the earlier time, so a second was sent to support it. The Germans were then able to stop the attack at the set time.

Crowded roads forced IV Corps' assault troops to move in 'artillery formation over the fields, now drenched by the heavy rain', making 37th Division, the New Zealand Division and 63rd Division late.[138] The tanks had to withdraw to safety as soon as the mist cleared, leaving the infantry pinned down in front of Bapaume. An outflanking attack north of the town was then cancelled at dusk because 'it was suspected that [37th Division's] telegraph message ordering the attack must have been tapped.'

The Germans were eager to abandon the old Somme battlefield and V Corps' pursuit passed through Le Sars, the Butte de Warlencourt, Eaucourt l'Abbaye and

---

135 Stewart, *The New Zealand Division 1916-1919, Vol. II*, p. 429-31.
136 Edmonds, *Military Operations: France and Belgium, 1918, Vol. IV*. The circumstances of DePree's sacking are explained on p. 254.
137 Ibid. The VI Corps' attack is covered on pp. 274-8.
138 Stewart, *The New Zealand Division 1916-1919, Vol. II*, p. 442. The IV Corps advance is detailed on Edmonds, *Military Operations: France and Belgium, 1918, Vol. IV*, pp. 270-4.

High Wood. Mametz Wood was only lightly held but many Germans had been overlooked in the mist and some even tried to capture one of 38th Division's brigade headquarters.[139]

VI Corps' started early on 26 August and 52nd Division cleared the Hindenburg Line on Third Army's left before nine tanks followed the infantry across Cojeul stream onto Hénin Hill. Meanwhile, 56th Division's attack floundered in heavy rain, as it cut through the five belts of wire protecting Croisilles.[140]

The weather interfered with IV Corps' operations but 5th Division still captured Beugnâtre at dawn.[141] The New Zealanders sent 'fighting patrols dribbling forward and scuppering the machine gun nests' covering Bapaume.[142] However, 63rd Division encountered strong resistance around Thilloy because the Germans were holding out until all the ammunition had been evacuated from the area.

V Corps faced a nightmare crossing the 1916 battlefield and some men became lost whilst Germans who had remained hidden, emerged to counter-attack. The new enemy line was eventually encountered around Ligny-Thilloy and Delville Wood.[143]

Fourth Army, 22-26 August

Fourth Army faced the old Somme battlefield, an 8-mile deep belt of overgrown trenches, wire and shell holes. Lewis guns drowned out the sound of the tanks before 18th Division advanced through Albert early on 22 August.[144] The advance stopped along three lines; along the River Ancre, on the east edge of the town and finally beyond a line of strongpoints. The engineers then had to remove dozens of mines and charges from the roads and bridges. Men swam across the Ancre south of the village during the night, to secure two footbridges before dawn. It meant the tanks could cross the Dernancourt causeway, while the barrage covered the advance east of the river.

Gas shells caused many tanks to be late, but the rest led 12th Division around Méaulte and Bécourt until they had all broken down. The result was the infantry bunched together in thick mist and they lost the barrage.[145]

Ten tanks led 47th Division through the mist and smoke, finding the Germans across Happy Valley were willing to surrender.[146] However, poor map reading meant

---

139 Edmonds, *Military Operations: France and Belgium, 1918, Vol. IV*, V Corps' pursuit is explained on pp. 267-70.
140 Ibid. The VI Corps' attack is explained on pp. 303-4.
141 Ibid.
142 Stewart, *The New Zealand Division 1916-1919, Vol. II*, p. 444.
143 Edmonds, *Military Operations: France and Belgium, 1918, Vol. IV*. The V Corps advance is covered on pp. 299-301.
144 Ibid., pp. 201-2.
145 Ibid., pp. 200-1.
146 Ibid., pp. 199-200.

the infantry dug in ½ mile west of their objective, meaning they would never catch up with the barrage. Four supply tanks had carried entrenching tools forward so the Londoners could dig in, but observation balloons spotted them when the mist lifted; a supply tank was eventually sent forward loaded with ammunition, so they could hold their position. All the Whippets had broken down, so the cavalry had to explore behind the German line on their own and they could not cross the enemy entanglements. A counter-attack at the head of Happy Valley captured some of the Londoners but they had been 'excellently schooled in the way they should behave if captured, and they gave very clever, evasive answers.'

The Germans spotted the Australians assembling in the moonlight early on 22 August and their artillery shelled the deployment area until a mist formed. It made some of the tanks late and while the rest led the infantry forward at 4.45 am, the Germans regrouped when they paused on the first objective.[147] Anti-tank guns picked off the tanks when the mist cleared and it was down to the infantry of 3rd and 1st Australian Divisions to deal with them.

The Germans were falling back from Cappy and Chuignes to defensive positions which were nothing more than 'isolated shell-holes and wooden notice boards on short poles with the pretentious inscription Second Main Line of Resistance.'[148] Resistance was so weak at one point that Lieutenant Lawrence McCarthy of 16th Australian Battalion was able to single-handedly clear 500 yards of trench in the 'most effective piece of individual fighting in the history of the AIF'.[149]

Fourth Army's artillery fired 'crash barrages' at selected targets before the creeping barrage started the advance at 1 am on 24 August.[150] The early hour had been chosen to take advantage of the bright moonlight, only it was too bright and 12th Division was pinned down in Happy Valley. On the right, 47th Division had more luck, 'silently working their way behind a line of posts, without the enemy being aware of what happened.'[151] Stokes mortars pinned 250 men inside Lochnagar crater when it was light, while 18th Division advanced across the Chapes spur. Five tanks also helped the Londoners advance lengthways along Happy Valley, to help 12th Division.

The 3rd Australian Division relied on supporting fire from all angles as they crossed the spurs and valleys north of the Somme. Delays in getting out orders sometimes meant the mist had often lifted and the advance involved a lot 'sneaking in small groups along banks, old trenches and sunken roads.'[152]

---

147 Ibid., pp. 197-9.
148 Ibid. An unidentified quote attributed to the German 243rd Division history is provided on p. 236.
149 Edmonds, *Military Operations: France and Belgium, 1918, Vol. IV*, p. 214.
150 Ibid., p. 239.
151 Alan Maude (ed.), *The 47th (London) Division, 1914–1919 by Some who Served with it in the Great War* (London: Amalgamated Press, 1922), p. 190
152 Bean, *The Official History of Australia in the War, Vol. VI*, p. 767

Both III Corps and the Australian Corps pushed forward without becoming too heavily engaged on 25 August, but it became difficult to direct the artillery and barrages sometimes landed too far ahead to help. Troops usually advanced across country, because the German artillery was shelling the roads and advanced guards of infantry, Whippet tanks and cavalry continued the advance the following day, until it started to rain heavily.

First Army, 26 August to 1 September

General Henry Horne planned to start First Army's advance astride the Scarpe on 26 August, with the Drocourt-Quéant Line, or *Wotan Stellung*, 8 miles to the east, as its objective; it was 'among the strongest on the Western Front'.[153] The Canadian Corps had just relocated after its success with Fourth Army and it had been busy probing the German lines, in what they referred to as 'hole-boring'.[154] The Germans were expecting an attack, so Currie chose to attack behind a barrage at 3 am on 26 August, to confuse them.[155] Eighteen tanks followed, ready to assist but they were 'not to be used ahead of the infantry unless definite resistance demanded their employment.'[156] Overhead four squadrons bombed and strafed targets while two more squadrons kept a look out for German reinforcements. The 3rd Canadian Division outflanked Orange Hill and cleared Monchy-le-Preux with a pincer attack. The 2nd Canadian Division kept pushing until it crossed the Cojeul stream.[157]

German observers spotted the eight tanks as they advanced at 4.55 am on 27 August and they were all knocked out, leaving 3rd Canadian Division holding a jagged front line. Zero for 2nd Canadian Division was delayed to 10 am and there was then struggle to cross the Sensée stream, so it just established a bridgehead in the Rouvroy-Fresnes Line.

The entire corps' field guns staggered their firing to help 3rd Canadian Division straighten its line the following morning. The different zero hours alerted the Germans but the volume of artillery fire silenced all the machine-gun teams.[158]

The 3rd Canadian Division broke the Fresnoy-Rouvroy Line then swung north to seize the high ground beyond the following day. However, the 2nd Canadian could not cut through the wire covering Cagnicourt because the troops 'were mentally and physically worn out'.[159]

---

153 Nicholson, *Official History of the Canadian Army in the First World War*, p. 426.
154 The same as Australian 'peaceful penetration', probing the enemy line to test the men and their defences.
155 Nicholson, *Official History of the Canadian Army in the First World War*, p. 428.
156 Ibid., p. 427.
157 Ibid., pp. 428-9.
158 Ibid., p. 430.
159 Ibid., p. 431. The battalions were weak, and the men had been in constant action for several days.

Planes swooped low at 4.40 am on 30 August while the Canadian Corps' artillery fired 'an ingenious barrage that rolled from right to left.'[160] The 1st Canadian Division made pincer attack against the ends of the Vis-en-Artois Switch and took two battalions 'completely by surprise'. It meant the Drocourt-Quéant Line was in reach and the Canadian heavy guns could move forward to cut the wire.[161]

Summary, 21-26 August

Third Army's success north of the Somme meant that Haig could tell Byng and Rawlinson 'to take risks, which a month before would have been criminal to incur, ought now to be taken as a duty.'[162] Meanwhile, the Secretary of State for War, Lord Alfred Milner, had warned Haig there was a shortage of conscripts and he had to conserve enough manpower to attack the Hindenburg Line. The German Army was also facing a manpower crisis because all divisions were reporting of men and 'it was really impossible to talk about companies; they were merely weak platoons.'[163] OHL would eventually issue orders for a general withdrawal from the 1916 Somme battlefield on 26 August, giving everyone just twenty-four hours to prepare.

Third Army, 27-29 August

All the divisions along Third Army's line were weak and tired but prisoners correctly stated that a withdrawal was due. The German gunners were seen to be shooting all their surplus ammunition while the infantry had orders to hold on until all the supplies had been evacuated from Bapaume. Machine guns were the backbone of the defence but they also left 'behind single field guns and sections in woods and copses...'[164] IV and V Corps had wait for the Germans to evacuate Bapaume because 'it was no part of the High Command's purpose to ram their heads against a brick wall'.[165]

The rest of Third Army's advance began at different times on 27 August with 62nd Division starting behind a 'practically perfect' barrage on VI Corps' right flank at 7 am.[166] The Guards Division had to postpone their zero hour because it was believed prisoners had given it away, and its attack began at 9.30 am. Both 52nd and 56th Divisions advanced over Hénin Hill thirty minutes later, after hearing how the Canadians were progressing on XVII Corps left.

160 Ibid., p. 433.
161 Edmonds, *Military Operations: France and Belgium, 1918, Vol. IV,* p. 365.
162 Ibid., p. 513.
163 Ibid. An unidentified quote from German 243rd Division's history given on p. 236.
164 Ibid., p. 315.
165 Stewart, *The New Zealand Division 1916-1919, Vol. II,* p. 448.
166 Edmonds, *Military Operations: France and Belgium, 1918, Vol. IV.* The advance on 27 August is covered on pp. 325-7.

Although 52nd Division crossed the Sensée at Fontaine, it took 56th Division all night to get through the wire north of Croisilles and reach the stream. The rest of the divisions were also having problems. The Guardsmen lost the barrage while clearing St Léger Wood before coming under enfilade fire from Croisilles, where 56th Division should have been. It required a battery of field guns to deploy in full view of the enemy to stop the counter-attack. The machine-gun teams covering Vaulx-Vraucourt had also pinned down 62nd Division.

Hendecourt was taken by 56th Division on 28 August but it had to fall back to avoid being surrounded.[167] Later that night, the Germans withdrew from Bapaume after setting fire to anything they could not remove, then the 'flares about the western faubourgs became less numerous, and his machine guns noticeably less aggressive. And at last there was silence.'[168] The 5th Division, the New Zealand Division and the 42nd Division then moved cautiously through and past the town. Aerial observers 'brought reports of fires lit behind the German front' around Thilloy and 21st Division, 17th Division and 38th Division were able to follow up the withdrawal south of Bapaume.

A 12.30 pm zero hour was chosen on 29 August, to catch the Germans in Hendecourt resting after their midday meal.[169] However, 52nd Division had to withdraw because no one had advanced on its flanks, while a second barrage had to be fired far ahead, because no one knew where of the new front line was. It overshot the German machine-gun teams and Riencourt had to be abandoned when the Germans closed in. It took 56th Division many hours to work its way along the Hindenburg Line around Bullecourt. Meanwhile, 62nd Division's bombing teams used flares to coordinate their advance along two trenches towards Vaulx-Vraucourt, while Lewis gun teams gave covering fire above ground. Some sections manned the captured trenches while others cleared strongpoints between them.

The south end of the Drocourt-Quéant Line joined the Hindenburg Line opposite XVII Corps. However, General Byng's plan was to wait until the Germans had abandoned the triangle of trenches. Meanwhile, VI Corps faced stiff resistance when it attacked the fortified villages along the Hirondelle at 5 am on 30 August.[170] The Germans then withdrew across the stream.

Zero hour was fifteen minutes later on IV Corps' front and the German artillery were firing a counter-barrage by the time seven tanks led 5th Division during a tough fight for Beugny. Another four tanks led the New Zealand Division through Frémicourt and Bancourt, east of Bapaume. The mist had cleared by the time 42nd Division advanced just before 6 am but it could not get along old trenches into Riencourt.[171]

---

167 Ibid., pp. 334-6.
168 Stewart, *The New Zealand Division 1916-1919, Vol. II*, p. 448. Faubourgs are a French term
     for suburbs.
169 Edmonds, *Military Operations: France and Belgium, 1918, Vol. IV*, p. 344-7.
170 Ibid., pp. 363-4.
171 Ibid. The IV Corps attack is covered on pp. 362-3.

A surprise pre-dawn attack by 38th Division failed to take Morval while 17th Division twice failed to get into Le Transloy.

Several tanks led German infantry down the Bapaume road early on 31 August and it was some time before the New Zealander's SOS signals were seen through the mist. Machine-guns teams firing armour piercing bullets stopped two tanks while a gun battery firing over open sights forced the rest to retire.[172] Meanwhile, 21st Division had failed to find their forming-up line in the dark, so their pre-dawn attack failed to outflank Beaulencourt. Gas shells then cause the men to sneeze, so a counter-barrage disrupted 17th Division's dawn attack while 38th Division captured Morval. One of 17th Division's brigade-major was hit while reconnoitring Le Transloy and his brigadier stayed with him. It meant the jumping off line was placed in the wrong position and a second attack failed.[173]

Fourth Army, 27 August-1 September

III Corps' advance towards Delville Wood and Trônes Wood started at 4.55 am on 27 August but it was slow going because the divisions had just been given a new batch of conscripts. One battalion had 'just received 350 recruits whose ages varied from 18 ½ to 19 ½.'[174] Later that night, 3rd Australian Division moved silently through Vaux Wood, cutting off the spur next to the River Somme.

The advance on III Corp's left had to stop when 18th Division reached Combles ravine but 12th Division was able to reach Maricourt on the Somme. The Australians continued moved slowly on the opposite river bank but it was easier going to the south, where patrols advanced 'over the open moorland until sharply fired on; the companies coming up to the patrols at each convenient stage, and the patrols then walking on again.'[175]

All along Fourth Army's line, artillery observers accompanied the infantry companies, so bombardments could be called down quickly, while battery and battalion commanders worked side-by side. Up ahead the Germans rear guards fired off all their ammunition and then made a run for the bridges before the engineers blew them up. The railway bridge south of Péronne was wired up and the artillery shelled the area when the Australians approached, detonating the explosives.[176]

III Corps wheeled field guns forward to silence machine-guns teams during the advance south of Combles.[177] The Germans eventually retired to the Canal du

---

172 Stewart, *The New Zealand Division 1916-1919, Vol. II*, p. 454-5.
173 Edmonds, *Military Operations: France and Belgium, 1918, Vol. IV.* V Corps' failure to advance is detailed on p. 362.
174 Scott, *History of the 12th Division in the Great War, 1914-1918*, p. 199.
175 Bean, *The Official History of Australia in the War, Vol. VI*, p. 780.
176 It had either been too dangerous or too difficult to set up to detonate by hand.
177 These single field guns were called sniping guns.

Nord late on 31 August, but it was too dangerous to follow them down the slope in daylight hours.

Monash wanted 2nd Australian Division to capture Mont St Quentin,[178] to outflank Péronne even though his brigadiers said the attack 'will fail; the men and the officers are too knocked out'.[179] The battalions were weak while field guns had to move close behind the infantry because there was no time to arrange a barrage.[180] The Australians advanced across Mont St Quentin at 5 am, catching the Germans in the middle of a relief and they either 'threw down their arms and ran forward to be captured' or ran back.[181]

On 1 September, 3rd and 2nd Australian Divisions cleared the ground around Mont St Quentin in rain and mist.[182] Meanwhile, 5th Australian Division cleared Péronne, 'advancing at a half run, as fast as they could go … shooting from the shoulder and giving the [Germans] no time to stop'.[183] South of the town, 32nd Division bridged the Somme Canal but could not cross the lagoons and marshes, flanking the river beyond.

Breaking the Drocourt-Quéant Line and Beyond, 2 to 11 September

All was going well but the Chief of the Imperial General Staff, General Sir Henry Wilson, warned Haig not to lose too many men because it would make the War Cabinet anxious about attacking the Hindenburg Line. He did not pass the concerns to his army commanders.[184]

First Army[185]

The Canadian Corps faced the Drocourt – Quéant Line (D-Q Line) south of the River Scarpe and the Buissy Switch which connected it to the Hindenburg Support Line. It was 'one of the most powerful and well organized German defence systems' and Generals Horne and Currie had agreed to 'not to attack it until we are ready and then to go all out' against it.[186] Nine tanks had to wait until 4th (British) Division had silenced the anti-tank guns covering the only crossing over the Sensée stream. Then

178 Edmonds, *Military Operations: France and Belgium, 1918, Vol. IV,* Monash's conference is discussed on p. 357-8.
179 Bean, *The Official History of Australia in the War, Vol. VI,* p. 796.
180 Edmonds, *Military Operations: France and Belgium, 1918, Vol. IV,* the capture of Mont St Quentin is covered on pp. 367-9.
181 Bean, *The Official History of Australia in the War, Vol. VI,* p. 811.
182 Edmonds, *Military Operations: France and Belgium, 1918, Vol. IV,* p. the capture of Péronne is detailed on pp. 373-5.
183 Bean, *The Official History of Australia in the War, Vol. VI,* p. 838.
184 Edmonds, *Military Operations: France and Belgium, 1918, Vol. IV,* the telegram is on p. 383.
185 Ibid., Lieutenant General Currie's orders are detailed on pp. 396-7.
186 Nicholson, *Official History of the Canadian Army in the First World War,* pp. 433-4.

'as each post was located, it was at once engaged by rifle and Lewis gun fire, under cover of which [men] then started to work around to a flank.' The Germans withdrew during the night.

The plan was to break the German line at 'Arras-Cambrai road, and then swing outward to roll up the German defences to north and south.'[187] Aircraft flew low to drown out the sound of tank engines, as they joined the Canadian advance at 5 am on 2 September. The tanks would head back after taking the D-Q Line, reaching their assembly area by the time the mist lifted.[188] The Canadians moved down the 'long, exposed crest of Mont Dury' at 5 am while the tanks sprayed smoke to blind the German anti-tank gun teams.[189] They led 4th and 1st Canadian Divisions through the Drocourt – Quéant Line and then did an about turn to help the support troops mop up the position.[190] In one brigade, both the tanks and the infantry deployed late, and missed the creeping barrage. Fortunately, many Germans surrendered while the rest capitulated when the tanks caught up. The tanks were heading back to their assembly areas before the mist cleared.

The main resistance came beyond the crest around Dury, where the German machine-gun teams and batteries had deployed out of sight of the Canadian artillery. Casualties were high because there was no creeping barrage, no tanks and no smoke, but the infantry kept moving in platoon rushes, extending the advance to over 4 miles in places. The Canadian Corps then made false preparations to cross the Sensée stream and the Canal du Nord, to draw attention away from Third Army's attack to the south. Currie later said; "whether our victory of yesterday or of August 8th is the greatest, but I am inclined to think yesterday's was."[191]

Third Army, 4-11 September[192]

As 57th Division tried in vain to cross the canal at Moeuvres, both the Guards Division and 2nd Division checked out the Hindenburg Line, where it ran close to the Canal du Nord. The tunnel was the weak point in the German line, but IV Corps' artillery accidently shelled the Germans surrendering near Havrincourt Wood.[193] It meant the New Zealand Division had to outflank the west part of the wood while the heavy artillery convinced the Germans to abandon the rest.

Both 42nd and 17th Division crossed the canal tunnel at 6 am on 4 September, before fanning out beyond it. Patrols believed the Germans could not see into the

---

187 Ibid.
188 Edmonds, *Military Operations: France and Belgium, 1918, Vol. IV*, p. 396.
189 Ibid. The assault is covered on pp. 399-403.
190 Nicholson, *Official History of the Canadian Army in the First World War*. The Canadian Corps' attack is covered on pp. 436-8.
191 Ibid., p. 440.
192 Edmonds, *Military Operations: France and Belgium, 1918, Vol. IV*, pp. 439-41.
193 Stewart, *The New Zealand Division 1916-1919, Vol. II*, p. 466.

Etricourt cutting, so a platoon ran down to the canal on 4 September. Suppressive fire allowed others to cross the damaged bridge and 38th Division had soon cleared the canal bank. All along Third Army's front, the Germans fell back to old British trenches and Byng correctly believed they would hold out there while the Hindenburg Line was prepared.

Fourth Army, 4-11 September

Machine guns hit the Canal du Nord bridges while II Corps' artillery shelled the ridge beyond, but 18th Division struggled to get beyond Riverside Wood on 4 September.[194] Meanwhile, 47th Division over-extended itself east of Moislains, only to be told to pull back so the artillery could shell the area. Many Londoners chose to shelter in German dug-outs rather than retire and then joined the pursuit, which was led by cavalry and cyclist patrols, backed up by field guns. The Germans withdrew from Nurlu and Templeux, on III Corps' flanks as 12th and 74th Division advanced from the canal following day.

Cavalry and cyclists led 3rd and 5th Australian Divisions east of the Somme but they rarely saw the enemy, only the 'horizon ahead, lurid with burning villages.'[195] Artillery shelled the rearguards in the villages, while the infantry had 'to outflank one machine-gun post after another', as they moved across country.[196] No one saw the Germans withdraw from the Somme late on 4 September but 32nd Division was across around Brie the following morning. The bridgehead was reinforced, and the Germans were found dug in around Holnon Wood.[197]

Stormy weather hampered operations on 8-9 September and then Rawlinson received bad news. The Australian Corps was going to be withdrawn from the line. A no conscription vote had left battalions short of men and the veterans were going to be sent on home leave, after three years in action.

The Allies Strike Back Summary

The capture of Le Hamel on 4 July was the BEF's first combined arms offensive for eight months but it illustrated that the BEF had not forgotten how to use artillery, infantry and tanks effectively together. Deception played a major part in deceiving the Germans as to the time and place of the attack. The tanks once again led the infantry while the artillery used shrapnel, high-explosive and smoke to good effect to stun the

---

194 Edmonds, *Military Operations: France and Belgium, 1918, Vol. IV.* The passage the Canal du Nord is covered on pp. 444-8.
195 Bean, *The Official History of Australia in the War, Vol. VI*, p. 883.
196 Ibid., p. 884.
197 Edmonds, *Military Operations: France and Belgium, 1918, Vol. IV.* The Australian advance east of the Somme is chronicled on pp. 447-8.

Germans. Fighting tanks then covered the infantry while they dug in, while supply tanks carried huge amounts of equipment and ammunition forward.

The Allied counter-offensive to the last German offensive of the war started on 18 July on the Marne. Four British divisions took part but their attacks were poorly organised and it was success on the French front that led to a general withdrawal after a week of inconclusive fighting. It marked the beginning of the end for the Germans.

The attack on 8 August was a bigger version of Le Hamel, both in width and depth and again, great lengths were taken to conceal the deployment. Scouts guided the tanks and they in turn led the infantry through the smoke and dust in an efficiently organised advance. Well planned arrangements to move infantry, artillery and tanks forward resulted in what GHQ had wanted for many months; a breakthrough. It may have been a victory for the infantry and artillery but too many tanks had been lost and it left the BEF short of them until the end of the war.

Third Army extended the attack front and it too used cavalry and Whippet tanks to clear the German outpost zone, starting on 21 August. Difficult fighting across the 1916 Somme battlefield followed but the rapid transfer of the Canadian Corps Arras meant the BEF's attack could expand further north. The breaking of the Drocourt-Quéant Line on 2 September finally precipitated a withdrawal to the old British trenches in front of the Hindenburg Line.

10

The Final Advance
12 September-11 November 1918

Third Army, 12-18 September

On 12 September, the Guards Division established posts across the Canal du Nord under cover of smoke. Meanwhile, 62nd Division relied on a complicated artillery barrage to cover two brigades as they squeezed through the bottleneck between the Spoil Heap and Havrincourt chateau moat. IV Corps' centre was secured by 37th Division while the New Zealand Division advanced from Havrincourt Wood and Gouzeaucourt Wood, 'close to the barrage in splendid style'.[1] An SOS barrage delayed a counter-attack towards Havrincourt until heavy rain forced the Germans to retire.[2]

Everyone knew Moeuvres was the best place to cross the Canal du Nord and 52nd Division was engaged in the 'worst ordeal that they ever endured' around the ruins between the 17th and 21st.[3] A counter-attack across the canal on 18 September was 'no kid glove affair' either.[4]

The next stage of Third Army's advance involved clearing the trenches dating back to the battle of Cambrai. Byng's artillery smothered the German batteries with gas every night, but there was no preliminary bombardment because there was little wire to cut. Trench mortars fired a hurricane bombardment, and there was a three-layer creeping barrage, some 800 yards deep.[5] The infantry advanced behind a smoke

---

1   Stewart, *The New Zealand Division 1916-1919, Vol. II, New Zealand*, p. 481.
2   Sir James E. Edmonds, *Military Operations: France and Belgium, 1918, Vol. IV: 8 August to 26 September: The Franco-British Offensive* (London: HMSO, 1947), pp. 469-72.
3   TNA WO 95/2897/3: 1/7th Royal Scots War Diary.
4   TNA WO 95/1423/6: 2nd Royal Scots War Diary.
5   Edmonds, *Military Operations: France and Belgium, 1918, Vol. IV*, p. 490. The 60 pounders covered 400 to 800 yards; the 6-inch howitzers covered 200 to 500 yards; half the 18-pounders fired just in front of the infantry. The rest of the 18-pounders and the 4.5-

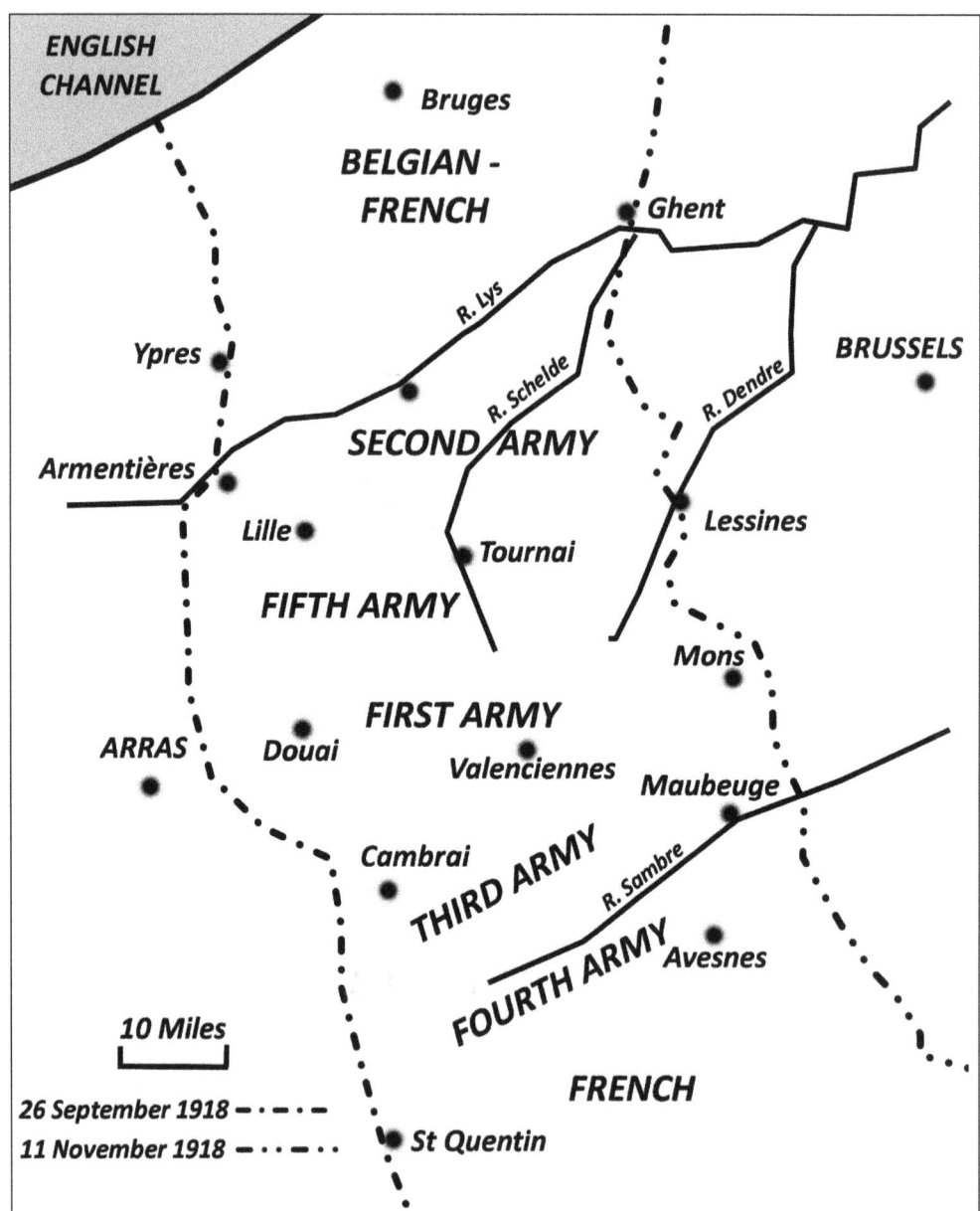

Map 10. Final Advance, 12 September-11 November 1918: Great distances were covered during the last weeks of the war, but the withdrawing Germans always managed to keep one step ahead.

screen in 'appalling weather' at 5.20 am on 18 September, and took the Germans by surprise.[6] All four divisions made good progress around Gouzeaucourt, Gauche Wood and Chapel Hill, while a couple of supply tanks carried ammunition forward to 17th Division so it could take 'an armoured machine-gun nest' in Gauche Wood.[7]

An unfortunate mix up with orders resulted in 5th Division having to give up ground on the left flank, while Fourth Army's failure to capture Peizière, on the right flank held up 21st Division. Late orders meant that 38th Division did not advance past Gouzeaucourt during the night while contact planes warned about counter-attacks against Havrincourt Wood and Chapel Hill. The attack ended with 33rd Division engaged in four days of bloody fighting across the ridges and ravines south of Villers Guislain.[8]

Fourth Army, 12-26 September

The beginning of the end came for the Australian Corps when Lieutenant General Monash had to send 800 married men to Marseille; they had been in service since 1914. A second ship would be waiting to take another batch of men to Australia straight after the attack on 18 September.[9]

Fourth Army faced the three old British trenches which had once faced the Hindenburg Line and they had been converted to face in the opposite direction. They would be approached in reverse order; the Green Line, the Battle Line and the Outpost Line. In particular, extra steps had been taken to fortify the villages around the weak point in the Hindenburg Line; the St Quentin tunnel. The German artillery soaked Fourth Army's assembly areas with mustard gas, but they found few artillery batteries to shell before zero hour.

Only sixteen tanks were available, because the rest were being saved for the attack on the main Hindenburg position. They deployed in small groups to silence strongpoints, while dummy tanks were placed at other parts along the line. They were made from 'wooden frames covered by painted hessian... and would be moved a little distance by pioneers with long drag ropes to points where the Germans would see them after dawn.' Nearly 1,500 artillery pieces opened fire at 5.20 am in the pre-dawn mist.

---

inch howitzers hit lucrative targets with searching barrages. Extra companies reinforced the machine-gun barrage.

6   Edmonds, *Military Operations: France and Belgium, 1918, Vol. IV,* pp. 489-93.
7   A. Hillard Atteridge, *History of the 17th (Northern) Division* (University Press, Glasgow, 1929) p. 412. The strongpoint was made from four derelict British tanks dating from the Cambrai battle.
8   Edmonds, *Military Operations: France and Belgium, 1918, Vol. IV,* pp. 493-4 covers the German counter-attacks.
9   Ibid., pp. 481. Conscription had been rejected and both Birdwood and Monash had rejected the reorganisation of Australian divisions, as British divisions had done earlier in the year. They said it 'would complicate tactics and destroy the *esprit de corps*'.

III Corps, 12-26 September

One tank helped 58th Division get through Pezières, while 12th Division cleared its assembly area ready to attack at 6.50 am.[10] Two tanks were knocked out while one of 58th Division's drove past, firing on the British infantry as they cleared Epéhy.[11] Engineers placed dummy tanks in the valley west of Ronssoy, but the Germans never saw them in the mist. Four tanks led 18th Division along the ridge through Ronssoy and Lempire, while the support companies followed the trampled grass to keep direction in the mist.[12] Three tanks were unable to lead the troops any further east until the afternoon, because it took six hours to tell the artillery where they were. On the right, 74th Division advanced beyond Templeux-le-Guérard until the supporting barrage stopped it capturing Malakoff Farm.[13]

A dozen tanks advanced east of Lempire at 5.40 am on 21 September. Five were knocked out while the rest had to withdraw because 18th Division's infantry had been driven back by machine-gun fire. All four tanks with 74th Division were knocked out and it took until the following morning to capture the Quadrilateral.

The Australian Corps, 12-18 September

The 4th Australian Division advanced across abandoned ground to get close to the Germans on 12 September, encountering resistance in the British Battle Line around Le Verguier.[14] It was even harder to take the British Outpost Line after the mist lifted but the Australian troops could see the 'dense wire belts and white parapets of the Hindenburg Outpost Line' in the distance. Eight tanks then led 1st Australian Division through mist on 18 September, catching many Germans sheltering in shell holes and trenches. The troops could now see across the St Quentin Canal and the entrance of the Bellicourt tunnel.[15]

IX Corps, 18-26 September

The Germans withdrew across the St Quentin Canal around Bellenglise on 18 September. Then 1st Division fought to clear Pontruet, Fresnoy-le-Petit and Gricourt. A gas barrage on Holnon Wood forced 6th Division to march around it before the Quadrilateral scattered the infantry and knocked out their four tanks. There was then

10   Edmonds, *Military Operations: France and Belgium, 1918, Vol. IV,* pp. 486-9.
11   Ibid., p. 488.
12   Ibid., pp. 485-6.
13   Ibid., pp. 483-5.
14   Ibid., pp. 476.
15   Ibid., pp. 481-3.

'great difficulty circulating the necessary operation orders on time' the following day and another eight tanks were hit while the infantry struggled to get through the wire.[16]

Early on 22 September, 46th Division made a flank attack to divert the Germans' attention around Pontruet from the main frontal attack seventeen minutes later. However, the assault was disorganised because the troops encountered a new trench which had been dug during the night. They then had to abandon Pontruet when the smoke cleared.[17] The Germans eventually evacuated Pontruet and Fayet on 26 September and 46th Division could see the Hindenburg Line defences along the canal, when they moved up.

First Army, 27 September-3 October

The Germans were dug in beyond the half-finished Canal du Nord. The plan was for the 1st and 4th Canadian Divisions to cross the dry section of the canal around Sains-lez-Marquion early on 27 September. They would fan out to the north and south, enabling the engineers to bridge the water-filled sections. It meant the deployment was so cramped that the Germans could not fail to spot an attack was looming.[18]

Aerial observers reported that the enemy trenches were shallow, so the artillery focused on cutting the belts of wire when the order to attack was issued on 18 September. There was no preliminary barrage and the typical three-layer creeping barrage included 50 per cent shrapnel, 40 per cent high-explosive and 10 per cent smoke.[19]

VIII Corps

VIII Corps 'adopted a role of peaceful penetration, occupying ground relinquished by the retreating enemy, as and when the opportunity occurred, but avoiding, unless absolutely necessary, a pitched battle.' The artillery fired four fake barrages to make the Germans stay in their dugouts before 8th Division advanced towards the Rouvroy-Fresnes Line early on 23 September.

More ground was taken on 27 September, with 58th Division moving past the north side of Lens, while a gas barrage hit the town. Both 20th and 8th Division advanced closer to the Rouvroy-Fresnes Line, while Chinese attacks were made just

---

16   Ibid., pp. 475-6. The Official History pays scant attention to IX Corps' initial battle for the Quadrilateral.

17   Ibid., pp. 499-502.

18   Sir James E. Edmonds and Lieutenant-Colonel R. Maxwell-Hyslop, *Military Operations: France and Belgium, 1918, Vol. V: 26 September to 11 November: The Advance to Victory* (London, HMSO, 1947). The Canadian Corps' plan is covered on pp. 19-20.

19   Edmonds and Maxwell-Hyslop, *Military Operations: France and Belgium, 1918, Vol. V*, p. 20.

after the Canadian zero hour, to pin down German reserves opposite VIII and XXII Corps frontage.[20]

The Canadian Corps, 27-28 September

Twenty-four Mark IV tanks advanced alongside two waves of Canadian skirmishers at 5.20 am on 27 September, with the rest of the infantry following in section columns. The tanks would return from the third objective, ready to be used again the following day. The gunners had to deploy deep on the narrow front, so batteries were ready to move forward in stages once the engineers bridged the canal, so they could maintain a steady barrage.

On the left, 56th Division advanced astride the Canal du Nord while the engineers bridged the watercourse, so that 11th Division could cross at Sains-lez-Marquion.[21] The first battalion was pinned down and the barrage had moved on by the time the support battalion arrived, but they still took Oisy-le-Verger. Two tanks were knocked out clearing the Marquion Line, while four tanks led 1st Canadian Division past Sains-lez-Marquion.[22] The barrage then crept back, as the infantry and tanks took the canal side position from the rear. Eight tanks crawled across the dry canal channel north-east of Moeuvres and then used the smoke dischargers attached to their exhausts to keep their vehicles hidden. A smoke screen also hid 4th Canadian Division but the creeping barrage fell short, so a second one had to be arranged for the advance towards Bourlon.[23]

The Germans were seen withdrawing around Aubencheul-au-Bac on 28 September, so 11th Division moved up to the Sensée Canal. Four tanks led 3rd Canadian Division towards Fontaine-Notre-Dame at 6 am but 'unmapped wire' stopped the advance through the Marcoing Line.[24] Zero had been delayed until 9 am for 1st Canadian Division, because it was ahead the troops on its flanks, and it was light by the time the troops heard they had to withdraw behind the barrage line.[25] Many were hit pulling back and there were many more casualties advancing over the same ground. A second attack by 3rd Canadian Division was delayed until dusk, because the gunners needed more ammunition.

For a second time, many men were hit when 1st Canadian Division was told to withdraw from the barrage line in daylight on 29 September. The late start meant that

20   Ibid., pp. 28-9.
21   Ibid., pp. 26-8 covers 56th and 11th Divisions' attacks.
22   Ibid., pp. 22-6.
23   Ibid., pp. 22-4.
24   Nicholson, *Canadian Official History*, p. 448. A brigade from 4th Canadian Division also took part, capturing part of the Marcoing Line.
25   Edmonds and Maxwell-Hyslop, *Military Operations: France and Belgium, 1918, Vol. V*, pp. 55-6. The artillery wanted the creeping barrage to follow a straight line, while the infantry line was jagged.

4th Canadian Division had to assemble far back out of sight, before advancing 1,400 yards to catch up with the barrage. It was unable to clear the Douai railway, so 1st Canadian Division was forced to fall back.[26] Three tanks led 3rd Canadian Division through the Marcoing Line only to be pinned down in front of more 'unmapped wire' protecting the Cambrai-Douai road and the Douai railway.[27] A second barrage landed too far ahead, because the gunners did not know where the front line was and the day ended in the 'most desperately fought engagement of the war'.

An attempt to capture Blécourt the following day failed because smoke shells failed to screen 4th Canadian Division, while 3rd Canadian Division struggled to advance north of Cambrai.[28] At 5 am on 1 October, 1st Canadian Division captured Blécourt, Bantigny and Cuvillers but counter-attacks drove it out of the exposed valley, when it was light. The 3rd Canadian Division found it impossible to cross the Schelde Canal but the 'identification of a large number of regiments and battalions' proved that the Germans were determined to hold on for as long as possible.[29]

The Canadians' success north Cambrai of sparked a general withdrawal on First Army's left. Fires and explosions were seen behind the German line while no one fired at planes flying low over enemy territory. It meant 20th Division could advance through Méricourt, Acheville and Fresnoy on 2 and 3 October.[30]

Third Army, 27 September-5 October

General Sir Julian Byng's orders to attack the Hindenburg Line at 5.20 am on 27 September were issued on 20 September. Third Army's left and centre would push through the Hindenburg Line to the Schelde Canal, while the right only had to move forward a short distance. There were concerns that VI Corps had to advance along the valley called the Grand Ravin before IV Corps seized Highland Ridge on its right flank. So, Byng postponed its zero hour, meaning VI Corps would be advancing in daylight.[31]

Old belts of wire hidden in the long grass delayed 52nd Division and the Scots had to resort to bombing after losing their barrage. Most of the tanks were lost in tank traps but the infantry still reached the Hindenburg Support Line around Lock 8. Stokes mortars covered 63rd Division when it crossed the canal at 5.5 am but all of its tanks were knocked out clearing the Hindenburg Support Line.[32]

Tanks crossed a dry section of the Canal du Nord east of Demicourt with the Guards Division, before turning south along the Hindenburg trenches. Three tanks

---

26 Ibid., pp. 123-4.
27 Ibid., pp. 123-4.
28 Ibid., pp. 150-1.
29 Ibid., pp. 153-4.
30 Ibid., pp. 129-30.
31 Ibid. The unsuccessful compromise is explained on pp. 31-2.
32 Ibid. The XVII Corps initial attack is detailed on pp. 33-6.

were knocked out in front of a sugar factory, so an 'artillery crash' was organised to suppress the garrison while infantry led a fourth tank along a sunken road, to outflank the position.[33]

The Germans were firing so many flares that the support divisions did not spot the ones telling them to advance until it was getting dark. Troops falling back in the face of a counter-attack from Anneux disorganised 57th Division; the British SOS barrage stopped the advance altogether.[34] Meanwhile, 2nd Division failed to take the Cantaing Line despite a smoke barrage and the Germans only withdrew after the Canadians had outflanked Bourlon Wood to the north.[35]

A smoke barrage covered 3rd Division's right flank, because VI Corps would advance three hours later, but the Germans were still waiting beyond the first ridge.[36] Eight tanks helped clear the Hindenburg Support Line past Flesquières but a delay around Ribécourt caused 62nd Division to lose its barrage. It meant the charge down the slope towards the St Quentin Canal around Marcoing ended in disaster.[37]

IV Corps advanced in stages, with part of 42nd Division and 5th Division moving off at 7.52 am as drums of blazing oil exploded across Highland Ridge. The rest of 42nd Division advanced along the Hindenburg trenches on Trescault ridge at 8.20 am.[38] Nearly all of the eighteen tanks were knocked out and then the infantry had to form defensive flanks because they were under counter-attack.

On Third Army's right, a single tank had led 33rd Division into Villers Guislain at 3.30 am while 21st and 33rd Divisions advanced down Targelle Ravine and towards Gouzeaucourt, two hours later.[39] Counter-attacks retook Villers Guislain and captured two of 33rd Divisions' battalions in the ravine, while 21st Division was forced to withdraw at dusk. It would re-enter Gouzeaucourt after the Germans abandoned it during the night.

Third Army, 28 September

The first to attack was 42nd Division and it overran Highland Ridge trenches, on Third Army's right, at 2.30 am.[40] The Scots took so many prisoners that 'they simply waved them to the rear and the Boches meekly obeyed, too glad to be out of the

---

33   Ibid., pp. 37-39. An 'artillery crash' was a specially arranged hurricane bombardment of an enemy position which refused to surrender. Every available gun hit the target for a short period before it was attacked again.
34   Ibid., p. 36.
35   Ibid., pp. 39-40.
36   Ibid., pp. 40-2.
37   Ibid., pp. 42-3.
38   The staggered start times were needed because the Hindenburg Line ran at an angle to the British line.
39   Edmonds and Maxwell-Hyslop, *Military Operations: France and Belgium, 1918, Vol. V*, p. 45.
40   Ibid., IV Corps' attack is detailed on pp. 47-9.

fighting to take advantage.' Unfortunately, late orders meant the Germans were ready for 5th Division, resulting in a tough fight for Welsh Ridge. It proved difficult to distribute orders in the rain and darkness in time for 62nd Division's support of IV Corps' crossing of the Schelde Canal at Crèvecoeur at 4.35 am.

Thirty minutes later 2nd Division attacked the Cantaing Line, only to find the Germans had the canal crossings covered. Some men crossed the bridges around Marcoing, but the rest of the men had to wait until dusk before they could cross the lock gates.[41]

The guides failed to turn up after 62nd Division's second advance into Marcoing at 6.30 am, so 'there was no time for nothing, a few hasty orders and away they went... And how well it succeeded!'[42] The men were filing across a plank bridge when it collapsed into the canal and the delay cost them dearly when they attacked the Marcoing Line.

Third Army, 29 September-4 October

Fog covered the Schelde Canal early on 29 September, allowing 63rd Division to cross pontoon bridges and canal locks around Cantaing, while 57th Division used an aqueduct to establish a bridgehead.[43] Meanwhile, 2nd Division crossed the canal by two footbridges until artillery fire smashed them. Machine-gun fire from Mont sur l'Oeuvre stopped part of 62nd Division advancing north of Rumilly, but the rest cleared Masnières and les Rues Vertes.

The New Zealanders advanced along the old trenches on Welsh Ridge and Bonvais Ridge behind a barrage at 3.30 am.[44] They took over 500 prisoners and twenty-eight artillery pieces before coming under cross fire on Bonvais Ridge because of delays around La Vacquerie. They were then hit by enfilade fire because 5th Division's advance to the south had been delayed until 8.30 am. The advance was pinned down for a time but the New Zealanders were soon firing across the Schelde Canal, 'engaging transport lorries, guns and motor tractors, scattering horses and personnel' escaping from IV Corps.[45]

Meanwhile, a 'very bad barrage' landed too far ahead of V Corps' advance, so neither Gonnelieu nor Villers Guislain could be taken.[46] Many from 33rd Division were taken prisoner because the messenger sent to order them back was captured,

---

41   Ibid., pp. 50-1.
42   TNA WO 95/3087/3: 2/4th Hampshire Regiment's War Diary.
43   Edmonds and Maxwell-Hyslop, *Military Operations: France and Belgium, 1918, Vol. V*, pp. 120-1.
44   Ibid., pp. 147-8.
45   Stewart, *The New Zealand Division 1916-1919, Vol. II*, p. 501.
46   Edmonds and Maxwell-Hyslop, *Military Operations: France and Belgium, 1918, Vol. V*, pp. 116-7.

while 21st Division's advance soon broke down because one battalion was late and another was held up.

Neither 57th nor 63rd Division could make any progress through the southern suburbs of Cambrai but many prisoners were captured in the Marcoing Line on 30 September.[47] It took until late the following day before 2nd Division cleared Mont sur l'Oeuvre, along with its 400 strong garrison. Then 62nd Division could clear the trenches around Rumilly, and one battalion used forty captured machine guns to stop a counter-attack. However, both 2nd and 3rd Division had to withdraw during the night, so the morning's barrage could be made in a straight line.[48]

The plan for the New Zealand Division to cross the Schelde Canal before dawn without a barrage on 30 September had to be altered because the messengers got lost in the mist.[49] A barrage was fired at 5.45 am, alerting the Germans who stopped anyone crossing at Crèvecoeur. Meanwhile, the infantry advanced to the canal at Les Rues des Vignes before the barrage began and they were then not ready when the guns opened fire for a second time. However, 5th Division saw the enemy withdrawing from the Hindenburg Line towards the Schelde and while a few men crossed the canal, the Germans had soon returned to defend it. A new barrage convinced the Germans to abandon Gonnelieu and Villers Guislain but both 21st and 33rd Divisions discovered that the Germans had crossed the Schelde Canal and blown the bridges around Banteux.[50]

The New Zealanders eventually crossed the Schelde by a demolished bridge and a raft made of duck boards strapped to cork slabs at Masnières and Crèvecoeur early on 1 October.[51] The Germans abandoned the rest of the canal opposite IV Corps late on 4 October rest of the line fell back up to 3 miles, leaving the 37th, 21st and 33rd Divisions to find them in the Hindenburg Support Line the following morning.[52]

Second Army 28 September-2 October

On 16 September General Plumer was instructed to get ready to advance east of Ypres and across the Messines Ridge. The chosen date was 28 September, making it the second of the three BEF's great attacks over just three days. There would be no extra air activity, no extra artillery fire and extra batteries assembled in secret.

---

47   Ibid., p. 149.
48   Ibid. The VI Corps' attack is covered on pp. 148-9.
49   Stewart, *The New Zealand Division 1916-1919, Vol. II,* p. 505.
50   Edmonds and Maxwell-Hyslop, *Military Operations: France and Belgium, 1918, Vol. V,* pp. 146-7.
51   Stewart, *The New Zealand Division 1916-1919, Vol. II,* pp. 510-2.
52   Edmonds and Maxwell-Hyslop, *Military Operations: France and Belgium, 1918, Vol. V,* pp. 151-2.

The guns opened fire a few minutes before zero, to warn the infantry.[53] Then at 5.30 am the barrage crept forward through the mist, which blinded the Germans who were deployed across the 1917 crater field. The infantry fired flares to control the speed of the barrage and to report progress to the contact planes overhead.

The long advance required the artillery to move forward and battery positions had been built close to the front line, ready for the guns to occupy them. It meant the creeping barrage covered the infantry for 4,000 yards.[54] The guns then fired observed bombardments at pre-determined targets, to conserve ammunition. However, there was close cooperation between the artillery and infantry at all levels, and they dealt with targets as soon as they appeared.[55] The assault troops also called for smoke when the mist started to clear.

Both II and XIX Corps encountered little resistance because the maze of craters and pillboxes dating from the 1917 battle were difficult to defend.[56] They eventually stopped around Becelaere, Gheluvelt, Zonnebeke and Kortewilde because the few roads were booby trapped, while some of the British heavy guns were firing short.

There was a fierce battle around the St Eloi craters and Damm Strasse, at the northern end of Messines Ridge. The Lewis gunners had subdued the Germans by the time a second barrage was fired, and it hit 34th Division's advancing troops. There was little opposition on the ridge itself, but orders to take Wytschaete did not reach one battalion in time, while the other could not clear it on its own.[57] It was also impossible for 30th Division to clear Messines and so 31st Division had to send troops to outflank the ruins. Traffic congestion made it difficult to move in the dark, while the Germans coordinated their withdrawal with flares.

General Friedrich Sixt von Armin was shocked that Second Army had captured more ground in one day than during the entire Third Ypres campaign, the previous year. He told Crown Prince Rupprecht that Fourth Army could 'no longer stand up to a serious attack'.[58] Prisoners reported that their comrades were preparing to hold the Flanders I and II Lines, while a new defensive line was built behind the River Lys.

Second Army might have advanced a great distance, but it was struggling to supply its troops, because the 'roads were choked. The only tolerable ones among them were the Menin and Zonnebeke roads. Upon each was a solid mass of transport, which

53 Ibid., p. 60. The Belgian Army, on Second Army's left, fired a three-hour preliminary barrage. General Plumer was against this because it would be fired in the dark and he believed it would merely alert the Germans.
54 Ibid., pp. 61-2 explains the artillery organisation and post zero movements in detail.
55 Artillery brigades worked with infantry brigades, batteries with battalions and gun sections with companies.
56 Edmonds and Maxwell-Hyslop, *Military Operations: France and Belgium, 1918, Vol. V.* The rapid advance of the two corps is detailed on pp. 65-70.
57 Ibid. The battle for Messines ridge is explained on pp. 70-1.
58 Ibid., p. 73.

often for hours at a time remained immobile.' The German bombers could hardly fail to miss when there were breaks in the rain and mist.

The difficulties on the roads meant there were insufficient guns to create a satisfactory barrage at 9 am on 29 September. Instead, trench mortars had to be used to fire smoke which screened the weak battalions as they advanced.[59] Machine-gun teams were 'cleverly disposed in depth behind hedges or buildings' but II Corps forced their way through the Flanders I Line.[60]

A 4 am attack by 41st Division surprised the Germans along the Comines Canal, but a later attack by 35th Division went in the wrong direction.[61] There was success on the Messines Ridge where XV Corps' advance sparked a general withdrawal to the Lys but no one dare enter Armentières, in case the buildings were booby trapped.

For the second day running, there had been a long advance but there had been no rout because of several problems. The weather was poor, the ground was bad, and Second Army was inexperienced at moving fast in the open. It meant the Germans were able to retreat in good order while fresh divisions moved to Flanders to hold the River Lys.[62]

Early on 30 September, 36th Division advanced towards the Flanders II Line in heavy rain and high winds.[63] The artillery was too far back to hit Hill 41, so smoke was used to hide the troops as they reached the summit; a counter-attack drove them off. Both 29th Division and 35th Division faced a tough fight getting through the Gheluwe Switch but 41st Division found huge piles of abandoned stores in Comines.

After waiting for the divisions to catch up on either flank, 9th Division attacked the Flanders II Line under cover of smoke on 1 October. The weather had improved, so the Royal Air Force were able to support the infantry by locating machine-gun posts for the artillery; field guns were often manhandled forward to knock them out.[64] The Germans stopped 41st Division taking the Gheluwe Switch before withdrawing at dusk, leaving rearguards behind in pillboxes to stall the advance. Second Army's advance towards the Lys was going well but the Belgians were lagging on the left, while 36th Division would not clear Hill 41 until 12 October.

59   Some were as low as 25 per cent strength due to casualties and sickness. Spanish flu was starting to cause problems for all the armies, because the soldiers were living outside, in poor weather conditions and sometimes short of rations.
60   *Falls, The History of the 36th (Ulster) Division*, p. 264.
61   Edmonds and Maxwell-Hyslop, *Military Operations: France and Belgium, 1918, Vol. V*, pp. 77-8.
62   Ibid., p. 83.
63   Ibid. The fighting on 30 September is covered on pp. 85-7.
64   Ibid. The advance on 1 October is detailed on pp. 88-9.

Fourth Army, 27 September-3 October

On 22 September Rawlinson issued orders to attack the Hindenburg Line and American II Corps joined Fourth Army the following day, forming a composite Australian and American Corps. The two divisions were double the size of a British division and while 27th Division relieved III Corps' right, opposite the Bellicourt tunnel, 30th Division relieved the Australian Corps' left, opposite Bellicourt village.

Monash had resigned himself to the fact that the artillery would not be able to smash the many bunkers along the Hindenburg Lane, so a prolonged barrage started at 10.30 pm on 26 September, with nearly 600 medium and heavy howitzers targeting headquarters and batteries with the first British made mustard gas shells. It forced the Germans to put on their masks before the guns switched to high-explosive and shrapnel. The gunners were working to an old captured plan of the 3-mile-deep system of trenches which had been updated with aerial photographs. One task they attempted was to blow a hole in the canal embankment, to try and drain it, but it the bombardment did nothing more than alert the Germans.

Preliminary Attack, Australian-American Corps, 27 September[65]

The II American Corps had been reinforced by sixty tanks but 27th American Division had to make a preliminary attack, to clear the Outpost Zone and get in line with 30th American Division. Zero was set for 5.30 am but 27th American Division's sector was too wide and many of its officers were on training courses. The infantry bunched up in the mist and smoke, to avoid the counter-barrage, and then became disorientated. Many dug outs were overlooked and there were too few moppers up, leaving the tanks knocked out and the Americans pinned down with little ammunition, when the air cleared.

The Main Attack, 29 September

Neither 12th Division nor 18th Division made much progress through the mist towards Vendhuille at 5.40 am on 29 September. The Germans then pulled back in front of III Corps and crossed the canal during the night.[66]

The aerial observers could not locate the Australian-American Corps' new front line, but it was clear it was not as far forward as expected. Monash asked if the start line could be changed but it was too late to tell the artillery, so zero hour had to be

---

65 This disastrous preliminary attack is not mentioned in Edmonds and Maxwell-Hyslop, *Military Operations: France and Belgium, 1918, Vol. V.*
66 Edmonds and Maxwell-Hyslop, *Military Operations: France and Belgium, 1918, Vol. V*, pp. 109-10.

brought forward an hour to 4.50 am, on 29 September.[67] The barrage had to land 1,000 yards ahead to miss the Americans and it alerted the Germans right along the Hindenburg Line. The Americans experienced the same problems, with men bunching up in the mist while too many dugouts were overlooked. Many of the forty-five tanks were hit or ditched crossing the Hindenburg Line, while the infantry was left pinned down again.

The mist thickened when 30th American Division joined the advance an hour later and it suffered from the same issues as the 27th American Division.[68] Many of the thirty-three tanks and armoured cars were knocked out when it cleared. Despite all the problems, the Americans still cleared the Main Hindenburg Line and took many prisoners inside the tunnel.

The Australians marched towards the front, unaware of the problems; they soon were.[69] Eight tanks were disabled crossing an old British minefield while another eight tanks were knocked out before they reached the start line. The 3rd Australian Division then found 'many Americans [laid] dead or wounded among the yellow half trampled wheat. Small parties, clearly Americans, were seen ahead.' There were too many Germans still firing and it was impossible to fire a supporting barrage, so the Australians tried again when the mist returned. Meanwhile, the 5th Australian Division advanced in the same mist, which was so thick the 'troops closed up in file, each able to tap the back of the man ahead', as far as the Bellicourt tunnel embankment. A weak barrage, which did little more than alert the Germans, supported a further advance by the two divisions at 3 pm.

IX Corps faced the St Quentin Canal and 46th Division had practiced the crossing on the River Somme, only the day before. At 5.50 am on 29 September, they ran down the open slope and clambered down the wall into the canal cutting.[70] Some ran across an abandoned footbridge and others paddled across on rafts. The men equipped with life preservers had to jump into the 'stagnant, fetid water, uninviting for an early morning dip' and swim across.

The journey sounds daunting but the canal cutting protected the men from the machine-gun teams for a time. They then climbed the opposite side and then negotiated the smashed wire to enter the Hindenburg Line. They found 800 men hiding in the Bellicourt Tunnel and tunnellers had to go inside to disarm the explosives set to blow it up. Eight tanks crossed the canal bridge, but most were knocked out when the mist cleared in front of Magny-la-Fosse and Lehaucourt. The division had taken 4,200 prisoners and 72 guns and had suffered only 800 casualties.

On IX Corps' right flank, 1st Division had fought its way to the canal at Bellenglise, while 6th Division had drawn attention away from the main attack. The headquarters

---

67   Ibid., pp. 106-7.
68   Ibid., pp. 107-8.
69   Ibid. The Australian Corps attack is detailed on 108-10.
70   Ibid., pp. 101-6.

of 46th and 32nd Divisions had been set up together, to coordinate the later stages of the advance. However, there were delays getting forward and the advance began at dusk, 'unfortunately too late to reap the full advantage of the success of 46th Division'.[71] All six tanks were either late or knocked out but 700 prisoners were still taken in the Hindenburg Support Line.

Despite the difficulties, the Germans knew they were in serious trouble and there were serious discussions at a Council of War that morning. Both Hindenburg and Ludendorff demanded 'an immediate armistice in order to save a catastrophe.'[72]

Fourth Army in the Hindenburg Line, 30 September-1 October

Eleven tanks joined 3rd and 5th Australian Divisions, but heavy fire from Bony forced the infantry to bomb their way into the Hindenburg Support Line.[73] There were still worries about the stranded Americans on 1 October and while bad weather meant planes could not locate them, artillery could not be used either. Half a dozen Whippets were knocked out, but 3rd Australian Division still cleared Hindenburg Line around Bony and Tunnel Hill, while 5th Australian Division discovered that Joncourt had been abandoned.

IX Corps reported that the 'enemy's opposition lacked the determination of the previous day'.[74] The bend in the St Quentin Canal was cleared by 1st Division but 32nd Division could not take Joncourt, despite help from eight Whippets. It then needed a 'crash barrage' at dusk to make the 400 strong garrison in Levergies surrender. Joncourt was abandoned during the night but attacks against the Hindenburg Reserve Line (commonly known as the Beaurevoir Line) on 1 and 2 October failed to take Ramicourt or Sequehart.[75]

Fifth Army, 5-23 October

The Germans started a 'slow and deliberate retirement' opposite XI Corps and I Corps on 2 October and they crossed the flooded Haute Deule Canal over the next forty-eight hours.[76] There was then a long pause until the Germans retired again past Lille, starting on 15 October. It was down to 57th Division to enter Lille on 16 October and the 'reception accorded the troops was historic.[77] The men were decorated with French and Belgian colours and flowers by the civilian population, who cheered and shouted

---

71   Ibid., p. 105.
72   Ibid. The council of war, and whether Ludendorff used the word 'catastrophe' is discussed on pp. 111-2.
73   Ibid., pp. 135-6.
74   Ibid., pp. 133-4.
75   Ibid., pp. 139-41.
76   Ibid., pp. 125-8.
77   Ibid. The occupation of Lille is covered on pp. 410-1 and 413.

in delight.' The soldiers soon discovered that the Germans had robbed everything of value from Lille, Tournai and Antoing or smashed what they could not carry. They had left food for the civilians in Lille but they had evacuated other centres of population. Prisoners were rounded up to disarm the booby traps left in many buildings.

XI, I and III Corps all reached the Schelde Canal a few days later and began to look for ways to cross to flooded area.[78] Men swam or scrambled across ruined bridges to take telephone wires across. They were used to pull chains across which were rigged up to makeshift rafts and footbridges. All but one of the bridgeheads had to be abandoned because the far bank was flooded. The only group which could stay on the far bank occupied an island surrounded by a loop of the old river.[79]

Fourth Army, Breaking the Beaurevoir Line, 3-7 October

Rawlinson issued orders to attack the final part of the Hindenburg Line, often referred to as the Beaurevoir Line, at 6.5 am on 3 October and he was so confident of a breakthrough that he put the Cavalry Corps on standby. Two attempts to make the Germans withdraw from Le Catelet failed and then the mist cleared, forcing 50th Division to withdraw.[80] Meanwhile, 2nd Australian Division was cutting through the Beaurevoir wire by hand when seventeen tanks caught up and made gaps for the men to pass through.[81] Many Germans fled but one anti-tank gun knocked out five Whippets in quick succession, forcing the rest to withdraw to a safe distance. The infantry persevered, with the Lewis gunners firing from the hip, and they crossed the ridge overlooking Beaurevoir. Unfortunately, they discovered that the trenches 'had merely been spit-locked a foot deep, except for short lengths beside the pill-boxes.'

Eleven tanks led 46th Division through the Beaurevoir Line and the Germans fell back after the loss of Montbréhain and Mannequin Hill.[82] Up ahead the 'German transport or guns were seen withdrawing but again, the lack of direct communication from battalions to the artillery caused many opportunities for shelling the movement to be missed.' There was the same problem when Montbréhain was counter-attacked.

The attack on the rest of the Beaurevoir Line, at 6 am on 4 October, was far less organised. Some of 25th Division's battalions 'did not then know whether they were to attack', until ten minutes after zero.[83] Some of the batteries received their orders late and they hit 2nd Australian Division when they opened fire. All eleven tanks were

78   Ibid., pp. 413-4.
79   TNA WO 95/3021/10: 25th King's (Liverpool) Regiment War Diary.
80   Edmonds and Maxwell-Hyslop, *Military Operations: France and Belgium, 1918, Vol. V*, pp. 166-7.
81   Ibid., pp. 164-7.
82   Ibid., pp. 160-3.
83   TNA WO 95/2244/3: 9th Devonshire Regiment War Diary.

late, while four were knocked out supporting the Australian attack on Montbréhain.[84] The main success was 32nd Division's pincer attack on Sequehart with the help of four tanks and a smoke screen on their open flank.[85] The tanks then withdrew, leaving the infantry to use 200 captured machine guns to halt enemy counter-attacks.

Fourth Army took more ground over the next three days, but it had taken far longer and had been far costlier than Rawlinson had expected. The troops had, however, pushed beyond the final Hindenburg Line and Haig told his army commanders to prepare for open warfare after four weeks of hard fighting.

Fourth Army, Advance to the Selle Stream, 8-19 October

Third Army's early attack on 8 October alerted the enemy, so 66th Division came under fire as it advanced behind a smoke screen created by planes dropping phosphorus bombs. Most of the Whippets and twelve out of nineteen Mark V tanks were knocked out around Villers Outreaux and Usigny ravine, as soon as the smoke cleared. Meanwhile, seven tanks helped 25th Division take 1,400 prisoners along the Le Cateau road, before it expanded its frontage to contact the Americans on their right flank.[86]

The 30th American Division discovered the Germans were withdrawing from around Montbréhain when it advanced at 5.10 am on 8 October.[87] Thirty-six Mark V and Whippet tanks helped the infantry round up 1,500 prisoners and thirty artillery pieces but half of them were knocked out around Brancourt and Prémont. Rawlinson thought a breakthrough was possible, so he ordered the Cavalry Corps across the Canal du Nord. Both 1st and 2nd Cavalry Divisions struggled to move forward along the busy roads and only a few squadrons managed to squeeze past the infantry.[88]

IX Corps' plan to clear the Beaurevoir Line east of Sequehart involved three Whippets putting down suppressive fire at 5.10 am, while 6th Division cleared the ridge north of Méricourt. Nearly 700 prisoners had been taken by the time the infantry reached Mannequin Hill, but the outflanking move into Sequehart valley at 8.37 am failed, because no one had told the artillery to support the attack. Instead, Major General Marden sent more of his troops into the French sector and they made a successful advance under cover of smoke at 1.20 pm.

XIII Corps' artillery fired late on 9 October, hitting 66th and 25th Divisions as they advanced through the fog towards Elincourt and Honnechy.[89] Rawlinson again thought there was a chance of a breakthrough, so 3rd Cavalry Division was sent

84   Edmonds and Maxwell-Hyslop, *Military Operations: France and Belgium, 1918, Vol. V*, p. 169.
85   Ibid., p. 165.
86   Ibid. The XIII Corps' attack is detailed on pp. 192-5.
87   Ibid. The American assault is chronicled on p. 192.
88   Ibid. The Cavalry Corps' problems are explained on pp. 195-6.
89   Ibid., pp. 215-6.

forward, only to be stopped by machine-gun fire and wire fences. Only six tanks were available to help the Americans clear Busigny and Becquigny but IX Corps found that the Germans had abandoned Bohain and Méricourt.[90] They found 4,000 civilians and 'vast quantities of war materials but few prisoners' waiting for them.

Three 'real' tanks led 6th and 46th Divisions through the mist into Riqueval Wood while dummy tanks and figures drew fire away from them. They discovered that the Germans had abandoned the woods and they soon discovered why, when it was targeted by gas shells.[91]

The 3rd Cavalry Division made another attempt to disrupt the German withdrawal to the Selle. They took plenty of prisoners but did not turn the retirement into a rout nor get across the steam. All the cavalry had done was block the roads, delaying the advance rather than speeding it up; they had also given the German pilots a tempting target.[92] It was down to the infantry to move up close to the stream. All along Fourth Army's front the troops discovered that 'banks of the Selle heavily wired', with the Germans digging in on the far side.

Second Army, Crossing the Lys, 14-19 October

Poor weather delayed the preparations for breaking the Flanders I and II Lines, giving the Germans time to withdraw to the Lys. The general barrage would start at 5.32 am on 14 October, giving the infantry a three-minute warning to deploy, before they advanced through the smoke and mist at 100 yards every two minutes.[93]

Time and again, field gun teams cantered forward to support 9th, 36th and 29th Division as they fought past Hill 41, Moorslede and Ledeghem. Both 35th and 41st Divisions cleared the Gheluwe Switch across XIX Corps' front, having captured nearly eighty guns. On X Corps' front, 34th Division followed a smoke and thermite barrage through the Gheluwe Line and Flanders I Line at 5.25 am on 14 October. Some even went beyond the Flanders II Line, until the rearguards drove them back. Meanwhile, 30th Division cleared the Switch Line and a position along the Menin-Comines railway. XV Corps had the shortest distance to go to reach the Lys and it crossed first on 14 October, where a curve in the old river had formed an island opposite on 14th Division's front.[94]

Cyclists and motorbikes mounting machine guns then led II Corps towards the Lys on 15 October, with orders to establish bridgeheads across the river 'without

90   Ibid., p. 215.
91   Mustard gas lingered around for a long time in undergrowth, making woods dangerous to occupy.
92   Edmonds and Maxwell-Hyslop, *Military Operations: France and Belgium, 1918, Vol. V*. The last major cavalry action of the war is covered on pp. 216-9.
93   Ibid. The 14 October attack is detailed on pp. 273-6.
94   Ibid., p. 276

undue loss'.[95] A crossing was made north of Courtrai during the night, but artillery kept destroying the flimsy footbridges. Planes tried dropping supplies into 29th Division's bridgehead but there were never enough, and Lewis gunners had to cover the withdrawal across the river.

The Germans had abandoned Menin and Wervicq during the night and withdrawn across the Lys, in front of XIX Corps.[96] The engineers built a bridge out of barges for 34th Division, while others crossed 'one man at a time, on an improvised ferry raft'. Engineers tied duckboards to a line of rafts, so 30th Division could cross to an island in the river. On XV Corps' front, 14th Division discovered that the Germans had abandoned Comines, so 31st Division was able to send men across on boats around Deulemont. The artillery spent the day silencing the machine guns across the Lys, so the engineers could build a bridge out of barrels and planks. Men then formed a human chain across the rubble of Harlebeke bridge and passed ammunition to 9th Division's slender bridgehead.

An officer who had lived in Courtrai before the war was sent into the town early on 16 October.[97] He reported the Germans had withdrawn, so the barrage was stopped and 36th Division marched in to be greeted by 'scenes of great enthusiasm among the citizens, who came forth into the streets from their cellars.' A smoke screen then covered two pontoons filled with infantry as they across the Lys and they held on while the engineers rigged up a footway across the damaged road bridge. Shell fire soon destroyed the crossing beyond repair and infantry had to withdraw from the bridgehead.

XV Corps across the Lys by 16 October and both divisions advanced past Tourcoing while aerial observers watched the Germans heading for the Schelde. Those who entered the town were greeted by 'enthusiastic demonstrations of gratitude'.[98] Meanwhile, 40th Division crossed the La Basse Deule stream and canal around Wambrechies, 'encouraged by crowds of cheering children who lined the towpath.' Engineers then put a footbridge across the Roubaix Canal, because the water was too shallow for their pontoons, and Roubaix was cleared.

Artillery fire stopped the engineers launching two bridges across the Lys for 35th Division late on 17 October but they eventually built a narrow plank bridge between two sunken barges. The Germans then abandoned the rest of the Lys late on 18 October and II, XIX and X Corps started ferrying men across in earnest, while the engineers started work on bridges for the artillery to cross.[99] The men who entered Courtrai early the following morning 'received an ovation from the inhabitants. Coffee was freely offered to the men; it was all they had to offer.' They were then

---

95   Ibid.
96   Ibid. The operations of 15 October are covered on pp. 277-81.
97   Ibid. The operations of 16 October are covered on pp. 284-7.
98   TNA WO 95/2358/1: 11th East Lancashire Regiment War Dairy.
99   Edmonds and Maxwell-Hyslop, *Military Operations: France and Belgium, 1918, Vol. V*. The operations of 18 October are covered on pp. 287-9.

greeted by 'crowds of liberated civilians' as they moved through the villages between Courtrai and Tourcoing.

North of Harlebeke, 36th Division crossed the Lys on footbridges and pontoons during the night on 19 October, but it took time to find enough material to build a bridge for the artillery.[100] Then 9th Division crossed the following evening, on boats, rafts and a bridge made of duckboards and barrels.

Second Army, Crossing the Schelde, 20-27 October

Second Army's left had the longest distance to go reach the Schelde and the pursuit began in earnest after a messenger carrying orders to retire to the river was captured.[101] Both 35th and 30th Divisions used ditches and hedges for cover, as they broke through the Courtrai Switch. They reached the Schelde by dawn on 21 October, finding that the German engineers had blown the bridges and escaped on rafts.

A counter-attack disrupted both 29th and 41st Divisions' advance along the banks of the Bossuyt Canal, and the troops missed the creeping barrage. Despite the problems they were told to attack at all costs, and they advanced across the waterway.[102]

Second Army's right flank had the furthest to go but 36th Division was troubled by the delays to the French advance.[103] It struggled to clear the low ridge between Anseghem and Ingoyghem on 25 October while 9th and 41st Divisions reported 'every farm was a centre of resistance and furious conflicts were being waged behind the objective'.[104] The Germans eventually fell back across the Schelde when the high ground was taken around Ingoyghem. Civilians reported that Avelghem had been evacuated the following day, allowing 41st Division to close up Second Army's line along the canal.

More civilians reported that the Germans were retiring towards the Schelde on 27 October, so 36th, 31st and 35th Divisions moved up to the canal. The Germans machine-gun teams were using tracer ammunition to aim, making it easy to spot their positions. One officer also bravely dressed as a civilian and crossed the canal to pinpoint them exactly for the artillery. The 14th Division then crossed the Schelde around Warcoing.

Bad weather on 31 October meant the RAF could not fly, ground patrols could not cross the river and prisoners were saying nothing, leaving Second Army blind to what lay ahead.[105] The advance to the Schelde began at 5.25 am, moving at 100 yards every three minutes. Twenty French tanks had been given to 34th and 31st Divisions but

---

100 Ibid. The operations of 19 October are covered on pp. 290-2.
101 Ibid. XIX Corps operations are detailed on pp. 428-30.
102 Ibid. II Corps' advance is detailed on pp. 430-2.
103 Ibid. The continuation of the advance is covered on pp. 440-5.
104 TNA WO 95/1767/1: 5th Cameron Highlanders War Diary.
105 Edmonds and Maxwell-Hyslop, *Military Operations: France and Belgium, 1918, Vol. V.* The advance on 31 October is explained on pp. 447-50.

the German machine-gun teams remained silent until the guides had led the tanks past. Fortunately, 'an almost unique amount of artillery' stopped the Germans cutting the infantry down, because they were 'blasted off the bank of the river'.

First Army, 8-20 October

Third Army's left flank advanced south of Cambrai early on 8 October and the Canadian Corps started clearing the area between the Sensée and the Schelde at 1.30 am, north of the town, the following morning. First Army then moved in three sectors, starting on the left, as the Germans fell back to the canals running between Lens, Douai and Cambrai.

Both 12th and 8th Divisions passed through the Drocourt-Quéant Line and Rouvroy-Fresnes Line, starting on 8 October and then 58th Division followed the Lens Canal spur.[106] Floods made it difficult to get close to the Haute Deule Canal and the Germans breached the bank on 13 October, forcing 8th Division to withdraw from the flooded area. Even so, 58th Division managed to cross near Pont à Vendin two days later.[107]

A Chinese attack by 1st Canadian Division had triggered a strong enemy response along the La Trinquise stream, in First Army's centre on 8 October. Three days later the Germans abandoned the D-Q Line south of the Scarpe Canal and the Senseé stream, in line with the withdrawal to the north. The artillery shelled targets across the Sensée Canal on 12 October, while 1st Canadian Division ran to the embankment, only to find all the bridges were down.[108] Men of the 56th Division crossed in silence on 12 October and were able bring back 200 prisoners, even after their footbridge collapsed. Patrols were sent across on floating footbridges two days later, but the Germans fought hard to hold the Sensée. An assault over the canal was called off because prisoners believed a withdrawal to the Schelde Canal was imminent.

There were also signs that the Germans planned to withdraw opposite First Army's right, so 2nd Canadian Division was told to stop the Germans escaping across the Sensée and Scheldt Canals.[109] Its attack at 1 am on 9 October 'was a complete surprise and it caught the enemy in the midst of preparing for a withdrawal'. Later, 3rd Canadian Division followed up the withdrawal across the Schelde Canal and entered Cambrai. The Germans had planned to burn the city down, but they were taken by surprise and the engineers tackled the fires while the infantry disposed of piles of combustible material.

Half a dozen enemy tanks counter-attacked 2nd Canadian Division around Avesnes-le-Sec but a battery of field artillery cantered up and forced them to retire. It

---

106 Ibid., p. 227.
107 Ibid., pp. 256-8, 261-2.
108 Ibid., pp. 258-9, 261-2.
109 Ibid., pp. 226-7.

was then the turn of 51st and 49th Divisions to get to the Selle as quickly as possible, but artillery fire and strafing planes interfered with the advance.[110] The Scots had to 'gain this objective by exploitation' but a later attack by 49th Division, north of the Cambrai road, surprised the Germans. A counter-attack by eight A7V tanks delayed the advance but a second advance reached the high ground overlooking the Selle in the afternoon.[111] A rushed attempt by 49th Division to cross the stream at 9.30 am on 12 October ended in disaster.[112] The artillery had not been given time to register their targets, while the infantry had not located all the enemy machine-gun posts.

First Army was now along the Haute Deule and Sensée Canals and it was time to start crossing the waterways. Men from 12th Division crossed the Haute Deule Canal on duckboards tied to cork rafts and the damaged Pont a Sault bridge on 16 October. Both VIII Corps and the Canadian Corps fired an artillery barrage each morning but they received no response on 17 October, because the Germans had unexpectedly withdrawn from canals.[113]

As 8th and 56th Divisions advanced fast north of Douai, 1st, 4th and 2nd Canadian Divisions moved south of Douai. They were met by hungry French civilians waving Tricolours, shouting 'Vive la France'. They had been left with no food, however, they still handed over gifts of cigars and coffee. Cavalry, cyclists armoured cars and motorcycles carrying machine-guns moved fast towards the Schelde, only to find the Germans had blown up every bridge.[114]

XXII Corps took over the line, south of Denain on 19 October, only to hear that the Germans were withdrawing from the Selle stream because they did not want to get trapped against the l'Escaut Canal. Both 51st and 4th Divisions found them waiting behind the Ecaillon stream the following day.

On 20 October, men from 12th Division crossed on barrel rafts at Thun while 8th Division's men crossed a plank bridge at Hergnies. Everyone had to withdraw because the Germans had opened all the sluices, flooding the area between the river and the Canal du Jard, making it impossible to dig in. Late on 22 October 4th Canadian Division negotiated the floods and entered Valenciennes.

XXII Corps' patrols had found it impossible to find how wide the Ecaillon stream was before 4 am on 24 October, so some foot bridges were too short. Some of men used a wire strung over the stream to cross, while others waded across. The barrage was lost and 51st Division was engaged in a fierce battle for Mont Houy. Lieutenant General Currie refused to take over until it was cleared. Meanwhile, 4th Division persuaded a German officer who spoke English to surrender the Monchau garrison and then scrambled over the Rhonelle stream on the ruins of a demolished bridge.

---

110 Ibid., pp. 259-60.
111 Ibid., pp. 255.
112 Ibid., pp. 262.
113 Ibid. The crossing of the canals is covered on pp. 330-1.
114 Ibid. The advance to the Schelde is covered on pp. 332-4.

First Army had been unable to catch the Germans up and it now had to pause on the Schelde while the rest of the BEF moved up. Currie blamed poor logistics for the slow advance: 'Our higher authorities do not seem well enough organised to push their railheads forward fast enough.' But the men were having to make long marches, the engineers were having to repair roads and bridges while the support services were having to feed and treat thousands of civilians.

Third Army 8-24 October

The bombardment started on 6 October. Four tanks helped 21st Division clear the last part of the Beaurevoir Line in front of Villers Outreaux, at 1 am on 8 October, bringing Third Army's flank in line with Fourth Army. However, 38th Division could make no progress through the belts of wire.[115]

The main attack began at 4.30 am. Batteries put down a smoke screen around a burning Cambrai, while 57th Division moved past.[116] South of the town, the 63rd, 2nd, 3rd and New Zealand Divisions were advancing through Niergnies, Forenville and Seranvillers when eleven tanks counter-attacked in the mist.[117] Most were captured British tanks and it was some time before it was realised that they had crosses on them.[118] An attempt to restart the advance in the afternoon failed because 2nd and 3rd Divisions failed to coordinate their movements.

On IV Corps' front, four tanks with the New Zealand Division knocked out two enemy tanks.[119] At the same time two of 37th Division's battalions moved north of the Bel Aise salient and took the position in the rear with the help of three tanks. The artillery could not shell Caudry, because it was full of civilians, so it was left to the tanks and infantry to make a pincer attack on it.

Six tanks led 21st Division across the Sargrenon stream, but the Germans had already abandoned the Beaurevoir Line. Two tanks were lost around Villers Outreaux, so 38th Division needed three more to take it.[120] Elements of both 17th and 33rd Divisions spotted civilians waving Tricolours were repairing the roads up head, so they knew it was safe to advance. They could then see transport queuing to cross the Solesmes bridge and a few shots from field guns sent men fleeing to the Selle.

Patrols from 57th Division entered Cambrai early on 9 October, meeting Canadian patrols in the centre. At 5.20 am, the rest of Third Army advanced, only to discover that the Germans had withdrawn behind the Ereclin stream. Both VI and IV Corps relied on barrages to cover the infantry, while sections of field artillery stayed close

115 Ibid., pp. 200-1.
116 Ibid., pp. 208-10.
117 Ibid., pp. 206-8.
118 Stewart, *The New Zealand Division 1916-1919, Vol. II*, p. 526-7.
119 Edmonds and Maxwell-Hyslop, *Military Operations: France and Belgium, 1918, Vol. V*, pp. 203-5.
120 Ibid., pp. 201-2.

ready to deal with any enemy tanks.[121] Meanwhile, V Corps used advanced guards, each supported by a brigade of artillery ready to fire when required. This method of the infantry leading the artillery was found to be faster than the traditional method of the infantry following a barrage.[122]

The Germans had fallen back across the Selle by the time the artillery was ready to target the new line on the 12th.[123] Cavalry and motorbikes mounting machine guns moved onto the ridge overlooking the Selle, where they could see rearguards covering the bridges while engineers wired up the bridges for demolition and dammed the stream.

The next few days were spent evacuating the sick and elderly from the villages along the Selle, while the engineers prepared temporary bridges. A few troops probed the far bank, only to find that the Germans had based their defensive line along a railway embankment and cutting.

Officers were issued electric torches and the men provided with white brassards. Every man studied aerial photographs of their objective and passwords were given out.[124] Patrols forced the German outposts to withdraw from the east bank, so engineers could carry their footbridges quietly forward on handcarts, marking them with numbered lanterns.

The German artillery usually opened fire around 4 am, so the plan was to launch an early surprise attack on 20 October, when the moon was full. There would be no preliminary bombardment and the twenty-four tanks were held in reserve, so they would not alert the Germans. [125] The men deployed silently on the far bank in rain, mist and smoke ready to advance after a hurricane bombardment by 6-inch mortars at 2 am. They cut through two aprons of wire by hand while the field artillery fired the creeping barrage which moved forward at 100 yards every four minutes. Some guns fired thermite shells to mark the flanks of the infantry battalions, guiding the company officers through the mist. Most of the heavy guns hit the enemy batteries while the machine guns sprayed the far bank with bullets. Lorry mounted mortars were on hand to knock out machine-gun posts.

Both 19th Division and the Guards Division crossed the Selle on floating footbridges and advanced to the Harpies stream with relative ease.[126] Only shrapnel could be fired at Solesmes because it was full of civilians. Rubble from a demolished railway bridge had caused the Selle causing a flood, so 62nd Division's first wave waded across and

121 Ibid., pp. 219-23.
122 Ibid., p. 219.
123 Ibid. The advance to the Selle is covered on pp. 238-42, 249-54.
124 Wyrall, *The History of the 62nd Division (West Riding) Division, 1914-1919*, p. 111.
125 Edmonds and Maxwell-Hyslop, *Military Operations: France and Belgium, 1918, Vol. V*, the infantry and barrage plan are detailed on p. 335-6.
126 Ibid., pp. 341-3.

surrounded it from the north and south.[127] The support waves bypassed the town and joined the advance to the ridge overlooking the Harpies.

Fourth Army's earlier attack alerted the Germans opposite Third Army's right flank and an SOS barrage hit IV and V Corps' assembly areas. It delayed the four tanks allocated to 42nd and 5th Divisions and they were pinned down along the Beart stream.[128] Four runners were killed before a fifth got the message back to the gunners, to fire a new creeping barrage. Two tanks were knocked out leading 17th Division, so a second barrage including smoke had to be organised. Meanwhile, the bridges collapsed, and the single tank sent to help 38th Division struggled to cross the Selle around Montay. A second tank helped establish a bridgehead, forcing the Germans to retire.[129]

The engineers completed pontoon bridges over the Selle on 21 October, so dozens of field batteries could cross. The same method was used to cross the Harpies; patrols cleared the far bank before 19th, 2nd and 3rd Divisions filed over footbridges. Zero hour had been set early, at 3.20 am on 23 October, so the garrisons of Vertain and Romeries could be taken by surprise.[130] Two more divisions crossed and the New Zealanders pursed the Germans across the St Georges stream, using 'covering fire and rushing alternate sections down the slopes, [they] plunged through and pressed up the eastern bank'.[131] Lorry-mounted mortars failed to silence the machine-guns teams across the stream, so 37th Division had to wait until the artillery caught up.

Fourth Army's earlier attack had warned the Germans opposite Third Army's right, so they were waiting for the 2 am advance.[132] Two tanks were knocked out and the third drove south into 33rd Division's area as 21st Division crossed the Harpies stream. The infantry were hit by machine-gun fire from Poix du Nord, across the St Georges stream, but the artillery was banned from retaliating because the village was full of civilians. Three tanks were disabled during 33rd Division's advance but the infantry 'advanced by sections in easy rushes as if on the parade ground. Their advance was covered by well-directed fire from the batteries' until they were pinned down in front of the Herman II Line.

Third Army's centre had broken through, but its flanks had to catch up and a third advance was timed for 4 am on 24 October. The artillery missed the wire on XVII Corps' front, so the 61st Division could not get far. Both the 2nd and 3rd Divisions found the Ecaillon stream to be deeper than expected and then some companies

127 Ibid., pp. 339-41. The civil population hid in their cellars during the attack.
128 Ibid., pp. 338-9.
129 Ibid., pp, 337-8.
130 Ibid., pp. 367-9.
131 Stewart, *The New Zealand Division 1916-1919, Vol. II*, pp. 547-50.
132 Edmonds and Maxwell-Hyslop, *Military Operations: France and Belgium, 1918, Vol. V*, pp. 362-4.

mistook the objective in the dark.[133] However, VI Corps had reached its objective by the afternoon.

On IV Corps' right, 37th Division reached Ghissignies, despite a difficult deployment in the dark and then the New Zealand Division joined in.[134] The barrage had been cancelled because the New Zealanders had captured extra ground during the night. However, no one told V Corps' artillery and its barrage hit the New Zealanders instead.[135]

In V Corps' sector, the artillery and machine guns fired rapidly for five minutes as 21st and 33rd Divisions' first wave ran forward at 4 am.[136] They then slowed their rate of fire while the next line of platoons prepared to advance. This process was repeated right through the Hermann II Line, across the St Georges stream and beyond Poix du Nord.

The Germans withdrew across the Rhonelle stream during the night and V Corps headquarters believed Englefontaine had been abandoned. Patrols proved otherwise, so 33rd Division sent two battalions around the flanks at 1 am on 25 October, to seal it off.[137] Two more battalions then cleared the village, taking many prisoners who believed 'what is the good of going on, as we are beaten.'[138]

Fourth Army, 17-25 October

Prisoners said the Germans soon planned to withdraw rapidly behind the Sambre. That involved a long advance through the Mormal Forest for Fourth Army's left, while the right only had a short distance to go. They also reported that the engineers were preparing bridges for demolition along the canal and closing locks or opening sluices to flood the surrounding fields.

Rawlinson set staggered zero hours, beginning at 5.20 am, for the morning of 17 October. The Selle stream between Le Cateau and the Andigny Forest had been dammed and the rain had made it deeper in places.[139] The Hermann Line did not have any deep trenches but it was protected by plenty of wire entanglements.[140] It also had lots of hidden machine-gun posts and many strongpoints based around buildings.

---

133 Ibid., pp. 378-9.
134 Ibid., pp. 377-8.
135 Stewart, *The New Zealand Division 1916-1919, Vol. II*, pp. 553-5.
136 Edmonds and Maxwell-Hyslop, *Military Operations: France and Belgium, 1918, Vol. V*, p. 376.
137 TNA WO 95/2427/1: 1/4th King's Regiment War Diary.
138 TNA WO 95/1371/1: 1st Berkshire Regiment's War Diary.
139 It was normally no more than waist deep.
140 Edmonds and Maxwell-Hyslop, *Military Operations: France and Belgium, 1918, Vol. V*, p. 228. 'The Hermann Position existed for the most part only on paper' whilst 'air photographs taken on the 14th did not show the Le Cateau-St Souplet position' except for a few trenches and rifle pits.

The bombardment started early on 15 October and it was split into four types; counter-battery fire, harassing fire against communications, targeting of the Sambre crossings and a gas bombardment of the Andigny Forest.[141] Poor flying conditions prevented the RAF from taking photographs and made it difficult to register guns. Troops established bridgeheads and cut holes in the wire beyond the Selle on 15 October, while the engineers spanned ruined bridges and built footbridges.

A dam had flooded the Selle around St Benin, so a barrage was fired at Le Cateau at 5.20 am, while six tanks crossed the stream on fascines north of St Souplet.[142] The men of 50th Division could not find them in the mist but the German machine-gun teams could not see any targets either.[143] A second thirty-minute barrage preceded 66th Division's crossing at 8.5 am and both divisions then cleared the railway cutting beyond. A counter-attack struck 50th Division when the mist lifted, because of a lack of cooperation with American troops on their flank. It would take all night to clear Le Cateau, but it proved impossible to take the railway triangle, south-east of the town.

Only one tank got stuck in the Selle as II American Corps crossed between St Souplet and Molain but nine were knocked out crossing the railway line beyond. A counter-attack hit 27th American Division, because of the lack of cooperation with 50th Division on its flank.[144] Molain delayed 30th American Division's left and the mist cleared while the right waited for it to catch up. The Germans were waiting for the Americans when they renewed the advance at 11.30 am and they had to wait IX Corps to clear Ribeauville before they could take Mazinghien.[145]

IX Corps advanced towards Andigny Forest at 5.30 am but some of the tanks headed north out of 6th Division's area.[146] The barrage was lost while the remaining five tanks cleared the area east of Vaux Andigny and the infantry had to follow trenches into the forest. A Chinese attack had occupied the Germans in Riqueval Wood while three tanks led 46th Division toward the south part of Andigny Forest in the mist.

Six tanks led 1st Division through the north side of Andigny Forest but they were knocked out as soon as the mist cleared.[147] There was insufficient time to tell the artillery where the new front line was, so they could not help the second advance north of the forest. A German gas bombardment later forced everyone to abandon Andigny Forest.[148]

---

141 Ibid., pp. 295-6.
142 They crossed in II American Corps sector before turning north into XIII Corps area.
143 Edmonds and Maxwell-Hyslop, *Military Operations: France and Belgium, 1918, Vol. V*, pp. 309-14.
144 Both the 50th Division and the 27th American Division blamed each other for the lack of support.
145 Edmonds and Maxwell-Hyslop, *Military Operations: France and Belgium, 1918, Vol. V*, pp. 305-8.
146 Ibid. The first part of IX Corps' advance is detailed on pp. 299-303.
147 Ibid., pp. 303-5.
148 Mustard gas lingered in undergrowth, making wooded areas dangerous places, effectively denying it to both sides.

XIII Corps' objective on 18 October was at an angle to jumping off line, so the artillery started firing a ripple effect barrage at 5.30 am, with each brigade joining in at three-minute intervals. However, the first sound of gun fire alerted the Germans and the counter-barrage caused many problems.[149] The railway triangle south of Le Cateau was captured as a train arrived full of reinforcements, while Lewis gun teams stopped the German artillery limbers withdrawing towards the Sambre Canal.

The II American Corps advanced in the morning mist but had to withdraw due to artillery fire as soon as it cleared. The Germans withdrew towards the Sambre during the afternoon and both the 27th and 30th American Divisions followed up.[150]

Planes dropped smoke bombs to cover 1st Division's advance north of Wassigny at 11.30 am, taking the Germans by surprise. 'All night long, loud explosions were heard' as the Germans withdrew across the Sambre and IX Corps was close to the canal by nightfall.[151]

The German Situation

Crown Prince Rupprecht thought the war had been lost some time ago, because withdrawing was bad for morale. His armies were short of everything, but supplies were having to be abandoned or destroyed during the retirement to the incomplete Hermann Line, was approximately 10 to 20 miles behind his line.[152]

Ludendorff told the War Cabinet that he thought the Allies were tiring and he believed the German Army could hold on over the winter, if it received the men it had been promised. But the meeting ended in stalemate because Ludendorff said the German Navy had to continue unrestricted U-boat warfare, while the Chancellor, Prince Max von Baden, threatened to resign if it did not stop.[153]

Fourth Army, 23-25 October

The artillery fire before zero was restricted to counter-battery fire and harassment, to conserve ammunition. Machine-gun teams opened fire at 1.28 am on 23 October, to warn XIII Corps to advance under a full moon two minutes later. That would allow it to get into line with both Third Army and IX Corps, ready for when they advanced forty minutes later.[154]

Many batteries had been unable to find their positions in time, so 18th Division's creeping barrage was patchy while the infantry stopped short of their objective by

---

149 Edmonds and Maxwell-Hyslop, *Military Operations: France and Belgium, 1918, Vol. V*, pp. 320-1.
150 Ibid., pp. 319-20.
151 Ibid., pp. 321.
152 Ibid. Rupprecht's full statement is given on pp. 327-8.
153 Ibid. Details of the meeting are given on pp. 316-7.
154 Ibid. Fourth Army's plan is provided on pp. 352-3.

mistake.[155] All four tanks were put out of action while crossing the Richemont stream, but many prisoners were taken when the Germans then withdrew. Troops from the adjacent division interfered with the final advance and the barrage was lost, so six more tanks were sent forward and German morale collapsed. Only two tanks accompanied 25th Division across the Richemont stream and one then shot up the infantry it was supposed to be supporting. Even so, the advance continued apace through L'Evêque Wood.

Nine tanks ripped holes in the hedges laced with wire for 6th Division but the barrage was still lost crossing the St Maurice stream. The infantry then moved parallel with the rides in L'Evêque Wood, rather than at an angle to them, until the Germans made a run for the Sambre Canal around Ors.[156] A barrage followed them through the wood while machine-gun teams caught those trying to escape across the canal. On IX Corps' right, 1st Division just had to move up to the Sambre because the Germans had already withdrawn across it around Catillon.

The advance restarted at 4 am on 24 October but 18th Division was delayed cutting through hedges strung with wire and there were no tanks left to help them.[157] The only other option was to pass through gateways and gaps cut by the Germans, and they were usually covered by machine-gun teams. Six tanks smashed gaps through the hedges for 25th Division but it too encountered strong resistance in L'Evêque Wood.[158]

A final attempt to clear the high ground north of Bousies by 18th Division failed at 1 am on 26 October. The problem was, both divisions had run into the Hermann II Line and 'nothing had been previously known of this line of trenches.'[159] It was time to pause while the supply routes caught up, ready to break this new line and cross the Sambre Canal.

Summary

The Kaiser blamed OHL for failing to stop the Allied attacks when Hindenburg and Ludendorff asked him to reject President Woodrow Wilson's terms. They both offered to resign but only Ludendorff's offer was accepted. Meanwhile, the Germans would soon lose their Allies, when an armistice with the Ottoman Empire came into effect on 31 October. Another was agreed with the Austro-Hungarian Empire on 4 November, after Hungary withdrew from the Empire.[160]

---

155 Ibid., pp. 357-61.
156 Ibid., pp. 356-7.
157 Fourteen out of 23 tanks had been lost the previous day.
158 Edmonds and Maxwell-Hyslop, *Military Operations: France and Belgium, 1918, Vol. V*, pp. 373-5.
159 TNA WO 95/2247/3: 9th Green Howards Regiment War Diary.
160 Edmonds and Maxwell-Hyslop, *Military Operations: France and Belgium, 1918, Vol. V*. Ludendorff's dismissal is covered on pp. 400-3.

Second Army, 31 October-11 November

Men had crossed a lock when the Germans pulled back behind a flooded stream, allowing 14th Division to cross the Schelde around Warcoing by 29 October.[161] Engineers had completed three bridges by the time the Germans withdrew on 8 November. More bridges were launched in heavy rain and aerial spotters saw columns of troops heading east when the skies cleared. The men of XIX Corps then crossed as fast as they could before dawn on 9 November.[162] Some scrambled over lock gates and sluices, others filed across footbridges and pontoon bridges while the rest paddled across on rafts and canvas boats. It was the same on X Corps' front and cyclist and cavalry patrols immediately headed for the River Dendre.

Fifth Army, 30 October-11 November

Fifth Army had reached the Schelde on its left and right flanks but the area north of Tournai was flooded. Men of 58th Division crossed in pontoons on 30 October, but poor visibility meant the aerial observers had not seen the Germans leaving the Tournai and Antoing bridgehead. So, it was down to III Corps' patrols to find out they had gone on 8 November. Men of 74th Division used Tournai's medieval city wall to cross the river during the day, while 55th Division crossed at Calonne on rafts and boats when it was dark.[163] The engineers then spent the night building bridges, so cavalry and cyclist patrols could lead mixed groups of infantry, machine guns and field guns towards the Dendre.

The three divisions of I Corps used rafts, floats and ruined bridges to get their infantry across around Antoing on 9 November.[164] Engineers could then launch floating bridges, allowing combined arms group to moved rapidly east. They had reached the Dendre some 15 miles away by the time of the Armistice.

First Army, 1-11 November

The floods along the Schelde had subsided by the end of October, allowing both 12th and 8th Divisions to launch bridges. However, one bridge collapsed while the bridgehead had to be abandoned because the ground between the Schelde and Jard Canals was water-logged.

Valenciennes was full of civilians and so Currie and Godley decided the Canadian Corps and XXII Corps would force their way past the south side of the town, using the combined power of their artillery. Seventeen field brigades fired a 'rather unique

---

161 Ibid., p. 446.
162 Ibid., pp. 547-51.
163 Ibid., pp. 539-42.
164 Ibid., pp. 540, 544.

artillery barrage' of 2,000 tons of shells while the heavy guns provided 'enfilade and even reverse fire.'[165] Twelve batteries of machine guns contributed to what would be the heaviest barrage fired in support of a single brigade during the entire war.

The 4th Canadian Division crossed the Schelde on 'collapsible boats and cork float bridges' to be met by Germans who 'surrendered in large numbers, stupefied by the overpowering barrage'.[166] Meanwhile, both 49th and 4th Divisions had crossed the Rhonelle stream on duckboards and cleared the area on the Canadians' flank.[167] There was then fierce fighting around Marly steelworks until the Germans withdrew from what Currie later reported as 'one of most successful operations the [Canadian] Corps has yet performed'.[168]

The advance beyond Valenciennes was difficult because 'most of the roads had been blown up by the enemy and transport was impossible.' The troops had no rations so 'aeroplanes dropped a certain amount of bully beef and biscuits which temporarily satisfied the hunger of the troops.'[169]

A mobile force of cavalry, cyclists and motor-cycles carrying machine guns led the Canadian Corps through the coal mining area south of the Condé Canal. They experienced 'a mixture of street fighting against enemy die-hards and a warm welcome from the civilian inhabitants.'[170] Artillery units used churches as report centres and logistics units were given 'meeting points' along the route of advance but the roads were cratered, bridges were down and the distances to the railheads getting were longer. It sparked a withdrawal north of the canal on 8 November, so that VIII Corps could finally cross the Schelde Canal. Men avoided the bridges, in case they were booby-trapped, and some filed across lock gates and footbridges while others paddled across on rafts.

XXII Corps had driven the Germans from the Rhonelle stream by 7 November. From then onward, the advance became 'practically a route march'. Isolated machine-gun detachments and sporadic artillery 'exacted their toll in what was no longer a battle but a pursuit.'[171] But the 'conditions were awful. The weather was very bad, rain was falling all day and night while the ground was a morass'.[172] The men were suffering from living outdoors most of the time and many succumbed to world-wide epidemic which would become known as Spanish Flu.

The Canadian captured Mount Erebus, south of Mons, on 10 November and while it threatened the German line of retreat, 'heavy mist, poor communications and

165 Nicholson, *Canadian Expeditionary Force*, p. 473.
166 Ibid., p. 473.
167 Edmonds and Maxwell-Hyslop, *Military Operations: France and Belgium, 1918, Vol. V*, pp. 457–8.
168 Nicholson, *Canadian Expeditionary Force*, p. 464.
169 TNA WO 95/1809/3: 2nd Green Howards War Diary.
170 Nicholson, *Canadian Expeditionary Force*, p. 479.
171 Douglas Jerrold, *The Royal Naval Division* (London: Hutchinson, 1923) p. 327.
172 TNA WO 95/1809/3: 2nd Green Howards War Diary.

strong enemy fire' made it impossible to catch them.[173] Patrols from 3rd Canadian Division crossed the Canal du Centre and entered Mons during the early hours of 11 November, encountering only a few rearguards in the town. The men of 2nd Canadian Division reached St Symphorien, to the south-east, where the BEF had fought its first battle on 23 August 1914.

Third Army, 1-11 November

On 1 November 61st Division crossed the Rhonelle stream and advanced beyond St Hubert, keeping Third Army's left in line with First Army. Byng had set zero for 5.30 am on 4 November but V Corps' right had to attack forty-five minutes later, in cooperation with Fourth Army.

Le Quesnoy was surrounded by earthworks, walls and dry moats; it was also full of civilians. Two flares at 5.20 am on 4 November signalled that the New Zealanders had withdrawn to a safe distance and barrels of burning oil hit the town ramparts ten minutes later. Smoke then smothered the walls as the infantry surrounded the town.[174]

The garrison wanted to surrender but the officers wanted to fight on, so the New Zealanders had to scale the outer walls. Prisoners were sent to their officers with surrender messages, while a plane dropped a similar note.[175] A trench mortar barrage sent the Germans underground as the New Zealanders crossed the moat and scaled the inner walls. They then rounded up the garrison before forcing them to put out fires and disarm booby-traps.[176]

At the same time, oil drums exploded around Louvignies and Englefontaine, on the edge of the Mormal Forest.[177] A handful of tanks tore holes in the hedges laced with barbed wire, so 37th, 17th and 38th Division could follow the shrapnel barrage at a safe distance, to avoid falling tree branches.[178] Once inside the forest 'there was little undergrowth, several large clearings and the trees had been thinned'. Some batteries moved up and fired 'sudden concentrations of fire on the edges of woods or clearings...'[179] A few machine-gun teams covering the roads and rides, but the main problem was how to fill in the craters and drag the trees astride to clear them.

---

173 Nicholson, *Canadian Expeditionary Force*, p. 479.
174 Stewart, *The New Zealand Division 1916-1919, Vol. II*. The advance past Le Quesnoy is detailed on p. 573-84.
175 Ibid., p. 586-93. The text of the message is given on 589.
176 Ibid. The surrender of Le Quesnoy is described as 'one of the most outstanding days for the New Zealand Division. The event is covered on p. 483.
177 Ibid., pp. 479-82.
178 High-explosive shells armed with instantaneous fuses were too dangerous because they exploded prematurely in the tree-tops. Standard fuses were of little use against troops deployed in the open.
179 Ibid., p. 478.

IV Corps emerged from the Mormal Forest and reached the Sambre Canal. The pontoons were not delivered to 42nd Division in time, so civilians helped the soldiers use the debris around the demolished Haumont bridge to bridge the canal. Meanwhile, 5th Division crossed on pontoons, so that cyclists and cavalry patrols could led the advance beyond the Solre stream.[180]

Men of 21st Division crossed a lock and bridge, before the Germans could blow them up, so the engineers could bridge the Sambre. The German artillery targeted the sites as the engineers used logs, cork rafts, limbers and ropes to cross. Some men even swam across, pushing rafts loaded with ammunition, to keep 33rd Division's bridgehead supplied.[181]

It took time to clear Maubeuge's outlying forts but a captured order stated that the town was to be abandoned, so patrols were sent in as cavalry and cyclist patrols moved up to the Sambre. Both 17th and 38th Divisions continued the advance on 8 November and the Germans made a brief stand along the Maubeuge-Avesnes road, before withdrawing to the Thure stream, near the Belgian border.[182] They had withdrawn as fast as possible and when it was prudent to do so. The 'advance was governed mainly by the state of the roads and the difficulty of getting rations to the troops in the forward area.'

Fourth Army, 4-11 November

Engineers needed ten days to bridge the Sambre around Catillon, ready for a staggered attack, starting on 4 November. IX Corps would cross at 5.45 am, while XIII Corps followed thirty minutes later. Three battalions of Mark V's, a battalion of Whippets and a battalion of armoured cars would join the advance, while the cavalry waited in reserve.[183]

Fifteen tanks led 18th and 50th Divisions' advance through the Mormal Forest, only to find that machine-gun teams posted along the west edge were letting troops pass by, hoping to cut them off.[184] But resistance collapsed when XIII Corps' support waves moved forward and they advanced parallel with the rides through the trees, following the 'edges of the uncut portions'. The Germans fell back across the Sambre Canal but 50th Division captured three footbridges around Hachette. It meant a bridgehead could be formed and the engineers built a pontoon bridge.

A German officer galloped forward to blow up the Landrecies bridge, but 25th Division still found two footbridges and a trestle bridge across the Sambre Canal. An engineer sergeant swam across la Vielle Sambre stream, to disarm the explosives

---

180 Ibid., pp. 503-4.
181 Ibid., pp. 508-9.
182 Ibid., pp. 528-31.
183 Ibid. Planning for the crossing of the Sambre is detailed on pp. 464-6.
184 Ibid., pp. 473-6.

on the bridge south-west of the town. The rest of the men were then ferried across on planks strapped to petrol tins.[185] Over the next twenty-four hours, both 50th and 25th Divisions waded, paddled or scrambled across the Petite Helpe stream and then waited while the engineers could build pontoon bridges.

Three tanks helped 32nd Division get closer to Landrecies, but heavy fire prevented the engineers from launching a pontoon to bridge a damaged structure. Men could not cross on boats to the north, but they crossed a bridge of kerosene tins to the south of Ors, so sturdier bridges could then be built.[186]

Catillon was still in German hands while reservoirs along the west bank of the Sambre meant XIII Corps needed two bridgeheads. The infantry deployed along hedges close to the Sambre, while engineers launched four bridges before 6.10 am. Only they were too short, so two were tied together to create one crossing, while the rest of 1st Division crossed by lock gates or on collapsible boats.[187] It allowed 46th Division to cross during the afternoon. The Sambre and Oise Canals had been crossed along a 15-mile front and 4,000 prisoners and eighty guns had been taken.

The Germans continued to withdraw at speed, blowing up all the bridges, before the aerial spotters could report their positions to the artillery. It left the infantry scrambling across rubble or paddling across the water in canvas boats. In places, civilians helped dump material into the streams, so they could clamber across. The armoured cars, field guns and cavalry needed pontoon bridges, while the heavy guns more substantial trestle bridges. The Germans stopped briefly on the high ground around Avesnes on 8 November before withdrawing across the Belgian border.[188]

Armistice

Attitudes during the last hours of the war varied between men. Some had no desire put their lives in danger, knowing that the fighting was to end' while others wanted to kill as many Germans as possible before the war ended. The news on the morning of 11 November 'was received with apathy and perhaps a tinge of disappointment that the pursuit of a routed and disorganised foe was not to be continued.'[189] 'There was no cheering or excitement amongst the men, they seemed too tired and no one seemed able to realise that it was all over.'[190] The 'officers and men took the news very calmly; it seemed too good to be true.'[191]

185 Ibid., pp. 471-3.
186 Ibid., pp. 470-1.
187 Ibid., pp. 467-70.
188 Ibid., pp. 519-21.
189 Hussey and Inman, *The Fifth Division in the Great War*, p. 256.
190 Dudley Ward, *The Fifty Sixth Division 1914–1918*, p. 313.
191 Geoffrey Powell, *The History of the Green Howards* (Barnsley: Pen and Sword, 2015.

The Final Advance Summary

The last major attack of the war involved all four armies attacking over three days, illustrating how well organised and supplied the BEF was. It began with First Army crossing the Canal du Nord, while Third Army cleared the northern part of the Hindenburg Line. Second Army then crossed the crater field east Ypres, covering more ground in one day than it had covered during the whole Third Ypres campaign. Finally, Fourth Army broke into the adjacent section of the Hindenburg Line. All four armies kept up the pressure over the days that followed and then the race was on to catch the Germans, as they fell back behind rivers and canals.

The limited reserve of tanks was deployed only when necessary, providing support to the infantry when they faced strongpoints. Artillery batteries also worked closely with the infantry, either firing barrages in support of set-piece attacks or at fleeting targets; but always at short notice.

The BEF's greatest difficulty in the final days of the war was how to keep up with the Germans. Troops had to cross demolished bridges and negotiate crated roads, always knowing that their enemy could choose where to make their next stand. The infantry relied on improvisation to cross the many watercourses while the engineers relied on the experience gained during the advance to the Hindenburg Line, back in the spring of 1917, to bridge them.

The British troops had to contend with welcoming refugees, large numbers of prisoners, booby-trapped buildings and demolished bridges, but they kept moving as fast as they could. All arms were worked together quickly to draw up attack plans on the move, when necessary. However, the Germans were always able to retire faster than the BEF could advance, allowing the politicians extra time to negotiate an Armistice.

11

Summarising the Learning Process

The warfare faced by a British soldier in the autumn of 1914 was very different from that experienced four years later in the final battle for the Hindenburg Line. Tactics had changed, new weapons had been introduced, organisations had been updated, communications had been upgraded and new technology had changed the face of warfare. Those who support the 'lions led by donkeys' dogma believe the generals were guilty of ignoring failure and did nothing to change their methods. We have seen how every campaign and most actions contributed something to the BEF's learning process and that it learnt in four different ways.

Firstly, methods were learnt when plans were spoiled by mistakes or unanticipated difficulties. Secondly, failure caused by enemy action led to new methods being tried. Thirdly, lessons were learnt by analysing unexpected results which resulted from luck. Finally, new methods evolved after studying how the enemy tackled problems. In all four cases, the results were reported and reviewed and then acted on.

The BEF's learning process was not always a positive one because faulty methods were sometimes tried but they were not used again in most cases. However, the process was complicated by the fact that the Germans were constantly changing their own fighting methods. The case of Aubers Ridge in May 1915 is a prime example because First Army failed to spot that the Germans had upgraded their defensive measures; it resulted in disaster.

Past Lessons and Ideas for the Future

The BEF which went to war in the summer of 1914 had been trained and organised according to lessons learnt during the war in South Africa, between 1899 and 1902. The irregular Boers had frequently beaten the professional British soldiers, with the help of modern weapons and tactics. The British Army took onboard the lessons and introduced new training regimes between 1906 and 1912, to suit its contemplated role as the Empire's police force.

The changes were completed just before the First World War and the tactics designed for colonial engagements served the BEF well at the battles of Mons and Le Cateau. The infantry and guns used controlled rapid fire and concealment to counter superior numbers and proved skilful at withdrawing from battle. They were able to march fast and knew how far to go with the information provided by the cavalry and the Royal Flying Corps.

The advent of trench fighting illustrated that the BEF was too weak in men and guns to break the German line when it was on the offensive, such as on the Aisne. But it was able to hold its own against overwhelming odds when it was on the defensive, in the spirit of past colonial conflicts. There was, however, no time to improve how it fought in the autumn, because it was too busy surviving around Ypres.

The BEF's last action of 1914 illustrated that its thoughts on offensive actions left a lot to be desired. There was little coordination between the artillery and infantry, while orders were merely statements of intent rather than detailed instructions. However, there was a complete rethink over the winter months.

Neuve Chapelle was a small battle by later standards but it was significant one in the BEF's learning process, because it became the blueprint for future offensives. Feasibility studies about what could be achieved and assessments over the arrival of German reinforcements were made. Tests showed how long the preliminary bombardment had to be to destroy the wire and the parapets, while an attack timetable let the artillery jump forward in steps as the infantry advanced to objectives. All these factors set the benchmark for future battles, so let us summarise the key factors of the 'Learning Process' between the spring of 1915 and the winter of 1917.

The Art of Deception

Several deception techniques tried during the battle of Neuve Chapelle were improved over the months that followed. The artillery deployed to camouflaged positions during the hours of darkness and then registered targets a few guns at a time. Chinese attacks were used to draw attention away from the attack but they had to be used carefully because premature shooting alerted the Germans, as it did before the Festubert battle. Widening the barrage to the flanks also disguised attack limits.

The gunners demonstrated that they were able to use deception to take a position as early as March 1916, when regular salvos were used to condition the enemy's response. Three months later, random barrages were then used to confuse Germans into recognising when zero hour. Batteries were soon taking various steps to register their guns without alerting the Germans, either firing at random or as part of a normal day's shooting, to disguise the build-up of guns. All kinds of barrages, some fired at an incorrect time, some aimed at a different place and some completely fake, were used to confuse the Germans during the Somme campaign.

One of the biggest deception plans of 1917 was Operation Hush; the false information put out concerning the quarantining of an entire infantry division. It allowed thousands of men to spend several weeks training for an amphibious assault on the Flanders coast under the guise that they had a contagious illness.

Digging and Capturing Trenches

One problem resolved in 1915 was how to create the best layout of trenches before an attack. The infantry used dummy trenches to draw attention away from the real camouflaged assembly trenches before the Neuve Chapelle battle but it required a lot of manpower. A lack of assembly trenches exposed the attack front to the Germans while it was unwise to make the assault troops dig extra ones, because it left them too fatigued. Russian saps (shallow tunnels) were dug into No Man's Land for the Loos battle, so that assembly trenches could be dug closer to the enemy wire just before zero hour.

A shortage of communication trenches was a common problem throughout 1915 because it left reinforcements unable to get forward, while casualties could not be evacuated. So, 'Up' and 'Down' trenches were introduced for the Loos battle to ease movement, while keeping trenches narrow enough to give protection. Effective consolidation plans had also been introduced by the summer of 1915, as men carried enough tools, sandbags and ammunition forward to stop counter-attacks.

Artillery fire could be so heavy and concentrated by early 1916 that it was impossible to capture a small sector. The problem intensified in the summer because the preliminary bombardments were destroying the German trenches the assault troops were detailed to occupy. Counter-barrages also made it impossible to hold exposed positions, like Pozières and Skyline Ridge.

By the autumn of 1917, the decision was taken to ignore captured trenches and pillboxes because they had also been designed to suit the defence. The Germans also knew where to bombard and how to attack their lost position, so it was far safer to dig new trenches the Germans did not know about.

The Artillery

A lack of guns and good quality shells meant that the heavy artillery could only fire limited preliminary barrages during the 1915 battles. Aerial reporting and photographs helped identify and neutralise targets but too much firing could stir up dust, interfering with observation. The action at the Bluff in March 1916 illustrates that the artillery had learnt how to fire different barrages to serve different purposes.

The prolonged bombardment plan for 1 July 1916 was a highly organised affair, in which aerial observers systematically searched for enemy batteries for the artillery. Ground observers then used flash spotting and sound ranging, while aerial observers visually adjusted fire. However, Fourth Army was over confident about the effectiveness of the heavy artillery, while the field artillery struggled to cut the wire on the undulating ground. It resulted in a huge disaster for the infantry.

The artillery used a short bombardment, ending with an intense barrage which prompted the troops to crawl forward through the darkness on 14 July. It marked a change in preliminary bombardments, in which the goal was to deceive rather than destroy the enemy. Over the weeks that followed, a variety of fake barrages, practice barrages and different intensity barrages were used. Sometimes there was no preliminary bombardment, leaving the infantry relying on surprise to take a position.

The gunners found it difficult to master unobserved fire, often failing to hit targets behind crests or woods during the Somme campaign. They also found it desirable to have a straight front line, so they could give the infantry effective support. The occasions when different zero hours were used, to account for different widths of No Man's Land, simply alerted the Germans.

By August 1916, the gunners were using practice barrages and fake creeping barrages to confuse the enemy. The barrages were also so accurate and effective that the Germans hid in craters to avoid them, leaving the gunners needing to shell all the enemy territory. The autumn weather then made it difficult for the artillery to identify targets through the frequent periods of mist and rain.

The artillery had often reorganised during the first two years of trench warfare but had been formed into three groups by the time of the Arras campaign. 'Counter Battery Groups' targeted the enemy artillery, 'Super Heavy Groups' fired at villages and 'Trench Groups' hit the infantry targets. Generals were now allowed to determine the preliminary barrage to suit the objective. For example, First Army chose a prolonged bombardment before reducing the rate of fire before zero hour, to relax the Germans holding Vimy Ridge. Third Army wanted to fire a short hurricane bombardment but GHQ overruled General Byng and the bombardment lasted for five days. The gunners then extended their range for a time before dropping it back to hit No Man's Land at zero hour, to confuse the Germans east of Arras.

The quantity of shells and the time available to redeploy the batteries sometimes dictated what sort of preliminary bombardment was fired, such as during the autumn of 1917. Seven-days of shelling preceded the attack on 20 September, while a twenty-four-hour barrage was fired before the 26 September assault; there was no barrage on 4 October.

Predicted fire was introduced at Hill 70, in August 1917, but it made its big impact near Cambrai in November. The guns were calibrated and weather conditions were assessed, so that precise shooting calculations could be made. It meant the gunners were confident the first shots at zero hour would hit their target. It meant there was a greater chance of surprise, that less ammunition was required and that the ground was left intact for the tanks to cross.

Throughout 1915, the protective barrage fired after zero hour jumped between the objectives and it was always too far ahead of the infantry. The problem increased as the Germans became quicker at manning their trenches, ready to decimate the advancing waves of infantry. Artillery officers started working closer with the infantry after Neuve Chapelle, but poor reporting meant that it was difficult to give close support after zero hour. It proved even more difficult to give support once a breakthrough had been made, such as on the second day at Loos.

An inflexible approach meant there were no plans to change the protective barrage if there were delays, such as on 1 July 1916. Communications between the infantry and artillery remained a problem throughout the Somme campaign but sound was used to warn the infantry that the barrage would advance in November.

Firing a creeping barrage to protect the infantry was considered in the spring of 1916 and it was introduced as soon as the gunners were proficient enough to create one, during the early stages of the Somme campaign. The ground conditions, terrain and strength of the enemy position dictated how fast the barrage moved forward in front of the infantry. Steps to improve the accuracy of the artillery included studying weather conditions and calibrating guns. The innovative double shrapnel screen introduced in November 1916 kept the Germans underground much longer.

One temporary setback was the introduction of gaps into the barrage, to accommodate the tanks on 15 September 1916. But too many broke down, leaving the infantry vulnerable and it was not used again. On the positive side, the combination of different ammunition and the mixture of air and ground bursts improve the deadliness of the creeping barrage in the autumn battles.

Communication between the guns and the infantry during the Third Ypres campaign was achieved by using smoke and different rates of fire. There were enough guns and ammunition to fire a five-layer creeping barrage by September 1917 and heavy and medium calibre shells first drove the Germans underground. A machine-gun tempted them back into their trenches but the field guns followed up with high explosive shells; a screen of shrapnel protected the advancing infantry. High explosive shells were sometimes used to supress pillboxes as assault teams moved through smoke to outflank them.

Zero Hour, Smoke and Gas

Zero hour usually took place around dawn in 1915, so the final preparations could be made under cover of darkness. The first night attack (and all the problems that came with it) was made at Festubert in May 1915 but they would not become a regular feature until the Somme campaign. Attacks in the middle of the day were also tried, so the assault troops could consolidate their position before dusk, leaving the Germans to counter-attack in the dark.

Eventually, visibility became the deciding feature for zero hour with pre-dawn attacks being a favourite. The time when the assault troops could see far enough to advance in unison, while the enemy machine gunners could not see their targets was determined to be ideal. But it also became too obvious, so mist or smoke was used to limit the enemy's visibility during attacks made later in the day.

Late changes to zero hour caused problems, either because the artillery or infantry received the message too late to act on. One example of such an error took place on 3 May 1917, when there was no time to reset the barrage or the objectives. No one had appreciated the moon would silhouette the advancing troops before the dust thrown up by the barrage blinded them.

Zero hour was sometimes linked to the weather, such as with the wind direction and the gas attack at Loos, in September 1915. However, the effect it could have on offensive action became far more involved over the months that followed, aside from the usual impact of rain. The gunners needed to know the air pressure and wind conditions, so they could fire an accurate barrage, while mist and clouds interfered with aerial spotting and gun registration. Sunlight, moonlight and mist could either highlight or hide the advancing infantry.

Gas became associated with zero hour in 1915 and a rudimentary mask was invented immediately after the Germans breached the Ypres Salient in April. An improved hood was introduced while GHQ considered using gas to make up for the lack of artillery. A shortage of cylinders resulted in the use of smoke candles, to deceive the Germans around Loos in September, but the cloud disorientated and choked the assault troops. Misunderstandings over how far the wind would blow the gas and a reliance on the weather meant that a new delivery system was required before gas and smoke could be used effectively.

Good discipline against phosgene gas in the Ypres Salient in December 1915 prevented a disaster, while new box respirators gave the men confidence to stay put during gas attacks the following spring. So, gas was used to impair the men's effectiveness instead, while shells meant that it could be accurately directed against distant targets.

The introduction of mustard gas ushered in a new purpose for chemical warfare in the summer of 1917. It was used to deny areas to the enemy, such as battery positions and headquarters. The gas was particularly effective at driving troops out of wooded areas because it stagnated in undergrowth. Tear and sneezing gas were also introduced, to impair the men's ability to fight without putting an area off limits.

Infantry Tactics, Training and Weapons

Rudimentary training had been introduced for Neuve Chapelle, with the infantry practising advancing in waves. Training had become more realistic by early 1916, as full-scale models made from aerial photographs were built to practice on. All the experiences of 1915 were put together into pamphlets but there were too few trainers and too little time for effective training.

The basic tactics for 1 July 1916 were to use four waves of infantry to clear the German defences, after the artillery had bludgeoned a way through. However, the failure to knock out the enemy machine-gun teams, inflexible tactics and the tendency to reinforce failure rather than success resulted in a bloody failure. Despite the huge setback, the infantry continued to advance between set objectives, with waves passing through one another (or leap frogging), for the rest of the campaign. However, more emphasis was placed on clearing (or mopping up) captured trenches.

The anticipated rate of advance of the infantry set the pace of the creeping barrage as the campaign progressed. But the speed had to be decreased when the autumn weather made the ground difficult to cross, until it was almost too slow to be successful. So, more surprise attacks were made, with men creeping forward in the dark to take an enemy position by surprise. Flares were also used to control the speed of the barrage.

After so long in the trenches, the infantry found it difficult to advance in the open during the advance to the Hindenburg Line in the spring of 1917. However, it was back to fighting in trenches during the Arras campaign and training now included practising across full scale models slowly and then at the correct speed. The artillery continued to smash the wire, while the infantry cleared the first trench system, by fire and manoeuvre. The tanks then supported the deep advance beyond field gun range.

The density of infantry required was calculated on the frontage and defences faced during the Third Ypres campaign, however, the numbers of men required to clear the vast belts of pillboxes around the Salient were sometimes underestimated. By now, the creeping barrage always stood still as the first wave deployed, while the support waves took precautions to avoid the inevitable counter-barrage.

Small unit tactics which used the various infantry support weapons were formalised in the SS-143 pamphlet and they were practised until everyone knew how to play their part. The standard tactic was for the Lewis gun teams and rifle grenadiers to suppress a target, while the riflemen outflanked it under cover of smoke. Once close enough, they would assault the position with bayonet and grenade. Definite defensive arrangements had also been put in place at battalion, brigade and division level, making it easier to drive counter-attacks off with the artillery's help.

The first big test against counter-attacks came on 30 December 1917, when the Germans struck back near Cambrai. Well-practised defensive tactics could stop an attack in its tracks when there was adequate warning and enough visibility to see the enemy coming. However, it was impossible to stop a strong attack when it was misty, until local reinforcements arrived on the scene.

The first grenades were dangerous home-made models but they gave the infantry an indirect close support weapon, which was useful in trench fighting. The safer Mills No. 5 grenade appeared late in 1915 while the No. 23 grenade could be fired from a rifle. The Stokes mortar added another short-range indirect weapon which was light enough to be carried forward. It could fire a large number of rounds per minute, either creating suppressive fire or a smoke screen at short notice.

The Lewis gun was introduced early in 1916 and the number issued to battalions increased until each infantry platoon had its own direct fire support weapon. The number of Maxim (and later Vickers) machine guns per battalion had also been increased but they were too cumbersome to carry across the battlefield under fire. They were organised into companies and then battalions, so they could be deployed to give long-range tactical support. They fired overhead at roads and tracks, to catch the Germans falling back, during the Arras campaign and then provided part of the artillery barrage during the Messines campaign.

The BEF also tried the Livens flame projector, but it was too cumbersome to deploy but the much smaller Livens projectors could cover an enemy trench with blazing oil. Pipe pushers were used to blow up trenches, to blast holes in wire and to create shallow ditches across No Man's Land, to facilitate the digging of communication trenches.

The Engineers

The engineers carried out many tasks which indirectly supported operations on the Western Front. But the main one was to keep the troops supplied with ammunition and food, a huge task which required the building and maintaining of miles of roads, tracks and light railways across difficult ground, often under fire. They also supervised the building of entanglements, trenches and pillboxes, as well as the construction of billets, stores and host of rear area facilities.

However, two important areas in which the engineers directly affected offensives were in mapping and mining. Mapping was inaccurate and limited until the BEF settled down over the winter of 1914-15. The engineers had soon prepared accurate maps of Flanders, for plotting bombardments and planning attacks. They used ground surveys to draw the BEF's trenches while the Royal Flying Corps helped them plot enemy trenches with the help of aerial photographs. The coordinate system proved to be complicated, so the artillery upgraded to a zone system for calling down barrages quickly. The infantry's informal system of naming trenches and terrain features was also adopted because they made it easier to reference locations.

The BEF sought experienced tunnellers to dig under the German trenches at the beginning of 1915. Mines were used to capture tactical points but it soon became clear that the Germans were better at capturing the craters. The tunnellers skilfully employed a double layer of mines to dig under the Hohenzollern Redoubt, in the spring of 1916. Prudent use of small, shallow mines called camouflets allowed them to destroy the German tunnels without disturbing the surface, as they continued to dig their deep galleries.

The timing of mine detonation proved to be problematic because the explosion warned the Germans over a wide area that an attack was imminent. The detonation of the two large mines on 1 July 1916 gave them a ten-minute warning before zero hour, increasing the magnitude of the disaster. The tunnellers reverted to blowing up tactical points during the rest of the Somme and Arras campaigns, but the attack against Messines Ridge on 7 June 1917 was the pinnacle of mining warfare. They dug many tunnels and then laid the large mines which destroyed the German morale. It was, however, the end of mining because of the wet ground conditions in the Ypres Salient and then the fast-moving nature of battles in 1918.

Tanks and Planes

The First World War saw many new innovations, but two which changed the face of battle forever were the tank and the plane. Secrecy surrounding the tanks meant there were no training opportunities for the infantry, severely limiting cooperation on 15 September 1916. The tanks were supposed to crush the wire beyond field gun range but breakdowns and broken ground meant too few did so. Infantry teams had been introduced to guide them forward by the end of the campaign while the designers in Britain were taking note of the feedback from the battlefield.

Tanks followed the infantry over the broken ground at Arras, ready to lead them through the wire protecting the second line of trenches. Machine-gun fire was being used to cover the sound of the tanks but a late decision to use them caused problems at Bullecourt on 11 April.

Messines saw the arrival of the Mark IV, which had hardened steel, a larger fuel tank and improved reliability. The crews worked closely with the infantry, while improved maintenance and refuelling facilities meant they could stay in the field longer. The infantry and tank officers billeted together before the Third Ypres campaign, to further improve coordination, and some tanks helped mop up strongpoints while the rest led the later stages of the advance. But the soft ground limited them to the roads, resulting in many being knocked out, so they were often reduced to carrying ammunition and stores forward.

Dummy tanks were used for the first time in the summer of 1917 to unsettle the Germans, but the Tank Corps' big chance came at Cambrai on 20 November. Accurate predicted artillery meant that the ground would not be cratered, while the tanks cut the wire. The infantry was given time to practice with the tanks, giving them extra confidence, but the tactics failed on the occasions when they became separated. The tanks may have created a break in at Cambrai, but a shortage of repair, maintenance and fuelling facilities for such a large action, meant they could not break through.

The Royal Flying Corps added an extra dimension to the battlefield and its contribution became more sophisticated and valuable with each campaign. Some air crews photographed the enemy trenches, so attacks could be planned, while others kept the enemy planes at bay so troops could deploy without in secret. They also found targets for the artillery and then monitored their destruction before zero hour. They watched the infantry's progress, reported new targets for the artillery and kept a look out for counter-attacks during the battle.

Pilots eventually used Klaxon horns and Very lights to communicate with the infantry and the men on the ground responded by lighting flares. Wireless messages or marked up maps dropped at corps report centres meant that the reports could be passed onto the artillery quickly. The introduction of special flares, which were easier to spot, and improved wirelesses in August 1917 meant that the aerial observers were able to report targets faster than ever before.

Command and Control

Trench warfare posed immense command and control problems during the First World War but many refinements were tried, with varying degrees of success. The panic following the gas attack at Ypres in April 1915 resulted in several command problems; not least the shortage of staff which resulted in disorganised attacks by inexperienced men. Ineffective staff work resulted in the reserves taking too long to exploit the break in on the first day of the battle of Loos, while a lack of planning for the second day ended in disaster. But the biggest command failure was to rely on New Army divisions which had never been in the trenches before to make an assault.

The attack on 1 July 1916 illustrated how quickly inflexible plans fell apart in the face of problems. It then took far too long to report the break in made on 14 July and the delayed deployment of the cavalry resulted in another disaster. There had to be full commitment to an attack by all levels of command if it was to have any chance of success. One example which illustrates a half-hearted level of support was the disastrous attack at Fromelles on 20 July 1916. GHQ took time to appreciate the many lessons learnt on the Somme and its appraisals were not circulated fast enough. Both the Reserve and Fourth Armies were also struggling to make all the arms work together, while the arrival of the tanks on 15 September further complicated matters.

It proved difficult to pass reinforcement divisions through the line east of Arras, on 9 April 1917, while it was impossible to get large numbers of cavalry forward. Strategy changed after the disaster east of Ypres, on 31 July 1917, where a counter-attack overran the over-stretched assault troops. Instead, limited bite and hold advances were used, so the artillery did not have to redeploy during an advance.

Cambrai was a return to a breakthrough strategy, in which the tanks seized ground for the infantry to occupy. However, the age-old problem of getting the artillery and cavalry forward had not been solved. Third Army failed to prepare to counter the German attack on 30 November and the situation was only saved by the brave actions of the local reserves. GHQ quickly moved up infantry and guns to shore up the line, before Third Army withdrew to a shorter line.

Communications were always a problem for the BEF during offensives but many methods were tried. Flags could not always be seen at Neuve Chapelle, while the artillery found it difficult to estimate distances when they gave supporting fire. It was noted that the Germans used flares to coordinate their infantry and artillery activity during the gas attacks around Ypres in April 1915. British troops started using them at Festubert, while head lamps and torches reported progress in the dark. By the summer of 1915, triple cables had been added to the rear area communications system but it was often down to pigeons to relay messages through the smoke of battle and they could only fly one way. Flares continued to be used during the Somme campaign but messages were misunderstood when too many were fired, while there was confusion between friendly and enemy flares.

The rapid retreat to the Hindenburg Line in the spring of 1917 caused problems because headquarters continued to rely on trench telephones rather than using signalling methods suited to open warfare. The infantry did, however, use flares to control the artillery during their advances when the gunners could see them. A variety of power buzzers, amplifiers and wireless sets were used to compliment visual communications during the Arras campaign. The infantry improved their reporting by introducing message maps for explaining tactical situations during the battle of Messines.

As noted, spark-based wireless sets had been tried for some time, with varied results. The introduction of continuous wave sets at the end of the Third Ypres campaign was an insight into why radio communications would transfer how battles were fought.

Offensives and Counter-Offensives in 1918

The BEF had been reorganising its artillery, machine guns and support arms at regular intervals throughout 1916 and 1917, in response to the increase in weaponry and evolving tactical situation. It was the turn of the infantry in the early part of 1918 and the reduction from twelve battalion down to nine battalion infantry divisions was carried out quickly and efficiently. GHQ expected to come under attack in the spring of 1918 because Russia's surrender allowed the Germans to transfer tens of thousands of troops from the Eastern Front to the Western Front. It put plans in place to meet a large offensive but there were insufficient men to carry them out, because of the extension of the front as far south as the River Oise.

The German two offensives, in March and April 1918, threatened to drive the Allies back beyond the important rail centres of Amiens and Hazebrouck. But in both cases, the tenacity of the BEF's soldiers and the Germans' inability to control their logistics stopped them. There was no time for lessons to be learnt in these battles of survival, it was down to the officers on the ground to concoct ad-hoc plans and decided when to fight and retire.

As the German offensives came to an end, the BEF planned how to strike back while 'peaceful penetration' and 'hole-boring' techniques probed the German defences for weak spots. The action at Le Hamel on 4 July 1918 may have been the first combined arms attack in the British sector for seven months, but it demonstrated that the BEF had combined the lessons learned over the past three years.

Targets were registered in routine bombardments, so the build of guns remained secret, while planes flew overhead to drown out the noise of the tanks. Zero hour was chosen so it was light enough to identify a uniform at 20 yards while smoke made the Germans put their gas masks on. The barrage warned the first wave to deploy while the rest advanced quickly to avoid the counter-barrage.

High explosive shells stunned the Germans hiding underground while extra layers of smoke blinded those who remained above it. The first wave of tanks cut off the enemy front line, while the second accompanied the infantry; supply tanks each carried the same amount of supplies as one hundred men. The action ended with some planes scouting for anti-tank guns, while others dropped ammunition for machine-gun teams. The tanks then withdrew as soon as a new trench had been dug and consolidated.

The advance east of Amiens on 8 August 1918 was a much bigger version of the Le Hamel attack. A greater degree of secrecy was required because of its size and detailed orders were issued only forty-eight hours before the attack. Great steps were also taken to get the thousands of infantry and dozens of tanks into place in secret. New batteries stayed silent before the attack while established batteries relocated just before zero hour, to avoid the counter-barrage. The guns finally opened fire as skirmishers guided the tanks past the assault troops and then columns of infantry followed them through the smoke. There was good control over the reserves moving through to exploit the break in, while supply tanks carried machine-gun teams forward to occupy the final objective. Whippet tanks and armoured cars then worked with the cavalry to clear the area ahead during the exploitation phase.

The troops struggled to adapt to the fast-moving battles over the days that followed but the main drawback was the heavy losses to the Tank Corps on 8 August, caused by letting the tanks stay in enemy territory after the smoke had cleared. The Royal Air Force also lost many planes because they had switched to attacking the Somme bridges at the last minute.

Third Army's artillery hit the villages rather than fire a creeping barrage into the mist, when the BEF's attack front extended on 21 August. But communications again proved problematic as the infantry, artillery and tanks struggled to coordinate their efforts. Tanks had to be used sparingly and they always back before the mist lifted. Smoke dischargers were added to tanks, so they could lay screens to cover their tracks when needed. Single field guns, called sniping guns, often worked alongside the infantry, while the first self-propelled howitzer made an appearance.

It took the BEF nearly two weeks to clear the old British trenches, giving the Germans time to repair the dilapidated Hindenburg Line. First and Third Armies did not use a preliminary barrage on 27 September, but followed a flexible three-layer creeping barrage across the Canal du Nord instead. Fourth Army made the mistake of using inexperienced US troops who failed to mop up to lead its attack and were left stranded in No Man's Land. There were heavy tank losses during the main attack two days later but the infantry persevered and crossed the St Quentin Canal and tunnel. The Beaurevoir Line was soon cleared and the retreat then began in earnest.

The Germans proved to be skilled at causing problems as they fell back; they blew up bridges, cratered roads, flooded areas and set booby traps. The BEF proved equally resourceful at dealing with the problems but they were often delayed by hungry civilians and prisoners. The end, however, soon came because the BEF swept aside every attempt to stop them before the Armistice was declared on 11 November 1918.

Bibliography

National Archives of the United Kingdom (Kew)

WO 95/1911	15th Division, Headquarters, Branches and Services, General Staff,
WO 95/2128	21st Division Headquarters Branches and Services, General Staff
WO 95/2662	46th Division, Headquarters, Branches and Services, General Staff,
WO/1979	46 Brigade
WO 95/2151/1	62 Brigade
WO 95/1666/2	91 Brigade
WO 95/2456/3	101 Brigade
WO 95 2614/2	121 Brigade
WO 95/2928/5	166 Brigade
WO 95/721/1	1/4th Royal Welsh Fusiliers
WO 95/1270/3	1st Loyal North Lancashire
WO 95/1271/2	1st Northamptonshire
WO 95/1281/2	2nd Welsh
WO 95/1371/1	1st Berkshire
WO 95/1372/2	23rd Royal Fusiliers
WO 95/1423/5	2nd Royal Scots
WO 95/1423/6	2nd Royal Scots
WO 95/1429/2	13th King (Liverpool)
WO 95/1430/3	1st Northumberland Fusiliers
WO 95/1432/2	12th West Yorkshires
WO 95/1571/1	1st Cheshire
WO 95/1609/4	1st Somerset
WO 95/1656/2	2nd Gordon Highlanders
WO 95/1670/2	1st South Staffordshire
WO 95/1767/1	5th Cameron Highlanders
WO 95/1772/2	6th King Own Scottish Borderers
WO 95/1795/2	4th South African
WO 95/1809/3	2nd Green Howards

WO 95/1937/2	9th Black Watch
WO 95/1495/5	1st Hampshire
WO 95/1946/2	13th Royal Scots
WO 95/2040/1	8th Norfolk
WO 95/2043/1	7th Bedfordshire
WO 95/2049/1	7th Buffs (East Kent)
WO 95/2078/2	1/4th Shropshire
WO 95/2079/1	9th Cheshires
WO 95/2092/2	9th Welsh
WO 95/2093/1	2nd Wiltshire
WO 95/2244/3	9th Devonshire
WO 95/2247/3	9th Green Howards
WO 95/2250/1	11th Cheshire
WO 95/2277/3	1st Suffolk
WO 95/2279/2	2nd Buffs (East Kent)
WO 95/2329/3	6th Green Howards
WO 95/2358/1	11th East Lancashire
WO 95/2427/1	1/4th King's (Liverpool)
WO 95/2655/1	1/7th Lancashire Fusiliers
WO 95/2756/1	1/7th Royal Warwickshire
WO 95/2764/1	1/4th Oxford and Buckinghamshire
WO 95/2897/3	1/7th Royal Scots
WO 95/2924/1	1/4th Loyal North Lancashire
WO 95/2926/2	1/6th King (Liverpool)
WO 95/2929/2	1/5th South Lancashire
WO 95/3021/10	25th King
WO 95/3050/3	1st Duke of Cornwall Light Infantry
WO 95/3087/3	2/4th Hampshire
WO 95/3115/1	Hood Battalion
WO 95/3946/1	2/3rd Gurkha Rifles
WO 95/3948/2	1st Black Watch

Official Publications

Australian

Charles E. W. Bean, *The Official History of Australia in the War, Vol. III: The Australian Imperial Force in France, 1916* (Sydney: Angus and Robertson, 1941)

Charles E. W. Bean, *The Official History of Australia in the War, Vol. IV: The Australian Imperial Force in France, 1917* (Sydney: Angus and Robertson, 1941)

Charles E. W. Bean, *The Official History of Australia in the War, Vol. V: The Australian Imperial Force in France during the Main German Offensive, 1918* (Sydney: Angus and Robertson, Sydney, 1941)

Charles E. W. Bean, *The Official History of Australia in the War, Vol. VI: The Australian Imperial Force in France during the Allied Offensive, 1918* (Sydney: Angus and Robertson, 1942)

British

Sir James E. Edmonds, *Military Operations: France and Belgium, 1914: Vol. I: Mons, the Retreat to the Seine, the Marne and the Aisne, August to October 1914* (London: HMSO, 1922)

Sir James E. Edmonds, *Military Operations: France and Belgium, 1914: Vol. II: Antwerp, La Bassée, Armentières, Messines and Ypres, October and November 1914* (London: HMSO, 1925)

Sir James E. Edmonds and Captain G.C. Wynne, *Military Operations: France and Belgium, 1915: Vol. I: Winter 1914-15: Battle of Neuve Chapelle: Battles of Ypres* (London: HMSO, 1927)

Sir James E. Edmonds, *Military Operations: France and Belgium, 1915: Vol. II: Battles of Aubers Ridge, Festubert, and Loos* (London: HMSO, 1928)

Sir James E. Edmonds, *Military Operations: France and Belgium, 1916: Vol. I: Sir Douglas Haig's Command to the 1st July: Battle of the Somme* (London: HMSO, 1932)

Captain Wilfrid Miles, *Military Operations: France and Belgium, 1916: Vol. II: 2 July 1916 to the end of the Battles of the Somme* (London: HMSO, 1938)

Captain Cyril Falls, *Military Operations: France and Belgium, 1917: Vol. I: The German Retreat to the Hindenburg Line and the Battles of Arras* (London: HMSO, 1940)

Sir James E. Edmonds, *Military Operations: France and Belgium, 1917: Vol. II: Messines and Third Ypres (Passchendaele)* (London: HMSO, 1948)

Captain Wilfrid Miles, *Military Operations: France and Belgium, 1917: Vol. III: The Battle of Cambrai* (London: HMSO, 1948)

Sir James E. Edmonds, *Military Operations: France and Belgium, 1918: Vol. I: The German March Offensive and its Preliminaries* (London: HMSO, 1935)

Sir James E. Edmonds, *Military Operations: France and Belgium, 1918: Vol. II: March and April: Continuation of the German Offensives* (London: HMSO, 1937)

Sir James E. Edmonds, *Military Operations: France and Belgium, 1918: Vol. III: May to July: The German Diversion Offensives and the First Allied Counter-Offensive* (London: HMSO, 1939)

Sir James E. Edmonds, *Military Operations: France and Belgium, 1918: Vol. IV: 8 August to 26 September: The Franco-British Offensive* (London: HMSO, 1947)

Sir James E. Edmonds and Lieutenant-Colonel R. Maxwell-Hyslop, *Military Operations: France and Belgium, 1918: Vol. V: 26 September to 11 November: The Advance to Victory* (London: HMSO, 1947)

Canadian

G.W.L. Nicholson, *Official History of the Canadian Army in the First World War: Canadian Expeditionary Force, 1914-1919* (Ottawa: Roger Duhamel, 1962)

New Zealand

Colonel H Stewart, *The New Zealand Division 1916-1919, The New Zealanders in France, Vol. II* (Uckfield: Naval and Military Press 2009 reprint of 1921 edition)

South African

Anon., *Union of South Africa and the Great War 1914-1918* (Uckfield: Naval and Military Press 2015reprint of 1924 edition)

Formation and Unit Histories

Anon., *A Brief History of the 30th Division from July 1918 to 11 November 1918*, (London: War Narratives Publishing, 1919)

A.H. Atteridge, *The History of the 17th (Northern) Division* (Glasgow: Robert Maclehose & Co, 1929)

F. W. Bewsher, *The History of the 51st (Highland) Division 1914-1918* (London: Blackwood, 1921)

Rev. J. Coop, *The Story of the 55th (West Lancashire) Division* (Liverpool: Liverpool Daily Post, 1919).

H. M. Davson, *The History of the 35th Division in the Great War* (London: Sifton and Praed, 1926).

Cyril Falls, *The History of the 36th (Ulster) Division* (Belfast: McCaw, Stevenson & Orr, 1922)

Cuthbert Headlam, *History of the Guards Division in the Great War, 1915-1918 Vols. I & II* (Edinburgh: John Murray, 1924)

A.H. Hussey and D.S. Inman, *The Fifth Division in the Great War* (London: Nisbet and Co., 1921).

G. Seton Hutchinson, *The Thirty Third Division in France and Flanders 1915-1919* (London: Waterlow & Sons, 1921)

Lieutenant Colonel M. Kincaid-Smith, *The 25th Division in France and Flanders* (London: Harrison & Sons,1920)

Captain V.E. Inglefield, *The History of the Twentieth (Light) Division* (London: Nesbit, 1921)

Douglas Jerrold, *The Royal Naval Division* (London: Hutchinson, 1923)

Major General J. Latter, *The History of the Lancashire Fusiliers, 1914-1918, Vols. I & II* (Aldershot: Gale and Polden, 1949).

Major General T. Marden (ed.), *A Short History of the 6th Division, 1914 to 1919* (London: Hugh Rees, 1920).

Alan H. Maude (ed.), *The 47th (London) Division, 1914-1919* (London: Amalgamated Press, 1922)

Lieutenant General Ivor Maxse, *Eighteenth Division in the Battle of the Ancre 1916* (France: 18th Division Printers, 1917)

J. Mereweather and Sir Frederick Smith, *The Indian Corps in France* (New York: E. P. Dutton, 1918)

J. E. Munby, *A History of the 38th (Welsh) Division* (London; H. Rees, 1920)

G.H.F. Nicholls, *The 18th Division in the Great War* (Edinburgh: William Blackwood and Sons, 1922)

F. Loraine Petre and Major General Sir H. Cecil Lowther, *The Scots Guards in the Great War, 1914-18* (London:John Murray, 1925).

Lieutenant Colonel Rt. Hon. Sir Frederick Ponsonby, *The Grenadier Guards in the Great War* (London: Macmillan and Co.,1920).

Geoffrey Powell, *The History of the Green Howards* (Barnsley: Pen and Sword, 2015)

Major General Sir Arthur B. Scott, *History of the 12th Division in the Great War, 1914-1918* (London: Nisbet, 1923).

J. Shakespear, *The Thirty Fourth Division, 1915-1919: The Story of its Career from Ripon to the Rhine* (London: Witherby, (1921)

Major General C. R. Simpson, *The History of the Lincolnshire Regiment, 1914-1918* (London: Medici Society, 1931).

J. Stewart and J. Buchan, *The Fifteenth (Scottish) Division 1914–1919* (Edinburgh: Blackwood, 1926)

C. Dudley Ward, *The Fifty Sixth Division 1914-1918* (1st London Territorial Division), (London; Murray, 1921).

Everard Wyrall, *The History of Second Division 1914-18, Vols. I & II* (London; Thomas Nelson and Sons, 1921)

Everard Wyrall, *The History of the Fiftieth Division, 1914-1919* (London: P. Lund, 1939).

Everard Wyrall, *The Story of the 62nd (West Riding) Division, 1914-1919* (London: The Bodley Head, 1924)

Miscellaneous Sources

David Blanchard, *Aisne, 1918* (Barnsley: Pen and Sword, 2015)

Stephen Bull, Trench: *A History of Trench Warfare on the Western Front* (Oxford: Osprey, 2014)

Dale Clarke, *World War I Battlefield Artillery Tactics* (Oxford: Osprey, 2014).

Major General Charles Foulkes, *Gas! The Story of Special Brigade* (London: Blackwood & Sons Limited, 1934)

Dominick Graham, *Against Odds: Reflections on the Experiences of the British Army, 1914-45* (London: Palgrave McMillan, 1999).

Maxwell Hundleby, Strasheim, Rainer, *The German A7V Tank and the Captured British Mark IV Tanks of World War I* (London: Haynes Foulis, 1990)

John W. Jenkins, *The World War and Historic Deeds of Valour from Official Records and Illustrations of the United States and Allied Governments, Vol. 5* (Minnesota: National Historic Publishing Association, 1919)

H. A. Jones, *The Air in the War, Vol. IV* (Oxford: Clarendon Press, 1934)

Michael LoCicero, *A Moonlight Massacre. The Night Operation on the Passchendaele Ridge, 2 December 1917: The Forgotten Last Act of the Third Battle of Ypres* (Solihull: Helion & Company, 2014).

Erich Ludendorff, *My War Memories, 1914-18, Vol. II* (London: Hutchinson, 1919)

Anthony Saunders, *Reinventing Warfare 1914-18: Novel Munitions and Tactics of Trench Warfare* (London: Continuum, 2012)

Electronic Sources

Instructions for Training of the British Armies in France (General Staff, June 1917) <https://www.army.gov.au/sites/g/files/net1846/f/instructions_for_the_training_of_the_british_armies_in_france_1917_uk_0.pdf>

Transport and Supply during the First World War <https://www.iwm.org.uk/history/transport-and-supply-during-the-first-world-war>

Landships Homepage <https://sites.google.com/site/landships/home/narratives/1917/cambrainarratives/tank-tactics-at-cambrai>

Index

MILITARY FORMATIONS

Armies

Corps

Lightning Source UK Ltd.
Milton Keynes UK
UKHW021942050819
347442UK00006B/328/P